UNKNOWN TEXAS

OTHER BOOKS BY JONATHAN EISEN

The California Dream (edited with Dennis Hale)
The Age of Rock: Sounds of the American Cultural Revolution
The Age of Rock II
Twenty-Minute Fandangos and Forever Changes
Altamont: Death of Innocence in the Woodstock Nation
Unknown California (edited with David Fine and Kim Eisen)
The Nobel Reader

OTHER BOOKS BY HAROLD STRAUGHN

The Five Divorces of a Healthy Marriage

UNKNOWN
TEXAS

EDITED BY

JONATHAN EISEN AND HAROLD STRAUGHN

COLLIER BOOKS
MACMILLAN PUBLISHING COMPANY
New York

Collier Books
Macmillan Publishing Company
866 Third Avenue, New York, NY 10022
Collier Macmillan Canada, Inc.

Library of Congress Cataloging-in-Publication Data
Unknown Texas.
    1. Texas—History. I. Eisen, Jonathan.
II. Straughn, Harold.
F386.5.U54 1988   976.4   87-27850
ISBN 0-02-019760-8 (pbk.)

Macmillan books are available at special discounts for bulk purchases for sales promotions, premiums, fund-raising, or educational use. For details, contact:

Special Sales Director
Macmillan Publishing Company
866 Third Avenue
New York, NY 10022

10 9 8 7 6 5 4 3 2 1

PRINTED IN THE UNITED STATES OF AMERICA

Unknown Texas is also published in a hardcover edition by Macmillan Publishing Company.

This book is lovingly and gratefully dedicated to

BOB AND CARMEN RIGGS
and to
ALEXIA DORSZYNSKI

I cannot give you much.
I give you the images I know.
Lie still with me and watch.

Anne Sexton

CONTENTS

III • OIL AND DUST AND DREAMS OF GLORY

IV • JUST AS IT IS

EPILOGUE

FOREWORD

"DAD" JOINER'S EAST TEXAS DISCOVERY well in 1930 lifted Texas out of the Great Depression and catapulted it into a boom mode in much the same way that a tornado lifts a house three hundred yards and grounds it with a completely new orientation.

Although oil production in the state dated back to 1901, the Joiner well and the East Texas field had a bombshell effect on the state. Texas and Texans were never the same again. It changed the way people looked, the way they acted, the way they appeared to the rest of the world, and the way they regarded themselves. The boom led to the development of a braggadocio spirit based on Texas's primacy in geographic size, resources, and prosperity, facts which were duly observed but not particularly appreciated by the rest of America still suffering from the effects of the depression.

Walter Prescott Webb, the noted historian, wrote, "As long as the region was church-rat poor, there was nothing for the other sections to be jealous of. But today . . . we in Texas have become a sort of whipping boy for the other regions. Wherever we go, people tell us stories, most of them unfavorable to Texas . . . Texans may have done things to foster this attitude of not-too-delicate criticism and incentive. But there is no doubt that a good part of the hostility stems from the fact that Texas is booming."

It is unusual to be able to name an exact date and time to designate the beginning or end of an era. Not so in the case of Texas. The state only recently has come off of a fifty-year boom that started near midnight on October 5, 1930, in Kilgore, Texas, when the East Texas oil field blew in, and it came to a sickening, jerking stop when the price of oil fell to $9.75 at 11:32 A.M. on March 31, 1986.

It was during this span of time, more than a half century, that the Texas portrait was painted, or if you will, the Texas caricature was drawn. Boom times have a peculiar effect on humans and particularly so if the time lapse is as long as this one.

The oil crisis of the 1970s pushed the price up to a peak of $40.25, creating a state of euphoria in an industry that had prospered when oil prices varied from $.51 per barrel in 1931 to a rough average of $3 for a fifteen-year period, 1954 to 1970.

When oil went up to $40.25 per barrel "there was dancing in the streets." When it went down jobs dried up, companies closed their doors, mortgages were foreclosed.

The precipitous drop in the price of oil has affected virtually everyone in the state, for whether individuals owned an interest in an oil well or a share of oil stock, worked in the oil fields or in a gas station, practiced law or medicine, they were in the oil business and affected by the price of oil.

John Bainbridge in "The Super Americans," written for *The New Yorker* and later published in book form, captured the spirit of the place, the people, and the times when he wrote, "This exuberant, razzle-dazzle approach to life is sometimes referred to in Texas as the 'wheeler-dealer' spirit." It startled the establishment, for it was the first critical piece written about Texas and Texans.

Now is a propitious time to organize an anthology of Texan writings, a good portion of which were written as far back as the time of Texas's birth. While many are reflections of the oil boom period, together they give an adequate and fair view of what Texas was. At this moment in the midst of the energy depression, it's hard to visualize what Texas is going to be like when the doom and gloom disappear and the state stages a recovery. It won't be the same, for sure, because a boom coming from the quick and fortuitous discovery of national resources is different than an economy based on more slowly acquired wealth.

There will be fewer wildcatters and gamblers in the next decades; they will be replaced by stockbrokers, corporate executives, and prudent investors—more subdued, less colorful. The Texas world will not come to an end, but the individuals whose works will appear in the next anthology, forty years hence, are not likely to be as exciting and as interesting as those in this book.

The mix of writers in this anthology, ranging from the renowned explorer Cabeza de Vaca and the defeated General Santa Anna to the native observors like J. Frank Dobie and William Humphrey, from Texas heroes Davy Crockett and Sam Houston to outlanders such as Frederick Law Olmsted and Stephen Crane, and commentators on the oil age, ranging from A. C. Greene and Larry McMurtry to Dan Rather and Willie Morris, constitute a pungent potpourri of literary experiences and expressions.

—Stanley Marcus

ACKNOWLEDGMENTS

Permission to use the following previously published material is gratefully acknowledged:

"At the Seven Mile Ranch, Comstock, Texas," by Naomi Shihab Nye. In *Hugging the Jukebox*. Dutton, 1982. By permission of the author.

"Adventures in the Unknown Interior of America." In *The Journey of Alvar Núñez Cabeza de Vaca,* translated by Fanny Bandelier. Rio Grande Press, 1905. Reprinted in 1964.

"The Christian and the Pagan," by Bill Porterfield. In *A Loose Herd of Texans*. Texas A&M University Press, 1978. By permission of the author.

"The Last of the Caddoes," by William Humphrey. In *The Collected Stories of William Humphrey*. Delacorte/Seymour Lawrence, 1985.

"The Big Thicket," by William O. Douglas. In *Farewell to Texas*. McGraw-Hill, 1967.

"Longhorns," by J. Frank Dobie. In *Up the Trail from Texas*. Random House, 1955.

"Colonel Crockett's Texas Exploits," by Davy Crockett. In *The Autobiography of Davy Crockett*. Charles Scribner's Sons, 1923.

Excerpt from *The Mexican Side of the Texan Revolution,* by Antonio López de Santa Anna, et al., translated by Carlos E. Castaneda. P. L. Turner Company, 1928.

"Speech at Brenham, March 31, 1861," by Sam Houston. In *The*

Writings of Sam Houston 1813–1863, edited by A. W. Williams and E. C. Barker. University of Texas Press, 1938.

Excerpt from *My Master: The Inside Story of Sam Houston and His Times,* by Jeff Hamilton as told to Lenoir Hunt. Manfred, Van Nort and Company, 1940.

Excerpts from *A Journey Through Texas, or A Saddle-Trip on the Southwestern Frontier,* by Frederick Law Olmsted. Burt Franklin Company, 1969.

"Scraps of Early Texas History," by Mary Sherwood Wightman Helm. In *Texas Tears and Texas Sunshine: Voices of Frontier Women,* edited by Jo Ella Powell Exley. Texas A&M University Press, 1985.

"Indianola Scrap Book," by Eudora Inez Moore. In *Texas Tears and Texas Sunshine: Voices of Frontier Women,* edited by Jo Ella Powell Exley. Texas A&M University Press, 1985. By permission of the Calhoun County Historical Committee.

Excerpt from *Letters of an Early American Traveller,* by Mary Austin Holley. Southwest Press, 1933.

Excerpt from *Interwoven,* by Sallie Reynolds Matthews. University of Texas Press, 1974.

"The Bride Comes to Yellow Sky," by Stephen Crane. In *McClure's* magazine, February 1898.

"Holiday," by Katherine Anne Porter. In *The Collected Stories of Katherine Anne Porter.* Harcourt Brace Jovanovitch, 1965. By permission of Isabel Bayley.

"How the Oil Came," by A. C. Greene. In *A Personal Country.* Texas A&M University Press, 1979.

"Memoirs of an Oilfield Smoothneck," by Kathleen McConnell. 1987. By permission of the author.

"The Fishers: 1932," by Hughes Rudd. In *My Escape from the CIA (and into CBS).* Dutton, 1976.

"Boy in Search of Something," by Woody Guthrie. In *Bound for Glory.* Dutton, 1943.

"A Glorious Fourth," by John Henry Faulk. In *The Uncensored John Henry Faulk.* Texas Monthly Press, 1985.

"The American Redneck," by Larry L. King. In *Of Outlaws, Con Men, Whores, Politicians, and Other Artists.* Viking, 1973.

"The Killings," by Bill Brett. In *There Ain't No Such Animal and Other East Texas Tales.* Texas A&M University Press, 1979.

"The Town," by James A. Michener. In *Texas.* Random House, 1985.

"The Sad Irons," by Robert Caro. In *The Years of Lyndon Johnson: The Path to Power*. Knopf, 1982.

Excerpt from *The Gay Place*, by Billy Lee Brammer. Houghton Mifflin, 1961.

"Trip," by Frederick Barthelme. In *Moon Deluxe: Stories.* Simon and Schuster, 1983.

"A Mojo Hand," by Frank X. Tolbert. In *Tolbert's Texas*. Doubleday, 1983.

"The Last Picture Show," by Larry McMurtry. In *The Last Picture Show*. Dial, 1966. By permission of the JCA Literary Agency.

"Gifts from My Father," by William C. Martin. In *Texas Monthly* magazine, October 1978.

"The Last History Ever of Fatigue in Texas," by William C. Gruben. In *The Atlantic* magazine, September 1985.

Excerpt from *North Toward Home*, by Willie Morris. Houghton Mifflin, 1967. By permission of the John Daves Agency.

Excerpt from *The Rites of Fall*, by Al Reinert. University of Texas Press, 1979.

"Don Meredith Remembers," by Don Meredith. In *The Rites of Fall*, by Al Reinert. University of Texas Press, 1979.

"A Little Learning," by Dan Rather and Mickey Herskowitz. In *The Camera Never Blinks*. Morrow, 1977.

"The Prince Appears," by Shelby Hearon. In *A Prince of a Fellow*. Doubleday, 1978. By permission of the Julian Bach Literary Agency.

"Surgical Spirits," by Stephen Brook. In *Honkytonk Gelato: Travels Through Texas*. Atheneum, 1985.

"Janice, Bobby, and Sarah," by R. E. Smith. By permission of the author.

"Tongues of Men and of Angels," by William Goyen. In *Had I a Hundred Mouths: New and Selected Stories 1947–1983*. Clarkson Potter, 1985. By permission of Doris Roberts and the Charles William Goyen Trust.

"The Death of the Marlboro Man," by Gary Cartwright. In *Confessions of a Washed-Up Sportswriter*. Texas Monthly Press, 1982. By permission of the author.

"Remembering Bob Wills," by Al Stricklin with Jon McConal. In *My Years with Bob Wills*. Naylor, 1976.

"Just As I Am: Willie Nelson, Country Outlaw," by Lola Scobey. In *Willie Nelson, Country Outlaw*. Kensington, 1982.

"Born in the U.S.A. (And Living Under the Watchful Eyes of the

UNKNOWN TEXAS

A WORD BEFORE

TEXAS HAS ALWAYS BEEN an enigma having an affair with a contradiction. Besides Vermont, it is the only state in the Union to have been an independent republic. Texas is still in many ways that independent nation—aloof and apart in an age of high technology, interdependence, and space exploration.

Texas is quite as much a state of mind as it is a place on the map. And this book is a bit like a travel guide to that state of mind. It will lead you to some of the iridescence and the horror, the summits and declivities of a culture and history that in many ways justify the legendary Texas pride. And perhaps, hopefully, it will take you beyond.

We hope this will be a book of surprises for Texans and non-Texans alike. It is a book that reflects the richness and diversity of numerous cultures at war and at peace, developing not so much a self-image as a continuous struggle, though that struggle is not without its humor.

The Texas identity is the product of a combined effort on the part of longtime natives as well as explorers who came and moved on. It is the result of newcomers and outsiders looking in, and of insiders looking out. Appropriately, some of the writers who reveal the Texas mind in these pages come from families with roots deep in the soil. Others are travelers and warriors or newcomers with "perspective."

The book unfolds in four parts, not strictly chronologically. It travels around in time, ebbing and flowing, going off on its natural tangents, though always returning to the core of consciousness that is this state of mind, this place in the heart.

In "Roots" we go back to the time when a sense of boundlessness marked the Texas experience. It was a time when all seemed possible and geographical boundaries were hardly a problem. But it was also a time of territorial imperative, of cultural clash and the conquest of native Americans and of the land itself. We find here the diaries of Cabeza de Vaca, washed ashore in a storm with his men desperate to the point of cannibalism. They are befriended by the local residents, a friendly, helpful and civilized lot who are horrified by the white man's barbarity.

In "Heroes and Hardships" we find ourselves at the beginning of contemporary consciousness. From Davy Crockett's autobiography we get one side of the Alamo story; from General Santa Anna we get another. We find here the letters and diaries of some of the most perceptive travelers of the time, evoking the harsh panorama of the old west. We end the section with one of the most evocative westerns you may ever read.

"Oil and Dust and Dreams of Glory" reveals the romance as well as the underbelly of the down-home Texas myth. From Woody Guthrie to Kathleen McConnell, we view the feelings at the deepest core of the struggle to cope.

And finally, "Just As It Is" takes us to the precipice of the collapse of illusion. We look at urban Texas and the sharpened contrast between dreams fulfilled and hopes defeated, between the hard exterior of macho and the tender heart of country and western; between the romance of early space flight in Houston and the romance of Willie Nelson, country outlaw balladeer. Somewhere at the center we hear music and laughter and some crying, too. We witness greed and the transcending of greed, suffering and the mitigation of suffering.

In these pages you will find humor raucous and subtle; passion sacred and profane; mystery up against the wall of banality; you will find the sensual interrupting the philosophical. The writers we have chosen to include together form an amalgam of startling and arresting perspectives, like Texas itself. Theirs may be among the most valuable of all the contributions Texas has given—and is giving—to the world.

This book is their most precious gift, and it is ours to you.

—Jonathan Eisen and Harold Straughn

Naomi Shihab Nye

Naomi Shihab Nye (b. 1943) has twice received the Texas Institute of Letter Poetry Prize and the American Library Association "Notable Books" Award for 1982. Her books include Yellow Glove, Different Ways to Pray, *and* Hugging the Jukebox, *from which this selection is taken.*

AT THE SEVEN-MILE RANCH, COMSTOCK, TEXAS

I live like I know what I'm doing.

When I hand the horses a square of hay,
when I walk the road of stones
or chew on cactus pulp,
there's a drumming behind me,
the day opens up to let me pass through.

I know the truth,
how always I'm following each small sign that appears.
This sheep that materialized behind a clump of cenizo bushes
knows I didn't see him till he raised his head.

Out here it's impossible to be lonely.
The land walking beside you is your oldest friend,
pleasantly silent, like already you've told the best stories
and each of you knows how much the other made up.

I • ROOTS

Alvar Núñez Cabeza de Vaca

Alvar Núñez Cabeza de Vaca (ca. 1490–ca. 1557) wrote the earliest description of Texas by a European—a harrowing account of adventurers undergoing shipwreck, capture and enslavement followed by escape, living by their wits, being decimated by disease until only a handful survived—including the leader, who recorded it all in a priceless historical and literary achievement.

ADVENTURES IN THE UNKNOWN INTERIOR OF AMERICA

A Sinking and a Landing

Our two barges continued in company for four days, each man eating a ration of half a handful of raw corn a day. Then the other barge was lost in a storm. Nothing but God's great mercy kept us from going down, too.

It was winter and bitterly cold, and we had suffered hunger and the heavy beating of the waves for many days. Next day, the men began to collapse. By sunset, all in my barge had fallen over on one another, close to death. Few were any longer conscious. Not five could stand. When night fell, only the navigator and I remained able to tend the barge. Two hours after dark he told me I must take over; he believed he was going to die that night.

So I took the tiller. After midnight I moved over to see if he were dead. He said no, in fact was better, and would steer till daylight. In that hour I would have welcomed death rather than see so many around me in such a condition. When I had returned the helm to the navigator, I lay down to rest—but without much rest, for nothing was farther from my mind than sleep.

Near dawn I seemed to hear breakers resounding; the coast lying low, they roared louder. Surprised at this, I called to the navigator, who said he thought we were coming close to land. We sounded and found ourselves in seven fathoms. The navigator felt we should stay clear of the shore till daylight; so I took an oar and pulled it on the shore side, wheeling the stern to seaward about a league out.

As we drifted into shore, a wave caught us and heaved the barge a horseshoe-throw out of the water. The jolt when it hit brought the dead-looking men to. Seeing land at hand, they crawled through the surf to some rocks. Here we made a fire and parched some of our corn. We also found rainwater. The men began to regain their senses, their locomotion, and their hope.

This day of our landing was November 6.

What Befell Oviedo with the Indians

After we ate, I ordered Lope de Oviedo, our strongest man, to climb one of the trees not far off and ascertain the lay of the land. He complied and found out from the treetop that we were on an island. [This was Galveston Island.]* He also said that the ground looked as if cattle had trampled it and therefore that this must be a country of Christians.

I sent him back for a closer look, to see if he could find any worn trails, but warned him not to risk going too far. He went and came upon a path which he followed for half a league to some empty huts. The Indians were gone to shoal-flats [to dig roots]. He took an earthen pot, a little dog, and a few mullets and started back.

We had begun to worry what might have happened to him, so I detailed another two men to check. They met him shortly and saw three Indians with bows and arrows following him. The Indians were calling to him and he was gesturing them to keep coming. When he reached us, the Indians held back and sat down on the shore.

Half an hour later a hundred bowmen reinforced the first three individuals. Whatever their stature, they looked like giants to us in our fright. We could not hope to defend ourselves; not half a dozen of us could even stand up.

The Inspector and I walked out and greeted them. They advanced, and we did our best to placate and ingratiate. We gave them beads and bells, and each one of them gave us an arrow in pledge of friendship. They told us by signs that they would return at sunrise and bring food, having none then.

The Indians' Hospitality Before and After a New Calamity

As the sun rose next morning, the Indians appeared as they promised, bringing an abundance of fish and of certain roots which taste

*Bracketed text are translator's annotations.

like nuts, some bigger than walnuts, some smaller, mostly grubbed from the water with great labor.

That evening they came again with more fish and roots and brought their women and children to look at us. They thought themselves rich with the little bells and beads we gave them, and they repeated their visits on other days.

Being provided with what we needed, we thought to embark again. It was a struggle to dig our barge out of the sand it had sunk in, and another struggle to launch her. For the work in the water while launching, we stripped and stowed our clothes in the craft.

Quickly clambering in and grabbing our oars, we had rowed two crossbow shots from shore when a wave inundated us. Being naked and the cold intense, we let our oars go. The next big wave capsized the barge. The Inspector [Solís] and two others held fast, but that only carried them more certainly underneath, where they drowned.

A single roll of the sea tossed the rest of the men into the rushing surf and back onto shore half-drowned.

We lost only those the barge took down; but the survivors escaped as naked as they were born, with the loss of everything we had. That was not much, but valuable to us in that bitter November cold, our bodies so emaciated we could easily count every bone and looked the very picture of death. I can say for myself that from the month of May I had eaten nothing but corn, and that sometimes raw. I never could bring myself to eat any of the horsemeat at the time our beasts were slaughtered; and fish I did not taste ten times. On top of everything else, a cruel north wind commenced to complete our killing.

The Lord willed that we should find embers while searching the remnants of our former fire. We found more wood and soon had big fires raging. Before them, with flowing tears, we prayed for mercy and pardon, each filled with pity not only for himself but for all his wretched fellows.

At sunset the Indians, not knowing we had gone, came again with food. When they saw us looking so strangely different, they turned back in alarm. I went after them calling, and they returned, though frightened. I explained to them by signs that our barge had sunk and three of our number drowned. They could see at their feet two of the dead men who had washed ashore. They could also see that the rest of us were not far from joining these two.

The Indians, understanding our full plight, sat down and lamented for half an hour so loudly they could have been heard a long way off.

It was amazing to see these wild, untaught savages howling like brutes in compassion for us. It intensified my own grief at our calamity and had the same effect on the other victims.

When the cries died down, I conferred with the Christians about asking the Indians to take us to their homes. Some of our number who had been to New Spain warned that the Indians would sacrifice us to their idols. But death being surer and nearer if we stayed where we were, I went ahead and beseeched the Indians. They were delighted. They told us to tarry a little while, then they would do as we wished.

Presently thirty of them gathered loads of wood and disappeared to their huts, which were a long walk away; while we waited with the remainder until near nightfall. Then, supporting us under our arms, they hurried us from one to another of the four big fires they had built along the path. At each fire, when we regained a little warmth and strength, they took us on so swiftly our feet hardly touched ground.

Thus we made their village, where we saw they had erected a hut for us with many fires inside. An hour later they began a dance celebration that lasted all night. For us there was no joy, feasting, or sleep, as we waited the hour they should make us victims.

In the morning, when they brought us fish and roots and acted in every way hospitably, we felt reassured and somewhat lost our anxiety of the sacrificial knife.

News of Other Christians

That very day, I saw an Indian wearing a trinket which I knew we had not given. Inquiring whence it came, we learned from our hosts' signs that it had come from men like ourselves, who bivouacked farther back. At this, I sent two Christians, with two Indians for guides, to contact them.

It so happened that the latter were at that moment on their way to see us; for the Indians had told them of us as us of them. My detail met them therefore nearby.

They turned out to be Captains Andrés Dorantes and Alonso del Castillo with their entire crew [of 48]. When they came up, they were appalled at our appearance and sad that they had no other clothes than what they then wore.

They told us that their barge had capsized a league and a half from here the 5th of this month [i.e., the day before Cabeza de Vaca's barge was cast ashore] and that they escaped without losing a thing.

We decided to repair their barge, so that those who were strong enough and willing could resume the voyage, while the others stayed until their health allowed them to walk along the coast, and one day God our Lord should bring us all alike to a land of Christians.

We set directly to work but, before we could wrest the barge out of the water, Tavera, a gentleman of our company, died; and then the unseaworthy barge sank.

With most of us naked and the weather discouraging walking or swimming across rivers and coves—also with no food supply or even anything to carry one in—we resigned ourselves to remaining where we were for the winter.

We did, however, decide that four of our most robust men should set out now for Pánuco, which we believed close. Should God our Lord prosper them, they could report our destitute existence on this island. The four were: Alvaro Fernández, a Portuguese carpenter and sailor; a certain Méndez; Figueroa, an *hidalgo* from Toledo; and Astudillo of Zafra—all excellent swimmers. They took with them an Indian of the island of Auia [which presumably was the Indian name of Galveston, though another island could possibly have been meant].

Why We Named the Island "Doom"

Within a few days of the departure of the four Christians, the weather turned so cold and stormy that the Indians could not pull up roots; their cane contraptions for catching fish yielded nothing; and the huts being very open, our men began to die.

Five Christians quartered on the coast came to the extremity of eating each other. Only the body of the last one, whom nobody was left to eat, was found unconsumed. Their names were Sierra, Diego Lopez, Corral, Palacios, and Gonzalo Ruiz.

The Indians were so shocked at this cannibalism that, if they had seen it sometime earlier, they surely would have killed every one of us. In a very short while as it was, only fifteen of the eighty who had come survived.

Then half the natives died from a disease of the bowels and blamed us.

When they came to kill us, the Indian who kept me interceded. He said: If we had so much power of sorcery we would not have let all but a few of our own perish; the few left did no hurt or wrong; it would be best to leave us alone. God our Lord be praised, they listened and relented.

We named this place *Malhado*—the "Island of Doom."

The Malhado Way of Life

The people we came to know there [Capoques and Han, as identified later in the narrative] are tall and well built. Their only weapons are bows and arrows, which they use with great dexterity. The men bore through one of their nipples, some both, and insert a joint of cane two and a half palms long by two fingers thick. They also bore their lower lip and wear a piece of cane in it half a finger in diameter.

Their women toil incessantly.

From October to the end of February every year, which is the season these Indians live on the island, they subsist on the roots I have mentioned, which the women get from under water in November and December. Only in these two months, too, do they take fish in their cane weirs. When the fish is consumed, the roots furnish the one staple. At the end of February the islanders go into other parts to seek sustenance, for then the root is beginning to grow and is not edible.

These people love their offspring more than any in the world and treat them very mildly.

If a son dies, the whole village joins the parents and kindred in weeping. The parents set off the wails each day before dawn, again at noon, and at sunset, for one year. The funeral rites occur when the year of mourning is up. Following these rites, the survivors wash off the smoke stain of the ceremony in a symbolic purgation. All the dead are lamented this way except the aged, who merit no regrets. The dead are buried, except medicine men, who are cremated. Everybody in the village dances and makes merry while the pyre of a medicine man kindles, and until his bones become powder. A year later, when his rites are celebrated, the entire village again participating, this powder is presented in water for the relatives to drink.

Each man has an acknowledged wife, except the medicine men, who may have two or three wives apiece. The several wives live together in perfect amity.

When a daughter marries, she must take everything her husband kills in hunting or catches in fishing to the house of her father, without daring to eat or to withhold any part of it, and the husband gets provided by female carrier from his father-in-law's house. Neither the bride's father nor mother may enter the son-in-law's house after the marriage, nor he theirs; and this holds for the children of the respective couples. If a man and his in-laws should chance to be walking so they would meet, they turn silently aside from each other and go a crossbow-shot out of their way, averting their glance to the ground. The woman, however, is free to fraternize with the parents and relatives of her husband. These marriage customs prevail for more than fifty leagues inland from the island.

At a house where a son or brother may die, no one goes out for food for three months, the neighbors and other relatives providing what is eaten. Because of this custom, which the Indians literally would not break to save their lives, great hunger reigned in most houses while we resided there, it being a time of repeated deaths. Those who sought food worked hard, but they could get little in that severe season. That is why the Indians who kept me left the island by canoe for oyster bays on the main.

Three months out of every year they eat nothing but oysters and drink very bad water. Wood is scarce; mosquitoes, plentiful. The houses are made of mats; their floors consist of masses of oyster shells. The natives sleep on these shells—in animal skins, those who happen to own such.

Many a time I would have to go three days without eating, as would the natives. I thought it impossible that life could be so prolonged in such protracted hunger; though afterward I found myself in yet greater want, as shall be seen.

The [Han] Indians who had Alonso del Castillo, Andrés Dorantes, and the others of their barge who remained alive, spoke a different dialect and claimed a different descent from these I lived among. They frequented the opposite shore of the main to eat oysters, staying till the first of April, then returning.

The inhabitants of all these parts go naked, except that the women cover some part of their persons with a wool that grows on trees [Spanish moss], and damsels dress in deerskin.

The people are generous to each other with what little they have. There is no chief. All belonging to the same lineage keep together. They speak two languages: Capoque and Han.

They have a strange custom when acquaintances meet or occasionally visit, of weeping for half an hour before they speak. This over, the one who is visited rises and gives his visitor all he has. The latter accepts it and, after a while, carries it away, often without a word. They have other strange customs, but I have told the principal and most remarkable of them.

In April [1529] we went to the seashore and ate blackberries all month, a time of *areitos* [dance ceremonies] and *fiestas* among the Indians.

How We Became Medicine Men

The islanders wanted to make physicians of us without examination or a review of diplomas. Their method of cure is to blow on the sick, the breath and the laying on of hands supposedly casting out the infirmity. They insisted we should do this too and be of some use to them. We scoffed at their cures and at the idea we knew how to heal. But they withheld food from us until we complied. An Indian told me I knew not whereof I spoke in saying their methods had no effect. Stones and other things growing about in the fields, he said, had a virtue whereby passing a pebble along the stomach could take away pain and heal; surely extraordinary men like us embodied such powers over nature. Hunger forced us to obey, but disclaiming any responsibility for our failure or success.

An Indian, falling sick, would send for a medicine man, who would apply his cure. The patient would then give the medicine man all he had and seek more from his relatives to give. The medicine man makes incisions over the point of the pain, sucks the wound, and cauterizes it. This remedy enjoys high repute among the Indians. I have, as a matter of fact, tried it on myself with good results. The medicine men blow on the spot they have treated, as a finishing touch, and the patient regards himself relieved.

Our method, however, was to bless the sick, breathe upon them, recite a *Pater noster* and *Ave Maria,* and pray earnestly to God our Lord for their recovery. When we concluded with the sign of the cross, He willed that our patients should directly spread the news that they had been restored to health.

In consequence, the Indians treated us kindly. They deprived themselves of food to give to us, and presented us skins and other tokens of gratitude.

Bill Porterfield

*Bill Porterfield is the preeminent portrayer of "Texas characters"
as a way to get to the heart of the Texas character. His essays
appear in regular newspaper columns and many national magazines.*

THE CHRISTIAN AND THE PAGAN

Indians are no different from white people when the preacher
comes calling in the middle of supper, and the Lewises could not hide
their discomfort. As their fried potatoes grew cold, they swallowed their
inclination to go on with the meal and hung there in a slack-jawed and
grudging gesture of hospitality. The hot little room was heavy with his
intrusion, and the Reverend Bertram E. Bobb sensed it. But he would
not be deterred. He was a big, beefy Choctaw, as resolute in his Christian mission as only a fundamentalist can be, and he went on talking to
them in that way that preachers do in the living rooms of backsliders.

"Charles," he said to the man of the house, "Now I want you to come
join us, you hear? We need you and you need us. Lots of fellowship, for
you and the wife and baby." He smiled benignly at the little Apache girl
in the crib.

Charles was miserable. He sweated through his T-shirt and fogged
his glasses. He was embarrassed because his wife lay lacerated and
bandaged on the couch, a testament to the meanness and violence that
came over him whenever he stumbled home drunk. He knew the
preacher knew why she had been in the hospital, and Charles had a
sinking feeling that this Christian witch doctor was on to him, that Bobb
and his missionaries would hound him mercilessly until he had no
choice but to fall into sobriety and salvation. When the preacher finally
left, leaving his card, Charles closed the door with a shudder.

"A little reluctance there," Brother Bobb said to his companion,
"but he'll come around."

Reverend Bobb's friend, his right-hand man, he often said, was Richard Soontay, a Kiowa-Apache. Richard was a mild-mannered Christian
man with a Creek wife and four kids. This had not always been so.
Before he met Reverend Bobb, Richard had done his share of boozing
down on the Corner. A sad place, the Corner. A clutter of shabby bars
at North Peak and Bryan streets where red men drank themselves into
oblivion.

There are more Indians in Dallas than Custer met at Little Bighorn, and they have been streaming in off the reservations of the Southwest for the past thirteen years. The government sends them to trade schools here in the hope that they will become productive members of the American mainstream. And so most of them have. They have tended to settle in and around Oak Cliff, Casa Linda, and Garland.

For many of them, however, the move into the city is a wrenching experience. This is especially true of the tribes from the desert states. Out there on the isolated mesas they have kept much of their Indian-ness in spite of government schools and Christian missions, and the life they encounter in Dallas is alien to them. Tenacious in the old tongue and in the old ways, harboring some deep racial memories of their near genocide at the hands of the white man, they come here reluctantly, and some continue to live here in a bitter self-destructiveness that finds expression in the beer joints along the Corner.

It is a challenge for any preacher, and for an Indian like Reverend Bobb, the Corner is an irresistible hunting ground for sinners. He found a song leader there in the Kiowa-Apache, Richard Soontay, and now he was on the Christian warpath again, searching for lost souls with which to fill his little Open Door Bible Church in Oak Cliff. He and Soontay had handed out cards on the Corner that morning, and now at noon they were going from door to door on Annex Street, a row of apartments a few blocks from the Corner where most of the Indians new to Dallas live. The mailboxes in the lobbies show the cultural schizophrenia of these aboriginal Americans: Phillip Bluebird, C. Eagle Road, Jerimiah Joe, Noreen Two Crow—anglicized versions of Indian names which have passed into the obscurity that is the fate of oral traditions.

They came to the door of Chavez LeValdo, a Navajo-Acoma with the name of his people's Spanish conquerors. LeValdo asked them in. He was a slender young man, modishly dressed in flared pants and a beaded belt. His hair, silky and black, fell below his shoulders. He wore a headband and a stony expression on his high-boned face. He listened patiently to the Choctaw preacher and his Kiowa-Apache sidekick, and then when they were through with their pitch he asked them some questions and expressed his own religious beliefs, which to Reverend Bobb harked of paganism. The preacher had run into this before with Indians, and it always stimulated him to work harder at spreading the gospel. He tried to get a commitment from LeValdo to attend one of his services, and failing that, he urged the young man to listen to his Christian Indian radio broadcast on KSKY.

Reverend Bobb left feeling that LeValdo was beyond the pale and would probably remain so.

Bertram Bobb was a single-minded savior of men, but sometimes he had to admit that the devil had gotten there first and had done his damage to some poor souls, rendering them beyond redemption. One had to take these losses in stride. The way of the righteous was straight and narrow, and many fell by the wayside. Bobb himself had always seen the way very plainly, thanks to his parents. They had been Methodist missionaries among the Choctaws. Bobb had begun his own ministry in the Methodist church, but he had left it because of the liberal theology he thought it had begun promoting. He was now an independent preacher, connected with no church but his own out in Oak Cliff, and he saw his mission as that of meeting the spiritual needs of the growing Indian population in Dallas.

He had been fairly successful, if he did say so himself. He could count twelve tribes on the membership roll of his church. The preaching and praying was in English because none of the tribes could understand one another in Indian. Indians, from tribe to tribe, were as different as white men from nation to nation. Well, that was not entirely true, Bobb was fond of pointing out; the Choctaws, Chickasaws, Creeks, and Seminoles could converse fairly well among themselves. But when they sang in Reverend Bobb's church, they often sang in Indian, first one tribe's tongue and then another's. Many of the hymns they sang were first sung on the Trail of Tears in the 1830s, when thousands of Indians died as they were forced to march to the new reservations in Oklahoma. The songs had what the Indians called a mourning sound.

Still, Reverend Bobb lamented, Christian work among American Indians was very slow. And often it was of the wrong kind. He believed in the literal truth of the Bible, and he felt that too many of the denominations were getting away from the Word. The shame of it, he thought, was that the basic religious nature of the Indian was being wasted on paganism. Its hold was still strong on the Indian: young Chavez LeValdo was an example. Bobb couldn't help but like LeValdo. The boy had a good mind. He wondered if LeValdo was on peyote. He sighed and went on about his business.

And then one Sunday he looked up from his pulpit to see Chavez LeValdo in the congregation. It was true LeValdo sat on the very last row, next to the door, and that there was about him an air of subtle defiance—he wore dark sunglasses and his arms were sternly folded— but nonetheless he was present, presumably to listen with an open mind.

The Christian and the Pagan | 17

Even in a congregation which was mostly Indian, LeValdo stood out because of his long hair and headband. There were others there just as Indian in their blood—Creek, Cherokee, Chickasaw, and Comanche, Cheyenne and Sioux and Seminole—but not so Indian, perhaps, in their dress or attitude.

Reverend Bobb made note of LeValdo to the congregation. Every face turned to the young man. He sat there awkwardly for a moment and then rose hesitantly to his feet to acknowledge the introduction.

The singing began. Good old fundamentalist hymns. "Come Thou Fount," first in English and then in Choctaw.

The song "He Hideth My Soul" said it all for Reverend Bobb. It was his reason for being, and he saw no conflict between being both a Choctaw and a Christian.

> He hideth my soul
> In the cleft of a rock
> That shadows a dry thirsty land;
>
> He hideth my life
> In the depths of his love
> And covers me there with his hand.

He sang his love for Christ in English, and now he sang it in Choctaw.

And then he prayed it and preached it.

But Chavez LeValdo was unmoved.

This was the second time the young man had ever sat in on a Protestant service, and he felt the same disappointment as he had before. The word *sacred* came to mind. Sacredness was what was missing here, it seemed to him. LeValdo had been taught, as a child, in a Catholic school on the reservation at Shiprock, New Mexico, and although he was now wrestling with himself over Catholicism—more and more he felt himself being drawn to the faith of his Acoma forefathers—he still liked the mystic feeling and formality of the Roman church. There was a magic, an otherworldliness in the rites of the Catholics and the Acomas that was missing in this plain little church next to the Central Expressway.

He did not question Reverend Bobb's sincerity, but what he regretted in this Choctaw Christian preacher was his Anglo-Saxon informality, his rather pedestrian and matter-of-fact approach to the spiritual. A "Rally Day" banner hung above the pulpit. Bobb could have been a well-fed coach speaking to the quarterback club or a program chairman at a Rotary luncheon. As LeValdo left the church, shaking the preacher's hand at the door, the only generous thing he could say was that he liked the Choctaw hymns although he could not understand the words.

And yet there were similarities between LeValdo and Reverend Bobb. They were both brown-skinned aboriginal Americans, both had been raised in Indian communities—Bobb in Oklahoma, LeValdo in New Mexico—both had attended Christian schools in their youth, and both had served in the U.S. Navy— Bobb during World War II and LeValdo aboard an aircraft carrier off Vietnam.

The difference between them, perhaps, was that out in the desert of LeValdo's youth the memory of the ancients was stronger and more binding than it was in Reverend Bobb's Oklahoma. It was a fact that the Choctaws—Bobb's tribe—were one of the Five Civilized Tribes, so called by the white man because they had more easily adapted to the white man's ways than had other Indians. On the other hand, the Navajo and the Acoma—whose blood and heritage LeValdo carried— had been among the last to capitulate to the white man. High up in the hot cliffs of the Acoma, LeValdo knew that Catholicism was a white man's medicine which had not entirely replaced the notions and potions of Pueblo prophets.

The old prayers and practices yet remained, the externals of a spirit pervasive after four hundred years of excommunication. It was true that LeValdo would have his baby daughter baptized by a Catholic priest, but it was also true that he fancied himself being buried, when his time came, in the Indian way with his moccasins and war paint on. The ways of his ancestors rose up in him and made him reluctant to cut his hair, and they worked in him when he carved dolls and made drums and shields of rawhide.

Chavez LeValdo did not consider himself a throwback to the past. There was enough of the white man's influence in him to cause him to count time and to measure it by the Newtonian dimensions of past, present, and future. And he saw himself as being in tune with these three references, like the *paisano* bird which was painted on Indian drums. The *paisano* had four toes on each foot. Two pointed to the back, the past, and two pointed to the front, the future. The leg itself came right down upon the ground of the present. And here was LeValdo himself, living in the urban clot of modern Dallas, taking advantage of a government grant which allowed him to learn how to repair and maintain a computer. He spoke six languages: Navajo, Acoma, English, Fortran, Cobol, and Compass—the last three being computer idiom.

Pagan? Peyote?

Well he had never tasted the cactus bud, and he had never understood why white men called the faith of his forefathers pagan. The Old Man of the Sky was the husband of the Old Woman of the Earth, and all things came from their union, just as Raquel came from Chavez's union with his wife Eunice. Mankind and the animals, the earth and the sky with their elements, all had the same kind of life. And a person had to be in harmony with the life in all things. The way was in religion, in a prayerful reverence for every stick and stone and bird and flower and brother. It was beautiful, he thought.

Chavez LeValdo went home to his apartment and got out his *kethawn* box. It had been given him by one of the elders of his tribe, an old Navajo who had taught him the ancient chants. It was a case made of cloth, and in it were prayer sticks and talismans of his people's sacred rites. He burned a stick and rubbed soot on his face and sang the magic chants that were said to ward off evil influences. Now he felt clean again and strong enough to cope with the white man's world. He was also hungry. He went into the kitchen and made a peanut butter sandwich.

William Humphrey

William Humphrey (b. 1924) is a native of Clarksville. His fondness for East Texas settings in his stories of family love and conflict is reminiscent of William Faulkner's frequent use of Yoknapatawpha County. His writings include the novels Home from the Hill *and* The Ordways; *critical essays* (Ah, Wilderness!); *and collections of short stories, from which this selection is drawn.*

THE LAST OF THE CADDOES

I

By the shores of the Red River, in Texas, lived a boy named Jimmy Hawkins, who learned one day to his surprise that he was, on his father's side, part Indian. Until then Jimmy had always thought he was just another white boy.

A curious reluctance had kept Jimmy's mother from ever telling him about his Indian blood. She had felt it from the time he first began to question her about himself, about the family. She shied away from it warily, almost as though in fear. This was very silly of her, of course. Just childishness. Some old bogeyman left over from her early childhood, nothing more. She had never seen a live Indian in her life. The savages, even in Texas, had long since been pacified, not to say exterminated. Being afraid of Indians in these days and times, when the only ones left were celluloid Indians, Saturday-matinee horse-opera Indians! *Ugh. How. Me big chief Squat-in-the-Mud. Heap big medicine.* Ridiculous! It was quite plain that what she really felt was not fear at all, it was in fact a touch of jealousy, possessiveness. For it was not she but his father from whom the child got his Indian blood, and obviously she was jealous of that part of him, small as it was, that was alien to her. Not that this was not equally silly of her, of course. Not that the Indian in himself was not equally alien to her husband. Certainly he would never try to use this bond to draw the boy closer to himself, away from his mother. There was really no reason for it. And that was it, precisely. That explained entirely why Mrs. Hawkins, and, following her lead, Mr. Hawkins, had let their Jimmy reach the age of twelve without ever mentioning this trifle about himself: there was no reason to.

Yet all the while Jimmy's mother felt she really perhaps ought to just mention it. There were times, indeed, when it was as though she were being urged from all sides to tell him, reproached for her silence, even almost commanded to speak out without further delay. "But what on earth difference does it make?" she would argue. "Nowadays what difference does it make? None whatever." Though in fact it might have made a great difference to Jimmy. The boy was simply crazy about Indians: read about nothing else, dressed himself up as one, made himself beadwork belts, sewed his own moccasins; his mother might have guessed that to be able to claim he was part Indian would have pleased him as nothing else could. "But it's only the tiniest little fraction," she would rejoin. "Hardly enough to count." Or, again: "It isn't as if I had deliberately not told him. Heavens! Why on earth would I do that? What's it to me, one way or the other? The subject has simply never come up, that's all. If it ever should, why then, of course . . ." Just who it was she was arguing with at these times she never knew.

It came out unexpectedly one day when they were having one of their rows. Lately it had gotten so all they ever did, it seemed, was fuss and quarrel. Jimmy was passing through a difficult phase. Going on thirteen now, and feeling new powers stirring within him, he was forever testing his strength, trying his mother, seeing just how far he could go, how much he could get away with. This one was their third fight in two days. Jimmy had done something he knew not to do, had been scolded and punished, and had turned sullen and defiant. His punishment would end, he was told, when he confessed he had been bad and said he was sorry; the set of his jaw proclaimed that he had vowed he would sooner die. He could be very stubborn. He was getting to be more than a match for his mother, as he well knew: too big for her to switch anymore—the very threat had begun to sound absurd—almost too big for his father to correct; and he soon reduced her to that frazzled state where, as she would say, she didn't know what to do. He grew bolder and more impudent until at last he said something so sassy she slapped his face. This made dart from Jimmy's black eyes two poisoned arrows of hatred. "Oh!" cried his mother, pierced by his look, "I don't know what gets into you at times like this!" Then before she knew it: "It must be the Indian in you coming out."

Jimmy instantly forgot his burning cheek. The Indian in him! Did she mean it? Real Indian? Which tribe? What part Indian was he? How long had this been known? Why had she never told him before?

But his mother had already told him more than she ever meant to. "You get it," she said dryly, "from your father, not me." To her surprise, and her chagrin, she found herself trembling, positively seething with anger. She felt somehow as though she had been tricked into letting it out. What was most exasperating was to find herself so vexed over a mere trifle. But what she felt was not altogether anger, and she knew it. One of her heartstrings had just been tied tight in a hard little knot of fear.

Jimmy's antics, meanwhile, did nothing to soothe her temper. His disobedience, his mother's displeasure, the sentence of punishment he was still under all forgotten, he was circling round and around her doing an Indian war dance. Brandishing an invisible tomahawk, he stamped his feet, ducked his head, then flung it back, all the while patting his mouth as he whooped, "Wah wah wah wah wah wah—" Until, shaking with rage, she hissed at him, "Little savage! Treat your mother with no more consideration than a wild savage! Well, that's just what you are! So act like one, that's right! Be proud of yourself for it!" Then she broke down in tears and ran sobbing from the room.

Thus, not until he was twelve, almost thirteen, and then only by accident (or so it seemed at the time), did Jimmy Hawkins learn that he was part Indian. And that that was the part his mother blamed for all she disliked in him.

II

How big a part? Which tribe? These questions, and others, Jimmy did not again put to his mother, eager as he was for an answer to them—not after her angry outburst. His hurt pride would not let him.

She had said he got it from his father, so Jimmy went to him. But he checked himself long before he got there. Not much pondering upon the matter was needed to make Jimmy even less willing to question his father than he was to question his mother. More Indian by half than he, his father had connived at, or at the very least had acquiesced in, keeping from his son the knowledge of his Indian ancestry. There was a name for men like his father, and a punishment decreed for them. His father was a renegade, and so without further ado Jimmy drummed him out of their tribe—whichever that might prove to be.

To be an Indian, even if only in part, was to Jimmy so glorious a fate it was impossible for him to imagine anyone feeling differently. But any lingering doubts he may have had about how differently his mother felt were soon dispelled. For although she had meant never to mention it—unless, that is to say, it just came up by itself, of course—once it was out and there was no taking it back, she found herself saying again and again, whenever he goaded her to it, which was often enough as the warfare between them went on, "That's the Indian in you coming out, that's what that bit of deviltry is. Little savage!" Though each time she said it it seemed to draw tighter that hard little knot in her heart.

And it was no sooner said than something awful began to happen. Something truly sinister. Something quite uncanny and even unbelievable, and yet precisely the sort of thing that might have been expected. Indeed, it now seemed to have been a premonition of this very thing that had kept her from ever speaking out before. Overnight Jimmy began to look like an Indian. He really did. What made this sudden transformation the more uncanny was that, strictly speaking, he looked no more like an Indian than he ever had, or ever would for that matter, with his corn-silk hair and pale, almost white eyebrows and lashes, his fair, not to say pallid, skin. His only feature that might have been Indian was his glittering black eyes—brown, actually, but a brown so dark, especially being set in that pale face, as to be really black. Yet all the same he really did begin to look like an Indian—more so every day—more so each time he was reproached with being one. More sullen and sly: more Indian.

It had certainly made a change in him: Jimmy could see it for himself. And no wonder. For although it may have come out accidentally, the revelation that he was an Indian found him already prepared to be one. He knew all there was to know about Indians. All his reading, ever since he learned to read, had been about the Indians, and in the accounts of the wars between them and the white settlers he had always taken their side. Now at last he knew why. They had been calling to him, blood calling to blood.

The things about himself that Jimmy had not understood before were explained now. His outbursts of temper, his touchy pride, his moods of contrariness, his impulses of cruelty, the stubborn streak that so irritated his mother: his Indian blood not only accounted for all these, it absolved him from blame for them. If he behaved sometimes like a little savage it was because he was a little savage. It was not his fault. He was what he was. He felt a burden of guilt lifted from him. He was through forevermore with apologizing for himself. It was not his fault that he was part Indian. He could not change that. He could not have done anything about it even if he had wanted to.

Being an Indian was not going to be all fun then. It never had been: this Jimmy knew from his reading; to be one in his day and time was harder than ever, it seemed. Situated where he was, cut off from his people, not even knowing yet who his people were, he was alone, surrounded by the enemy. He would need to be very crafty, very cunning, very wary. He would need to tread softly. He would have to sleep always with one eye open. He would need to grow up very fast. At his age an Indian boy was already training to be a brave.

He no longer joined in childish games. It did not befit his new dignity. To be an Indian was a serious responsibility. He seldom smiled, never laughed anymore. He comported himself with the gravity of a sachem, spoke with the sententiousness of one of Fenimore Cooper's sagamores. He exulted inwardly to see that his new disdainful silence was more exasperating to his parents and his schoolteachers than open defiance had ever been. When stung by one of his mother's slurs upon his Indian blood, he betrayed none of his resentment; he stored these up with Indian patience, all to be repaid with interest one day.

Meanwhile the more he brooded upon it the more he resented never being told that he was what he was. And who knew how much longer he might have been kept in ignorance? Had she not lost her temper that day and let it slip, his mother might never have told him. The prospect of this appalled Jimmy. When thought of that way it was not just the pleasure and the pride of being part Indian that he would have been deprived of: that would have been never really to know *what* he was.

It had come out despite them. Blood, they said, would out, and

Indian blood, more powerful than any, would out though it were only a drop. There was an unseen power at work here. The spirits of his long-denied red forefathers had spoken to him at last (ironically enough, through his mother's own mouth) and claimed him as one of their own. Only who, exactly, were they? What was he? Indian, but what kind? Heir to what renown?

There was just one person who might be able to tell Jimmy the answers to his questions.

III

That his Grandfather Hawkins was half Indian, or more, was plain for all to see, yet Jimmy saw it for the first time when next the family went for a visit out to the farm. He who had been looking all his life for an Indian to adore!

But how were you to recognize the Indian in a man who dressed always in baggy, patched old denim overalls and a tattered denim jumper out at the elbows? Who, as Jimmy had seen, let his old wife cut his hair using an oatmeal bowl as a form instead of wearing it down to his shoulders in braids? Who when he came into town came not riding bareback on a horse but in a creaky old farmwagon drawn by a team of plodding gray mules? Sixty-five years of plowing, hoeing, picking cotton had taken all the noble savage out of the man.

"Grandfather," Jimmy said, "I've just been told that I am part Indian, and that I get it from you."

"Who told you?"

"My mother."

"Did, did she? Well, sonnyboy, our side of the family is ever bit as good as yore mother's, and you can tell her I said so. She's got a lot to brag about, now ain't she? Them Tylers. What did e'er a one of them ever amount to? Old Dub Tyler, jake-legged from all the bootleg corn liquor he's drank, in debt to everybody in town: he's something to be proud of, I reckon? That's yore other granddaddy. So any time yore mother's in the mood to trade compliments about—"

"What I want to know is, why didn't anybody ever tell me about this before?"

"I'd of told you if you'd ever of ast me. Whether yore mother liked it or not. Think I wouldn't? Tell anybody. Not that it's anybody else's business but my own. Son, what a man is born don't matter a hill of beans. It's what you make of yoreself that counts."

"If you're not what you are then what are you?" said Jimmy. "You're not anything. Tell me now about myself."

"Tell you what?"

"Tell about your father. My great-grandfather. The Indian."

"Why, what do you want to know about him?"

"Everything! I want to know all there is to know."

"Well, he was not what you would call a big man. Neither was he a little man. More what you would call middling-sized. Bothered with stomach trouble all his life, though what killed him was not that but something else. Died of—"

"What kind of Indian was he?"

"What do you mean, what kind of Indin was he?"

"I mean like Comanche, or Cheyenne, or Apache. You know. What tribe?"

"Oh. Well, I wouldn't know nothing about that. Indin, that's all I can tell you, boy."

"What was his name?"

"His name? Mr. George P. Hawkins, same as mine."

"If he was an Indian, where did he ever get a name like that—Mr. George P. Hawkins? That's not an Indian name. Indians are named names like Rain-in-the-Face or Crazy Horse, or something like that. I expect he just never told you his true name."

"Must of been a Hawkins in the woodpile back somewheres along the line, just where and when I can't tell you, 'cause I wasn't there myself. I can tell you one thing though: I'm grateful I haven't had to go through life named George P. Crazy Horse. Yes, sir, I'm sure grateful I haven't had to go through—"

"How about your grandfather? Tell me about him."

"Never knowed the man. Dead 'fore ever I was born."

"Didn't your father ever tell you about him when you were a boy?"

"When I was a boy I never had no time to waste setting around talking about my granddaddy. And I ain't got none for it now. Maybe he was the Hawkins."

Another renegade. It ran in the family. Jimmy felt he had much to atone for.

IV

Before the coming of the white man, the northeastern part of Texas where Jimmy Hawkins lived with his father and mother was the domain of the Caddo Indians. The local tribe was one which, although he was born and raised there, and notwithstanding all his Indian lore, Jimmy had never heard of until he began delving into his pedigree.

To learn that he belonged to such an obscure tribe was a surprise, and for a moment something of a disappointment. He had rather set his heart on being a Comanche. However, he liked the name Caddo. He knew he was one: he felt a thrill of recognition the first time he read the word.

Specimens preserved in various museums, he read in the small guide book in the small town library, proved the Caddoes to have been the most talented potters of all the Indians of North America.

But who were their famous chiefs? Who were the Caddo Pontiac, the Caddo Sitting Bull, the Caddo Geronimo? Who were their most renowned warriors? Where were their great battles fought?

The Caddoes it was, he read, who had reared the numerous large burial mounds still to be found in that part of the state and adjacent Louisiana (in the one on his grandfather's farm did his own forefathers lie sleeping?), which, along with the name of nearby Caddo Lake, were at this late date (the book had been published in 1907) the only reminders left of this once large and powerful tribe.

Where had all the Caddoes gone?

Like the Mohicans, the Caddoes were no more. Their numbers depleted by their war against the white settlers, and by the diseases which the settlers brought with them, their last surviving remnant had been forcibly removed to Oklahoma in 1854 and resettled on government reservations, where, through intermarriage with and adoption into other tribes, the Caddoes had lost their separate identity.

The little book told no more; none other told as much.

He had been orphaned of his entire nation. He was the last of the Caddoes.

V

What Jimmy Hawkins had always known was now confirmed: he was meant for no common fate. He had been born with a horror of the ordinary, and had always known he was not what he seemed to the world to be. He had often wondered who he really was, and had felt that like the changeling prince in the fairy tale he had been cheated of his birthright and brought up in a meaner station of life than fate and his gifts had intended him for. The reason, as he now knew, was that he was the last of the Caddoes: rightful heir to all that he surveyed, with blood in his veins that cried out for vengeance: a dangerous person, a permanent threat to those who had wronged him. So they must have been warned by the bad fairy (herself Indian) who was not invited to his christening but who appeared at it all the same. "You may bleach him whiter than the snow, give him a white man's name, and bring him up in ignorance of his people," she had pronounced in a raspy voice, shaking a bony brown finger at them, "he is what he is. What will be will be." So Jimmy had always known he was ordained, marked out, chosen to perform some bold feat; now he knew it would be something to vindicate his dispossessed, destroyed, and all but forgotten race. He awaited the revelation of what it would be. Once he knew the name of his tribe he felt the constant presence of his red forebears molding him, training him, preserving him until such time as he should be ready and his mission be revealed to him.

They taught him to see what before he had overlooked, what others, outsiders, still overlooked: the relics everywhere of their immemorial stay in the land from which they had been driven out. In plowed fields they showed him arrowheads that generations of plowmen, though their eyes were seldom lifted from the ground, had not seen. In stones that the unknowing took to be just stones he recognized the mortars in which his people had ground their maize and the pestles with which they had pounded it, the flint knives with which they had skinned their game, the tomahawks with which they had brained their foes.

He felt them most powerfully in the woods. In the green stillness he could see their spirits flitting among the trees and in the whispering together of the branches could hear their voices. He knew no fear, for they were with him. They were the lords of the forest and he their only son, their sole survivor, the last arrow from the once-full quiver of their wrath. And when at home or at school he was whipped for his disobedience, they lent him fortitude. With them at his side he could endure without flinching whatever any white man could mete out. Not a whimper could they draw from him; he sneered in the faces of his tormentors. The last of the Caddoes brought no stain of dishonor upon the spirits of his proud dead.

If to be an Indian was a career in itself, to be the last of one's tribe was a calling. To be the sole repository of a nation's history, its traditions, its laws, its beliefs, and its rituals, and to know nothing of that history, those traditions, laws, beliefs, and rituals, and to be just twelve years old, was to carry an almost crushing weight of responsibility. No wonder Jimmy was aged and sober beyond his years. That with all this on his mind he should have no time for friends, for games, or for schoolbooks.

His confirmation time was fast approaching. He would turn thirteen that summer, would enter upon his manhood, and as soon as school was out Jimmy obeyed the call he had heard to make a pilgrimage to his ancestral shrine: the Caddo burial mound on his grandfather's farm. He was to spend the summer in the country. His parents were relieved to see him go, glad of a rest. The prospect of having him always about the house, of a whole long summer of wrangling, was more than his mother could face. It was his own idea; she need not accuse herself of getting rid of him. After a few months' separation maybe they would get along a little better. Hopefully, a summer in the open, swimming, going fishing, exploring the farm, would make a happier boy of him, a better pupil when school reopened in the fall.

VI

"He don't do a thing but dig in that damn dirt pile," his grandfather reported when Jimmy's parents drove out to celebrate his birthday. "He's at it all day long every day and Sunday. Can't even get him to stop long enough to eat his dinner. If you all weren't here he'd be out there right now. Wouldn't you?" Over his shoulder the old man flung a scowl at the great mound of earth that rose like a single gigantic grave out of the field below the house.

"Well, I must say it seems to have done him good. He's so changed I wouldn't have known him. Would you, Mother?" said Jimmy's father, and turning to his wife, received a look that blazed with exasperation.

For no, she would not have known Jimmy, he was so changed, and she was in torment while his father beamed. It was not her boy but a stranger she found awaiting her, a stranger whom she had brought into the world with her pain on this day of the year. He had grown like a weed, had in just these few weeks away from her shot up half a head taller. The last of the baby fat had thinned from his cheeks, which now showed their bones, and his baby fairness was gone: he was as brown as a penny. No longer was he the soft round ungendered little sausage she remembered; his shoulders had wedged out, his little pot been trimmed away neat and flat and hard. The change in his chemistry had coarsened his skin, his hair, thickened his muscles, deepened his voice. Yet though his mother ached to be proud of his new manliness, she could not. She was no part of it. She was a little afraid of him. She felt the misgiving every mother feels when suddenly one day her son comes to present her with his bill for the many slights and indignities of his boyhood.

His manner confused and disarmed her. She had expected on his birthday to find him cocky and impertinent, and had come prepared to overlook it for the occasion. Her forbearance would not be wanted, thank you. Instead she found him subdued, withdrawn, grave. This gravity grated her as no amount of impudence would have done. How

The Last of the Caddoes | 29

dared he treat her with such cool courtesy, as though there were no history of any troubles between them! To learn now that he had spent his time digging so fanatically in that old Indian mound instead of in the harmless pastimes she had imagined made her feel she had been betrayed and mocked.

"Must think he's going to find some buried treasure. Well, you're in for a big letdown if you do," said Jimmy's grandfather. "The Indins, why, they were all so piss-pore they never hardly had enough to eat, much less any silver or gold. What have you found? Just what I told you you'd find. Nothing but skeltons and a lot of old broken crocks."

Jimmy was used to his grandfather's disapproval of his project. The burial mound sat square in the middle of his grandfather's cotton patch. While Jimmy dug on top of the mound his grandfather chopped the cotton in the field below. Whenever the old man's progress down the row brought him parallel with the mound he would stop and rest and watch Jimmy dig. He refused ever to face the mound, he would only lour at it over his shoulder, leaning on his hoe handle with one foot crossed over the other and his behind stuck out. But if the sight of his grandson's foolishness disgusted him, the sight of his grandfather's degradation filled Jimmy with shame and despair. Commanded by the voice of his people to know himself through knowing them, Jimmy had bared the buried history of the Caddoes, delving backward in time from their end to their beginning. He had measured the antiquity of his lineage in countless shovelfuls of earth. The handiwork of his tribe had shown him the strangeness of his heritage, his own difference. From the mound's topmost layer, where the bodies, unceremoniously interred, had been so closely packed ("their numbers depleted by their war against the white settlers") that the bones were inseparably mixed, and where the little bones of children were numerous ("and by the diseases which the settlers brought with them"), he had dug down to the splendid rotting cerements, the broken, once-magnificent urns, the weapons of flint and obsidian worthy to accompany a great chief to the happy hunting grounds, of the days of their greatness: from desolation down to grandeur that made the desolation all the keener. Then to look down and see his grandfather, the man with more of the blood of the Caddoes in his veins than any other living man, hoeing his way down the rows of scraggly cotton: it was a constant reminder of how art the mighty fallen.

"I remember digging in there myself when I was a boy," said Jimmy's father. "I never found anything worth keeping."

"Maybe you didn't dig deep enough," said Jimmy.

"Why, what all have you found?"

"Oh, things."

"What sort of things?"

"Oh, just things."

"Well, some people collect old Indian things. Mr. Will Etheridge in town, for instance. He'll pay a dime apiece for flint arrowheads. Whole ones, that is, of course. I'll speak to him about you next time I see him. You can take and show him what you've found, see if he'll offer you something for it."

A laugh came from Jimmy's mother like the sound of breaking glass. "Jimmy isn't after buried treasure," she said. "And he wouldn't think of selling any of the things he's found. Would you, dear?" she said, turning to him with a spiteful simper. "They're sacred, isn't that right? Yes. You see, I'm the only one who understands, aren't I, my little Hiawatha? I can read you like an open book."

"Are we going to fight on my birthday, Mother?" asked Jimmy.

"Why, what better day for it?" she cried, regretting what she said even as she said it. "I was only trying to be friendly, but if you want to fight, what better day for it than your birthday?"

It was a shocking thing to say. She herself was quite taken aback. She had not known she was going to say that, it had just come out by itself. Thus she was all the more taken aback when Jimmy said, "I knew you were going to say that, Mother."

"He wants to work I'll put him to work and pay him for doing it," said Jimmy's grandfather. "Chopping cotton, fifty cents a day. It ain't near as hard work as spading in the ground. Fifty cents a day. Save it up and buy yoreself something nice. Damn foolishness to work for nothing when you could be earning pay. Buy yoreself a twenty-two rifle. A banjo. Get you a bicycle, then you can carry a paper route, earn money all year round. Tell you one thing, sonnyboy: prices of goods what they are today, if you was mine you wouldn't be out there wasting time when you could be bringing in a little something towards yore room and board and yore education."

Lest his wife say it first, Jimmy's father said he believed they could manage without that.

"Do you think I've grown, Mother?" asked Jimmy.

"I think you're looking thin," she said.

"I knew you were going to say that!" said Jimmy.

"Thin and flushed," she continued, ignoring the interruption. "Not well at all. I wonder if you're not coming down with something?" Truth was, she herself felt flushed and as though she might be coming down with something. She felt terribly out of sorts.

"It's because I'm excited," Jimmy said. "It's my birthday!"

He was excited. Something was going to happen. He had no inkling of what it would be—perhaps something not at all pleasant. But something momentous, he knew. It was imminent in the air like a break in the weather. This birthday would not end without bringing about some fundamental change in things.

"Well," said his mother, "you've had enough to be used to them and you've got a great many more to come. So you'd better begin calming down."

"But this one is special! This is my thirteenth birthday. Today I become a man."

"What! Is that what you think? Ha-ha! You've got a long way to go before you get to be a man, my son. You're still just a little boy. And I advise you not to forget it."

There was a birthday cake with fourteen candles—one to grow on—and when "Happy Birthday" had been sung Jimmy blew them all out with one breath. The presents were then opened and admired. Afterward Jimmy's father said, first submitting a glance to his wife, "Yes, I can remember digging in that old mound myself when I was your age. Though like I say, I never had any luck. So you're interested"—another appeasing glance toward his wife—"in the Indians. Well, that's natural. Most boys are. Let's go and see just what you've been up to. Mother? Let's go and see what Jimmy's dug up, shall we?" He was being the peacemaker. Show a little interest in the boy's hobby, said the look to his wife, which Jimmy caught.

"You really don't want to see," said Jimmy.

"You mean you really don't want us to see," said his mother. "Well now, I think I do want to have a look. Maybe you've got hold of something you ought not to have."

"Why, Mother," said her husband. "What sort of thing could you have in mind?"

"I have in mind," she said, fixing him with her look, "something nasty. We all know what the Indians were like."

His indignation rose with a taste as sour as gorge. Yet she demeaned only herself. They were beyond her spite, as they were beyond her understanding; nothing she might say could smirch them. And he felt slightly dizzied. Again as previously he had known the instant before what his mother was about to say. He had actually heard her words seconds before they were spoken. It was like what happened sometimes with the phonograph, when you heard distantly the opening bars of the music before the record actually began to play. It had happened several times today, so that now Jimmy had the sense of being clairvoyant. It was as though he were in some sort of occult communication with his mother's unconscious mind. But if, for all her quarrelsomeness, his mother had been delivered into his power, Jimmy did not feel like gloating. It was too uncanny.

Once today his mother had read Jimmy's thoughts. He did not want his parents to visit the mound. Not for the reason his mother suspected but because it was hallowed ground and they were infidels who would profane it, the one with his idle curiosity, the other with her hatred and scorn. But both were determined now to be taken there, his father intent on making peace, his mother on making mischief.

She hated the thing, the mound, on sight. Before, hearing of Jimmy's dedication to it, she had viewed it as no more than a red rag of his meant to taunt her. But seeing it sitting there so squat and alien and old she hated it. Brown and bare, it rose like a single enormous grave out of the field of dazzling white cotton. That it was man-made was obvious; no one could ever have mistaken it for a natural mound. Rectangular in form, it stretched two hundred feet, was fifty feet wide, rose twenty feet from the ground. She pictured the dead savages inside it packed like sardines in a tin, and she shuddered with revulsion. Such promiscuous burial offended her as not only uncivilized but obscene. If she had her way these ugly reminders of barbarism would all be leveled to the ground. And her son was under its spell. She could see it working in the dark depths of his eyes. It was an atavism in him, a taint in his blood.

But the place had a power. Undeniably it did, if even she was forced to acknowledge it. Standing to adjust her vision inside the black shadow it cast upon the glaring cotton she could feel its solemn spell. The single grave of a whole clan of people! She felt herself belittled by its bulk and its antiquity, and despite herself, reverent. She could gauge the power it had to attract her son by the power it had to repel her. Her sight sharpened and she saw him going ahead, his pace quickening with each step, drawn to it like an iron filing to a magnet, and her heart misgave her. She felt they were hopelessly sundered. As if a snake had coiled at her feet to strike, she sensed something stir somewhere nearby. The sensation was overpowering that her approach had alerted the hostile hosts of the dead. Her courage, born of her contempt, forsook her, and for a moment she stood quaking with superstitious dread.

Jimmy's father was impressed by the size of the opening he had made in the mound. More than impressed, he was awed, dumbfounded. Starting at about the middle of one of the long sides, at the spot where, on his first visit to the mound, he had received the command to dig, he had removed a slice six feet wide and six feet deep all the way down to the base. There was nothing slipshod, nothing boyish about his excavation; it was all quite amazingly professional-looking, like a photograph in the *National Geographic,* which was where he must have gotten his ideas from, of a field camp on the site of a "dig" of an archaeological expedition. He must have dug furiously, almost frantically, and yet his cuttings had been made systematically and with care— indeed, they had been made with reverence; his findings sorted and labeled and cataloged. To house them he had erected a tent on top of the mound. He had cut in the face of it a flight of steps leading there.

On the tent floor laid out in rows were neat stacks of human bones each crowned by its grinning gap-toothed skull. With each stack was carefully preserved its owner's beaded medicine bag, his tomahawk, his clay pipe, and in those cases where it had survived intact, the pouch containing parched corn that was to have fed him on his journey to the happy hunting grounds. Being but freshly unearthed, the skulls were not bleached white but were still a waxen yellow. To some adhered coverings of pursed brown skin drawn back from toothless gums in everlasting howls. Nobody to hear them but one thirteen-year-old boy of mixed blood and divided loyalties. And his was but one of many such mounds. They were numerous throughout that part of the state and adjacent Louisiana. Sights for tourists, spots for picnickers, curio seekers. On their slopes children romped and around their bases farmers gathered their crops while a nation groaned underground and no one heard. Only he heard. To him each and every skull he uncovered screamed its plea for pity, its demand for justice. It all came down to him. He was all they had. His heart was their last war drum; on it they beat night and day.

Asked by his father what he meant to do with all these Jimmy replied that he meant to put them back where he found them.

Put them back? his father wondered.

Wasn't that what he would do? One of those might be his great-great-grandfather.

In her hands Jimmy's mother held a clay jug, one of the few he had managed to salvage unbroken. Perfect in condition, perfect in form and in decoration, it demanded to be picked up and handled, demanded it even of a person in whom it produced an aversion exceeding what she felt in looking at the grimacing yellow skulls. It seemed fresh from the hand that had made it centuries ago. The design was of diamonds in bands that coiled about it shrinking and expanding in conformity with its shape, a treatment that must have been suggested to the potter by his own procedure in coiling his rope of clay. If, as has been said, the soul of a people is to be found in its pottery, then the soul of the mound builders, as expressed in this piece, was one of boundless self-assurance, superb and haughty, implacable and utterly without remorse, possessed of some inner harmony that gave them a careless mastery of life. Unconquerable, the spirit of the people who could produce one such thing!

She tore her eyes from it to look at her son. He stood gazing at the vessel in her hand with an expression that shrank her heart. There was nothing of pleasure, nothing of fond possession in his look—rather the reverse: a look of his belonging body and soul to it, and an ineffable sadness: the look a priest might give to the chalice of the mass or the reliquary of the founder of his order. A shudder of revulsion shook her soul, she dashed the jug to the ground, where it burst like a grenade, and as Jimmy drew back—for he had already heard the words she was about to utter—she hissed, "A snake in your mother's bosom, that's what you are! A snake in your mother's bosom!"

They stood staring into one another's eyes in mute wonder. She was merely aghast, but he was both aghast and enlightened. What was to have happened had happened. On his thirteenth birthday an Indian boy becomes a brave, a man, and is given his man's name. The spirits of his ancestors, speaking through their enemy's own mouth, had just told him his.

VII

Snake-in-His-Mother's-Bosom, in whose new name was contained his mission, returned home in September after his summer in the country most unwillingly. He dreaded ever to see his mother again. He was not afraid of his mother, he was afraid for her, and thus for himself.

He knew now that his mother's telling him about his Indian blood had been no accident. She had been tricked into it against her will by her enemies, the spirits of his dead tribesmen. And he knew why. If he had not known before, he knew now, after excavating the mound—that hive that like hornets had lived and died all for one and one for all. Digging down through layer upon layer, generation upon generation, he had come to know the importance to them of preserving the tribal continuity, the sacrilege it would be to them should ever the chain be broken, especially in its last link. He knew now how inexhaustible was the Indian patience in waiting for revenge, the refinements of Indian cruelty in exacting it. He had not read these things written on buckskin or bark or carved in stone. He had seen them in the grin of Indian skulls, in the incisions on Indian jugs, in those geometric designs endlessly repeated that always came full circle, returning in the end to their source. His mother's crime against them was to have brought him up in ignorance of them. For this she must be made to pay, and Indian justice decreed that her punishment was that her son be a snake in her bosom, Indian subtlety that out of her own mouth must come the discovery that he was theirs, that she herself must bestow upon him his tribal name, that out of her very mouth must come— That was what he dreaded. What message would they next transmit through her to him? Not knowing what she was saying, what would she say next?

One thing his mother was determined never to say again was that he was a snake in her bosom. She regretted saying that. It was a terrible thing to say. Dreadful! She had meant to hurt him, and could see that she had; but not nearly as much as she had hurt herself. What made it doubly awful was that it was also rather laughable. Stiff, stagey, like something out of an old-fashioned play, like "Never darken my doorway again!"—not at all her usual way of expressing herself. And this comical old-fashioned stiffness somehow made the memory of it all the more embarrassingly painful. Her excuse was, she had not really meant to say it. She had gotten carried away and it had just popped out. If only she could have kept her vow never to repeat it! Before he had been back home two days, however, she did, provoked by his sullen refusal to answer to his name.

But that was not his name. Not anymore. He was Jimmy Hawkins no longer and never again would he answer to that name. When called by it, at home or at school, he would await silently and with a maddening little smile the question or the command that followed, but he would not answer to that name though beaten for his surliness until the principal's arm ached, until his father begged him to be allowed to quit. Hostile as he felt toward his mother, she was still his mother, and even the last of the Caddoes shrank from his terrible new appellation. But his people had spoken. Snake-in-His-Mother's-Bosom they had called him: Snake-in-His-Mother's-Bosom he must be. That the name fit him he had to admit. It fit him like a skin. And painful though it was, there was also strong medicine in the name. It encased him in an armor of scales. It enabled him to slink in silence. It gave to his brain the serpent's subtlety. It equipped him with a forked tongue for speaking to the enemies by whom he was surrounded. It armed him with fangs.

Because he would respond to none other, his mother was often goaded into calling him a name that was painful to her. Thus things went from bad to worse.

They could not be together for half a day now without a quarrel breaking out. Though she charged him with being the one who always started it, in fact it was she herself. In dread of what she might say, he wanted peace, no more quarrels. Yet he was Snake-in-His-Mother's-Bosom. And of course when riled he struck back. But she began it. The spirits egged her on.

It was as if, that day in the country, his birthday, they had lured her, using her very hatred of them as bait, to their mound, where, like a host of germs entering the bloodstream through some scratch, they had stolen inside her. Now she was like a person unconscious that a fatal disease is quietly eating him alive, as cancer is said to be painless and give no warning until its host is already past cure. In this case the organ invaded was the soul.

To watch them play with their victim was both horrible and fascinating. That he was himself a part of their scheme he knew, but was powerless to prevent. Besides, he rather enjoyed it. By making him remind her continually of them they rubbed her where she was rawest. Drop by drop the cup of her irritation would fill, then at some trifle brim over. Then she tore at her hair as though there were bats in it. Then she would not have peace. Then nothing so irritated her as his efforts to appease her. "You're good at starting trouble, aren't you?" she would taunt him. "But when the going gets rough you cry off. Soft! Can't take it, eh?" She would not let him give in to her. He shunned her; this enraged her. He fleeing, she pursuing, their arguments swept up and down stairs and through all the rooms of the house, doors banging, windows, walls, and furniture shuddering at the violence. He could not shake her off; she clattered after, attaching herself to him like a tin can tied to a dog's tail. When she had him cornered then he turned. Then he bared his fangs. They parried words. She always won, always had the last word: *they* put it in her mouth. And when she had said something at last that chilled him into silence, then she would quit the field in dubious triumph. For days, weeks—the torture was fiendishly drawn out—all their quarrels would end on the same double-edged phrase. So it had been from the start, with "That's the Indian in you coming out!" So it was later with "A snake in your mother's bosom, that's what you are!" So it was for a time with "I brought you into the world just to torment me!" Then, wrought to a pitch of outrage which that phrase had grown too worn to express, she would utter a new and more reckless one, something that left them both appalled, then retire to savor the bitter taste of her triumph. So she was led on from one Pyrrhic victory to another.

As he grew more morose she grew more cutting. "Aren't you the little joy to your mother, though? Mother's little joy! Other women's children bring sunshine and laughter into the house, but you, sullen creature—! You're a stranger in the house. You came into the world just to torment me, you snake in your mother's bosom, you little savage, you!" And he would glower at her out of those hooded cold black eyes, remote, hostile, alien, lashing her on to ever more bitter recriminations, drawing the net ever closer about herself, until in a fit of rage one day she said, "You will be the death of me!"

So ended the worst quarrel they had ever had, with both of them left gasping for breath. This time she feared she had gone really too far. Ah, but she had certainly given him something to think about! That she could see. As in the days when she used to wash him, her words had wiped his face clean of its black scowl, leaving him pale and blinking. In tones still more ominous she repeated, "You will be the death of me!"

VIII

Under cover of darkness Snake-in-His-Mother's-Bosom fled from home that night, never to return. He went to seek for himself a new home, new parents, a new name. He knew where to find them. Where not to be found by the ones he was leaving behind.

To postpone the discovery of his flight he left a dummy of himself in his bed as jailbreakers do. It looked so much like him lying there in his bed it made him feel it really was himself, the old him with all his troubles, with that heavy curse upon him, that he was leaving behind. By the time his trick was found out and chase given, he would be beyond recapture.

His mother would fume and rage when she found him gone. Doubting prophetess, eager victim, she would pursue her appointed executioner and be angry when he eluded her. Then having done her duty she would give up the search. His mother would receive condolences from family and friends, and look sad, and be secretly glad, and never know how much she had to be glad for.

The route taken by Snake-in-His-Mother's-Bosom was the same one along which the last surviving remnant of his people had been driven in 1854. His destination was the same as theirs. Across the Red River in Oklahoma among those Indian tribes with whom the earlier Caddoes exiled from Texas had found a home, and lost their identity, the last of the Caddoes hoped to find for himself a new home, a new mother and father, or many mothers, many fathers, lose his identity, and thereby evade his terrible fate. A Comanche, a Cherokee, a Choctaw, or a Creek: when Snake-in-His-Mother's-Bosom had been adopted as one or another of those and been given his new name then the Caddoes would truly be no more.

No more! The night around him groaned at the dismal thought. The moon veiled her face behind a cloud and through the treetops passed a long low sigh of woe. Over the dark land of the Caddoes the sentence of irrevocable doom rolled out in the muffled drum of the owl.

The road to the river and the ferry to Oklahoma, the road he was on, would take him within two miles of his grandfather's farm. Could Snake-in-His-Mother's-Bosom pass so near and not pay a last visit to his ancestral burial mound? At this season, early spring, before time for the planting of crops, his grandparents slept late. He could go and pay his respects and still get away unseen. Although it was from their prophecy that he was fleeing, the last of the Caddoes must not go forever from the land of his fathers without taking leave of his tutelary spirits.

He arrived shortly before daybreak. The house was still asleep as he passed it going down to the mound. In the field still stood the stalks of last year's cotton. A multitude of empty cottonbolls murmured in the wind. Day broke as he stepped on top of the mound. He advanced to the center and set down his suitcase. Looking at the ground he seemed to see into it, down into the depths where he had dug, down to the bottommost layer where the old first fathers lay in their lavish decay, smiling serenely, confident of the continuity of their kind, having gone into the grave before the white man's coming. Above them in successive layers of decline, those who had followed after: children laid on top of their parents, their children on top of them, and now on top of all himself, the last of the line, come to forswear his allegiance and bid them good-bye forever.

He prepared to deliver his farewell speech, and the silence grew attentive. He was about to begin when a sound, a rustle, at his back made him turn. From a hole in the ground quite near him a snake was emerging slowly like something being squeezed out of a tube. Out and out it came: its final four inches were rattles. It was an old snake. Its skin was dull and lusterless, its markings blurred, and it was half blind with a film clouding its eyes so that it groped its way with its tongue flickering constantly, tasting the air for unseen danger. It hitched itself along in angles as the knight moves on a chessboard. It passed within mere feet of him while he stood rigid and unbreathing. Yet he was not afraid of being bitten by the snake. No snake would bite him. He was of the clan of snakes. He was a snake himself. It was something else that he feared. This was the time of year when the ground's warming up roused snakes from their winter's sleep and brought them out. But in the emergence of this old, decrepit, possibly dying one coinciding with his visit here he feared some omen.

Every few feet the snake paused and half coiled itself to strike and reared its head and peered blindly about, its long forked tongue quivering like an antenna. Presently it came up against a stone. At once it began stroking its jaw against this stone. He could hear the rasping of its scales.

And suddenly with one long stroke, at the part dividing its nostrils, the snake's skin split and out of its dull wrapper popped a bright new head with keen new eyes that blinked at the raw daylight. Then rapidly it peeled itself its entire length, turning the old skin inside out as a finger comes out of a glove. Its glassy little scales tightly woven in a pattern of diamonds, it resembled nothing so much as a belt of Indian beadwork. A shiver of pleasure ran down from its head to its rattles as it felt the air for the first time on its new skin. It gaped, showing its fangs, coiled and reared itself high and slowly looked about with lordly menace. Then quick as a fish it flashed away and was gone.

Snake-in-His-Mother's-Bosom knelt and picked up the cast-off skin. Rising, he saw his mother's face appear over the top of the mound. He felt himself instinctively coil, his lips fly back to bare his fangs. "Ahhah," said his mother's smirk, "I knew where to find you, didn't I? You can't get away from me."

Beneath his feet all was silence. Silence and sly toothless grins.

Snake-in-His-Mother's-Bosom surrendered himself with a sigh to his fate. He could not get away from her—foolish ever to have thought he could. He was what he was; what would be would be. The snake might shed his skin, but only to grow another one the same as before.

In obedience to his victim's nod, Snake-in-His-Mother's-Bosom took up his suitcase and followed her down the steps and across the barren field to the car. In its rearview mirror he watched the mound diminish and finally disappear. The snakeskin rode on his lap. Now he must wait. Must wait for their next, their final command. It would not come soon; they sipped their pleasures slowly. Many times yet he would have to hear his mother say that he would be the death of her. So many times that when the final order came it would be almost welcome, a release. Distant and ghostly, it sounded already in the echoing silence of his mind. Over and over, like a phonograph record when the needle cannot find the starting groove. "Kill me at once then and be done with it!" his mother's voice was saying. One day the needle would find the groove. Then out would come the command loud and clear and with the sudden shock of long-expectedness. Then Snake-in-His-Mother's-Bosom would strike, accomplish his mission and fulfill the prophecy; and then at last the ghosts of the Caddoes could lie down at peace in their many-tiered mound and haunt the land and him no more.

William O. Douglas ──────────────

William O. Douglas (1898–1980) was U.S. Supreme Court Justice from 1939 to 1975. An outspoken voice for progressive causes, he was an early advocate of environmental protection. His eloquent plea for Texas's Big Thicket helped develop support for the present national preservation areas.

THE BIG THICKET

The Big Thicket originally contained more than 3 million acres and was described as the land between the Sabine River on the east and the Brazos River on the west. Today it is reduced to 300,000 acres due to oil drilling, pipe lines, highways, logging, and man's other "development" programs. Trinity River is its present western boundary and it is now confined to Polk, Tyler, Hardin, and Liberty counties in southeast Texas.

This area, not far from Houston, has an elevation between 100 feet above sea level to 400 feet. It is hardwood country streaked with yellow pine—loblolly, longleaf, shortleaf, and slash. The hardwoods include the American beech and the red maple of Appalachia. There are sweet gums, cypress, buckeye, and ash, the latter having eight species, and *Xanthoxylum clava-herculis* or the toothache tree. There are many oaks in the Big Thicket, from the patrician white oak to the scrubby blue jack. On the old Isaiah Fields Farm, cleared in 1835, stands a 500-year-old white oak with a spread that I paced off at 135 feet. The shagbark hickory, familiar in New York and Minnesota, is in the Big

Thicket. More unusual is the nutmeg hickory whose leaflets are silvery white underneath. Sycamores brighten many dark bottom lands with their mottled trunks and branches. Magnolia trees *(Magnolia grandi-flora)* are gargantuan. The mammoth gardenia grows 15 feet high with a 22-foot top spread. Persimmon and honey locust are here, the latter having huge thorns on the trunk. Texas has twenty species of hawthorn and many are in the Big Thicket. Indeed, there are at times hundreds of acres where the understory is nearly all hawthorn. Other spots show thousands of acres of the dwarf palmetto, whose stem, when cut open, chopped up, and cooked, makes a delicious cabbage-like dish. Different species of holly at times make up the understory. Near Hardin, on the road to Livingston out of Liberty, is a huge holly tree. This is a male tree, tall, symmetrical, broad-spreading. How old it is no one knows. But it was there 130 years ago when the land was cleared for farming. Wild plum, wax myrtle, sweetleaf, bay, chinquapin, azaleas, and dogwood often indeed make a thicket. The understory of the hardwood forests is at times so thick that a man on horseback probably could not penetrate it. A man on foot would have difficulty enough. The tight squeeze the traveler experiences in trying to penetrate these dense stands resulted in their being called the "tight eye."

There are bayous in the Big Thicket where the alligator, water moccasin, four kinds of turtles, catfish, and blue heron thrive. It was in the Big Thicket that I first heard of the baygall. I asked Jim Bowmer what it was and he said with a straight face, "I reckon it's a Yiddish doughnut."

A baygall, however, is a Big Thicket name for a small pond where seepage water has collected. It is there that the sweet bay *(Magnolia virginia),* red bay *(Persea borbonia),* and the gall berries *(Ilex coriacea)* are usually found; hence its name.

The bottom lands of the Big Thicket are clay. Larry Walker of Stephen F. Austin State College was with me and he took borings to sample this soil. For a depth of six inches or more the darkish clay was so free of impurities that it was the equivalent of modeling clay. Beneath this upper stratum was red clay which was almost impervious to water. The result is that newly formed pools linger on after heavy rains; the water table is high, nourishing hardwoods. In these bottom lands there are no earthworms, centipedes, and the like that give soil organic as well as mineral content by passing it through their bodies. The result is an almost total absence of topsoil at these lower levels. Leaves fall and are quickly oxidized, the mineral content entering the clay, the rest being washed or blown away. At higher elevations—say 400 feet—there are earthworms, and here the humus slowly accumulates.

The pines *usually* grow on higher ground than do the hardwoods. A few feet may mark the difference; and often the conifers follow that contour line for miles.

I said that the Big Thicket is now reduced to 300,000 acres and is confined to the four counties mentioned. Some disagree with that statement. During my field studies I had several outdoorsmen come to me with a map, showing far-flung pieces of the Big Thicket in other counties. One can, indeed, find scattered spots between the Sabine and the Brazos where the forest conditions typical of the Big Thicket still exist. But they are isolated pockets. The single contiguous area is the one I have described.

The Big Thicket was originally settled in the 1820s and 1830s, mostly by people from Tennessee and Georgia. The land then was Mexico's, which promised four thousand acres free to anyone with a family who would settle on the land—provided, however, he and his family joined the Catholic Church. Land-hungry people came in numbers, some bringing slaves. Their axes bounced off the hardwoods. Today a power saw fells a thousand-year-old magnolia in five minutes. The early settlers worked for days to fell one tree and weeks to blow out the stumps and burn the logs. Eventually they had broad fields where they planted cotton. They also grew corn and raised chickens and cattle. Hogs were introduced and they ran loose, feasting on the mast of the hardwood forests. The hogs also loved the taproot of the loblolly pine; then, as now, they dug deep for it until only their twitching tails were visible. The settlers marked the ears of the hogs so that when the roundups were made for butchering in the fall, everyone would get his own animal.

In time sawmills were introduced. They were small operations scattered throughout the Big Thicket and they started the decimation that the large companies continue to this day.

Lumber companies established complete sawmill communities with as many as five thousand people in places such as Old Fuqua, Votaw, Camden, Greyberg, Village Mills, Pineland—all ghost towns today. The sawmills explain in large part the network of roads in the Big Thicket. Post offices were set up. General stores were built at crossroads.

A Negro once went into one of these general stores looking for a pair of shoes that he could wear when getting married. He had never worn shoes before. The storekeeper had difficulty finding the young man's size. The pair that was closest fitting would not do, because the man's left little toe stuck so far out that the shoe would not go on. They debated what to do and finally reached a decision. The storekeeper took his hatchet and chopped off the man's little toe.

The first oil well was drilled at Saratoga in the 1860s and now the derricks are a common sight in the Big Thicket, as well as wide rights of way that many, many pipelines have cut across it. The Santa Fe Railroad finally crossed the Big Thicket.

In time the Baptists became the majority and their churches went up everywhere. Near Rye is the Concord Baptist Church, organized in 1845 and attended by Sam Houston. Behind the church and beyond a field where the spiderwort paints the ground blue is Cherry Creek and a baptismal hole.

The Assembly of God is also popular; and there are Presbyterians and Methodists, too. One day Dempsie Henley, when he stopped in the Big Thicket to visit with an old friend, missed the big hound dog that always greeted him.

"I swore I'd never sell him," the friend said. "But a man came by and offered me one hundred dollars for the dog."

"Did he pay you?"

"No, he said he'd pay me next week. Said I could trust him because he was a steward in the Methodist Church. What is a steward, Dempsie?"

"A steward in the Methodist Church is like a deacon in the Baptist Church."

The man shot up like a rocket, shouting, "My God, I've lost my hound dog."

The Big Thicket today is a land of God-fearing people who cling tightly to an old order even though schools, power saws, and bulldozers are moving them into oblivion at the rate of fifty acres a day. For decades they rightly assumed that the land was theirs for hunting, whoever might have the title. From the beginning they lived off the land and that tradition continues down to this day. Indeed, not until 1964 were the game laws enforced against them. Now game wardens are on patrol and their job is considered a "dangerous" occupation in the Big Thicket.

Towns such as Saratoga have modern school facilities and teachers as competent as any I know. So in a few decades the level of citizenship will rise and a new generation will realize the awful destruction which the lumber companies, the oil companies, the real estate developers,

the road builders, and the poachers have wreaked on one of the loveli-
est areas with which God has blessed this nation.

The old-timers, however, live pretty much in isolation in spite of
radio, television, and newspapers and are sometimes oblivious of the
distinction their neighbors have achieved. The Big Thicket has produced five governors of Texas—George T. Wood (1847–1849), Sam
Houston (1859–1861), Will P. Hobby (1917–1921), Allan Shivers (1951–
1957), and Price Daniel (1957–1963). Price Daniel has a brother, Bill,
who was governor of Guam. Both are spiritually very close to the Big
Thicket, Price Daniel living at Liberty on its very edge, and Bill at a
ranch within the Thicket. When Price was in the United States Senate
fixing to run for governor, two Thicketeers were visiting while waiting
for their mail.

"I wonder what happened to the Daniels?" one asked.

"I see Bill Daniel once in a while. But no one has heard of Price for
years."

I was talking with a ninety-year-old man who evinced no interest in
current events, local or national politics, or elections. I asked him if he
was a Democrat or Republican. He said he didn't know, as he never had
voted.

"Well, what presidential candidates got your vote?"

He looked at me quizzically before replying. "In all my years no one
ever ran for president that I figured was deserving. So I never voted."

The Hightowers and the Lockharts were early settlers, intermar-
ried, and brought distinction to the Big Thicket. Today Cameron Hightower II is in the state legislature from Liberty; Byron Lockhart
practices law in Austin.

Ross Hightower is county attorney, Polk County, Thomas J. Hightower is county attorney, Liberty County, and Lewis Buckner Hightower III is a judge in Beaumont.

Samuel Webster Lockhart came to the Big Thicket in 1847 and
married Josephine Graham, a schoolteacher, in 1856. Lewis Buckner
Hightower came in 1873. He was a Methodist and preached. He was
also a judge. He was known as the "Davey Crockett of East Texas" and
the "Bear Hunting Judge." . . .

Lewis Buckner Hightower II was also a famous judge of the Big
Thicket.

Judge Hightower I had nineteen children by four wives. His fourth
wife was Jane Lockhart, by whom he had nine children. Jane's brother,
Thomas Jefferson Lockhart, had seven children. Apart from one of

them, Lewis Buckner Hightower Lockhart, he named his children in chronological order after the letters of the Greek alphabet—Alpha Omega, Beta Gamma, Delta Epsilon, Theta Iota, Omicron Pi, and Upsilon Phi.

The Lockharts and the Hightowers, having been united, heavily populated the Big Thicket; and while today some have left, these two families are still prominent in Big Thicket affairs.

An unusual criminal case was once presented to Judge Hightower I. A settler, suspecting that a young man, whom he disliked, was visiting his daughter surreptitiously at night, put a bear trap outside her window. Sure enough, the suspect was caught the first night and a prosecution of sorts was instigated. After hearing the prosecutor's evidence, Judge Hightower dismissed the case, saying, "If they're going to use bear traps for this purpose, they might even catch a judge."

Judge Hightower I, who died in 1919, was running for reelection shortly before that time. He was noted for his fondness for alcohol, and an opponent who was "dry" tried to exploit that frailty. Price Daniel's father, also a "dry," came out for Hightower and helped him win, saying that "Hightower drunk" was a better judge than his opponent would be sober.

A Lockhart inadvertently gave rise to a scary rumor that there was a wild man in the Big Thicket. He was visiting a lady friend at night when her husband unexpectedly came home. Lockhart escaped by the window in such a hurry that he left all his clothes behind. He was tall, hairy, and naked as he stalked through the Thicket in the dim light of dawn, scaring the wits out of a few travelers who sounded the alarm that started a futile search.

There are ghost roads in the Big Thicket where at night eerie forms appear and disappear. They take bizarre shapes and sometimes run or dance. Small groups gather at strategic points even to this day to watch them. The phenomena are explained in terms of phosphorescent gases or insects or rabbits who have become impregnated with the gases.

Today no cotton is grown in the Big Thicket, those quotas having been moved west. Some rice has gone in; but mostly the farms are small and diversified, cash income coming largely from jobs in sawmills.

No one has better described the abodes of the Thicketeers than Mary Laswell in *I'll Take Texas:*

Hound dogs and blowing horns. Blackeyed peas and hog jowl. Sausage, with a flavor unrivaled, red-pepper-hot, solid pork-meat with some substance to it. Grits floating in fresh butter or redeye gravy. Hot biscuits and mayhaw jelly. Kids selling buckets of haws by the road spell it "may halls". A poky mule turning a syrup mill. The land where *The King and I* means nothing but an old-time gospel hymn. Gray silvered shacks with bitter oranges and chinaberry trees near them . . . the yard a bleached sweep of hard-packed earth, an iron washpot turned over near a round white spot on the ground where the suds from strong yellow lye-soap wash water had been emptied for years. The broomstick used to punch the clothes down, boiled to the color and smoothness of old ivory. Grove's Chill Tonic and Slaughterine for Pains. Crisper's Hot Shot Nerve Sedative.

The country where a midwife is a "granny woe-man"; one a 92-year-old mulatto woman with slender steely fingers who was said to have delivered a live baby from a dead mother. "White doctor say she daid, so I don't say she ain't." Signs saying "Wheels Spoked." Negro help leaping the fence to "git away fum de cunjerin' powder on de gate posts," placed there by some "cunjer" man or woman in the hire of an ill-wisher. East Texas, where they do things *right*, not cloddish. Negro children shouting "Santy Claw comin'? Santy Claw comin'?" when you want to take their pictures: "How he gon' know me on paper?" The stompin' ground of a blind, toothless guitar player: "Play me some blues." "I don't play no sinful songs, lady." His gigantic wife, Billie, emerging from out back hollerin' "An' me lookin' like Who'd-a-Thunk-It!" Razor-back hogs and hickory nuts. Light-bread and sweet milk. English walnuts and Irish potatoes, and firecrackers at Christmas. The smell of fresh-made lye hominy, and the lacquered cypress beams of the smokehouse. A hint of frost in the air, and the sweet mouth of a coon dog when he trees.

Supper in the Big Thicket is apt to be sweet milk, hot biscuits, honey, and butter. The honey is in a deep saucer at everyone's place. The butter is in a huge common jar and one reaches for it with his knife. A friend of mine, having such a supper with a family deep in the Big Thicket, relates how the mother slapped one of her sons in the face, saying, "How many times have I told you to lick your knife clean before putting it in the butter?"

Pokeweed *(Phytolacca americana)* has a large poisonous root. But its young leafy sprouts, many think, are sweeter than asparagus.

"Poke and catfish is about the best dish in the Big Thicket," Lance Rosier told me.

Some interesting recipes come out of the Big Thicket. We got from Mrs. H. L. Phillips of Kountze the following one for corncob jelly:

12–15 *red dry corncobs*
3½ *cups water*
4 *cups sugar*
6 oz. *commercial pectin (1 bottle Certo*
or 1 box Sure-Jell)

Cut corncobs in small pieces. Cover with water. Bring to boil, then simmer for one hour or until liquid has strong flavor. Remove from heat, cover, let stand for ten minutes. Strain through cloth to make three cups prepared juice. Add pectin, dissolve. Then add sugar. Boil hard for five minutes. Add coloring to color bright red. Cool five minutes. Pour in jars.

"If you want a whitish corncob jelly," Lance volunteered, "use ordinary white cobs."

A Social Security agent was recently taking a census in the Big Thicket. He asked one man in his twenties what his occupation was. The word was new to him so he could not answer. The agent rephrased it several times in terms of work and wages. The young man finally answered, "Last year I worked in a gravel pit."

The agent insisted he was interested not in last year but right now. "Right now I'm frog gigging."

I mentioned that the youngsters now being educated will turn out to be a different breed. And so they will. But even today things common to the city-bred child may be startling or unusual to them. When my helicopter put down on the lawn of the high school at Saratoga, all classes broke up and children streamed out of every door with wonder and curiosity.

Dempsie Henley, mayor of Liberty, has air conditioning in his car, with the blower on the extreme right of the dashboard. He picked up a nine- or ten-year-old boy on a hot summer day and put him in the front seat. The boy was so small that the stream of cold air hit him right between the eyes. It so bothered and interested the lad that he could not take his eyes off it. When Dempsie Henley let the lad off at his destination he said, "If I were you, mister, I'd sure fix that hole in your car before winter. If you don't, you're going to freeze to death."

There was a hot spell in September when Dempsie Henley had his air conditioner on in the car. He picked up an old man from the Big Thicket who, feeling the cold blast, pulled his coat collar tighter and tighter around his neck. After twenty minutes or so he asked to get out and go home. When asked why, he replied, "With this norther coming up it'll be ideal weather for hog killing."

Dempsie Henley, whose great-grandfather, Isaiah Fields, settled near Liberty in 1835, grew up there. "We were so poor," he told me, "that until I got into the army in World War II, I thought everybody else was poor, too."

To eke out a living he collected the Spanish moss *(Tillandsia usneoides)* that hangs from all the hardwoods in the Big Thicket. This moss is grayish in appearance. But that is the exterior. In the center is a small wiry fiber almost as strong as horsehair. That fiber is used as stuffing for pillows and chairs. The Thicketeers collect it. "The stuff is so light that you work hard for a whole week and you won't have even 100 pounds."

Dempsie Henley today is a great civic leader and a conservationist, one of the leading spirits behind the Big Thicket Association, organized in 1964, which is out to save at least islands of the 300,000 acres as parks or sanctuaries. Walter McCreight of Batson has written a stirring song, "Land of the Big Thicket," calling people to action.

Another leading conservationist of the Big Thicket is Lance Rosier, who lives in a small cottage behind the post office at Saratoga. Lance was born in the Big Thicket and has spent all of his sixty-odd years there. He is a slight, gnome-like man who, according to Mary Laswell in *I'll Take Texas,* would weigh 120 pounds "soaking wet." That's about right. He walks the woods quietly and reverently. He is on speaking terms with all that blooms, with all that crawls or swims, with all that flies.

He was considered an "oddball" by his contemporaries. His classmates taunted him for wanting to search out plants and identify them, rather than shoot birds. The people of Saratoga wanted him to become a "useful" citizen. But the Thoreau that was in him made him turn his back on the town and head for the Big Thicket.

"I sat for hours on a stump until at last I could tell the difference between the song of the white-eyed vireo and the red-eyed one," he told me. He sent away for books on birds and plants and began at high-school age the slow process of classification and identification that has made him Mr. Big Thicket, the outstanding naturalist of the area. I gather that the taunting by his contemporaries and their rejection of him hurt this sensitive man to the quick. His confidence in himself probably dates from his association with H. B. Parks and V. L. Cory, who published in 1938 their *Biological Survey of the East Texas Big Thicket Area.* He was with them in the Big Thicket for weeks on end as they did their field work for this and other books; and from them he received the only technical instruction in botany he ever enjoyed. With their keys at his disposal he went to work in earnest and now knows the common names, and the Latin as well, of the several thousand plants that grow in the Big Thicket.

People are always running to him with a specimen, as I did, and asking, "Lance, what is this?" And he always knows. He not only knows the name but the use, if any, that the Indians and early settlers made of it, and its present commercial value as well. One day a small circus came to Saratoga. Among the animals was a baboon that suddenly died. The circus people dumped the carcass by the roadside as they left town. The next day some local people found it and brought it to Lance, asking, "Lance, what is this?" Lance studied awhile and then solemnly replied, "Judging from the calluses on its rump, the stoop of its back, and the depressed look on its face, I reckon it's a Big Thicket domino player."

Lance told me about the bootlegging in the Big Thicket. It was an ideal place for whiskey making. The principal ingredient was corn, and the product was sold in fruit jars that held a little less than one-half gallon and hence were called a "short half." Steel drums were used, a drum of mash, sealed at the top except for one opening, being fired up. From the opening came a copper tube that ran through a running creek to another steel drum into which the final product dripped. Big Thicket whiskey, they say, tasted not like bourbon but like Drambuie. A prudent drinker, when offered a drink from a jar, closed the lid tightly and vigorously shook it before imbibing in order to distribute the fusel oil uniformly.

Aging was achieved by chopping chips from a red oak and dropping them in the distillate. After two weeks the whiskey was "aged."

In the old days a man by the name of Drew had a general store at Drew's Landing.

"Most honest man I ever knew," Lance told me. "He kept a sign out—Whiskey, $1.00 a gallon; Good Whiskey, $1.50 a gallon."

Even today Texas liquor officials seize more stills in East Texas than anywhere else. And some are still found in the Big Thicket. "Cover is necessary for a still," one official said. "And East Texas woods are hard to beat in that respect."

A few years ago one of the local citizens was brought before the local judge on a charge of making whiskey. This was the fourth offense. The old man's only defense was that he was not a whiskey seller, he only made the stuff for his own use. The judge remonstrated with him.

"George," he said, "the commercial distillers put out a real good product these days, and they sell it at a reasonable price. I know you don't have much money, but it would be far better for you simply to buy a bottle every now and then than to keep on making this stuff and keep on getting caught."

"I dunno, I dunno," said the defendant.

"Of course I'm right," the judge said. "I'll prove it to you. How much do you drink?"

"A half gallon a day for me," said the defendant, "and then there's the family."

The judge thought it over for a minute. "Forget what I just said, George," he said. "Maybe your way is the best way after all."

I traveled the Big Thicket with Lance when the bright leaves of the hardwoods were first showing and the flowering shrubs were at their peak. We stopped at a stand of cypress whose bright green leaves were bursting from the buds.

"Ever see a young mesquite in bloom?" asked Lance. "Doesn't the cypress leaf remind you a bit of it at this stage? Filigree like."

We stopped at a baygall where a huge cypress with many knees grows. While some others in the party undertook to measure it, Lance, with a knowing eye, squinted skyward and said, "One hundred thirty-five feet." And so it was. It was eleven feet in diameter and probably one thousand years old. It stood in isolated splendor dominating some twenty acres of fairly open woodland. A few water ash, water oak, and elm were on the stand. Pecans and hickories were there, too, but they showed no leaves.

"Dead?" I asked.

"No, no," Lance replied. "They are the last trees to bud. After they bud, there's no more cold weather. You can count on that."

A blue mint was thick and Lance picked a sample to show me how mint always has a square stem. Wisteria, which is native in the Big Thicket, was in bloom, reaching for treetops to put its flowers on full display. Buttercups sent streaks of yellow through the grass. Clumps of vetch were flourishing and wild roses were in their heyday. We sat on a log, drinking in the beauty of the spot. Suddenly we were greeted with an orchestration. The white-eyed vireo burst into song. A cardinal, a wren, and a nuthatch followed suit. The wood thrush chimed in. A mockingbird intruded, boisterous and aggressive, as if to break up the song fest. Then all was suddenly quiet as a sharp-shinned hawk skimmed the treetops.

Lance and Don Correll went into the baygall to gather an unusual water plant—*Hottonia inflata* (member of the Primula family and sometimes known as featherfoil or water violet)—whose roots scrape the bottom and whose tuberlike tops are inflated and float erect.

On the edge of this baygall was a toothache tree *(Xanthoxylum clava-herculis)*, also known as Hercules club or prickly ash, whose cousin *(X. fagara)* grows in bushy form in Central Texas. The one we saw this day was perhaps fifteen feet high with wartlike lumps on its bark. The inner wood of these welts deadens the mouth tissues; and it seemed especially powerful this spring, as the sap was running strong.

We scouted the edge of this baygall and all was desolation. Roads practically encircled it. Summer houses were going up; subdivision signs were on display. Heroic efforts would be needed to save even this twenty-acre tract, for, as we left, we heard of plans to turn it into a cow and horse pasture.

We went to the corner of Liberty, Polk, and Hardin counties, walking from the narrow dirt road, where we left the jeep, a short distance through a stand of loblolly pine. The soil was a sandy loam. The trees were tall and stately, showing no limbs for fifty feet or more. A few red maple were present but the forest was essentially pine. A light wind was blowing and when we stopped to examine shelf mushrooms on a tree, the music of the treetops picked up. It never reached the crescendo I was to hear in conifer stands of far-off West Texas. But it was a soft, barely audible orchestration of strings that would put a man to sleep.

Lance and I talked about backpacking this country. "Too hot in July," he said. "But in the fall, winter, and spring it's the only way to see the Big Thicket."

Most shelf mushrooms of the Big Thicket are edible; and the one we examined was, according to Lance, particularly juicy. "More protein in a pound than beef," he commented.

Larry Walker joined us to say that at this elevation—which was perhaps a dozen feet above the bottom lands—there would be an oak-hickory climax forest. That is to say, if it were left undisturbed it would, over the years, be dominantly oak and hickory. Lance agreed, but added, "Trouble is, man disturbs it by cutting. Even without cutting, it is disturbed."

"How?"

"Mostly fire. And when the fires come and destroy the hardwoods, pine comes in. Some pine are indeed fire-resistant and survive."

"Then the oak-hickory climax forest is largely theory?"

Lance and Larry nodded.

We came to this area not to see the pine but an ancient magnolia that stands perhaps a dozen feet from the point where the three counties meet. It was a grand tree maybe one thousand years old. But it had become newsworthy, not for its age and beauty, but because of the manner of its destruction. Magnolia, the first flowering tree each spring in Washington, D.C., has become associated in my mind wholly with aesthetic values. In Texas I learned that magnolia was valued as lumber for flooring and for paneling. On my visit to the Big Thicket, however, I saw it cut by the small sawmills for railroad ties. The Santa Fe that crosses the Big Thicket uses it extensively for that purpose. My heart sank as I saw the huge piles of ties piled near the Santa Fe and manufactured out of magnolia. But I was not prepared for what Lance showed me at the point where the three counties come together. In 1965 this thousand-year-old magnolia was thriving. By April, 1966, it was dead. Lance showed me the five holes that had been bored into the base of the tree.

"Why?"

"To poison it."

"With what?"

"Arsenate of lead."

"Who did it?"

"No one knows. A fellow like the one that killed President Kennedy."

"Why was this tree on the assassin's list?"

"Some of us want the Big Thicket made a national park. Others are opposed. The opposition is trying to make the area as unattractive as possible. That's why they poisoned the big magnolia."

"Vandalism?" I said.

"You haven't seen anything yet," Lance volunteered.

On the road to Fugah I saw what he meant. We traveled a dirt road, called a "push road."

"A bulldozer in one trip can push it into place," Lance explained. "That's why it's a push road."

On the road's edge dozens of magnolia lay freshly cut. They were magnificent specimens from eighteen inches to thirty inches through. They were not cut for flooring, for paneling, or for railroad ties. They were cut for sheer destruction and the trunks lay rotting.

"Why?"

"To make the forest less attractive for a park."

"Did the lumber company do it?"

"No one knows. They are on its land but vandals might have done it." . . .

A few huge cypress—more than two feet in diameter and probably two hundred years old—had somehow escaped the lumber operations that had ravaged Menard Creek and stood in splendor in damp places. We stopped to make a boring on a loblolly pine; it had a diameter of fourteen inches and was thirty-two years old.

"It's now big enough to be commercial," Lance volunteered.

We came across river birch *(Betula nigra),* the same species that we have in the Potomac Valley and the only native birch in Texas—semi-aquatic, tall, with dull red-brown bark peeling off in thin, curly flakes.

Menard Creek boasts a few American beech, which to my eye was the same as the beech of New Hampshire, though some botanists claim the beech of East Texas has minor variations and dub it a Carolina beech. It was like meeting an old, old friend and I walked up to it and put my hand on its light-gray, smooth bark, and caressed it fondly. Nearby was a twenty-foot ironwood tree (hop hornbeam) more than twelve inches in diameter, a tree sometimes used for fence posts. A huge American sweet gum—eighty feet or more high—was also in this alcove along Menard Creek. Closer to the water grew a huge water tupelo *(Nyssa aquatica).* Blackberries were thick in the open places, being very showy now that their blossoms were out. Lance stooped to show me the dewberry trailing and tough and almost ready to bloom.

"People of the Big Thicket like its berries best of all for jelly."

A sow cleared the creek easily but her little ones in panic struggled to get across.

We stopped our hike down Menard Creek at the point where Meeting House Creek comes in. The two form an irregular-shaped pool at this spot, perhaps one hundred by fifty feet and six or more feet deep. It is known as Barrett Swimming Hole and is famous in Big Thicket history. . . .

Menard Creek has cool, clear, spring-fed waters. Barrett Swimming Hole, as a sanctuary, rates with any that I know in all of Appalachia. Yet it is on the verge of destruction. Every day fifty acres of the Big Thicket are devoured. Men are converting every acre into dollars, although its greater values are spiritual and aesthetic.

Land that in 1960 sold for fifty dollars an acre was selling for three hundred dollars in 1966. Big development programs, in the form of subdivisions composed of small lots, are spreading everywhere. They and the ruthless cutting programs of lumber companies are appropriating the modern Naboth's Vineyard to an end that these wondrous pieces of God's creation do not deserve.

One part of the Big Thicket looks like a pine plantation. It is the area known as Kaiser's Burn Out. Jim Kaiser was an officer in the Confederate Army and went in search of Texans who avoided military service for the South by hiding in the Big Thicket. Over and again Kaiser sent troops combing the "tight eye" woods for the Jayhawks. But the latter were wily and resourceful and knew the Big Thicket better than did the soldiers. They easily eluded their hunters and few if any were apprehended. But the Jayhawks, numbering about one hundred, needed some staples in order to survive. So they maintained lines of communication with the settlements. They collected honey and left it at a designated spot—now known as Honey Island—where village women came to get it, leaving staples in return. (In the Big Thicket any site agreed on for a meeting point or depository is an "island.") They dressed hides for money with which to buy ammunition, coffee, and molasses. Tobacco was pressed in the heart of a tree, a block of a large tree being cut from one side and removed, the tobacco leaves inserted, and the slice of wood replaced and held by a tight tourniquet. Tobacco leaves mixed with molasses and so pressed made good Big Thicket chewing tobacco. The Jayhawks raised some corn and potatoes and kept a few cows. They made whiskey out of the corn that they grew and that their friends smuggled to them and traded wild honey for coffee. They trapped, fished, and hunted. There were plenty of deer then, as well as turkey and squirrel.

Some say that Kaiser courted a girl whose brother was a Jayhawk and she told Kaiser where they were. Others say a man named Lilly played the role of Judas—a man who was shot by the Jayhawks "in the fork of his galluses." Whatever may be the truth, Kaiser waited until the wind was right and then started a forest fire that roared toward the target. The Jayhawks escaped and are the great-grandfathers of many present-day Thicketeers. But the Kaiser Burn Out scorched the land so thoroughly that for more than sixty years nothing would grow. Finally, about 1930, a lumber company planted it in pine, and the planting was so orderly that today the area looks like a manicured park or plantation. . . .

In the early days a settler, anxious to learn how they settled disputes among themselves, asked one Indian, "Suppose Charlie Thompson had a bad horse and you had a bad fence and Charlie's horse gets in your field and destroys some of your corn and you want him to pay you for your corn?"

The Indian answered by saying, "Charlie got no bad horse; me no bad fence."

The settler then asked, "Suppose your hogs and Charlie's hogs run in the bottom together and your hogs look so much like his hogs that Charlie claims all of the hogs?"

The Indian answered, "Me know my hogs; Charlie knows his hogs."

"Suppose he does not know his hogs and claims yours?"

The Indian replied, "I give Charlie my hogs."

The reservation now has 360 inhabitants, all full-blooded, all devout Christians, mostly Presbyterians. . . .

This virgin forest is on rolling red clay land, perhaps three hundred feet above sea level. Its open effect brings lots of sunshine to the forest floor; and when I was there the whole floor litter had a yellowish cast from the host of buttercups that were at their peak.

We left the reservation at dusk to the music of the whippoorwills.

Pipelines without rhyme or reason have cut the Big Thicket into many pieces, condemning private lands willy-nilly with no power on the part of a state officer or of citizens to stop them.

Oil companies have ruined hundreds of acres by allowing salt water from their wells to flood the land. We stopped at one such place where Lance sadly reported, as though speaking at an inquest;

"Here used to be the finest stand of the pitcher plant in all the Big Thicket. Now nothing will grow." . . .

The great white heron is in the Big Thicket—pure white with yellow beak and greenish-yellow legs. By 1935 it was close to extinction.

These great birds came into our conversation as we got glimpses of them, some at a considerable distance, when we stopped to look at a half section that was blighted and blistered.

"Planes sprayed the hardwoods," Lance explained.

"Why?"

"To kill them so that pine would grow. You see, pine grows faster and makes more money for the lumber companies."

"Any side effects?" I asked.

Lance choked up with emotion, saying:

"This was a rookery that they sprayed at a time when hundreds of big birds were nesting—herons, American egrets, spoonbills, and anhingas."

"What happened?"

"All the birds were killed except seven. Counted them myself. Dozens of young ones lay in their nests, their heads hanging over the side. Worst vandalism I ever knew."

We saw other tracts similarly sprayed that were now patches of desolation.

The ivory-billed woodpecker is in the Big Thicket. It is larger than a crow, the male having a flaming red crest, the female a black one. It has an ivory-white bill and large white wing patches visible when the bird is at rest. It is close to extinction; but Lance knows where it lives in the Big Thicket. This woodpecker needs the dead or dying logs of a wild virgin area for nesting purposes, and for grubs and other insects on which it feeds. It has difficulty surviving where the forests are cleaned out.

Lance offered to take me to them.

"I usually don't do it," he said, "because once the word gets around, the poachers move in. When a species is near extinction, one bird becomes quite a trophy."

I declined the invitation with thanks, thinking that perhaps man's greatest contribution was to stay away from their environment, leaving them alone and introducing no element of anxiety.

But the Big Thicket is an anxiety breeding area. The environment perpetuates the poacher's tradition. In the nineteenth century man hunted for the joy of it. Judge Hightower, already mentioned, is reputed to have killed more than 200 bears in the Big Thicket, one with a bowie knife, and as many as four a day. Another hunter was Bud Bracken of Kountze, who has the record of killing 305 bears. He hunted with dogs, and once, when a huge bear charged, he ran out of ammunition and ended up using the gun as a club and running the barrel down the bear's throat with the result that the barrel was dented and would not shoot straight any more.

What grandfather did, grandson does today.

J. Frank Dobie

J. Frank Dobie (1888–1964) won the Presidential Medal of Freedom in 1964, after thirty years of teaching at the University of Texas at Austin while writing and compiling nearly fifty books of Texas folklore and folk tales. He once wrote: "I've been called a historian; I'm not one in the strictest sense, but I suppose I can be called a historian of the longhorns, the mustangs, the coyote and other characters of the West." Dobie is represented here with just such a "history of a character."

LONGHORNS

Climate, grasses, minerals in the soil, latitude and other factors of nature inevitably made their mark on Spanish stock introduced into Texas. It was further marked by some crossing with cattle brought from the United States. Also, English-speaking ranchers were more selective than Spanish-speaking ranchers in bulls left on the range to breed. By the time Texas was admitted as a state to the Union, the Texas long-horns were generally bigger animals and had longer, heavier horns than the Spanish cattle below the Rio Grande.

Never was a cow brute better adapted to the demands of nature than these longhorns. They could horn off the fiercest wolf, smell out the most cunning panther. When they were driven westward, longhorn bulls did not hesitate to engage with grizzly bears. Their worst enemies were screwworms; longhorn cows licked them out of their calves.

A longhorn did not grow meat on its carcass clean down to the hock, like the Hereford and other man-developed breeds, but the longhorn had "cow sense" to a supreme degree. A cow would hide her newly born calf in grass as cunningly as a doe hides her fawn, leaving it there while she grazed and went to water. She and a dozen or so other cows with calves would band together, two or three of them staying to guard the calves while the others went to drink, those on guard leaving for water as soon as they were relieved. It is the nature of little calves to lie down a great deal of the time; they cannot stay on their feet and travel like older cattle. During a very cold winter in North Dakota, a cowman saw an old Texas cow walking her young calf up and down a draw in which it had been born; she seemed to know by instinct that its feet would freeze if she allowed it to lie down.

Like all other cattle, the longhorns required water, but they some-times went for months on very little, getting it mostly in the form of prickly pear, which they chewed through thorns to eat. During drouthy times in the arid Southwest, hardier longhorns, especially old steers, used to graze out as far as twenty-five miles from water, coming in to drink maybe not more than twice a week. (Grass is always shorter, from constant grazing, near water than away from it.)

An old-time cowboy of the trans-Pecos country told me that during one drouth when there was no vegetation near water—that was before ranchmen had dug wells and scraped out reservoirs—he once followed a bunch of Texas steers ten miles out from a spring before they halted to snatch a mouthful of grass. He said that they went in a long walk all the way without once pausing. There is not in the United States today a herd of improved cattle that could or would pioneer with such hardi-hood.

The longhorns were long-legged, long-backed, and long-tailed. They were not only good walkers individually, but adapted themselves to herd movement. Low-built, short-legged cattle of highly improved breeds could never have trailed thousands of miles across deserts, mountains, and rivers as did the longhorns. Their hoofs were as hard as their horns. They were built for their times; and when the time came to ride to market instead of walking, the longhorn was bred out of existence.

It is to be remembered always that the native home of the longhorn was not the high plains but the thickets and prairies of the southern half of Texas. His instincts were all for the freedom of the wilds. He did not want to leave his native coverts. Here his horns were often ringed with age and as rough as bark—before he was captured to be driven north. Many cattle stayed hidden in brush by day like the deer, coming out to graze on the prairies only at night. No cow work was more exciting than waylaying them and roping them at night. On some ranges, the cow hunters kept dogs to help find and catch the wild cattle.

Cattle too wild and cunning to be caught by man were called outlaws. Their outlawry consisted of the passion and the ability to remain free. A ranchman named Roberts down in the brush country of lower Texas once captured a steer bearing a brand that had been discarded for twenty-five years. That means that the steer must have been at least twenty-six years old. During a quarter century he had been seen only a few times.

Roberts had a waterhole fenced in. Beside the gap entering the pen was a densely foliaged live oak tree. One day Roberts stationed himself in this tree to trap outlaws. After the big steer came into sight through the brush it was an hour before he got up to the gap. Then he smelled along the entire length of each of the ten gap poles lying on the ground. Then he smelled up and down each of the gap posts. No hand had touched them. Then he stepped inside. Immediately he whirled, and for five minutes or more stood facing the brush he had emerged from, motionless, watching. Thirst made him only more suspicious, more alert to danger. As is the nature of cattle and deer, he did not look up. After he at last walked to the water and then whirled for another look behind him before drinking, Roberts dropped from the tree and reached for a pole to close the gap.

Instantly the outlaw was racing toward him. Roberts stood his ground. At a distance of ten feet the outlaw halted and began pawing the ground. Then he moved off, and Roberts barred the gap. Before he was tied down the steer broke several ropes and it took all hands to secure him. He was killed on the ranch. It would have been useless to try to drive him out.

Many wild cattle could not be held even after they were caught.

One way to deal with them was to neck two together, or else neck one to a gentle ox. Another way was to tie the head down to a forefoot. Still another was to cut the knee tendon; an animal so "doctored" could walk but could not run. A method sometimes employed to keep "snaky" cows from running off was to sew up their eyelids. Thus temporarily blinded, they followed other cattle, depending on them for guidance. By the time the thread rotted and they could see again, they were gentle enough to stay in a herd—often in the middle of it, as far away as possible from the surrounding riders. Handling such cattle without pens or fences was labor for twenty-four hours a day.

Many an outlaw achieved more than a local reputation. A brindle steer branded Nine R withstood for nine years all attempts to dislodge him from the rough country about the headwaters of Devil's River in southwest Texas. He had escaped various roundups, had been tied down a half dozen times, and had even been driven three or four times to the shipping pens at Colorado City, 150 miles away, only to escape and return to his lair. In 1892 his owner sold out, and John Custer, who had been a trail boss, took a "cow crowd" to clean up the range. The bets were that "Old Nine R" would never be prodded over the gang-plank into a cattle car.

But Custer captured him. On the trail to Colorado City he tied him every night, and when the gates at the shipping pens were finally closed, a great yell from the spectators went up. Word had gone ahead that the Nine R brindle was coming, and over fifty men were assembled to see him.

"Old Nine R is going to roll this time," they said.

"Wait," said Custer.

A freight engine pulled a car up against the loading chute, and with other steers Nine R was crowded in. The "bull board" was fastened, the door was pinned shut.

"Old Nine R is gone now," a cowboy yelled.

"Wait," said Custer.

Presently, while another car was being loaded, Custer heard a commotion ahead. He looked. Nine R was racing across the prairie back toward Devil's River. He had somehow by hooking and kicking knocked the door down and jumped out. Custer mounted his horse, took after him, roped him, led him back, put him in another car, and tied him short in a corner.

"Now you can say," Custer announced, "that Old Nine R is safe."

Nine R's liberty, for which he had fought so fiercely, was at an end.

II · HEROES
AND HARDSHIPS

Hamlin Garland

Hamlin Garland (1860–1940) was a pioneer in the use of local color and naturalistic techniques to depict the individual's heroic struggle against a hostile environment. His high regard for Davy Crockett is reflected in this introduction to Crockett's autobiography.

INTRODUCTION TO DAVY CROCKETT'S AUTOBIOGRAPHY

Many years ago, while a student in Boston, I saw Frank Mayo play the title role in Murdock's comedy "Davy Crockett," and though I greatly enjoyed it, I can recall but two scenes: one in which the young hero sadly confesses to his sweetheart his inability to read and write, and the other an exciting moment wherein a band of wolves gnaw their way through the wall of the settler's cabin with such incredible ease that I wondered what kind of logs had been used in its construction. The first scene was altogether charming. The soft-voiced, bashful, handsome young hunter in his fringed buckskin jacket and coonskin cap quite won the hearts of the audience, and we were all grateful when the girl of his adoration offered to teach him his alphabet. The playwright had made of Davy a young Lochinvar of the Canebrake, endowing him with all the romantic virtues. He was chivalrous, generous, and a poet, the prototype of the long line of heroes, hunters, cowboys, and miners who from that day to this have filled a large place in our literature.

Influenced by this play I read the autobiographical works acknowledged by David Crockett and the books about him which he disclaimed and imprecated, and also a *Life of Martin Van Buren* which he inspired if he did not write. The total effect of this reading was to destroy my conception of Crockett as a Lochinvar of the Canebrake. As set forth in his own books he is a long way from being a poet, although he loved the wilderness as profoundly as he hated Jackson and Van Buren. Somewhere between the coarse, bragging, stump-speaking politician and the Davy Crockett of Murdock's play lies the real backwoodsman, whose fame is united with that of Daniel Boone as our typical pioneer.

The most characteristic figure of the New World for the first two centuries was the man of the "trace" or trail: the settler who, carrying a rifle and an axe, adventured into the wilderness and there hewed out a clearing, built a cabin, and planted corn; whose skill with the flint-lock provided meat for his family, skins for his clothing, and literally kept the wolf from the door. No other age or time could have produced his like. Europe colonized in clans or tribes; American immigration was individual. Men like Boone and Crockett moved alone, hunted alone, planted alone, and harvested alone—only in time of war against the savage did they come together in fellowship and active cooperation. To have a neighbor within six miles was helpful; to have one within sound of an axe was a nuisance.

In Crockett's autobiography the reader will find the picture of such a man, a blunt, bold, prosaic account of a life, epic in its sweep. That he wrote it as it stands is doubtful, but that he talked it is unquestionable. The internal evidence is unmistakably genuine. Other so-called lives of Crockett are spurious, but the *Narrative of the Life of David Crockett, of the State of Tennessee,* copyrighted by the hunter himself in 1834, bears every evidence of being substantially his own expression. No one else could have permitted such a singular mixture of naïve boasting and homely humor. "The whole book is my own," he declares, "every sentiment and sentence"; and this is the fact, although, as he admits, some little change was made here and there in the spelling and grammar. No hack writer would use such expressions as "lick me up," "get me some decent clothes," and "the balance of my money." The homely details of his life as wagon boy, his senseless wanderings as a youth, are all in this authentic narrative; so, too, is his boastful reference to the fact that at the age of fifteen he did not know a single letter of the alphabet. His use of "I know'd," "in and about," "parara," and "blizzard" brings his book down to my time, for many of these expressions were in use by the old men of Wisconsin in 1868. The inconsistencies of Davy's spelling are accounted for also by the statement that it was touched up a little here and there. He talked so much better than he could write that his book is but the limited expression of a man who could tell a story easily, racily, and with individual humor. His writing does him an injustice. At his best he wrote with sad inadequacy; at his worst he is commonplace. . . .

It is a curious commentary on political conditions of that day to read, in Crockett's own words, that when he was elected to the legislature of Tennessee he could barely write his name, had never read a newspaper in his life, and was living forty miles from a neighbor. His chief claims to political preferment were his record as a bear-hunter and his ability to tell a racy story. He seems to have possessed the politician's memory also. He never forgot a face, and this was of great value to him.

That his election to Congress some years later was based on his reputation as an "original" seems substantiated by his own words and acts in Washington. The fact that he had killed 105 bears in one year and could tell such vivid stories in the picturesque vernacular of the Canebrake gave him an exalted place in every hotel barroom and dining hall. He embodied the spirit of the West. His whimsical humor and his elemental dignity, combined with a frank confession of his ignorance concerning cities, books, and parlors, gave him so great a renown that someone, perhaps facetiously, suggested him for the presidency—a fact which he took mightily to heart. Thereafter he was never weary of alluding to himself as an opposition candidate to Van Buren, "the little Dutchman."

In the light of today that entire political period appears almost farcical. All that redeemed Crockett from ridicule was his loyalty to the Border and his sturdy honesty of purpose. So far as I can discover, he was never accused of bribery or double dealing.

That he was "whimsical" is undoubted. He was in a crude sort the direct progenitor of Lincoln and Mark Twain. He was always ready with a story and he had the authentic note of American humor, the element of exaggeration. At his highest, he was picturesque, vivid, and true to his locality. At his lowest, he reflected the tricks of the professional "Sam Slick" and "Sut Lovengood" humorists of his time. That he was sometimes coarse and that his stories are often without point is evident from the records we have of him, but the reader must also remember that the reporters of that day were not skilled in reproducing characteristic utterances and that David could not write himself down for the very "amusing cuss" he must have been. It is only by inference, by charitable interpretation, that we can arrive at the poetic figure which Murdock suggested and Mayo embodied.

There are many newspaper accounts of Crockett, and several biographies. A small book published in 1833 as *Sketches and Eccentricities of Col. David Crockett, of West Tennessee* appears to be, on the whole, trustworthy. It is a record of Crockett's home life by one who knew him, and yet the anonymous writer's descriptions are so vague that no clear notion of the famous hunter's features, voice, or diction remains. The most valuable chapter describes a visit to the hero's home.

"Obtaining directions, I left the high road and sought his residence . . . pursuing a small blazed trail, which bore no marks of being often travelled, and jogged on, wondering what sort of a reception I should meet with from a man who, by quirky humors unequalled, had obtained for himself a never-dying reputation. . . . I pursued my journey until a small opening brought me in sight of a cabin which, from description, I identified as the home of the celebrated hunter of the West.

"It was in appearance rude and uninviting, situated in a small field of eight or ten acres, which had been cleared in the wild woods; no yard surrounded it, and it seemed to have been lately settled. In the passage of the house were seated two men in their shirt sleeves, cleaning rifles. I strained my eyes as I rode up to see if I could identify in either of them the great bear hunter: but before I could decide, my horse had stopped at the bars, and there walked out, in plain homespun attire, with a black fur cap on, a finely proportioned man, about six feet high, aged, from appearance, forty-five. His countenance was frank and manly, and a smile played over it as he approached me. He brought with him a rifle, and from his right shoulder hung a bag made of a racoon skin, to which, by means of a sheath, was appended a huge butcher's knife.

"With a cordial invitation to enter the house, Crockett said: 'You see, we are mighty rough here. I am afraid you will think it hard times, but we have to do the best we can. I started poor and have been *rooting hog ever since;* but d—n apologies, I hate 'em; what I live upon always, I think a friend can stand for a day or two. . . .'

"His cabin within was neat and clean, and bore about it many marks of comfort. The many trophies of wild animals spread over his house and yard—his dogs, in appearance war-worn veterans, lying about sunning themselves—all told truly that I was in the home of the celebrated hunter. . . .

"His wife was rather grave and quiet, but attentive and kind to strangers; his daughters diffident and retiring, perhaps too much so, but uncommonly beautiful. . . . There are no schools near them, yet they converse well. . . . The colonel has no slaves; his daughters attend to the dairy and kitchen, while he performs the more laborious duties of his farm."

Without doubt these pages present the real David Crockett, for, by great good fortune, the writer of them was invited to go with the hunter to a shooting match, so that in the chapter which follows the reader may not only read a detailed description of a genuine old-fashioned backwoods rifle tournament, but may also see the most celebrated hunter of his day in action—the Robin Hood of the Canebrake. It is the most vivid, detailed, and convincing picture of a shooting match known to me. It is as if a careful modern reporter had seen it and recorded it, but the story, so valuable for its detail, is buried in a forgotten book. The unknown is to be pardoned if he favors his hero a little, for in his account Crockett was easily, proudly, negligently the victor. The picture here drawn restores the graceful, masterful figure of the member of Congress from "the Great Shakes." . . .

At dawn on the sixth of March, 1836, Crockett with five undaunted companions was captured by General Castrillon of the Mexican army. With a bloody bandage around his brow (he had been slashed by a saber) Crockett and his companions stood behind a barricade of those who had fallen before their weapons. Castrillon, moved by a soldier's admiration for a brave enemy, took them before Santa Anna. They were all that was left of the defenders of the Alamo.

"The steady, fearless step and undaunted tread of Colonel Crockett on this occasion, together with the bold demeanour of the hardy veteran, had a powerful effect on all present. . . . Castrillon addressed his excellency: 'Sir, here are six prisoners I have taken alive; how shall I dispose of them?' Santa Anna looked at Castrillon fiercely, flew into a violent rage, and replied, 'Have I not told you before how to dispose of them? Why do you bring them to me?' At the same time his brave officers plunged their swords into the bosoms of their defenceless prisoners. Colonel Crockett, seeing the act of treachery, instantly sprang like a tiger at the ruffian chief, but before he could reach him a dozen swords were sheathed in his indomitable heart; and he fell, and died without a groan, a frown on his brow, and a smile of scorn and defiance on his lips."

Whether precisely true to the historic fact or not, this passage—taken from the apocryphal and posthumous work called *Col. Crockett's Exploits and Adventures in Texas*—remains the only account of the great woodsman's death, and it is in character. He was among Travis's forces, and he fell with them: so much we know. Only one woman and a negro survived to give the story of the Alamo to the world. All other history must come from the testimony of Santa Anna and his men.

Whether a monument exists to mark the place of Crockett's burial or not I am unable to say, but he has no need of it. His fame, like that of Daniel Boone, is securely woven into the history of the Border, and with all his faults he will remain an almost perfect embodiment of the American trail-maker.

Davy Crockett

Davy Crockett (1786–1836) was a masterful storyteller, and a self-taught one. After a colorful ten-year career as a U.S. Representative from Tennessee, he headed for Texas in 1835, looking for land and a new start. By March of 1836 he was dead, one of the first to die in defense of the Texas Revolution at the Alamo. His autobiography, while written in the entertaining tall-tale style, is considered a reliable source by most historians.

COLONEL CROCKETT'S TEXAS EXPLOITS

The Siege of the Alamo

I write this on the nineteenth of February, 1836, at San Antonio. We are all in high spirits, though we are rather short of provisions, for men who have appetites that could digest any thing but oppression; but no matter, we have a prospect of soon getting our bellies full of fighting, and that is victuals and drink to a true patriot any day. We had a little sort of convivial party last evening: just about a dozen of us set to work, most patriotically, to see whether we could not get rid of that curse of the land, whiskey, and we made considerable progress; but my poor friend, Thimblerig, got sewed up just about as tight as the eyelet-hole in a lady's corset, and a little tighter too, I reckon; for when he went to bed he called for a bootjack, which was brought to him, and he bent down on his hands and knees, and very gravely pulled off his hat with it, for the darned critter was so thoroughly swiped that he didn't know his head from his heels. But this wasn't all the folly he committed; he pulled off his coat and laid it on the bed, and then hung himself over the back of a chair; and I wish I may be shot if he didn't go to sleep in that position, thinking every thing had been done according to Gunter's late scale. Seeing the poor fellow completely used up, I carried him to bed, though he did belong to the Temperance society; and he knew nothing about what had occurred until I told him the next morning. The Bee hunter didn't join us in this blow-out. Indeed, he will seldom drink more than just enough to prevent his being called a total abstinence man. But then he is the most jovial fellow for a water drinker I ever did see.

This morning I saw a caravan of about fifty mules passing by Bexar, and bound for Santa Fe. They were loaded with different articles to such a degree that it was astonishing how they could travel at all, and they were nearly worn out by their labors. They were without bridle or halter, and yet proceeded with perfect regularity in a single line; and the owners of the caravan rode their mustangs with their enormous spurs, weighing at least a pound a piece, with rowels an inch and a half in length, and lever bits of the harshest description, able to break the jaws of their animals under a very gentle pressure. The men were dressed in the costume of Mexicans. Colonel Travis sent out a guard to see that they were not laden with munitions of war for the enemy. I went out with the party. The poor mules were bending under a burden of more than three hundred pounds, without including the panniers, which were bound so tight as almost to stop the breath of the poor animal. Each of the sorrowful line came up, spontaneously, in turn to have his girth unbound and his load removed. They seemed scarcely able to keep upon their feet, and as they successively obtained relief, one after another heaved a long deep sigh, which it was painful to hear, because it proved that the poor brutes had been worked beyond their strength. What a world of misery man inflicts upon the rest of creation in his brief passage through life! . . .

Last Days at the Alamo

February 22. The Mexicans, about sixteen hundred strong, with their President Santa Anna at their head, aided by Generals Almonte, Cos, Sesma, and Castrillon, are within two leagues of Bexar. General Cos, it seems, has already forgot his parole of honor, and is come back to retrieve the credit he lost in this place in December last. If he is captured a second time, I don't think he can have the impudence to ask to go at large again without giving better bail than on the former occasion. Some of the scouts came in, and bring reports that Santa Anna has been endeavoring to excite the Indians to hostilities against the Texians, but so far without effect. The Cumanches, in particular, entertain such hatred for the Mexicans, and at the same time hold them in such contempt, that they would rather turn their tomahawks against them, and drive them from the land, than lend a helping hand. We are up and doing, and as lively as Dutch cheese in the dog-days. The two hunters that I have already introduced to the reader left the town this afternoon, for the purpose of reconnoitring.

February 23. Early this morning the enemy came in sight, marching in regular order, and displaying their strength to the greatest advantage, in order to strike us with terror. But that was no go; they'll find that they have to do with men who will never lay down their arms as long as they can stand on their legs. We held a short council of war, and, finding that we should be completely surrounded, and overwhelmed by numbers, if we remained in the town, we concluded to withdraw to the fortress of Alamo, and defend it to the last extremity. We accordingly filed off, in good order, having some days before placed all the surplus provisions, arms, and ammunition in the fortress. We have had a large national flag made; it is composed of thirteen stripes, red and white, alternately, on a blue ground, with a large white star, of five points, in the centre, and between the points the letters TEXAS. As soon as all our little band, about one hundred and fifty in number, had entered and secured the fortress in the best possible manner, we set about raising our flag on the battlements; on which occasion there was no one more active than my young friend, the Bee hunter. He had been all along sprightly, cheerful, and spirited, but now, notwithstanding the control that he usually maintained over himself, it was with difficulty that he kept his enthusiasm within bounds. As soon as we commenced raising the flag he burst forth, in a clear, full tone of voice, that made the blood tingle in the veins of all who heard him:—

"Up with your banner, Freedom,
　Thy champions cling to thee;
They'll follow where'er you lead 'em,
　To death, or victory;—
Up with your banner, Freedom.

Tyrants and slaves are rushing
　To tread thee in the dust;
Their blood will soon be gushing,
　And stain our knives with rust;—
But not thy banner Freedom.

While stars and stripes are flying,
　Our blood we'll freely shed;
No groan will 'scape the dying,
　Seeing thee o'er his head;—
Up with your banner, Freedom."

This song was followed by three cheers from all within the fortress, and the drums and trumpets commenced playing. The enemy marched into Bexar, and took possession of the town, a blood-red flag flying at their head, to indicate that we need not expect quarters if we should fall into their clutches. In the afternoon a messenger was sent from the enemy to Colonel Travis, demanding an unconditional and absolute surrender of the garrison, threatening to put every man to the sword in case of refusal. The only answer he received was a cannon shot, so the messenger left us with a flea in his ear, and the Mexicans commenced firing grenades at us, but without doing any mischief. At night Colonel Travis sent an express to Colonel Fanning, at Goliad, about three or four days' march from this place, to let him know that we are besieged. The old pirate volunteered to go on this expedition, and accordingly left the fort after nightfall.

February 24. Very early this morning the enemy commenced a new battery on the banks of the river, about three hundred and fifty yards from the fort, and by afternoon they amused themselves by firing at us from that quarter. Our Indian scout came in this evening, and with him a reinforcement of thirty men from Gonzales, who are just in the nick of time to reap a harvest of glory; but there is some prospect of sweating blood before we gather it in. An accident happened to my friend Thimblerig this afternoon. He was intent on his eternal game of thimbles, in a somewhat exposed position, while the enemy were bombarding us from the new redoubt. A three-ounce ball glanced from the parapet and struck him on the breast, inflicting a painful, but not dangerous wound. I extracted the ball, which was of lead, and recommended to him to drill a hole through it, and carry it for a watch seal. "No," he replied, with energy, "may I be shot six times if I do: that would be making a bauble for an idle boast. No, Colonel, lead is getting scarce, and I'll lend it out at compound interest. Curse the thimbles!" he muttered, and went his way, and I saw no more of him that evening.

February 25. The firing commenced early this morning, but the Mexicans are poor engineers, for we haven't lost a single man, and our outworks have sustained no injury. Our sharpshooters have brought down a considerable number of stragglers at a long shot. I got up before the peep of day, hearing an occasional discharge of a rifle just over the place where I was sleeping, and I was somewhat amazed to see Thimblerig mounted alone on the battlement, no one being on duty at the time but the sentries. "What are you doing there?" says I. "Paying my debts," says he, "interest and all." "And how do you make out?" says I. "I've nearly got through," says he; "stop a moment, Colonel, and I'll close the account." He clapped his rifle to his shoulder, and blazed away, then jumped down from his perch, and said, "That account's settled; them chaps will let me play out my game in quiet next time." I looked over the wall, and saw four Mexicans lying dead on the plain. I asked him to explain what he meant by paying his debts, and he told me that he had run the grape shot into four rifle balls, and that he had taken an early stand to have a chance of picking off stragglers. "Now, Colonel, let's go take our bitters," said he;—and so we did. The enemy have been busy during the night, and have thrown up two batteries on the opposite side of the river. The battalion of Matamoras is posted there, and cavalry occupy the hills to the east and on the road to Gonzales. They are determined to surround us, and cut us off from reinforcement, or the possibility of escape by a sortie. Well, there's one thing they cannot prevent; we'll still go ahead, and sell our lives at a high price.

February 26. Colonel Bowie has been taken sick from overexertion and exposure. He did not leave his bed to-day until twelve o'clock. He is worth a dozen common men in a situation like ours. The Bee hunter keeps the whole garrison in good heart with his songs and his jests, and his daring and determined spirit. He is about the quickest on the trigger, and the best rifle shot we have in the fort. I have already seen him bring down eleven of the enemy, and at such a distance that we all thought it would be a waste of ammunition to attempt it. His gun is first rate, quite equal to my Betsey, though she has not quite as many trinkets about her. This day a small party sallied out of the fort for wood and water, and had a slight skirmish with three times their number from the division under General Sesma. The Bee hunter headed them, and beat the enemy off, after killing three. On opening his Bible at night, of which he always reads a portion before going to rest, he found a musket ball in the middle of it. "See here, Colonel," said he, "how they have treated the valued present of my dear little Kate of Nacogdoches." "It has saved your life," said I. "True," replied he, more seriously than usual, "and I am not the first sinner whose life has been saved by this book." He prepared for bed, and before retiring he prayed, and returned thanks for his providential escape; and I heard the name of Catherine mingled in his prayer.

February 27. The cannonading began early this morning, and ten bombs were thrown into the fort, but fortunately exploded without doing any mischief. So far it has been a sort of tempest in a tea-pot, not unlike a pitched battle in the Hall of Congress, where the parties array their forces, make fearful demonstrations on both sides, then fire away with loud-sounding speeches, which contain about as much meaning as the report of a howitzer charged with a blank cartridge. Provisions are becoming scarce, and the enemy are endeavoring to cut off our water.

If they attempt to stop our grog in that manner, let them look out, for we shall become too wrathy for our shirts to hold us. We are not prepared to submit to an excise of that nature, and they'll find it out. This discovery has created considerable excitement in the fort.

February 28. Last night our hunters brought in some corn, and had a brush with a scout from the enemy beyond gun-shot of the fort. They put the scout to flight, and got in without injury. They bring accounts that the settlers are flying in all quarters, in dismay, leaving their possessions to the mercy of the ruthless invader, who is literally engaged in a war of extermination more brutal than the untutored savage of the desert could be guilty of. Slaughter is indiscriminate, sparing neither sex, age, nor condition. Buildings have been burnt down, farms laid waste, and Santa Anna appears determined to verify his threat, and convert the blooming paradise into a howling wilderness. For just one fair crack at that rascal, even at a hundred yards' distance, I would bargain to break my Betsey, and never pull trigger again. My name's not Crockett if I wouldn't get glory enough to appease my stomach for the remainder of my life. The scouts report that a settler by the name of Johnson, flying with his wife and three little children, when they reached the Colorado, left his family on the shore, and waded into the river to see whether it would be safe to ford with his wagon. When about the middle of the river he was seized by an alligator, and after a struggle, was dragged under the water, and perished. The helpless woman and her babes were discovered, gazing in agony on the spot, by other fugitives, who happily passed that way, and relieved them. Those who fight the battles experience but a small part of the privation, suffering, and anguish that follow in the train of ruthless war. The cannonading continued at intervals throughout the day, and all hands were kept up to their work. The enemy, somewhat emboldened, draws nigher to the fort. So much the better. There was a move in General Sesma's division toward evening.

February 29. Before daybreak, we saw General Sesma leave his camp with a large body of cavalry and infantry, and move off in the direction of Goliad. We think that he must have received news of Colonel Fanning's coming to our relief. We are all in high spirits at the prospect of being able to give the rascals a fair shake on the plain. This business of being shut up makes a man wolfish. I had a little sport this morning before breakfast. The enemy had planted a piece of ordnance within gun-shot of the fort during the night, and the first thing in the morning they commenced a brisked cannonade, point blank, against the spot where I was snoring. I turned out pretty smart and mounted the rampart. The gun was charged again, a fellow stepped forth to touch her off, but before he could apply the match, I let him have it, and he keeled over. A second stepped up, snatched the match from the hand of the dying man, but Thimblerig, who had followed me, handed me his rifle, and the next instant the Mexican was stretched on the earth beside the first. A third came up to the cannon, my companion handed me another gun, and I fixed him off in like manner. A fourth, then a fifth, seized the match, who both met with the same fate, and then the whole party gave it up as a bad job, and hurried off to the camp, leaving the cannon ready charged where they had planted it. I came down, took my bitters, and went to breakfast. Thimblerig told me that the place from which I had been firing was one of the snuggest stands in the whole fort, for he never failed picking off two or three stragglers before breakfast, when perched up there.

And I recollect, now, having seen him there, ever since he was wounded, the first thing in the morning, and the last at night, and at times, thoughtlessly playing at his eternal game.

March 1. The enemy's forces have been increasing in numbers daily, notwithstanding they have already lost about three hundred men in the several assaults they have made upon us. I neglected to mention in the proper place, that when the enemy came in sight we had but three bushels of corn in the garrison, but have since found eighty bushels in a deserted house. Colonel Bowie's illness still continues, but he manages to crawl from his bed every day, that his comrades may see him. His presence alone is a tower of strength. The enemy becomes more daring as his numbers increase.

March 2. This day the delegates meet in general convention at the town of Washington, to frame our Declaration of Independence. That the sacred instrument may never be trampled on by the children of those who have freely shed their blood to establish it, is the sincere wish of David Crockett. Universal independence is an almighty idea, far too extensive for some brains to comprehend. It is a beautiful seed that germinates rapidly, and brings forth a large and vigorous tree, but like the deadly Upas, we sometimes find the smaller plants wither and die in its shades. Its blooming branches spread far and wide, offering a perch of safety to all alike, but even among its protecting branches we find the eagle, the kite, and the owl preying upon the helpless dove and sparrow. Beneath its shades myriads congregate in goodly fellowship; but the lamb and the fawn find but frail security from the lion and the jackal, though the tree of independence waves over them. Some imagine independence to be a natural charter, to exercise without restraint, and to their fullest extent, all the energies, both physical and mental, with which they have been endowed; and for their individual aggrandizement alone, without regard to the rights of others, provided they extend to all the same privilege and freedom of action. Such independence is the worst of tyranny.

March 3. We have given over all hopes of receiving assistance from Goliad or Refugio. Colonel Travis harangued the garrison, and concluded by exhorting them, in case the enemy should carry the fort, to fight to the last gasp, and render their victory even more serious to them than to us. This was followed by three cheers.

March 4. Shells have been falling into the fort like hail during the day, but without effect. About dusk, in the evening, we observed a man running toward the fort, pursued by about half a dozen of the Mexican cavalry. The Bee hunter immediately knew him to be the old pirate who had gone to Goliad, and, calling to the two hunters, he sallied out of the fort to the relief of the old man who was hard pressed. I followed close after. Before we reached the spot the Mexicans were close on the heel of the old man, who stopped suddenly, turned short upon his pursuers, discharged his rifle and one of the enemy fell from his horse. The chase was renewed, but finding that he would be overtaken and cut to pieces, he now turned again, and, to the amazement of the enemy, became the assailant in his turn. He clubbed his gun, and dashed among them like a wounded tiger, and they fled like sparrows. By this time we reached the spot, and, in the ardor of the moment, followed some distance before we saw that our retreat to the fort was cut off by another detachment of cavalry. Nothing was to be done but to fight our way through. We were all of the same mind. "Go ahead!" cried I, and they shouted, "Go ahead, Colonel!" We dashed among them, and a bloody conflict ensued. They were about twenty in number, and they stood their ground. After the fight had continued about five minutes, a detachment was seen issuing from the fort to our relief, and the Mexicans scampered off, leaving eight of their comrades dead upon the field. But we did not escape unscathed, for both the pirate and the Bee hunter were mortally wounded, and I received a sabre cut across the forehead. The old man died, with out speaking, as soon as we entered the fort. We bore my young friend to his bed, dressed his wounds, and I watched beside him. He lay, without complaint or manifesting pain, until about midnight, when he spoke, and I asked him if he wanted any thing. "Nothing," he replied, but drew a sigh that seemed to rend his heart, as he added, "Poor Kate of Nacogdoches!" His eyes were filled with tears, as he continued, "Her words were prophetic, Colonel;" and then he sang in a low voice that resembled the sweet notes of his own devoted Kate,

> "But toom cam' the saddle, all bluidy to see,
> And hame cam' the steed, but hame never cam' he."

He spoke no more, and a few minutes after, died. Poor Kate, who will tell this to thee!

March 5. Pop, pop, pop! Bom, bom, bom! throughout the day. No time for memorandums now. Go ahead! Liberty and independence forever!

[*Here ends Davy Crockett's own story.*]

Antonio López de Santa Anna ─────────────

Antonio López de Santa Anna (1794–1876), while known as the general who annihilated the Alamo defenders and lost ingloriously at San Jacinto, was also loved and hated equally in his own country—he was six times elected president of Mexico, though ideologically illiterate (he led armies for monarchists, imperialists, republicans, and liberals). His autobiography bristles with elements of the self-serving and the self-pitying, and his appeals to patriotism seem coated with bathos—nowhere more evident than in his explanation of his conduct at the Alamo and San Jacinto.

THE MEXICAN SIDE OF THE TEXAN REVOLUTION

Never has the ambitious thought of obtaining universal approval for my actions entered my mind; nor have I been so pusillanimous that the fear of the disapproval of a few, or even of many, could have prevented

me from acting in a certain way when convinced, even though errone-
ously, of the propriety of my action. In the palace of Mexico as in this
humble hut, in the midst of the applause of a free people the same as
amidst the insolent hisses of the Texans who loudly called for my death,
I have realized that my conduct would always be criticized, for who has
not at least one enemy if fate has raised him above his fellow-citizens
and placed him in the public eye? I was not surprised, therefore, to see
the triumphs of Béxar and the Alamo tainted by the tireless and venom-
ous tooth of that envy which I have always despised, nor the defeat of
San Jacinto horribly portrayed by the unfaithful and disloyal brush of
an unjust animosity; much less was I surprised that by these means a
great part of a nation, zealous as it should be of its honor and anxious
that the cost of sustaining it should be reduced to a minimum, should
have been made to doubt the propriety of my war measures if not to
condemn them outright. But my misfortune having reached its limit,
this ill opinion has gone one step further, and, although I expected as
much, it has been all the more painful to me. Thus, when I placed foot
upon the soil of my native land, evoked as it were from the grave, after
having suffered for its cause, the most sacred of causes, a painful impris-
onment, a cruel separation, a great misfortune, the judgment of my
compatriots would like to banish me. This ill-deserved judgment has not
failed to inflict a mortal wound to my heart, in spite of the fact that I
recognize its noble origin in some cases. Still I expected, yea, I flattered
myself in the midst of my sorrows, that I would obtain the compassion
of my compatriots and that upon hearing me they would accept my
justification. . . .

At the age of thirty-five my military achievements had long since
carried me to the highest military rank, thanks to the liberality with
which my services were repaid. I held the first place among Mexicans
by their own generous vote. My name was known beyond the limits of
Mexico and a competent fortune assured me against poverty. To what
else could the ambition of a man who had just refused a dictatorship
offered to him, and who had fought those who had dared to make such
an offer, aspire? What else could he desire who, though able to live in
a palace in luxury and plenty surrounded by never-failing courtiers,
dwelt in a simple country home where his pride could only be flattered
by the sincere love of his wife and the innocent games of his children?
I was wrested from this peaceful life by my love for my country. I had
sworn that my sword should always be the first to strike the blow upon
the daring necks of her enemies, and the news that came from Texas
regarding the plight of General Don Martín Cós, besieged in Béxar by

the Texans, late in 1835, made me realize that they were the most formidable enemies that threatened our country at that time. . . .

I went to Mexico, therefore, in November 1835, to take charge of a war from which I could have been excused, for the fundamental law of the country offered me a decorous excuse that my broken health made all the more honorable. Nevertheless, aware of the adverse circumstances I have expressed, I still desired to try to serve my country. In a few days I gathered six thousand men, clothed and equipped. At the cost of immense sacrifices, rising above obstacles that seemed insuperable, this force set out from San Luis toward the end of December 1835. The difficulties arising from the need of securing food supplies sufficient for the army while crossing four hundred leagues of desert lands, and those attendant upon its conveyance, as well as the transportation of other equipment, arms, munitions, etc., were all difficulties that, though not pressing at the time of organization, were, nevertheless, of the utmost importance, particularly since the cost of transportation was extremely high in that long stretch. Hospitals had to be located and protected; a great number of rivers had to be crossed without bridge equipment, without even a single boat; the coast had to be watched and the ports kept open to receive provisions and to prevent the enemy from receiving reinforcements or from retreating—all of this with only one serviceable war vessel—and lastly, we had to raise a reserve force to come to our help in case of a reverse, a frequent occurrence in war, when, in order to complete the number of those deemed necessary for the campaign, we had had to use raw recruits. . . .

On the night of the fifth of March, four columns having been made ready for the assault under the command of their respective officers, they moved forward in the best order and with the greatest silence, but the imprudent huzzas of one of them awakened the sleeping vigilance of the defenders of the fort and their artillery fire caused such disorder among our columns that it was necessary to make use of the reserves. The Alamo was taken, this victory that was so much and so justly celebrated at the time, costing us seventy dead and about three hundred wounded,* a loss that was also later judged to be avoidable and charged, after the disaster of San Jacinto, to my incompetence and precipitation. I do not know of a way in which any fortification, defended by artillery, can be carried by assault without the personal losses of the attacking party being greater than those of the enemy, against whose walls and

---

*"Not one remained alive but they disabled over a thousand of our men between dead and wounded." Genaro García, *Documentos,* II, 35.

fortifications the brave assailants can present only their bare breasts. It is easy enough, from a desk in a peaceful office, to pile up charges against a general out on the field but this cannot prove anything more than the praiseworthy desire of making war less disastrous. But its nature being such, a general has no power over its immutable laws. Let us weep at the tomb of the brave Mexicans who died at the Alamo defending the honor and the rights of their country. They won a lasting claim to fame and the country can never forget their heroic names. . . .

Let it be said now in order to avoid repetition: the war against Texas has been as just on the part of the Mexican government as the lack of the slightest attempt on the part of those who forced it upon Mexico has been to try to justify their action. Few of the colonists, properly speaking, have taken up arms in the struggle. The soldiers of Travis at the Alamo, those of Fannin at Perdido, the riflemen of Dr. Grant, and Houston himself and his troops at San Jacinto, with but few exceptions, were publicly known to have come from New Orleans and other points of the neighboring republic exclusively for the purpose of aiding the Texas rebellion without ever having been members of any of the colonization grants.

Some Mexicans,* partisans of a former system of government, thought, perhaps in good faith, that the only effect of fanning the fire of war in Texas would be a political change in accord with their opinion. Their shortsighted ambition must be a terrible lesson to them as well as a source of eternal remorse. Too late, they now deplore having placed in jeopardy the integrity of our national territory.

Our country found itself invaded not by an established nation that came to vindicate its rights, whether true or imaginary; nor by Mexicans who, in a paroxysm of political passion, came to defend or combat the public administration of the country. The invaders were all men who, moved by the desire of conquest, with rights less apparent and plausible than those of Cortés and Pizarro, wished to take possession of that vast territory extending from Béxar to the Sabine belonging to Mexico. What can we call them? How should they be treated? All the existing laws, whose strict observance the government had just recommended, marked them as pirates and outlaws. The nations of the world would never have forgiven Mexico had it accorded them rights, privileges, and considerations which the common law of peoples accords only to constituted nations.

*Santa Anna is hinting at Zavala, who left Mexico City and joined the Texans. He was the first vice president of Texas.

*Sam Houston (1793–1863) resigned as governor of Tennessee in
1829 when his wife left him, and went to live with the Cherokees
in Arkansas Territory. Representing the tribe in its dealings with
the U.S. government, he once struck an Ohio congressman with
a cane during a debate on the House floor, for which he was
reprimanded. Shortly after moving to the Texas province of Mexico in 1833 he was named commander of the Army of Independence, and on April 21, 1836, he defeated the army of Mexican
President Santa Anna in the eighteen-minute-long Battle of San
Jacinto. As a U.S. senator and governor of the new state of Texas
he opposed secessionist sentiments, and was deposed from the
governorship for refusing to take the oath of allegiance to the
Confederacy. This selection is the only one in existence that expresses his feelings about being deposed, and about the disasters
he predicted were in store for Texas as a result of the Civil War.*

SPEECH AT BRENHAM, MARCH 31, 1861*

Fellow-Citizens: It was not my purpose or desire to address you
today upon the great issues now confronting our common country, but
old soldier comrades who fought with me at San Jacinto, and other dear

*A copy of this speech was sent to The University of Texas Library by S. A. Hackworth.
The *Brenham Inquirer,* April 3, 1861, mentions the speech, also the ominous threats
made against Houston's life should he try to make a speech at Brenham; it also states that
a "brave secession leader" addressed "the howling mob" stating that he would protect
General Houston while he made any speech he might wish to make. But *The Enquirer*
did not report the speech or any part of it; but it did give the date as March 31, 1861.

In sending the copy to The University of Texas, Mr. S. A. Hackworth wrote the
following letter which may be of interest:

Galveston, Texas [no date].

I herewith enclose to you a correct report of the great speech made by Governor Sam
Houston at Brenham, Texas, in 1861, immediately after he had been deposed from the
Governorship of the State, because he refused to take the Oath of Allegiance to the
Confederate Government. General Houston, accompanied by his family, was on his way,
by stage travel, from Austin to his home at Cedar Point, near the old battlefield of San
Jacinto. He did not wish to speak, but his old soldier comrades, and other friends at
Brenham insisted that he speak his sentiments. He firmly continued to refuse their
invitation, until some of the hot-blooded secessionists declared that he should not speak.
This aroused the old lion-hearted hero, and he then consented to speak. I remember the
scene as vividly as if it had been only yesterday. The excitement was intense; excited
groups of secessionists gathered upon the street corners, and declared that it would be
treason against the Confederate Government to permit Governor Houston to speak
against secession. The court house was densely packed, and as Governor Houston arose

friends, insist that I shall explain the reason why I refuse to take the oath of allegiance to the Confederate Government, and why I have been deposed from the Governorship of our beloved State. The earnest solicitations of my old soldier comrades outweigh my desire to remain silent until the whirlwind of passion and popular clamor have subsided and the voice of reason can be fairly heard.

I shall, therefore, speak my honest sentiments and convictions and I now submit to you the reasons why I could not take the oath of allegiance to the so-called Confederate Government, and thereby violate the oath of allegiance I took to the Federal Government when I entered upon the duties of the Chief Magistracy of Texas. It has always been the invariable rule of my life never to form an opinion or verdict upon any great public question until I have first carefully and impartially heard and considered all the evidence and facts upon both sides, and when I have thus formed my verdict, no fear of popular condemnation can induce me to modify or change such verdict. I have never permitted popular clamor, passion, prejudice nor selfish ambition to induce me to change an opinion or verdict which my conscience and judgment has once formed and tells me is right. My only desire is to be right, and for this reason I can not nor will not sacrifice what my conscience and judgment tells me is right. I love the plaudits of my fellow citizens, but will never sacrifice the principle of right and justice for public favor or commendation.

---

to speak, cries were heard: "Put him out; don't let him speak; kill him." At this moment, Mr. Hugh McIntyre, a wealthy planter of the community, and a leading secessionist, sprang upon the table and drew a large Colt revolver saying: "I and 100 other friends of Governor Houston have invited him to address us, and we will kill the first man who insults, or who may, in any way attempt to injure him. I myself think that Governor Houston ought to have accepted the situation, and ought to have taken the oath of allegiance to our Confederate Government, but he thought otherwise. He is honest and sincere, and he shed his blood for Texas independence. There is no other man alive who has more right to be heard by the people of Texas. Now, fellow-citizens, give him your close attention; and you ruffians, keep quiet, or I will kill you."

This warning had the desired effect and only frequent cheers interrupted the Governor during his address. His speech so deeply impressed me, that at the time I wrote it out from memory. I gave a copy of it to the editor of the *Brenham Enquirer* (Mr. Rankin), who complimented me on the correctness of the report, but he deemed it inexpedient to print it. I also gave a copy of it to Mr. Hugh McIntyre, and he, too, declared it correct in every detail. I may have failed to use Governor Houston's exact words in a few phrases, or sentences, but my report of his line of argument is perfect. So far as I know this speech has never been printed, and believing that it will be of interest to the people of Texas and other States to read that grand old hero's speech, which so prophetically and fearlessly predicted coming events of disaster to our people, I herewith submit it to you for publication.

S. A. Hackworth

The Vox Populi is not always the voice of God, for when demagogues and selfish political leaders succeed in arousing public prejudice and stilling the voice of reason, then on every hand can be heard the popular cry of "Crucify him, crucify him." The Vox Populi then becomes the voice of the devil, and the hiss of mobs warns all patriots that peace and good government are in peril. I have heard the hiss of mobs upon the streets of Austin, and also heard the hiss of mobs upon the streets of Brenham, and friends have warned me that my life was in great peril if I expressed my honest sentiments and convictions.

But the hiss of the mob and the howls of their jackal leaders can not deter me nor compel me to take the oath of allegiance to a so-called Confederate Government. I protest against surrendering the Federal Constitution, its Government and its glorious flag to the Northern abolition leaders and to accept in its stead a so-called Confederate Government whose constitution contains the germs and seeds of decay which must and will lead to its speedy ruin and dismemberment if it can ever secure any real existence. Its seeds of ruin and decay are the principle of secession which permits any one or more of the Confederate States to secede from the parent Confederate Government and to establish separate governments. Can any well-informed man doubt that the time will soon come when several of the Confederate States will secede and establish separate governments? Why will such results follow in the event the Confederate Government is established? Because in all the Confederate States there are ambitious secession leaders who will be aspirants for the Presidency of the Confederacy and to exercise controlling influence in its government and in all cases where their ambitions are frustrated these leaders will cause their respective States to secede and form separate governments wherein they may be able to realize their selfish political hopes. Within ten years we would have ten or more separate Confederate Governments, which would in time fall an easy prey to foreign Governments. The increase of secession leaders will be rapid and large in all the Confederate States and their contests against each other for political leadership will lead to discord, promoting continual conspiracies and revolutions, which will produce many Count Julians, or traitors, who will call to their aid foreign Governments to despoil the people who refuse to help them gratify their selfish ambitions.

Never will I consent to give up our Federal Constitution and our union of States for a Confederate constitution and government whose foundation principles of secession must and will prevent its successful establishment; or if it should triumph, its triumph would be only temporary and its short-lived existence end in revolution and utter ruin.

The Federal Constitution, the Federal Government and its starry flag are glorious heritages bequeathed to the South and all sections of our common country by the valor and patriotism of Washington, and all the brave revolutionary soldiers, who fought for and won American independence. Our galaxy of Southern Presidents—Washington, Jefferson, Monroe, Jackson, Taylor, Tyler and Polk cemented the bonds of union between all the States which can never be broken. Washington declared for an indivisible union and Jackson made the secession of South Carolina and of other States impossible. Jefferson by the Louisiana purchase added a vast empire of country to our union, and Polk followed his example by further extending our Union to embrace Texas, New Mexico, Arizona, Colorado, and California. Monroe established the Monroe Doctrine which for all time preserves and safeguards the Governments of the Western Hemisphere against foreign conquest. All our Northern Presidents have been equally patriotic and just to the South. Not a single Southern right has been violated by any President or by any Federal Administration. President Lincoln has been elected, because the secession Democratic leaders divided the Democratic party and caused the nomination of two separate Presidential Democratic tickets and nominees.

Both branches of Congress are Democratic; therefore it will be impossible for President Lincoln's administration to enact or enforce any laws or measures that can injure Southern rights. But grant for the sake of the argument that the time may come when both branches of Congress are Republican and laws are enacted and enforced which will injure or destroy Southern rights what shall we then do? I answer that sufficient unto the day is the evil thereof, nor would there be the least danger of the Republican party ever controlling both branches of Congress and all branches of the Federal Government if the secession leaders would permit the Democratic party to remain a solid indivisible party.

But if the day should ever come when Southern rights are ruthlessly violated or injured by the Republican party, we of the South will then fight for our rights under the Stars and Stripes and with the Federal Constitution in one hand and the sword in the other we shall march on to victory.

I believe a large majority of our Southern people are opposed to secession, and if the secession leaders would permit our people to take ample time to consider secession and then hold fair elections the secession movement would be defeated by an overwhelming majority. But the secession leaders declare that secession has already been peaceably accomplished and the Confederate Government independence and sovereignty will soon be acknowledged by all foreign governments. They tell us that the Confederate Government will thus be permanently established without bloodshed. They might with equal truth declare that the fountains of the great deep blue seas can be broken up without disturbing their surface waters, as to tell us that the best Government that ever existed for men can be broken up without bloodshed.

The secession leaders also tell us if war should come that European Nations will speedily come to our relief, and aid us to win our independence because cotton is King and European commerce and civilization can not long exist without cotton, therefore they must help us maintain and perpetuate our Confederate Government. Gentlemen who use such false and misleading statements forget or else are ignorant of the facts that commerce and civilization existed a long period of time before cotton was generally known and used.

They also forget or else are ignorant of the fact that the best sentiment of Europe is opposed to our systems of negro slavery. They also tell us if war comes that the superior courage of our people with their experience of the use of firearms, will enable us to triumph in battle over ten times our number of Northern forces. Never was a more false or absurd statement ever made by designing demagogues. I declare that Civil War is inevitable and is near at hand. When it comes the descendants of the heroes of Lexington and Bunker Hill will be found equal in patriotism, courage and heroic endurance with descendants of the heroes of Cowpens and Yorktown. For this reason I predict that the civil war which is now near at hand will be stubborn and of long duration. We are sadly divided among ourselves, while the North and West are united. Not only will we have to contend against a united and harmonious North, but we will also have to battle against tens of thousands of our own people, who will never desert the Stars and Stripes nor surrender the union of states for a Southern Confederacy of states, whose principles of secession must inevitably lead to discord, conspiracy and revolution, and at last anarchy and utter ruin. When the tug of war comes, it will indeed be the Greek meeting Greek. Then, oh my fellow countrymen, the fearful conflict will fill our fair land with untold suffering, misfortune and disaster. The soil of our beloved South will drink deep the precious blood of our sons and brethren. In earnest prayer to our Heavenly Father, I have daily petitioned him to cast out from my mind the dark foreboding of the coming conflict. My prayers have caused the light of reason to cast the baleful shadows of the coming events before me. I cannot, nor will I close my eyes against the light and voice of reason. The die has been cast by your secession leaders, whom you have permitted to sow and broadcast the seeds of secession, and you must ere long reap the fearful harvest of conspiracy and revolution.

Jeff Hamilton

Jeff Hamilton (1840–1942) was thirteen years old when he was bought as a slave by Sam Houston. Later as a free man he became Houston's personal valet. Years after, he wrote a lengthy journal describing such events as Houston's being deposed as governor and his freeing of his slaves. When Hamilton was over one hundred years old the journal came to the attention of historian Lenoir Hunt, who helped publish this rare first-person account of slavery in Texas.

MY MASTER: THE INSIDE STORY OF
SAM HOUSTON AND HIS TIMES

At last, the day came upon which Mr. Lincoln was elected our president.

For some months I had noticed that my master was aging fast. At times he would walk with a crutch, and used his cane all the time now. But his eyes were clear, and his mind as keen and sharp as ever. He was almost sixty-eight early in 1860. His old wounds, which I had dressed hundreds of times, were paining him more than usual, especially during the cold, damp winter months.

Early on the morning of election day, I drove my master down to the polls. I sat in the buggy in front of the Calhoun House, where the election was being held. It was raining like everything. Before the General went in to put his ballot in the box, he stood awhile under the balcony of the hotel and talked to some friends. I was not over two or three feet from them, and in spite of the rain could hear everything they said.

I heard the General say that slavery was a damnable thing at best, and that he didn't believe in human slavery nor in secession or disunion either. He said he hoped God in some way might perform a miracle as of old and save the country from destruction. There was the greatest excitement ever seen in this country over the election for president. The General went in to vote and within less than five minutes he came out and ordered me to drive him to his office in the State Capitol.

When we got to his office, Mr. Penland, the General's secretary, asked him if he had voted yet. When the General told him he had just voted, I could tell from the way Mr. Penland talked and acted that he was dying from curiosity to know exactly how the General had voted. Anyhow, it was not long until the secretary could stand it no longer, and simply had to ask the General how he voted.

I could see that my master did not like the question, as he looked at Mr. Penland in a kind of strange, dignified sort of way. But before he could answer one way or the other Major Cave, the secretary of state, rushed into the office and handed me some papers to take to town. I had to leave the office with my own curiosity unsatisfied, and was afraid when I got back to ask either the General or his secretary anything about it. I believe until this day that the General did not tell anyone how he voted. He made speeches for Senator Bell, but said in one of them that he didn't believe Senator Bell had a ghost of a chance. I have always thought that the General had reasoned it out that he ought not to throw his vote away on a losing horse like Senator Bell, and may have voted for Mr. Lincoln, believing that he would do more than anybody else to keep the Union together, but, outside of that point, the General did not agree with Mr. Lincoln on many other questions.

It was on January 28 that the State Convention of Secession met at Austin, in the capitol building. They drew up an ordinance of secession without wasting any time, and set February 1 as the date for the delegates to vote on it. Just before twelve o'clock noon that day, the Convention decided to ask the General to appear before it. They knew that nearly everyone of the delegates was for secession and that the General couldn't change a single vote at that late date. But they wanted to show him a courtesy on account of his long fight for Texas independence and annexation and all he had done for the State.

A committee of six members was appointed to ask my master to appear before them. The only two men I knew on the committee were

Mr. William Montgomery, a Baptist preacher, and Colonel William P. Rogers, who was a distant cousin of the General and who had fought with him in the Creek Wars under General Jackson.

The General accepted the invitation, and I hurried to bring him his coat and hat, also giving him his comb and brush to tidy up his hair. But he did not wear his hat. I followed my master and the committee up the stairs, but they hurried into the House of Representatives, and someone slammed the door in my face. But I had made up my mind nothing would keep me from the room. I ran up the stairway that opened into the balcony, and managed to get in without anyone seeing me. I crawled behind one of the posts where I could see and hear everything but where I could not be seen from the floor of the house.

There were many of my master's close personal and former political friends there who were members of the convention and who had joined the secession movement.

The General was given the seat of honor beside Judge Oran M. Roberts, who was called the "Old Alcalde" and who was then chief justice of the supreme court.

My master rose to speak. You could have heard a pin drop. I can remember only a few of the things he said, but I best remember how he said them and how he acted. He began by saying:

"All of you know that I am opposed to secession, and all of you know my convictions on the subject. I have taken an oath to support the Constitution of the United States and its flag and the Constitution of Texas and its flag. I almost died fighting for that flag, and I almost died fighting for the Texas flag. I have served Texas under both of those flags for a long time. Gentlemen, you cannot forget those two flags—you cannot withdraw from the Union.

"The country is just now in a state of prosperity. To secede from the Union and set up another government would cause war. I advise you to remain in the Union. For, if you go to war with the United States, you will never conquer her, as she has the money and the men. If she does not whip you by guns, powder, and steel, she will starve you to death. Now, if you go to war, it will take the flower of the country—the young men. I know what war is. I have been in it often and do not want any more of it. War is no plaything and this war will be a bloody war. There will be thousands and thousands who march away from our homes never to come back. There will be numberless mothers and children made widows and orphans. I advise you to settle this matter peaceably. Where there is union there is strength, and if you break the Union you will wreck the whole fabric of the Constitution. No, I will never agree to sign Texas away as a seceding state."

At this point in his speech, my master's voice choked with emotion, and tears—the biggest tears I ever saw in my life—rolled down his cheeks.

"I will show you the wounds I received in fighting for Texas and the Union you would destroy," added my master. And then my master placed his hand on his right thigh, bared his right arm, and pointed down to his ankle, and said:

"A barbed Indian arrow struck that thigh. I will take that wound to my grave. It has never healed. This arm and shoulder were shattered by Indian rifle balls. My ankle was broken to pieces at San Jacinto," he concluded and limped to his seat.

There was a deep silence, when Colonel Rogers rose and asked the General:

"Well, Sam, do you believe that your wife and daughters ought to scrub their clothes at a wash-tub and cook meals in pots over a hot fire? Before I would suffer my wife and daughter to cook and scrub, I'll wade in blood up to my neck!"

My master answered that washing and scrubbing were honorable and that no white woman had ever died from honorable work.

Then, Mr. Montgomery got up and raised a secession flag over the General's head, and asked him if he would rather give up the governor's office or join the secession plan.

My master answered:

"The reason I wanted to be governor of this state was to help it on its feet, and now everybody seems to be getting along nicely. I am not particular about the office. I have a home and livestock and can live without the office. I feel that the government has been paying me for past services in her hour of need rather than for present services. No, I will never give up the Constitution or the Union."

The convention then voted to adopt the Ordinance of Secession, which carried by a vote of 174 to 7 votes. The ordinance was then submitted to a vote of the people. The election was held on February 23, 1861, and the vote was 46,129 for secession to 14,697 against secession. March 5 was the day fixed for Texas to join the Confederate nation, and March 16 the time for state officials to take the oath of office.

On the latter date, the secretary of the convention began to call the roll of state officials, so that each one of them might take the oath of allegiance which the convention had prescribed. The first name called was that of "Sam Houston." The General had stayed away on purpose, and after his name was called several times, his office was declared vacant, and Mr. Edward Clark, the lieutenant governor, was sworn in as governor. The only other state officer who refused to take the oath was Major E. W. Cave of Houston, the General's secretary of state. My master had ended his long public career.

Between the time the first and second secession conventions met, my master made a trip to a number of the larger towns and cities in the state in a final effort to stop the secessionists. They could not stop my master from speaking at any place, although other Union speakers were driven out of town when they tried to talk. Uncle Joshua did a great deal of the driving that winter and spring.

As we came in sight of Belton (the very town where I now live!) a man riding a winded horse overtook us, waving something in his hand and shouting at the top of his voice.

As he reached the side of the buggy, he stopped and handed the General a big letter, sealed with wax.

My master got out his spectacles and opened and read the letter. With a very serious look on his face, he said sharply:

"Jeff, turn around; we must hurry back to Austin at once!"

When we got to Austin late that evening, he sent me with a message to four of his most trusted friends, having me tell them to meet him right away in the governor's office.

All of these four friends were true Union men. I built a roaring log-fire in the fireplace, and brought in a bucket of fresh water from the well just outside the capitol.

Without stopping to explain why he wanted to see them, my master read the letter aloud to them, and then passed it over to them, so each one could read it himself.

I heard every word of the letter the General read. It was from Mr. Abraham Lincoln, and it said that he would be president in about two weeks. He offered to make the General a major-general in the United States Army, and also to send to the Texas coast a fleet with fifty thousand Federal soldiers, so that my master might put down secession in Texas.

My master then left to a vote of his friends just what he should do about the matter. One of his advisers voted to accept the offer, but three of them voted against the proposition. The reason these three men voted against the idea, they said, was because over two-thirds of the voters of Texas had just voted for secession, and they didn't believe that even an army of half a million men could change the opinion of the Texas people, and that that kind of invasion would end with much needless slaughter. They also said that up to that time the state had not seceded from the Union in an official way.

The General took the letter, and went over to the fireplace. Throwing it into the blaze, he said:

"Gentlemen, I have asked your advice, and I will take it, but if I were ten years younger I wouldn't."

The General then had me take him down to Cedar Point, his summer home on Trinity Bay across from Galveston. I remember hearing him say he had bought the place back in 1837 for $8,500. After looking after some business there, he had Captain Palmer, who ran my master's sailboat, load the boat with salt and potatoes, and sail to Galveston.

The General had some posters printed and tacked on trees and buildings all over the town, which announced that he would speak there the next day. The secessionists tore down the posters, and threatened to hang the General if he tried to speak in Galveston. His friends came to him and begged him not to speak on account of the high feeling. But the General had made up his mind to speak, and I knew that no one could stop him. He went to the manager of the Tremont Hotel and paid him the money out of his own pocket for the right to speak on the balcony the following day.

It looked like there would be a riot when my master came out on the balcony and began his talk. But the crowd quieted down when they saw General X. B. DeBray, a Frenchman, who was a close personal friend of the General, surround the big crowd with a regiment of Confederate volunteers, and let it be known to everybody that if any man dared to touch my master, he would shoot him down. General DeBray also told them that while he was in favor of secession himself, he believed in fair play for both sides.

My master certainly was in fine speaking form that morning. He got a chance several times to take advantage of something that happened while he was speaking and turn it into the strongest kind of argument against what he called the "folly of secession." A horse got frightened while he was talking, and kicked himself out of his harness and almost wrecked the buggy. The General stopped a minute, and quietly said:

"Let old Dobbin alone; he is trying a little practical secession!"

About that time, the horse got tangled up in the bridle lines and stumbled to the ground. His owner began to beat him with his whip. As the horse finally got to his feet, and the teamster started to put the broken harness on him and hitch him to the buggy again, the General said:

"See how it works? You can see in what a fix he was brought back into the Union!"

The crowd couldn't help but roar with applause and laughter.

Having given up the office of governor of Texas rather than to take an oath against his conscience, the General got ready to leave Austin. Within a few days, Uncle Joshua started several wagons ahead, loaded with household goods, including barrels of glassware and ornaments, and several boxes of books and papers which the General always carried with him from place to place.

Then, Tom Blue drove the great yellow coach and its four horses up to the entrance of the governor's mansion. Soon, it was on its way with Mrs. Houston, the children and the colored maids. The rest of the Negroes followed in a wagon.

My master and his wife planned to visit her mother at Independence before going to Huntsville. I waited with the top buggy for the General, who was seeing some friends in the business part of town before leaving. When he came, we found a large amount of papers and other things which had been overlooked, and crammed them in the buggy and headed east.

Nobody will ever know how bad I felt about my master losing his office as governor. I felt that all of us were disgraced by the way the secessionists had practically thrown him out of the capitol. The only consolation I had was that I knew only once before (in his race for governor in 1857) had he lost a battle in war or politics.

I felt like the end of the world had come, but my spirits began to revive when I saw the grand way my master was hiding the grief I knew he must be suffering every time he thought about his own Texas leaving the Union and his fear that the Union would be wrecked. I was old enough now to have a pretty good idea of what was causing the war which everybody knew would start any time. I could also have some idea of the terrible suffering that would come with it.

Frederick Law Olmsted

*Frederick Law Olmsted (1822–1903) laid out New York's Central
Park, the Capitol grounds in Washington, D.C., as well as various parks in Boston, Chicago, and Brooklyn. As America's fore-
most landscape architect, he traveled widely in search of ideas.
His 1857 journal,* A Journey Through Texas, *is a classic piece of
naturalist observation.*

A JOURNEY THROUGH TEXAS, OR A
SADDLE-TRIP ON THE SOUTHWESTERN
FRONTIER

Trinity Bottom Lands

On landing on the west side of the Trinity, we entered a rich bottom,
even in winter, of an almost tropical aspect. The road had been cut
through a cane-brake, itself a sort of Brobdignag grass. Immense trees, of
a great variety of kinds, interlaced their branches and reeled with their
own rank growth. Many vines, especially huge grape vines, ran hanging
from tree to tree, adding to the luxuriant confusion. Spanish moss clung
thick everywhere, supplying the shadows of a winter foliage. . . .

We made our camp on the edge of the bottom, and for safety against
our dirty persecutors, the hogs, pitched our tent *within* a large hog-
yard, putting up the bars to exclude them. The trees within had been
sparingly cut, and we easily found tentpoles and fuel at hand.

Leon County

January 3.—From the Trinity to Centreville—county town of Leon
County. At some fork in the indistinct road we have gone wrong, and
are to the northward of the regular course. During the first part of the
day we went over small, level, wet prairies, irregularly skirted by heavy
timber, with occasional isolated clumps and scattered bushes. Most of
the prairies have been burned over. Both yesterday and to-day we have
been surrounded by the glare of fires at night. The grass is coarse and
reedy, and exceedingly dry. Our road was little better than a cow-track,
and once we followed a worn cattle-path for some two or three miles,
and were obliged to follow it back again.

After a few miles began post-oak, which changed to blackjack, and for the remainder of the day the country was as forbidding as a moor. We shot a few quails, which are very common, and saw, several times, turkeys and wild geese. During the day we passed but one house and one still saw-mill, in a narrow belt of pine. At night, rain threatening our canvas, we took shingle shelter in preference, in the

Centreville Hotel

The hotel was only a log cabin, and we suffered, as usual, from drafts of cold air. Our animals, however, were well sheltered.

Mentioning to the host our annoyance from hogs, he offered us a perfect protection in the shape of a sturdy bull-terrier. After examining her, we added her to our company. She was made up of muscle, compactly put together behind a pair of frightful jaws, and had a general aspect which struck awe into small Mexicans and negroes wherever she appeared. Hogs cared little for her eye; but at the word of command she would spring upon them like a hungry lion, and rout a whole herd.

"Judy" (this was her sonorous name) manifested some reluctance to join our party, and was, consequently, tied by a stout cord to the mule, and hung by the neck until she—came. She tried, from time to time, the experiment of going an independent route upon the opposite side of stumps and trees, with the result of being suddenly arrested, and quickly reappearing upon the other side, with the loss of much temper and some nose. She also manifested much disgust by yelps at the mud-puddles through which she was dragged without regard to delicacy. Finally, toward night of her first day's journey, having become much entangled in the mule's legs and her own, by some Providence, the cord parted, and she suddenly became the object of the tenderest epithets and sundry remnants of corn-bread, on which, not knowing what else to do, she came along, and frankly gave allegiance to her new masters. She suffered much from fatigue, and in process of time wore her feet to the bone, but by great care, which she certainly deserved, she accompanied us not only through Western Texas, but even accomplished, on foot, the whole distance back to Richmond, Va. Her tired bones have now found a last rest upon Staten Island. . . .

Saddle and Tent Life

Our days' rides were short, usually from twelve to twenty miles only, which is about the common distance, we found, in steady travel. We soon reduced the art of camping to a habit, and learned to go through the motions with mechanical precision, and the least possible fatigue.

As the shadows grow long we intimate to one another that it is time to be choosing a camp ground, and near the first house at which we can obtain corn, select a sheltered spot, where fuel and water are at hand. Saddles off and hampers—the horses are left free, save Fanny, who is tied for a nucleus. The mule instantly is down, and reappears with his four feet in the air, giving loud grunts of satisfaction. A tree, overhanging a smooth slope, is taken for the back-rope of the tent, the hampers, saddles, and arms placed by it. The tent is unrolled and hoisted to the tree, a pole is cut for its other end, the long tent-rope carried over it and made fast to a bush or a peg, and when the corners are pegged out by the flat iron pegs attached, our night quarters are ready, and our traps already under it, secure from dew. One of us, meanwhile, has collected fuel and lighted a fire, brought water and set it heating. Then there is a journey for corn, and a task to husk it. The horses are caught and offered their supper, each on his own blanket, as manger. They bite it from the ear, taking, now and then, especially the mule, some of the husks, as salad. By this time it is nearly dark, and we hastily collect fuel for the night, thinking, rather dolefully, what we may have for supper. If nothing have been shot or bought there is only the hot corn-meal, engaged at the cabin with the corn, to be sent for. This we discuss with some rancor and a cup of coffee. Then comes a ramble out into the vague, nominally for logs of fire-wood, but partly for romance. A little way from the fire-light glower indistinct old giants all about; sticks crack under the feet, the horses start and peer wildly, with stretched ears, after you; who knows what wild-cat, wolf, or vagabond nigger may be watching to spring upon you if you go further from the light. Then, leaning upon your elbow, you lounge awhile upon the confines of combustion, toasting your various fronts, and never getting warmed through. Then a candle and a book or pencil in the tent, hooded in blankets. Then a piling on of logs for a parting and enduring fire, and your weary bones, covered with everything available, stretch themselves, from a saddle-bag, out towards the blaze, and—the chilly daylight.

Venison

The following evening, beyond Centreville, we stopped at a small cabin, on a hill, in the edge of a prairie, which was occupied by the families of two herdsmen. They could not lodge us.

Could they provide us corn for our horses? They rather grumblingly consented to do so; the man who measured it out (and gave short measure, too) muttering that "they had to most slave themselves for travelers." Perhaps the woman would oblige us by making a pone or two of corn-bread? She supposed she must accommodate us. And, perhaps, they might have some meat? Yes, they had some venison and turkeys that they had shot that day. We should be glad to have a small slice of venison, if they could spare it. Yes, they would let us have some venison.

Instead of a small slice of venison, the man cut off a whole haunch and threw it into our corn-sack. For this the charge was only twenty-five cents. The pone was twenty-five cents and the corn one dollar per bushel. We went to the nearest wood and camped for the night.

The Prairies

In the morning we at first rode through the rich alluvial border of a creek, dark with the rank luxuriance of a semi-tropical vegetation; great trees, with many reclining trunks springing together from the ground, their limbs intricately interlaced with vines; grotesque cactus and dwarf palm, with dark, glossy evergreen shrubs, and thickets of verdant cane hedging in our bridle-path; the sunshine but feebly penetrating through the thick, waving canopy of dark gray moss which everywhere hung above our heads. . . .

After two miles' ride along the woodland border, the prairie opened fair in the course before us, and our trail led directly across it. The waving surface soon became regular, like the swell of the ocean after the subsidence of a gale which has blown long from the same direction. Very grand in vastness and simplicity were these waves. Four of them would cover a mile, and yet as we ascended one after another, the contour of the next would appear dark against the sky, following Hogarth's line of beauty and of grace with mathematical exactness. Vertically, the line of the swell bent before us, and on the left we saw in the hollow of the wave, or as its crest was there depressed, the far away skirt of the dark wood; on the right, only the remote line of the prairie swelling against the horizon. Here were red and black clouds of distant fires. The sky was nearly covered with gusty, gray clouds, with the clearest blue seen through them. The night had been unusually mild, and the forenoon was becoming sultry.

The First Norther

Once again we came to the brow of the swell; but instead of the usual grassy surface before us, the ground was dead black—the grass having been lately burned off. The fire must have been intense; for the whole surface of the ground appeared charred and black as ink. The air had been perfectly calm; but as we arrived near the next summit there was suddenly a puff of wind from the westward, bringing with it the scent of burning hay; and in less than thirty seconds, another puff, chill as if the door of a vault had been opened at our side; a minute more, it was a keen but not severe cold northerly wind. In five minutes we had all got our overcoats on, and were bending against it in our saddles. The change in temperature was not very great (12° in 12 minutes), but was singularly rapid; in fact, instantaneous—from rather uncomfortably warm to rather uncomfortably cool.

"Is this a norther?" asked we.

"I shouldn't wonder," said B.

It was our first experience.

Steadily the gale rose, and the cold increased during the day. And all day long we rode on, sometimes in the low, dark, and comparatively calm and mild "bottom lands," sometimes in the shelter of post-oak groves, but mainly across the high, broad, bleak, upland prairies. At sunset, we had seen no house for an hour or two, and were fearing that we should have to find a harbor in some sheltered spot, where we could stay our tent against the blast, and let our horses go unfed. As we came to the top of one of the prairie swells, we saw, about half a mile to the right of the road, a point of woodland, and a little beyond it, on a hill-top, was a house. We turned off, and with some difficulty made our way across the gullies between the hills, and approached the house. It proved to be deserted; but beyond it, on the top of the next and highest hill, there was another. . . .

A Grazier's Farm

It was a log cabin, of one room, fourteen feet by fourteen, with another small room in a "lean-to" of boards on the windward side. There was no window, but there were three doors, and openings between the logs in all quarters. The door of the "lean-to" was barricaded, but this erection was very open; and as the inner door, from sagging on its wooden hinges, could not be closed at all, the norther had nearly free course through the cabin. A strong fire was roaring in the great chimney at the end of the room, and we all clustered closely around it, "the woman" alone passing through our semicircle, as she prepared the "pone" and "fry," and coffee for supper.

Our host seemed a man of thirty, and had lived in Texas through all the "trouble times." His father had moved his family here when Texas was still Mexican territory; and for years of the young man's life, Indians were guarded against and hunted just as wolves now are by the shepherd. They had always held their ground against them, however, and had constantly increased in wealth, but had retired for a few weeks before the Mexican invasion. His father had no property when he came here, but the wagon and horses, and the few household effects he brought with him. "Now," said the son, "he raises fifty bales of cotton"— equivalent to informing us that he owned twenty or thirty negroes, and his income was from two to three thousand dollars a year. The young man himself owned probably many hundred acres of the prairie and woodland range about him, and a large herd of cattle. IIe did not fancy taking care of a plantation. It was too much trouble. He was a regular Texan, he boasted, and was not going to slave himself looking after niggers. Any man who had been brought up in Texas, he said, could live as well as he wanted to, without working more than one month in the year. For about a month in the year he had to work hard, driving his cattle into the pen, and roping and marking the calves; this was always done in a kind of frolic in the spring—the neighboring herdsmen assisting each other. During the rest of the year he hadn't anything to do. When he felt like it he got on to a horse and rode around, and looked after his cattle; but that wasn't work, he said—'twas only play. He raised a little corn; sometimes he got more than he needed, and sometimes not as much; he didn't care whether it was enough or not—he could always buy meal, only bought meal wasn't so sweet as that was which they ground fresh in their own steel mill. When he wanted to buy anything, he could always sell some cattle and raise the money; it did not take much to supply them with all they wanted.

This was very evident. The room was, as I said, fourteen feet square, with battens of split boards tacked on between the broader openings of the logs. Above, it was open to the rafters, and in many places the sky could be seen between the shingles of the roof. A rough board box, three feet square, with a shelf in it, contained the crockery-ware of the establishment; another similar box held the store of meal, coffee, sugar, and salt, a log crib at the horse-pen held the corn, from which the meal was daily ground, and a log smoke or store-house contained the store of pork. A canopy-bed filled one quarter of the room; a cradle, four chairs seated with untanned deer-hide, a table, a skillet or bake-kettle, a coffee-kettle, a frying-pan, and a rifle laid across two wooden pegs on the chimney, with a string of patches, powder-horn, pouch, and hunting-knife, completed the furniture of the house. We all sat with hats and overcoats on, and the woman cooked in bonnet and shawl. As I sat in the chimney-corner I could put both my hands out, one laid on the other, between the stones of the fire-place and the logs of the wall.

A pallet of quilts and blankets was spread for us in the lean-to, just between the two doors. We slept in all our clothes, including overcoats, hats, and boots, and covered entirely with blankets. At seven in the morning, when we threw them off, the mercury in the thermometer in our saddle-bags, which we had used for a pillow, stood at 25 deg. Fahrenheit.

We contrived to make cloaks and hoods from our blankets, and after going through with the fry, coffee and pone again, and paying one dollar each for the entertainment of ourselves and horses, we continued our journey.

The norther was stronger and the cold greater than the day before; but as we took it on our quarter in the course we were going during most of the day, we did not suffer.

Harbor in an Inn

Late in the same evening we reached the town of Caldwell, the "seat of justice" of Burleson County. We were obliged to leave our horses in a stable, made up of a roof, in which was a loft for the storage of provender, set upon posts, without side-boarding, so that the norther met with no obstruction. It was filled with horses, and ours alone were blanketed for the night. The mangers were very shallow and narrow, and as the corn was fed on the cob, a considerable proportion of it was thrown out by the horses in their efforts to detach the edible portion. With laudable economy, our landlord had twenty-five or thirty pigs running at large in the stable, to prevent this overflow from being wasted.

The hotel building was an unusually large and fine one; the principal room had glass windows. Several panes of these were, however, broken, and the outside door could not be closed from without; and when closed, was generally pried open with a pocket-knife by those who wished to go out. A great part of the time it was left open. Supper was served in another room, in which there was no fire, and the outside door was left open for the convenience of the servants in passing to and from the kitchen, which, as usual here at large houses, was in a detached building. Supper was, however, eaten with such rapidity that nothing had time to freeze on the table.

Texan Conversation

There were six Texans, planters and herdsmen, who had made harbor at the inn for the norther, two German shop-keepers and a young lawyer, who were boarders, besides our party of three, who had to be seated before the fire during "the evening." We kept coats and hats on, and gained as much warmth, from the friendly manner in which we drew together, as possible. After ascertaining, by a not at all impertinent or inconsiderate method of inquiry, where we were from, which way we were going, what we thought of the country, what we thought of the weather, and what were the capacities and the cost of our firearms, we were considered as initiated members of the crowd, and "the conversation became general."

One of the gentlemen asked me if I had seen "this new instrument."

"What instrument?"

"This *grand boojer.*"

"I never heard of it before; what is it?"

"I don't know, only that." He pointed to a large poster on the wall, advertising *"L. Gilbert's celebrated patent* GRAND BOUDOIR *and square piano-fortes."* I mention the circumstance as a caution to printers on the choice of words for the use of their emphatic type.

"Sam Houston and his eccentricities" formed a very interesting topic of conversation. Nearly every person present had seen the worthy senator in some ridiculous and not very honorable position, and there was much laughter at his expense. As he seemed to be held in very little respect, we inquired if he were not popular in Texas. He had many warm old friends, they said, and always made himself popular with new acquaintances, but the greater part of the old fighting Texans hated and despised him.

About Niggers

But the most interesting subject to Northerners which was talked of, was brought up by two gentlemen speaking of the house where they spent the previous night. "The man made a white boy, fourteen or fifteen years old, get up and go out in the norther for wood, when there was a great, strong nigger fellow lying on the floor, doing nothing. God! I had an appetite to give him a hundred, right there."

"Why, you wouldn't go out into the norther, yourself, would you, if you were not forced to?" inquired one, laughingly.

"I wouldn't have a nigger in my house that I was afraid to set to work at anything I wanted him to do at any time. They'd hired him out to go to a new place next Thursday, and they were afraid if they didn't treat him well, he'd run away. If I couldn't break a nigger of running away, I wouldn't have him any how."

"I can tell you how you can break a nigger of running away, certain," said another. "There was an old fellow I used to know in Georgia, that always cured his so. If a nigger ran away, when he caught him, he would bind his knee over a log, and fasten him so he couldn't stir; then he'd take a pair of pincers and pull one of his toe-nails out by the roots; and tell him that if he ever run away again, he would pull out two of them, and if he run away again after that, he told them he'd pull out four of them, and so on, doubling each time. He never had to do it more than twice—it always cured them."

One of the company then said that he was at the present time in pursuit of a negro. He had bought him of a connection of his in Mississippi; he told him when he bought him that he was a great runaway. He had run away from him three times, and always when they caught him he was trying to *get back to Illinois;* that was the reason he sold him. "He offered him to me cheap," he continued, "and I bought him because he was a first-rate nigger, and I thought perhaps I could break him of running away by bringing him down to this new country. I expect he's making for Mexico, now. I am a-most sure I saw his tracks on the road about twelve miles back, where he was a-coming on this way. Night before last I engaged with a man who's got some first-rate nigger dogs to meet me here to-night; but I suppose the cold keeps him back." He then asked us to look out for him as we went on west, and gave us a minute description of him that we might recognize him. He was "a real black nigger," and carried off a double-barreled gun with him. Another man, who was going on by another road westward, offered to look for him that way, and to advertise him. Would he be likely to defend himself with the gun if he should try to secure him, he asked. The owner said he had no doubt he would. He was as humble a nigger when he was at work as ever he had seen; but he was a mighty resolute nigger—there was no man had more resolution. "Couldn't I induce him to let me take the gun by pretending I wanted to look at it, or something? I'd talk to him simple; make as if I was a stranger, and ask him about the road, and so on, and finally ask him what he had got for a gun, and to let me look at it." The owner didn't believe he'd let go of the gun; he was a "nigger of sense—as much sense as a white man; he was not one of your kinkey-headed niggers." The chances of catching him were discussed. Some thought they were good, and some that the owner might almost as well give it up, he'd got such a start. It was three hundred miles to the Mexican frontier, and he'd have to make fires to cook the game he would kill, and could travel only at night; but then every nigger or Mexican he could find would help him, and if he had so much sense, he'd manage to find out his way pretty straight, and yet not have white folks see him. . . .

Manners and the Weather

We slept in a large upper room, in a company of five, with a broken window at the head of our bed, and another at our side, offering a short cut to the norther across our heads.

We were greatly amused to see one of our bed-room companions gravely *spit* in the candle before jumping into bed, explaining to some one who made a remark, that he always did so, it gave him time to see what he was about before it went out.

The next morning the ground was covered with sleet, and the gale still continued (a pretty steady close-reefing breeze) during the day.

We wished to have a horse shod. The blacksmith, who was a white man, we found in his shop, cleaning a fowling-piece. It was too d—d cold to work, he said, and he was going to shoot some geese; he, at length, at our urgent request, consented to earn a dollar; but, after getting on his apron, he found that we had lost a shoe, and took it off again, refusing to make a shoe while this d—d norther lasted, for any man. As he had no shoes ready made, he absolutely turned us out of the shop, and obliged us to go seventy-five miles further, a great part of the way over a pebbly road, by which the beast lost three shoes before he could be shod.

This respect for the norther is by no means singular here. The publication of the week's newspaper in Bastrop was interrupted by the norther, the editor mentioning, as a sufficient reason for the irregularity, the fact that his printing-office was in the north part of the house.

We continued our journey during the day in spite of the increased chilliness of the air, occasioned by the icy surface with which the sleet of the night had clothed the prairies, without any discomfort, until we were obliged again to enter one of these prairie houses. During the next night it fell calm, and the cold, as measured by the contraction of the mercury, was greater than at any time before. But the sun rose clear the next day and by noon, the weather was mild and agreeable as in the fairest October day in New York.

During the continuance of the norther, the sky was constantly covered with dense gray clouds, the wind varied from N.N.E. to N.W., and was also of variable force. Our thermometrical observations were as follows:

Jan. 5th, 10:30 A.M. - - 67° | 2 P.M. - - - - - - 47°
" 10:42 " - 55° | 4 " - - - - - - 42°
6 P.M. - - - - 40°
Jan. 6th, 7:30 A.M.- - - - - 25°

It continued at about this point during the following two days, when it fell (Jan. 8th, 7:30 A.M.) to 21°. . . .

Austin

Austin has a fine situation upon the left bank of the Colorado. Had it not been the capital of the state, and a sort of bourne to which we had looked forward for a temporary rest, it would still have struck us as the pleasantest place we had seen in Texas. It reminds one somewhat of Washington; Washington, *en petit,* seen through a reversed glass. The Capitol—a really imposing building of soft cream limestone, nearly completed at the time of our visit, and already occupied—stands prominent upon a hill, towards which, nearly all the town rises. From it a broad avenue stretches to the river, lined by the principal buildings and stores. These are of various materials and styles, from quarried stone to the logs of the first settlers. Off the avenue, are scatered cottages and one or two pretty dwellings. They are altogether smaller in number and meaner in appearance than a stranger would anticipate. The capital was fixed, in fact, upon a thinly-settled frontier, at a point the speculative, rather than the actual, centre of the state. There is one little church, with a pretty German turret, another of stone is in process of erection, and a Governor's mansion is to be built. There is a very remarkable number of drinking and gambling shops, but not one bookstore. A druggist, who keeps a small stock of books, sold us, at one dollar, giving his word that its cost was seventy-five cents to himself, a copy of "Eagle Pass" (one of Putnam's Semi-Monthly Library), the price of which, elsewhere, is forty cents. The population, at the census of 1850, was 629; the estimate, when we were there, 3,000; a large one, we thought. The country around the town is rolling and picturesque, with many agreeable views of distant hills and a pleasant sprinkling of wood over prairie slopes.

Hotels

We had reckoned upon getting some change of diet when we reached the capital of the state, and upon having good materials not utterly spoiled, by carelessness, ignorance, or nastiness, in cooking. We reckoned without our host.

We arrived in a norther, and were shown, at the hotel to which we had been recommended, into an exceedingly dirty room, in which two of us slept with another gentleman, who informed us that it was the best room in the house. The outside door, opening upon the ground, had no latch, and during the night it was blown open by the norther, and after we had made two ineffectual attempts to barricade it, was kept open till morning. Before daylight, a boy came in and threw down an armful of wood by the fire-place. He appeared again, an hour or two afterwards, and made a fire. When the breakfast-bell rung, we all turned out in haste, though our boots were gone and there was no water. At this moment, as we were reluctantly pulling on our clothing, a negro woman burst into the room, leaving the door open, and laid a towel on the wash-table. "Here!" we cried, as she ran to the door again; "bring us some water, and have our boots brought back." She stood half outside the door, and shaking her finger at us in a weird manner, replied: "Haant got no time, master—got fires to make and ebery ting"; and she vanished.

When finally we got to breakfast, and had offered us—but I will not again mention the three articles—only the "fry" had been changed for the worse before it was fried—we naturally began to talk of changing our quarters and trying another of the hotels. Then up spoke a dark, sad man at our side—"You can't do better than stay here; I have tried both the others, and I came here yesterday because the one I was at was *too dirty!*" And the man said this, with that leopard-skin pattern of a table-cloth, before him, with those grimy tools in his hands, and with the hostler in his frock, smelling strongly of the stable, just handing him the (No. 3). Never did we see any wholesome food on that table. It was a succession of burnt flesh of swine and bulls, decaying vegetables, and sour and mouldy farinaceous glues, all pervaded with rancid butter. After a few days, we got a private room, and then, buying wheat-bread of a German baker, and other provisions of grocers, cooked what was necessary for ourselves, thus really coming back to caravansarism. . . .

An Eastern Planter

Before leaving Eastern Texas behind us, I must add a random note or two, the precise dates of which it would have been uncivil to indicate.

We stopped one night at the house of a planter, now twenty years settled in Eastern Texas. He was a man of some education and natural intelligence, and had, he told us, an income, from the labor of his slaves, of some $4,000. His residence was one of the largest houses we had seen in Texas. It had a second story, two wings and a long gallery. Its windows had been once glazed, but now, out of eighty panes that originally filled the lower windows, thirty only remained unbroken. Not a door in the house had been ever furnished with a latch or even a string; when they were closed, it was necessary to *claw* or to ask some one inside to push open. (Yet we happened to hear a neighbor expressing serious admiration of the way these doors fitted.) The furniture was of the rudest description.

One of the family had just had a hemorrhage of the lungs; while we were at supper, this person sat between the big fireplace and an open outside door, having a window, too, at his side, in which only three panes remained. A norther was blowing, and ice forming upon the gallery outside. Next day, at breakfast, the invalid was unable to appear on account of a "bad turn."

On our supper-table was nothing else than the eternal fry, pone and coffee. Butter, of dreadful odor, was here added by exception. Wheat flour they never used. It was "too much trouble."

We were waited upon by two negro girls, dressed in short-waisted, twilled-cotton gowns, once white, now looking as though they had been drawn through a stove-pipe in spring. The water for the family was brought in tubs upon the heads of these two girls, from a creek, a quarter of a mile distant, this occupation filling nearly all their time.

This gentleman had thirty or forty negroes, and two legitimate sons. One was an idle young man. The other was already, at eight years old, a swearing, tobacco-chewing young bully and ruffian. We heard him whipping his puppy behind the house, and swearing between the blows, his father and mother being at hand. His tone was an evident imitation of his father's mode of dealing with his slaves.

"I've got an account to settle with you; I've let you go about long enough; I'll teach you who's your master; there, go now, God damn you, but I havn't got through with you yet."

"You stop that cursing," said his father, at length, "it isn't right for little boys to curse."

"What do *you* do when you get mad?" replied the boy; "reckon you cuss some; so now you'd better shut up."

We repeatedly heard men curse white women and children in this style, without the least provocation.

Literature

In the whole journey through Eastern Texas, we did not see one of the inhabitants look into a newspaper or a book, although we spent days in houses where men were lounging about the fire without occupation. One evening I took up a paper which had been lying unopened upon the table of the inn where we were staying, and smiled to see how painfully news items dribbled into the Texas country papers, the loss of the tug-boat "Ajax," which occurred before we left New York, being here just given as the loss of the "splended steamer Ocax."

A man who sat near said—

"Reckon you've read a good deal, hain't you?"

"Oh, yes; why?"

"Reckoned you had."

"Why?"

"You look as though you liked to read. Well, it's a good thing. S'pose you take a pleasure in reading, don't you?"

"That depends, of course, on what I have to read. I suppose everybody likes to read when they find anything interesting to them, don't they?"

"No; it's damn tiresome to some folks, I reckon, any how, 'less you've got the habit of it. Well, it's a good thing; you can pass away your time so."

Foreign Relations

The sort of interest taken in foreign affairs is well enough illustrated by the views of a gentleman of property in Eastern Texas, who was sitting with us one night, "spitting in the fire," and talking about cotton. Bad luck he had had—only four bales to the hand; couldn't account for it—bad luck; and next year he didn't reckon nothing else but that there would be a general war in Europe, and then he'd be in a pretty fix, with cotton down to four cents a pound. Curse those Turks! If he thought there would be a general war, he would take every d—d nigger he'd got right down to New Orleans, and sell them for what they'd bring. They'd never be so high again as they were now, and if there should come a general war they wouldn't be worth half so much next year.

There always were some infernal rascals somewhere in the world trying to prevent an honest man from getting a living. Oh, if they got to fighting, he hoped they'd eat each other up. They just ought to be, all of them—Turks, and Russians, and Prussians, and Dutchmen, and Frenchmen—just be put in a bag together, and slung into hell. That's what he'd do with them.

We afterwards noted a contrast when a German cotton-farmer, beyond the Colorado, expressed to us, apropos to the same probable depreciation of prices of the next year, the greatest *fear* lest the sovereigns should not permit a general war to take place, with its chances for the peoples. There are some hearts that swim above prices. God bless them.

Black Housekeeping

Remarking, one day, at the house of a woman who was brought up at the North, that there was much more comfort at her house than any we had previously stopped at, she told us that the only reason that the people didn't have any comfort here was, that they wouldn't *take any trouble* to get anything. Anything that their negroes could make they would eat; but they would take no pains to instruct them, or to get anything that didn't grow on the plantation. A neighbor of hers owned fifty cows, she supposed, but very rarely had any milk and scarcely ever any butter, simply because his people were too lazy to milk or churn, and he wouldn't take the trouble to make them.

This woman entirely sustained the assertion that Northern people, when they come to the South, have less feeling for the negroes than Southerners themselves usually have. We asked her (she lived in a village) whether she hired or owned her servants. They owned them all, she said. When they first came to Texas they hired servants, but it was very troublesome; they would take no interest in anything; and she couldn't get along with them. Then very often their owners, on some pretext (ill-treatment, perhaps), would take them away. Then they bought negroes. It was very expensive: a good negro girl cost seven or eight hundred dollars, and that, we must know, was a great deal of money to be laid out in a thing that might lie right down the next day and die. They were not much better either than the hired servants.

Folks up North talked about how badly the negroes were treated; she wished they could see how much work her girls did. She had four of them, and she knew they didn't do half so much work as one good Dutch girl such as she used to have at the North. Oh! the negroes were the laziest things in creation; there was no knowing how much trouble they gave to look after them. Up to the North, if a girl went out into the garden for anything, when she came back she would clean her feet, but these nigger girls will stump right in and track mud all over the house. What do they care? They'd just as lief clean the mud after themselves as anything else—*their time isn't any value to themselves.* What do they care for the trouble it gives you? Not a bit. And you may scold 'em and whip 'em—you never can break 'em into better habits.

I asked what were servants' wages when they were hired out to do housework? They were paid seven or eight dollars a month; sometimes ten. She didn't use to pay her girl at the North but four dollars, and she knew she would do more work than any six of the niggers, and not give half so much trouble as one. But you couldn't get any other help here but niggers. Northern folks talk about abolishing Slavery, but there wouldn't be any use in that; that would be ridiculous, unless you could some way get rid of the niggers. Why, they'd murder us all in our beds—that's what they'd do. Why, over to Fannin, there was a negro woman that killed her mistress with an axe, and her two little ones. The people just flocked together, and hung her right up on the spot; they ought to have piled some wood round her, and burned her to death; that would have been a good lesson to the rest. We afterwards heard her scolding one of her girls; the girl made some exculpatory reply, and getting the best of the argument, the mistress angrily told her if she said another word she would have two hundred lashes given her. She came in and remarked that if she hadn't felt so nervous she would have given that girl a good whipping herself; these niggers are so saucy, it's very *trying* to one who has to take care of them.

Servants are, it is true, "a trial," in all lands, ages, and nations. But note the fatal reason this woman frankly gives for the inevitable delinquencies of slave-servants, "Their time isn't any value to themselves!"

The women of Eastern Texas seemed to us, in general, far superior to their lords. They have, at least, the tender hearts and some of the gentle delicacy that your "true Texan" lacks, whether mistresses of slaves or only of their own frying-pan. They are overworked, however, as soon as married, and care gives them thin faces, sallow complexions, and expressions either sad or sour. . . .

Slavery with a Will

We were several times struck, in Eastern Texas, with a peculiarity in the tone of the relation between master and slave. Elsewhere at the

South, slavery had seemed to be accepted generally, as a natural, hereditary, established state of things, and the right and wrong of it, or the how of it, never to be discussed or thought of any more than that of feudal tenures elsewhere. But in Texas, the state of war in which slavery arises, seems to continue in undertone to the present.

"Damn 'em, give 'em hell," frequent expressions of the ruder planters towards their negroes, appeared to be used as if with a meaning—a threat to make their life infernal if they do not submit abjectly and constantly. There seemed to be the consciousness of a wrong relation and a determination to face conscience down, and continue it; to work up the "damned niggers," with a sole eye to selfish profit, cash down, in this world. As to "treasures in Heaven," their life is a constant sneer at the belief in them.

Texas as It Used to Be

I will add no further details upon the moral and social aspect of Eastern Texas. . . . Society has certainly made a great advance there in becoming even what it is. The present generation has, peculiarly, but the faults founded upon laziness. The past, if we may believe report, had something worse. In fact, in the rapid settlement of the country, many an adventurer crossed the border, spurred by a love of life or liberty, forfeited at home, rather than drawn by the love of adventure or of rich soil. Probably a more reckless and vicious crew was seldom gathered than that which peopled some parts of Eastern Texas at the time of its first resistance to the Mexican government.

"G.T.T." (gone to Texas) was the slang appendage, within the reader's recollection, to every man's name who had disappeared before the discovery of some rascality. Did a man emigrate thither, every one was on the watch for the discreditable reason to turn up.

Mr. Dewees, in his naive "Letters from Texas," thus describes (1831):

"It would amuse you very much, could you hear the manner in which people of this new country address each other. It is nothing uncommon of us to inquire of a man why he ran away from the States! but few persons feel insulted by such a question. They generally answer for some crime or other which they have committed; if they deny having committed any crime, or say they did not run away, they are generally looked upon rather suspiciously. Those who come into the country at the present time, frequently tell us rough, ragged, old settlers, who have worn out our clothes and our constitutions in the service of the country, that they have a great deal of wealth in the States which they are going after, as soon as they can find a situation to suit them. But we, not relishing this would-be aristocracy, generally manage to play some good joke upon them in return.

"One day, there were quite a number of these aristocrats, who seemed to think themselves better than those who were worn out by toil and hardships, seated at the dinner table, in a sort of tavern kept by a man named William Pettis, or Buck Pettis, as he was always called at San Felipe; these persons were boasting largely of their wealth, their land, their negroes, the ships they had at sea, etc. There was at the table an old man by the name of Macfarlane, a don't care sort of a fellow, who had married a Mexican wife, and was living on the Brazos when we first came to the country. He listened to them quietly for a while, at length he could restrain himself no longer. 'Well, gentlemen,' he said, 'I, too, once commenced telling that I had left a large property in the States, and, in fact, gentlemen, I told the story so often, that at length I really believed it true, and eventually started to go for it. Well, I traveled on very happily till I reached the Sabine river which separates this country from the United States. On its bank I paused, and now for the first time, began to ask myself seriously, What am I doing? Why am I here? I have no property in the States, and if I had, if I cross the river, 'tis at the risk of my life; for I was obliged to flee to this country to escape the punishment of the laws. I had better return, and live in safety as I have done. I did so, gentlemen, and since then have been contented without telling of the wealth I left in the States.' The relation of this story so exasperated those for whose benefit it was told, that they fell upon the old gentleman, and would have done him injury, had it not been for the interference of his friends. This, however, put a stop to long yarns."

If your life, in those times, an old settler told us, would be of the slightest use to any one, you might be sure he would take it, and it was safe only as you were in constant readiness to defend it. Horses and wives were of as little account as umbrellas in more advanced States. Everybody appropriated everything that suited him, running his own risk of a penalty. Justice descended into the body of Judge Lynch, sleeping when he slept, and when he woke hewing down right and left for exercise and pastime.

Out of this has come, with as much rapidity as could be expected, by a process of gradual fermentation and admixture, the present society.

Mary Sherwood Wightman Helm ────────────

Mary Sherwood Wightman Helm wrote one of the first historical accounts of early Texas. She participated in many important events as one of Stephen F. Austin's first colonists, and as the wife of early Texas land surveyor Elias Wightman.

SCRAPS OF EARLY TEXAS HISTORY

The usual time for sailing from New Orleans to Texas was seven days, so we only took provisions for sixty persons for seven days, and about the time that was consumed our water also became alarmingly scarce—half a pint a day to each person. Being sick, I could not drink the water, nor the tea and coffee made from it. A little vinegar and sugar, diluted with this bad water, sustained me. There were no conveniences for cooking, except a stationary sheet-iron boiler, so-called, in which we were allowed to heat water for our tea and coffee. Our Captain, one day, very kindly volunteered to make it full of vegetable soup for all the passengers, when we, or more especially the well ones, were nearly famished, and invited his sixty passengers to help themselves. And such a scrambling! It would have made a picture for Harper. Many could not procure vessels to get what they so much needed. It so happened that a small tin cup fell to my lot; it was very small at the top and took a long time to cool. I had been nine days without food and but very little to drink, because I could not eat and drink such as the vessel afforded, and having a fever did not crave much. Now came the tug of war. Those who could procure large vessels took too much. By the time I had cooled and consumed my gift of soup the boiler was empty. Looking down the hatchway I saw a family of three with a six-quart pan full, and reaching down my cup, I requested them to fill it. They parleyed and said they could not spare any. I would not report, to make trouble for my friends; but after I had retired in disgust they offered to fill my cup. I do not remember the sequel, only remember telling them of it years after, at which time, of course, they had forgotten the circumstance. After our cooked provisions had given out, crackers and hard sea bread sustained life; but when the water gave out, then real suffering commenced. And such water! I really supposed then that powder casks had been used for holding the water, not having learned then that it took time for water to become good. The well passengers could drink it made into coffee, but it so affected me that I could not endure the smell of coffee for several years. Mr. Pilgrim says that he gave his share of the water to the children, and sustained himself on whiskey and crackers.

Some of our men had the good fortune to shoot and kill a pelican, a most disgusting sea fowl that lives on fish, having a large pouch in front that holds his prey till time of need. Its flesh is black and tastes fishy. I had not tasted food for so many days, that I was constantly dreaming of soups and milk, or something to sustain life. We had a little sick boy, Laroy Griffeth, now more than sixty years of age, who also craved food. The bird was boiled and the boy promised the meat, but I not caring for the meat, craved the soup, worth more to me than its weight in gold. When, to my astonishment, the boy was in tears for fear "Aunt Mary would eat all the meat," while I was about as foolish about the soup. We had, a few days before, witnessed a burial at sea, and we naturally felt that unless relief came soon, it would be repeated. This was the first time I had ever experienced *want*—want of something to sustain life—and no wonder I worshipped the disgusting soup of the pelican, so that when a hurricane drove us into Aransas Bay, no wonder we did not think of Indians. And now, again, as we enter Matagorda Pass, Sunday morning, January 27, 1829, with all our fears of hostile Indians, whose telegraphic smokes told of our approach, a joyful thankfulness filled our hearts, for we were entering the land of promise. . . .

As no vessel had ever before entered the port [of Matagorda] great was the excitement in accomplishing that feat. The soundings of the channel had to be made so that it could not be done at once, and our friends on land sent out our poor weary and worn immigrants a sumptuous dinner on board the vessel—long before she made her appearance in port—of boiled hominy, pounded in a mortar, cooked meats of various kinds, also a variety of fish and fowl, and a large bucket of sweet milk and some sweet potatoes, the first they ever saw, bread minus, for the corn only produced a small fraction of meal, when the hominy was pounded by a contrivance like an old-fashioned well sweep. We had on board plenty of flour which we had no way of cooking, also groceries, portions of which we returned to our generous donors, and I will state in passing, that requests often came with visitors from a distance for small portions of flour to show their friends who had never seen wheat flour. Our sixty starving sea-worn passengers were thus welcomed to their long sought for post, after an absence of thirty-one days from New Orleans. . . .

By the time our vessel was ready to unload passengers, our fort was vacated. I shall ever remember the kindness of its late inmates, they seemed to vie with each other in giving material aid in fish, fowl and venison—deer being in droves of hundreds in every direction which had not yet learned to fear man, but would approach him if he would sit down to see what he looked like, and thus come within gunshot. Our friends also had plenty of cows and thus we had the long coveted milk I had dreamed so much about, when starving at sea. . . .

The surroundings of our new home, as it then appears, seemed to me quite romantic. Arriving in the night, I could only see a large enclosure, some fifty feet square. In one respect it was like Solomon's temple—no sign of tools or nails being visible about our edifice. A large fire in the centre, a mosquito-net covering a rude bed at each corner of the room, the whole building being without joists or tennents, but simply forked sticks drove in the ground to support poles on which cross-poles were laid to sustain the mattress, while perpendicular poles sustained the mosquito-net—a thing quite indispensable. Our door turned on a post, the lower end of which was driven in the ground. The whole edifice was enclosed by perpendicular posts some ten or twelve feet high. At intervals the posts were forked to support horizontal poles, upon which the roof rested, and which was also supported on the inside by poles. True, there were marks of an ax, but nothing more. Long, split, dry cypress boards (so called from float-timbers of some other coast cast upon the beach), formed a good substitute for shingles. . . .

For the want of material to build, as our fort let in much water in hard storms, we erected a sort of tent and covered it with long grass for a place to sleep, and the next move, was to tear down the fort, and build a smaller room to shut out the weather and rain. At last, an opportunity was offered to trade an order of five cows and calves for hewed logs sixteen feet long to build one room; we added a side porch and floored it with puncheon high and dry from the ground, and a shed kitchen from the leavings of the old fort; we had now lived one year on the ground floor, all this time the cooking was done in the open air, with the wind blowing a gale. The order of one cow and calf had by custom become a circulating medium for $10, hence the order for five cows and calves for these logs. Our relatives had all gone up the country, except the parents of my husband, E. R. Wightman, now more than seventy years of age. On June 20th, his mother died of fever; in six weeks after his father also died; those were the first graves in Matagorda cemetery—a mesquite tree marks the spot. A quantity of plank was thoughtfully taken on board at New Orleans on purpose for coffins, though no one knew the motive. Daniel Deckrow made both coffins, a yoke of oxen and a cart did the office of a hearse; kind friends dug the graves. No physician. No religious service soothed the lonely survivors, but all that sympathizing friends could do to soften the melancholy surroundings was done. . . .

At our new home everything seemed strange. We had never before traveled south of a latitude of 42°. At that time very little traveling was done; the very literature of common school books was borrowed from selections from the eminent lights of the old world. Western New York was quite a frontier, Indians being a fixture there, as also in Ohio and Indiana. . . .

The coast States, of course, had the advantage of direct intercourse with the old world, but the interior towns of all the States were so isolated that it took courage and a large stock of enterprise to make this colonization. The contrast of the idioms of language was most marked. Often when critically compared, the advantage would be in the favor of the untutored southerner, and their unassuming, free-and-easy, benevolent manners were most admirable. We did not expect such perfect Chesterfields in the garb of deerskin and mocassins, and such unselfish benevolence. All knowledge seemed practical, useful and fitted to any emergency, especially in children, which seemed so strange. They tread in the ways and manners of their elders without a rebuke, as with us, if we, when children, should presume to give our opinion to our elders; but I saw its advantages when these precocious youths were sent out on a message of fifty or a hundred miles alone through unsettled regions where he was obliged to assume the manhood he had been practicing from almost his infancy—for the very infant is expected to be introduced to every stranger and to give his little hand to everyone coming or leaving, thus cultivating the habits of social and benevolent feeling, while we northerners treat children as nonentities, and, unless business or necessity compels, the bashful youth, in consequence, shirks the society of his elders and superiors.

And then I could but notice that every boy was almost a knight errant. I noticed great deference paid to all the females: no man would remain sitting when one of us entered the house, fort or camp, and thus it was everywhere as we traveled or camped out. All the severe work on such occasions was done by the men of the company.

Flowers seemed to be the sport of the luxurious soil, instead of noxious weeds, which in other regions are ever ready without the aid of man to cover up its nakedness with the rich and variegated livery of nature. A continued and continuing variety carpeted our way for whole days together as we traveled, with scarce a sign of former traveler to mark the path, while large herds of deer in easy distance would stop grazing to look at us, and every way which the eye looked countless herds were seen in the distance. Many of these journeys, which so delighted me with their novelty and variety, were for the purpose of surveying town sites. As my husband was the founder of Matagorda, all paper town-makers made an effort to have him interested in such enterprises. Hence, my long journeys through unsettled regions to reach those sites for future cities, when we frequently fell in with large pleasure parties, who, like ourselves, had made long journeys from remote towns. On one occasion we rescued a young orphan girl from being married against her will, and gave her a home with us, at the head of the bay, forty miles distant. Another good subject for my story, without exaggeration, was when scores turned out to meet the Romans at given points to legalize the banns of matrimony. . . .

After our city of Matagorda had grown to quite a size many of our settlers still refused to have any dealings with the Indians, who were now so reduced in numbers as not to be dangerous, yet when the Indians would come to those settled on farms around the town offering to trade venison for corn or articles of clothing, the people refused to have anything to do with them, or even to be friendly.

Finally, an expedition was planned against them without Mr. Wightman's knowledge or consent, and the very day that I had fed a poor old Indian, covered with scars, he met his death at the hands of our settlers, who fell on them by surprise, and it seemed that each warrior claimed the honor of his slaughter, as he stepped forward to be a target while the women and children could have time to escape to the thicket. Of course all their goods and weapons fell into the hands of their conquerors.

After a few years a small party, evidently remembering who had fed them on the day of the fight, came to us. My husband became responsible for their good behavior, and set them to picking cotton, but before this they dared not venture into the town, only when they saw our boat coming down the Bay. There were no white settlements on the Peninsula, and the Indians had it all their own way there, but they were evidently afraid of another attack and so came and offered to work for us for protection.

I felt no fear whatever from these neighbors, but would sleep with all our doors open, with twenty-five or thirty Indians within call. It was amusing to see them parade the streets of Matagorda with their long plaid, red, blue, garments, which I had made for them, the tails tipped with ornamental feathers. One of the young women learned to speak very good English; I dressed her in my clothes, and one day thought to have some fun with her, invited her to take tea with me. But the joke turned to my own expense, for she not only used her knife and fork properly but her cup, saucer and plate like it was an every day affair. I asked her how they made out when our folks drove them off without anything. She answered that they traveled for days without food and no place to sleep, as the ground was all covered with water—which I recollected was the case. They had no means of fishing, but they kept close to the coast and at last the "Great Spirit" sent them a small vessel, after killing the crew they appropriated everything to their own use, and thus their lives were saved.

After a while they frequently had noisy nights, and upon inquiring what all this noise and dancing meant, with so many rude instruments of music, she replied that they were going west, as they had better health than with our way of living, and they were importuning the Great Spirit to give them success in stealing horses and other stock from the Mexicans who lived near the coast; and to protect them from hostile attacks. It took me a long time to become accustomed to their naked and hideous appearance, so that it did not shock me; I felt humiliated that I too was of the human species.

Their habits were idle and dirty in the extreme, but for their constant bathing in the river. The children almost lived in the water, would dive and bring up clams, etc., sometimes fighting in the water. The men would tread the water with heavy burdens on their shoulders walking erect with half their bodies dry. Our mode of living made them sickly and they were obliged often to resort to the coast. On one occasion a young wife ran off and the distressed husband applied to my husband to turn out with his skiff and help find her. They went up the river a few miles and found her at her mother's camp. She made a virtue of necessity and returned. To express his gratitude the happy husband offered to reciprocate the favor "whenever his squaw ran off."

Their few cooking utensils are made of a rude kind of pottery. Their drinking vessel is about ten inches wide at the top, coming to a point at the bottom. This is handed round for each one to take a swallow after the head man has worked it into a foam by a bunch of small sticks whirled with both hands; this serves them for their coffee cup and when all have drank the process is repeated, taking hours at a time at least twice a day. They also parch in this vessel their coffee—the leaves of an evergreen shrub resembling our garden privet. Their coffee pot in which it is boiled is of the same material, shaped like a double necked gourd, while a bunch of Spanish moss serves for a lid and a strainer.

When one of them dies his effects and his hut are burned the same day, and a corpse is never kept over night. When a chief dies the next heir to the throne, however young, marries the widow, however old. If he leaves no son after death, the nearest of kin, have periodical times of howling, generally before daylight. The women spend a great deal of time pounding a kind of root, on skins, which yields a kind of starch when washed and settled in water. Days will thus be spent in preparing what will only be a taste when divided among them. . . .

Alligator meat is a great luxury with them, and although supplied bountifully with fresh meat, they would be absent frequently, and return with pieces of cooked alligator tied between large pieces of bark swung over their shoulders. I have seen them killed. The creature is helpless when under the water and the Indians dive and stick him with a sharp knife.

They knew we did not approve of their stealing horses from the Mexicans and so when they left, they went on the sly. We got up one morning and found them all gone, and we saw no more of them for years.

In 1843, I spent some time in Matagorda when they made their appearance in a most wretched, filthy condition, few in numbers, offering to trade fish for whiskey. The young girl I had helped was dying. She formally gave away her only child to a white woman and the whole tribe formed a procession to go and deliver the child before the mother's death. I afterwards visited the child and found her at a little table with a white and a negro child, each about four years old, playing tea drinking, all speaking English together. On one occasion that summer, a stroke of lightning killed a man and his wife, but a child between them escaped unharmed, this made a profound impression upon the whole tribe. They felt it as a direct judgment from the Great Spirit for their drunkenness and bad behavior, and for days they scarcely moved or left the camp. As I left the country in 1843, I ceased to know more of these Indians. I believe that Mexico gave them a tract of land in one of her Eastern Provinces.

Eudora Inez Moore

Eudora Inez Moore (1848–1933) gives vivid witness to the rise and disappearance of the historic coastal town of Indianola. She spanned the lifeime of Indianola when it was one of the few Texas sites to be occupied by Union troops; as it survived a yellow fever epidemic in 1867; during its heyday of a population of six thousand; and through its violent end in 1886 following the second of two devastating hurricanes.

INDIANOLA SCRAP BOOK

Texas seceded from the Union on the 4th day of March 1861. The U.S. troops on the frontier were ordered back North. A company came to Indianola to embark. They marched with lively steps to the tune of Yankee Doodle, down to the wharf, where they boarded a vessel and started on their way rejoicing. They had not proceeded far when they were overtaken by Col. Van Dorn of the Steamer *Rusk,* joined by volunteers, some of them from Indianola, captured and brought back to the city where they were paroled and allowed to proceed on their way. . . .

We soon began to feel the privations which war entailed upon us, but we met them with brave hearts for we were full of patriotism in those days. Mrs. D. C. Proctor and other ladies took the lead in carding cotton, spinning thread, knitting and making comforts for our soldier boys. Companies were being formed and men drilled in military tactics. . . .

The Indianola ladies made a flag for a company raised there. At its presentation by Miss Amelia Rouff, Mr. F. S. Stockdale who received the flag said, "I can wipe up with a cambric handkerchief every drop of blood that will be shed in this war." Some people were quite optimistic, but they little knew. . . .

Mrs. Anderson took much interest in getting up entertainments for the benefit of soldier boys, they were usually held in the court house. I remember taking part in one in which "The Confederate Constellation" represented one of the acts. Eleven young girls, each with a flag appropriate for her state and reciting a patriotic verse, participated in it. . . .

When Dudley Woodward, or "Tip," as everybody called him, started to join his uncle's command, we girls went to see him off. He wore a handsome buck-skin suit and had a negro boy to attend him. He seemed quite a hero in our eyes, as in fact all the boys did who joined the army.

In the spring of 1862 a detachment of men was sent to guard Fort Esperanzo which commanded Pass Cavallo, the entrance to Matagorda Bay. That year yellow fever broke out among the men and Elija Stapp, son of Col. Darwin Stapp, took the fever and died. He was one of my early school mates and I mourned his death sincerely. His body was brought to Indianola and buried in the cemetery there. Jimmy Coates also took the fever and his mother went to Esperanzo to nurse him. He recovered but she succumbed to the fever. It soon spread to Indianola and a few died, a baby, Willie Gambol, and little Proctor Woodward fell victims to it. There had been an epidemic of fever there in 1853, my brother, Joe, took it while in town but would not come home on our account as it was considered very contagious. He was a thin, pale looking boy on his return.

The saying "Necessity is the mother of invention" was certainly exemplified in war times. Father bought a side of tanned leather for our shoe soles, the uppers were made of an old cloak of his, very heavy black material. Mother made a pair of pants out of a parlor table cover of wool, dyed it with the rind of pomegranates. Mr. Dan Sullivan, Sr., said he was going to have a pair made of the same kind of stuff, but just then his nephew sent him some material from the Rio Grande and the table cover was saved. I made hats for the boys out of shucks or palmetto and mother made them cloth caps for winter wear. After the Yankees left a great deal of cast off clothing was found. Mother boiled it in lye water, rinsed it thoroughly and dyed it with pomegranate rinds or pecan hulls and made it into clothes for the boys.

An iron mortar and pestle was used for pounding various things, as coarse salt, cloves, mustard, etc. Our bread was usually made of cornmeal as flour was scarce, but occasionally mother would make a batch of biscuits and we would count them to see how many there would be apiece. During the war we made tallow candles. Before that we used lamps with two tubes through which the wick passed at the tip and burned some kind of oil. It may have been the kind virgins used in Bible times for all I know.

In the spring and summer of 1863 a company of men under Capt. George was stationed at Indianola. They were a part of Hobby's regiment. The major was Ireland, afterwards governor of Texas. They were mostly from Seguin and vicinity. A number of the men boarded in private homes, some of them brought their families; Jep Dibrell, John

George, three LeGette brothers, Joe Zorn, Goodrich and Douglas were a few names I remember. Parties were given and plays consisting of tableaux and charades for the benefit of sick soldiers. I recall one in which I represented Pocahontas saving the life of Capt. Smith. Miss Mattie LeGette took great interest in helping get up the entertainments, at a party she looked quite pretty in her white dress trimmed with cedar and the red buds of the oleander. Natural flowers were used a great deal for decorative purposes in those days. On the 17th of November, which was my 16th birthday, a few friends were invited to our home, for refreshments we had molasses cookies and candy, it was truly simple fare, but many a poor soldier would have considered it fine eating. . . .

Fort Esperanzo was evacuated the last of November 1863, and the weather was very cold at the time, in a few days a Federal gunboat came up Matagorda Bay and demanded the surrender of Indianola, which was turned over to them peaceably by the mayor, Mr. Cleveland. No troops were stationed there at the time. They then went on to Port Lavaca and bombarded the town for some time. We could hear the cannonading very distinctly. They soon returned and a detachment occupied the town. On New Year's night of 1864 we were aroused from our slumbers by a dozen Yankees who demanded that they be allowed to enter the house, that they were about to freeze. They had been sent to guard a bridge over the bayou, when a fierce norther blew up bringing ice in its wake. My father opened the door for them and made a fire in the kitchen stove, suddenly they decided that they must search the house. I heard them coming up stairs and had the fright of my life. Father prevailed upon them not to enter my room (my door was locked) and they went on searching at other parts of the house. Not finding any Confederates they settled down for the rest of the night. . . .

The regiment commanded by Dan Perry camped on my father's place. He gave his men orders not to molest anything on the premises and they obeyed his instructions. After a time some new men were added to the regiment and the first night after they came our chicken house was invaded and a dozen fowls stolen, with them was a waif they had picked up somewhere, and one day he and my brother, Dolph Moore, had a fight and he bit my brother badly on the ear. . . .

For some reason the transports which were to take the troops failed to come at the appointed time; they had already broken camp when a young captain was taken sick and asked permission to stay at our house, which was granted. He seemed very grateful for the privilege and took the names and commands of my two brothers in the army, assuring mother that if they ever fell into his hands as prisoners of war he would befriend them.

While the Yankees were at Indianola some youths rode up west of town, a regiment with cannon went out on the prairie to meet them and fired a number of shells but I don't think any one was injured, though I heard a Yankee say "One saddle is emptied." The boys soon took their departure. This may have given rise to the statement about a battle having been fought in the streets of Indianola.

In the early part of the year 1864 all available troops were ordered into Louisiana. At Mansfield and Pleasant Hill many brave officers and men lost their lives. Col. Augustus Buchel of Indianola was mortally wounded while leading his regiment "The First Texas" in the charge at Mansfield and my brother, Joseph Moore, died soon after at Alexandria, La. . . .

When the main body of Federals under Gen. Warren arrived, they began digging rifle pits and building forts on the prairie back of town. All houses of Confederate soldiers were torn down to build barracks for the men. They would drive up herds of cattle and slaughter them, and by getting a permit from headquarters we could get some of our own beef to eat. It went mightily against the grain to do it, however.

The first Yankee that came to our house used very rough language to my mother and ordered her to get him something to eat, when told she had only corn meal and bacon, he said, "You need not trouble yourself, but I've got my eyes on you, old woman." A Yankee Chaplain was also rude to her but they were exceptions. It was rather hard on us to have to be cooped up in the house all the time. We couldn't even walk in the garden. One day I was in the back yard jumping over some boxes for exercise when I noticed a Yankee on the outside of our fence watching me. It is needless to say I quickly vanished indoors. . . .

After the Federals evacuated Indianola a vessel would occasionally come up the bay and land a few troops at Old Town, they would march down from there in order to capture any Confederate that might be in town. Our house was searched twice by them. Once father was hidden in a loft over the gallery. He took a notion that they might carry him off. Well for him they did not find him for they would probably have made him a prisoner under the circumstances.

During the Federal occupation of the town we never learned a word from our soldier boys. Brother Will had been shot through the body at the battle of Murfreesboro, Tenn., in 1862, after many days of anxiety, a letter came from him stating that he was out of danger and would rejoin his regiment as soon as he was able to ride. He had three horses killed under him in different entanglements. Brother Joe made us his last visit in 1863. I saw him mount his horse, Grey Eagle, and ride away never to return. Oh, war, cruel, cruel war. . . .

In this writeup it is my desire to be as accurate as possible, but I do not seem to get my dates in chronological order, so I shall have to go back to the surrender of General Lee, April 9, 1865. The war between the North and South was over as far as the actual fighting was concerned. The soldiers began coming home, but some of them were a long time in arriving. Brother Will came in August, he spent some time in Georgia, then visited an aunt in Mobile, Alabama, before returning; Mr. Bill Kyle of the Terry Rangers came about the same time, also Hays Yarrington and John Coates of the same regiment. The Yankees were here before them. . . . They occupied all coast towns; the first Federal troops that made their appearance at the close of the war were white, they seemed angry at being sent South and were reckless as to their conduct. Often we could hear shots rattling through the tree tops around our house, a bullet made a round hole in our kitchen window; mother stooped to bring in some wood when a ball whistled over her head and lodged in a shed nearby, my little brother, Baxter, came very near being shot by them. They were quite troublesome about cistern water, several would come into the yard, put their canteens under the faucet, not caring how much they wasted.

Soon a company of negro soldiers was stationed near us. They seemed to be turned loose at first and went shouting around our places like a lot of demons; presently they began driving off our hogs, when father went out to protest and threatened to report them at headquarters, they picked up sticks and told him they would beat his brains out if he moved a step farther. I rushed out and told them not to touch my father. In the meantime mother had gone out through the grapevine arbor and on to camp where she reported their depredations to their white officers. Immediately two of them mounted their horses and came dashing up to the house. At the sight of them the negroes fled like chaff before the wind. That night the two young officers came to our house to apologize for the conduct of their men; . . . the soldiers annoyed us so much we were obliged to apply for a guard. A negro was sent us, he seemed like an old plantation darky, was polite and unpretentious. It did me good to see the white soldiers walk around the fence not daring to come in. We had the same guard on two or three times, he liked to stay with us on account of getting better fare than he received in camp.

Finally, mother took an officer and his wife to board with us, as she felt we would be more secure with them in the house. We liked them both very well, Mrs. Archer seemed a kind hearted woman, she came down stairs one night to give my brother some of her homeopathic medicine to stop his coughing, she had remedies for every ailment under the sun. Lieut. Archer decided he wanted his wife to learn to ride, so he procured a horse and proceeded to give her riding lessons. She soon learned to stay on. I think that was the main thing about horseback riding in those days. After a time they gave a little party and invited me to be present to meet some of their officer friends, strange but I had an engagement away from home that night. One day the lieutenant had a negro to weed our flower bed, this he effectually did by pulling up every plant of our cherished verbena.

After a time a Yankee Captain with about twenty men came near our place to camp. He ordered his men to tear down the cow sheds at the lot, father reminded him that the war was over and he had no right to destroy private property. He ordered his men to shoot the d—d old rebel; our boys came running into the house crying, "They are going to kill father." Brother Will knowing that trouble was brewing, had gone to headquarters to report. The man was arrested and his shoulder straps removed. He had the audacity to come and tell father that he had been the cause of him losing his position. He had to board with us until he could get away. Brother was wearing his gray uniform with yellow trimmings and C.S.A. buttons. An officer advised him to remove them as he was liable to have them cut off, rather than to be a source of trouble he had plain buttons substituted for them. In writing these details I am only telling what happened in our immediate vicinity, things were bad enough in town. I was told of a Captain Cleveland who had given them offense in some way, as punishment they cut a hole in the top of a barrel large enough to go over his head and made him march back and forth with it resting on his shoulders.

At this time too the negroes were very impudent, while walking in town I saw three women approaching side by side and knew by their looks they would not make way for me, I walked as near the edge of the sidewalk as possible and they shoved me off. A lady spoke to a negro about getting a cook. The darky replied, "You want to know who your next cook is going to be? You go look in the glass." The negroes soon found out that Southern white people were their best friends and their attitude changed accordingly.

For a while I taught a little school at home, father had built a room for the boys separate from the house and this was my school room. My pupils were brother Ed, Mr. Fromme's son and a drayman's little boy, also the Harrison boys who lived on the other side of the lake, they were Henry, Frank, Willie and Ben, they crossed in a skiff. The family was very unfortunate in losing the wife and mother with cholera, caught supposedly from the negro soldiers camped near Old Town, a great many of them died. There was one girl named Adaline, about thirteen years old at the time of her mother's death, and six boys. The girl was industrious and did all she could for the family but she must have had a hard time of it at best.

Soon after the war closed a good many people came to town and engaged in various occupations, others that had moved away on account of Federal possession returned. We scarcely realized at first that the "tragic era" was upon us and that for a number of years we should be under the yoke of Reconstruction. . . .

Now, one more story of Reconstruction days, my sister-in-law, Gussie, had a friend in town whom she wished to visit and asked me to accompany her. We reached the house without molestation, after chatting a while we stepped out on the upper porch to look at a boat that was anchored in the bay on which Harriet expected to sail to Matagorda the following day; just as we turned back into the room we noticed a soldier had come up stairs and was about to enter. Harriet slammed the door shut and locked it. The man knocked violently at the door and insisted upon entering. Mr. Harrison came up the inside way and ordered the man to leave, by that time another drunken soldier had come up. Mr. Harrison pushed them down the stairway but they started up again using the most vile language I have ever heard. Mr. Prouty (who held some government office) was passing and heard the disturbance, he notified the officers and the men were taken away. We were a frightened set of girls and were almost afraid to go home by ourselves, we walked along the bay shore till we got opposite our home so as to avoid being near any camp. We heard the soldiers were sent to the Dry Tortugas which must be a dreadful place, almost as bad as Devil's Island, where Dreyfus was banished and lived for a number of years. Breaking into the house of a Union man probably made it worse for them. . . .

In July of that year yellow fever broke out in Indianola; we thought at the time it was brought there on a vessel by people who came from a fever-infested port, as the first person to take it was the drayman who carried their belongings up into town. It soon spread and there was scarcely a home that did not have one or more cases, it seemed to be more fatal with people who were not acclimated and there were quite a number of new residents. . . . I never had a list of all who passed away but there were many. I was anxious to go down town and visit some of my sick friends but mother begged me not to go, said she was afraid I would take the fever. I went to the cemetery, however, and located the graves of dear ones who had died. One day I was taken with a chill and my skin turned purple in spots, I sure enough had the fever, was quite ill for a week or more. Mother was my doctor and nurse too and a very successful one she proved to be, I was in low spirits over the loss of loved ones and scarcely cared to live. Father and brother Ed both took the fever but had it in a very light form and soon recovered, my dear mother was nurse through it all. . . .

In November of that year a young German couple came to Indianola and rented a house with the expectation of teaching music, in a short time the man died of yellow fever, the supposition was that the former occupants had the disease; it was very rare, in fact, thought impossible, for a person to have the fever that late in the year.

It took people a long time to find out that the mosquito was to blame, but "Knowledge is Power" and now we never hear of yellow fever epidemics in this part of the country any more. I am sorry to say, though, that mosquitoes still flourish in all parts of the coast country, after a rainy season there are millions of them but I guess they are the harmless kind, only their sting is just as bad as it ever was.

I have been asked the question: "Did many Federal soldiers die of yellow fever at Indianola?" The last two epidemics were in the years of 1862, 1867 and it will be remembered that the Yankees came there in December 1863, and left in March 1864. The statement about yellow fever raging there when the Yanks took possession was entirely without foundation as was also the manner of taking the place. Not a gun was fired and no Confederate soldiers were there.

After the war many negro soldiers died of cholera, some of them were buried at Old Town and a few in the cemetery at Indianola. A great deal of lime was used about their graves and in a few years their bodies were disinterred and taken to some national cemetery for final burial, I suppose.

Then and Now

Lines written during the visitation of yellow fever at Indianola, July 19, 1867:

A month ago our hearts were light,
Our words were gay; our smiles were bright,
We met together, laughed and sung,
All care upon the winds we flung.
We decked our hair with summer flowers
And danced away the fleeting hours,
Pleasure we sought for pleasure gained,
But now, oh now, we're sadly changed.
Sickness with polluting breath,
Has breathed and chilled our loved in death.
Nor age, nor infancy was spared,
But each its cold embrace has shared.
The forms that wandered by our side,
In all their strength and youth and pride,
Have gone from us forever more,
Death Angels steered their barks ashore.
The funeral hearse day after day
Carries our dead from us away,
Our well beloved, our darling dead,
Oh, in their deaths what bright hopes fled.
We cry, how long, Oh, Lord, how long?
Yet death with his sickle marches on
And in his tracks fresh victims fall
The earth seems one vast funeral pall.
Our hearts are sad, our pleasure o'er,
For those we love can come no more,
With restless fee[t] we wonder 'round
And seek for rest but none is found.
With anguished voice, Oh, Lord, we cry,
Have mercy on our misery.
Oh, send us health and strength once more,
And comfort our afflictions sore.

Mary Austin Holley

Mary Austin Holley (1784–1846) was a first cousin of Stephen F. Austin and niece of Moses Austin, the founders of Texas, and was author of the first book in English on Texas. She was born in Connecticut and married a clergyman of Unitarian views. Encouraged by her colonializing kin to move to Texas, she made a lengthy visit there after her husband's death in 1831 and kept a journal of her observations, which reveal her wit, charm, and cultivation, as well as a keen eye for the smallest details of social custom and a sophisticated sense of political and philosophical issues. Some historians point to her journal as having a major impact in influencing immigration to Texas—perhaps the first, and some would say the best, real estate developer's guide ever published.

LETTERS OF AN EARLY AMERICAN TRAVELLER

Bolivar, Texas, December 1831

The Comanches are a noble race of Indians, inhabiting the country to the north and northwest of San Antonio de Bexar. They are a wandering race, do not cultivate the earth for corn, but depend altogether upon the chase for subsistence. They follow the immense herds of buffaloe which graze the vast plains of this region, often to the amount of thousands in one herd. These plains are also stocked with wild horses, which run together in droves of many hundreds. These wild horses are called, in the language of the country, *Mustangs,* and hence the figure of speech to denote any thing wild and uncultivated, as a mustang girl, applied to a rude hunter's daughter. These horses are not natives, but descended from the stock brought over by the first Spaniards. Domestic animals, and man himself, become rude, when removed from the associations of civilized life. The Comanches catch and tame these wild horses, and when unsuccessful in the chase, subsist upon them.

These Indians always move on horseback. Besides the bow and arrows, the usual arms of the Indian warrior, they are armed with a long spear, having a sword blade for the point. A war party of these mounted Indians is sufficiently formidable. They are headed by two squaws, who by their shrill voices, serve as trumpeters, and have, like them, various tones, to denote the different evolutions and movements. When they descry an object of attack, or pursuit, they dart forward in a column, like lightning, towards it. At a suitable distance from their prey, they divide into two squadrons, one half taking to the right, and the other to the left, and thus surround it.

Though fierce in war, they are civil in peace, and remarkable for their sense of justice. They call the people of the United States their friends, and give them protection, while they hate the Mexicans, and murder them without mercy.

The Comanches have one head chief and many subordinate ones. They hold regular councils quarterly, and a grand council of the whole tribe once a year. At these councils all important matters are decided, and all prisoners taken for offences are tried. Their discipline is rigid. If a hunting party takes the life of a North American after making him prisoner, without bringing him before the council for trial, the offenders are punished with death. Not so with the Mexicans, who are considered as enemies and treated as such. This hatred is mutual, and fully reciprocated on the part of the Mexicans. Hence the origin of the epithet expressing odium, so general in all parts of Mexico. To denote the greatest degree of degradation, they call a person a *Comanche.*

The following adventure with a body of these Indians, was related to me by Col. Austin himself. Being illustrative of the character of the Comanches, I insert it here. It will show you also, an instance of the kind of hazard, both of life and limb, which this enterprizing man has encountered in accomplishing his noble project.

On his way to the city of Mexico, in the year 1822, with but two persons in company, arriving at San Antonio, he was told it was dangerous to proceed without an escort, for a war-party of Comanches was abroad, killing every unprotected person who came in their way, that some individuals had been murdered by them the day before, and that he, with so much baggage, being a valuable prize, could not possibly hope to escape.

Finding, however, no opportunity of obtaining an escort, and the business of the colony requiring his presence in the metropolis, he resolved, at all hazards, to proceed on his journey. They travelled the first day unmolested. On the morning of the second day, feeling somewhat indisposed, he undertook to prepare some coffee. There were no accommodations on the road, and it was necessary to carry provisions on a pack-horse, and cook by the way-side. His companions warned him, that if there were Indians near, they would be attracted by the smoke. He flattered himself, that by selecting a sheltered place, and making little smoke, it would be impossible for them to discern it.

Besides, his craving for the coffee was so great, being afflicted with a bad head-ache, he insisted he must have it, at all risks. They were upon an open plain, and they could see many miles around. No living creature at the moment, but themselves, was in view.

The men in company went to seek the horses, which had been hoppled the night before and let loose to feed. This is a mode of tying the horses' legs together to keep them from running away. The Colonel retired to a little ravine to enjoy his coffee. It was boiled, and in the act of putting the refreshing beverage to his parched lips, he heard a sound like the trampling of many horses. Raising his head, with the coffee yet untasted, he beheld in the distance, fifty mounted Comanches, with their spears glittering in the morning sun, dashing towards him at full speed. As the column advanced, it divided, according to their usual practice, into two semi-circles, and in an instant, he was surrounded. Quicker than thought, he sprang to his loaded rifle, but as his hand grasped it, he felt that resistance by one against a host, was vain.

The plunder commenced. Every article of the little encampment, with the saddle-bags, which he stood upon to protect if possible, was greedily seized. His presence of mind, however, did not forsake him. He calmly meditated for a moment, on what course to pursue.

Assuming great composure, he went up to the chief, and addressing him in Spanish and the few words of Indian he knew, he declared himself to be an American, and demanded if their nation was at war with the Americans. "No," was the reply. "Do you like the Americans?" "Yes—they are our friends." "Where do you get your spear heads, your blankets," &c. naming all their foreign articles, one by one. "Get them from our friends the Americans." "Well, do you think if you were passing through their nation, as I am passing through yours, they would rob you as you have robbed me?" The chief reflected a little, and replied, "No, it would not be right." Upon which he commanded his people to restore all the things taken.

Every article of value came back, with the same dispatch with which it had disappeared, except the saddle-bags. These, which contained all his money, were indispensable to the further prosecution of his journey. No one could tell any thing of the saddle-bags. Almost in despair of seeing them again, he observed in a thicket, at a little distance, a squaw, one of the trumpeters, kicking and belabouring her horse, to make him move off, while the sagacious beast would not stir a step from the troop. The Colonel instantly pursued the female robber, and, thanks to her restive mustang, secured his property, which was very adroitly hidden under the blankets and herself. The whole squadron then wheeled off, and were seen no more.

One little circumstance connected with this adventure must be added. A Spanish grammar, which the Colonel carried suspended at the saddlebow, that he might study it as he rode along (for he was not then familiar with the Spanish language), was missing. This grammar was afterwards found among the Indians by some traders, and having the owner's name in it, a report spread abroad, that he had been killed by the Comanches. This report reached the ears of his anxious mother and sister in Missouri, and it was many months before they learned that he had survived this dreary pilgrimage. . . .

Bolivar, Texas, December 1831

The first settlement of this colony by Colonel Austin and his little band of hardy pioneers, displays a spirit of noble enterprise not often surpassed. If the project of establishing such a colony in Texas did not originate with the Austins, it was the first proposal of the kind that was accepted by the Mexican authorities, and it cannot be denied, that the sagacity, the prudence, the industry and perseverance, displayed by Col. Austin in the successful execution of the undertaking, are worthy of all admiration. A short history of the origin of the colony, with some of the difficulties which embarrassed its first struggles for existence, cannot fail to be interesting.

The idea of forming a settlement of North Americans in the wilderness of Texas, it is believed, originated with Moses Austin, esq. of Missouri, and, after the conclusion of De Onis' treaty, in 1819, efforts were made by him to put matters in train for an application to the Spanish government in Old Spain. In answer to his inquiries as to the best mode of laying the subject before the Spanish government, he was advised to apply to the Spanish authorities in New Spain. A memorial was accordingly presented, and his application granted, on the 17th January, 1821, by the supreme government of the Eastern Internal Provinces of New Spain, at Monterrey. Authority was hereby granted to Mr. Austin to introduce three hundred families into Texas, on terms that were satisfactory to both parties.

At this juncture of affairs, before any location for the intended colony was fixed upon, in the midst of diligent preparations to fulfil his engagement, Mr. Moses Austin died. His health had suffered greatly by exposure to bad weather, from swimming and rafting rivers, and from want of provisions on his return to Missouri from Bexar; for at that time Texas was an entire wilderness from Bexar to the Sabine. A severe cold, occasioned by this exposure, terminated in an inflammation of the lungs, which finally put an end to his mortal life.

This gentleman was a native of Durham, in the State of Connecticut, and presents an eminent specimen of the enterprising character of the New England people. At a very early age, impelled by a thirst of knowledge, and an ambition to make a speedy fortune, he left his native state, and, at the age of twenty, was married to Miss Maria Brown, in Philadelphia. Shortly afterwards, in partnership with his brother, Stephen Austin, he purchased the lead mines, called Chessel's Mines, on New river, Wythe county, Virginia, to which he removed, and established a regular system of mining and smelting together with the manufacture of shot, sheet-lead, &c. Miners and mechanics to prosecute this business, were introduced from England, for at that time, manufactures, of this description, were in their infancy in the United States. Owing to causes beyond his control, this enterprise failed of success. Having received flattering accounts of the lead mines in Upper Louisiana, now Missouri, he resolved to visit that distant and unknown country. Accordingly, having procured the necessary passports from the Spanish minister, he visited Upper Louisiana in 1797, and procured a grant from the Governor General, Baron de Carondelet, for one league of land, including the Mine-a-Burton, forty miles west of St. Genevieve. After closing all his affairs in the United States, he removed his family, with a number of others from Wythe county, by a new and almost untried route, down the Kenhawa river, to his new grant, in 1799, and laid a foundation for the settlement, of, what is now called, Washington county, in Missouri. The early settlers of this county will bear ample testimony to this enterprise, public spirit, and honorable character. The exercise of these generous qualities, in fact, brought on another reverse of fortune, and compelled him to turn, with unabated ardour, in the decline of life, to a new and hazardous enterprise in the wilderness of Texas.

At his death, Mr. Moses Austin left a request, that his son, Stephen F. Austin, should prosecute the enterprise which he had thus commenced, of forming a settlement in Texas. Stephen F. Austin, whom I shall hereafter designate as Col. Austin, immediately entered upon the prosecution of the enterprise with vigour. After having first visited the capital of Texas, to make the legal arrangements, and having personally surveyed the country, without a guide, and at much risk, in order to select a favourable location, in December 1821 he arrived on the Brazos with the first emigrants, and the new settlement was commenced in the midst of an entire wilderness. Without entering into a detailed history of all the difficulties, privations and dangers that were encountered by the first emigrants, it is sufficient to say, that such a detail would present examples of inflexible perseverance and fortitude on the part of these settlers, which have been seldom equalled in any country, or in any enterprise. . . .

When, in the progress of years, the state of Texas shall take her place among the powerful empires of the American continent, her citizens will doubtless regard Col. Austin as their patriarch, and children will be taught to hold his name in reverence; for though there have been many other respectable men engaged in the work of colonization, yet Col. Austin began the work, and was the first to open the wilderness. All the subsequent labour of others has been comparatively easy.

Col. Austin has proved himself, both in point of talents and sound judgment, perfectly qualified for the arduous undertaking he took in hand. In the first place, we view him as the hardy and bold pioneer, braving all the dangers of a wilderness infested with hostile Indians, far out of the reach of civilized society, and all the most common comforts of civilized life, enduring with the humblest labour of the little band, all the exposure and privation of the camp, living for months upon wild horse-flesh, without bread or salt.

In the second place, we view him as the skilful negotiator in the capital of Mexico. His difficulties here, were of the most trying and discouraging kind, and required the greatest discretion to surmount; for his business was with the government, and that government in a constant state of revolution and counter-revolution. Twice was his business brought, as he had every reason to think, almost to a successful termination, when a change of government threw it out, and left him where he began months before, to commence anew. His difficulties were not a little increased by the number of petitions for grants of colonization similar to his own. Among these applications, was one from Gen. Wilkerson, formerly of the United States army. It argues not a little in favour of his own skilful management, that, of all these petitions, his alone was finally acceded to, at that time, by the Mexican authorities. . . .

We do injustice to the subject, and to the Austins, by regarding them merely as the founders of the colony which bears their name. They have, in fact, been the movers, either directly or indirectly, of the whole North American and Irish emigration to this country, and, whatever good may result to the great cause of liberty, of science, and human happiness, by the introduction into this vast region, of the English language, and of those principles of republican and constitutional government, which always accompany that language, may be very properly attributed to them,—to the father for conceiving the idea of such an enterprise, to the son for successfully accomplishing it. Few instances occur in the history of new settlements, in which results so important and permanent have been produced by means so comparatively feeble, and under circumstances so discouraging. The settlers of Austin's Colony were unaided by capital or support, either from the Mexican government or from any other quarter. They had no resources, whatever, to depend upon, except those afforded by the spirit and prudence of their leader, a total contempt of danger, obstacles, and privations, and a firm reliance on their rifles, themselves, and their God. Besides the natural difficulties of subduing the wilderness, they had to contend with the deeply fixed prejudices of the people in the United States, who were loath to remove to a country, which they had been taught to believe, was barren and savage, doomed to eternal pestilence and fevers, and, at least, but a refuge for fugitive criminals, pirates, and desperados. Other obstacles, not less appalling to some, arose from the revolutionary and distracted condition of the civil government of Mexico.

Until recently, neither the Mexican government nor the Mexican people, knew any thing of this interesting country, and, whatever value it now possesses in their estimation, or in the opinion of the world, is to be attributed, entirely, to the foreign emigrants. They redeemed it from the wilderness,—they developed its resources,—they have explored it, in its length and breadth, and made known its geography. All has been done by them, without the cost of a single cent to the Mexicans. This consideration, certainly gives to those emigrants, a natural and a just claim upon the liberality of their government, and authorises them to expect a system of colonization, of revenue and municipal law, adapted to their local situation and their infant state.

Bolivar, Texas, December 1831

One's feeling in Texas are unique and original, and very like a dream or youthful vision realized. Here, as in Eden, man feels alone with the God of nature, and seems, in a peculiar manner, to enjoy the rich bounties of heaven, in common with all created things. The animals, which do not fly from him; the profound stillness; the genial sun and soft air,—all are impressive, and are calculated, both to delight the imagination, and to fill the heart, with religious emotions.

With regard to the state of society here, as is natural to expect, there are many incongruities. It will take some time for people gathered from the north, and from the south, from the east, and from the west, to assimilate, and adapt themselves to new situations. The people are universally kind and hospitable, which are redeeming qualities. Every body's house is open, and table spread, to accommodate the traveller. There are no poor people here, and none rich; that is, none who have much money. The poor and the rich, to use the correlatives, where distinction, there is none, get the same quantity of land on arrival, and if they do not continue equal, it is for want of good management on the one part, or superior industry and sagacity on the other. All are happy, because busy; and none meddle with the affairs of their neighbours, because they have enough to do to take care of their own. They are bound together by a common interest, by sameness of purpose, and hopes. As far as I could learn, they have no envyings, no jealousies, no bickerings, through politics or fanaticism. There is neither masonry, anti-masonry, nullification nor court intrigues.

The common concerns of life are sufficiently exciting to keep the spirits buoyant, and prevent everything like ennui. Artificial wants are entirely forgotten, in view of real ones, and self, eternal self, does not alone, fill up the round of life. Delicate ladies find they can be useful, and need not be vain. Even privations become pleasures: people grow ingenious in overcoming difficulties. Many latent faculties are developed. They discover in themselves, powers, they did not suspect themselves of possessing. Equally surprised and delighted at the discovery, they apply to their labours with all that energy and spirit, which new hope and conscious strength, inspire.

You wish to know my opinion, if it will do for all sorts of people to emigrate to Texas, and if I would advise J—— and S—— to sell out and remove. On this point, I should say, industrious farmers will certainly do well, and cannot fail of success; that is to say, if abundant crops, and a ready market with high prices, will satisfy them. Substantial planters, with capital and hands, may enlarge their operations here to any extent, and with enormous profits. One gentleman, for instance, whom I visited, has ninety-three acres under cultivation, by seven hands. His crop, this year, consists of eighty bales of cotton, two thousands bushels of corn, five hundred bushels of sweet potatoes, besides other articles of minor importance.

Those persons, however, who are established in comfort and competency, with an ordinary portion of domestic happiness; who have never been far from home, and are excessively attached to personal ease; who shrink from hardship and danger, and those who, being accustomed to a regular routine of prescribed employment in a city, know not how to act on emergencies, or adapt themselves to all sorts of circumstances, had better stay where they are. There is no better advice, than, "to let well enough alone." All changes may be for the worse as well as better, and what we are used to, though not so good as might be, may suit us best. New shoes, though handsomer and better than old ones, may pinch and fret the wearer. Happiness is relative. A high standard for one person, is a low one for another, and what one prizes, another may think worthless. So that even conceding all the advantages I have claimed for Texas, it does not follow that the happiness of all would be promoted, by emigrating to this country. It depends much upon the spirit of the man.

He whose hopes of rising to independence in life, by honourable exertion, have been blasted by disappointment; whose ambition has been thwarted by untoward circumstances; whose spirit, though depressed, is not discouraged; who longs only for some ample field on which to lay out his strength; who does not hanker after society, nor sigh for the vanished illusions of life; who has a fund of resources within himself, and a heart to trust in God and his own exertions; who is not peculiarly sensitive to petty inconveniences, but can bear privations and make sacrifices, of personal comfort—such a person will do well to settle accounts at home, and begin life anew in Texas. He will find, here, abundant exercise for all his faculties, both of body and mind, a new stimulus to his exertions, and a new current for his affections. He may be obliged to labour hard, but riches are a very certain reward for his exertions. He may be generous, without fear of ruin. He will learn to find society in nature, and repose in solitude, health in exertion, and happiness in occupation. If he have a just ambition, he will glow with generous pride, while he is marking out an untrodden path, acting in an unhackneyed sphere, and founding for himself, and his children after him, a permanent and noble independence.

Sallie Reynolds Matthews

Sallie Reynolds Matthews (1861–1938) wrote her memoirs in 1936, looking back on her life as a member of an early West Texas ranching family who with her husband developed one of the largest cattle ranches in the nation. Entitled Interwoven, *her memoirs provide one of the most colorful and literate accounts of the Old West in print. This selection recalls her early years.*

INTERWOVEN

The Stone Ranch, so called by our family because it was all built of stone, even to the large corrals, lay in an open valley with beautiful hills to the south and, at a farther distance, to the west and northwest. Not far to the northeast there is a little peak which we have always called Buzzard Peak and beneath which flows the Clear Fork whose winding course came to within less than a mile of the ranch house. It was situated in what is now the southwest corner of Throckmorton County and was on the outside border of civilization. The country just northwest of us was occupied solely by Indians and wild animals for hundreds of miles; great herds of buffaloes, deer, antelopes and wild horses roamed the plains. The nearest ranch, Camp Cooper, was five miles east.

It was a bright sunny day when we came to the Stone Ranch, and although the house was not very large, it appeared to be a veritable fortified castle with its thick stone walls, and seemed a haven of peace and quiet to the family after having lived in the crowded fort.

The house stood on the north side of a little creek we called Walnut because of the many trees of that species which grew along its banks. Across the creek on the south was a spring, covered by a stone house, where we kept milk, butter, and meat in the warm weather.

The main building consisted of only two large rooms with a fireplace in each room, and a wide hall between with heavy double doors of oak opening on both north and south. The hall was made into a bedroom by closing one side. One room had a plank floor; the other room and the hall were flagged with stone. On the north was a detached building with two rooms, one with a fireplace. This we called the "bachelors' hall" as it was occupied by the young men and boys.

On entering the house, we found it in a state of disorder. Some of the windows were broken and the glass was lying on the floor. Some wild animal, a wolf or panther, perhaps, had evidently been in the house, as one of the inside doors had been badly gnawed on the edge. The sight of those glaring toothmarks gave me an eerie feeling; I could imagine many and all kinds of wild animals visiting us at night time. How such things impress children! I can see that dusty and glass strewn floor, and that door deeply marked by animal teeth, in my mind's eye now. The work of putting things in order was started at once when Mother began to sweep, and Brother George took the broom from her, saying, "Let me sweep."

There were a few pieces of furniture in the house when we took possession, some chairs and a little French bedroom suite in white, decorated with a spray of flowers on the head and foot boards of the bed and on the dresser drawers. To my childish eyes this furniture appeared about the last word in elegance.

One day Glenn was nosing around in the old rock quarry nearby when he spied a wooden box which on examination proved to be filled with dishes. I think there was almost a full dinner set of ordinary white queen's ware, decorated with tiny roses in relief. I remember there were several covered vegetable dishes. This was a rich find for the family as the supply of china had become so depleted that there was not enough with which to set the table, and tin ware was substituted. With all this new china the table appeared festive indeed.

There were other things found hidden in these rocks, cowbells, staples for ox yokes, and such, for all of which, together with the pieces of furniture, my father paid when the owners came back.

Finding all these articles made the family feel that any pile of rock might contain hidden treasure, so when a small mound of rock was discovered on a hill close by, the men at once proceeded to investigate in order to see what was hidden there. What they found was a tiny coffin. There was no mark of any kind about this mound of rock to indicate that it was a grave. Of course it was immediately replaced as found, and the little mound is still there, but to this day we do not know to whom the child belonged.

The room with the stone floor in the main house was an all-purpose room. Mother's bed was in one corner. At the opposite wall stood a long table at which could be seated twelve or fifteen people, and in some way Mother and Sister managed to set it always with a white cloth, clinging tenaciously to the refinements of life.

The cooking was done on the wide fireplace. On winter evenings after the ovens were set aside, the hearth swept and table pushed against the wall, the family gathered around the fire. Often the boys would be molding bullets, Mother and Sister sewing, knitting or mending. Many pecans, which had been gathered along the banks of the Clear Fork or

Walnut Creek, a short distance away, were cracked and sometimes roasted over the fire. Now and then the cured tongue of a buffalo would be buried in the ashes and roasted; if you have never tasted this special tidbit you have missed something to delight the taste of an epicurean.

Life was never monotonous to me even though there were no other little girls with which to play. I tagged along after my young brothers, Glenn and Phin, as they played. They would make traps and sometimes get a bird, which was always thrilling. They never put them in a cage, but would free them after playing with them a little while.

On the south side of the creek near the spring house, there stood two magnificent elm trees, the interlocking branches of which, like a huge umbrella, made a dense shade. The soil under the elms was moist and alluvial, a contrast to the rocky, arid hillsides.

One day Mother observed Glenn and Phin, very busy with hoe and rake under these trees. She asked them what they meant by all this work; they answered, "We're making a garden."

"Well," Mother replied, "Nothing will grow in that shade."

This was a wet blanket indeed on their spirit of industry. Phin dropped his hoe, saying, "Humph! I'm not going to work in the hot sun." Thus, garden making was over for the time.

Of course, I was too young to realize the seriousness of life, and it seemed a busy, happy time, full of cheerfulness and useful tasks; but as I look back upon it now, I know it was fraught with much anxiety, especially when the boys were out working with the cattle or scouting for Indians. It must have been lonely and rather desolate for my mother and sister with so little contact with other women. There would be an occasional visitor from Camp Cooper and Sister would sometimes ride down there with the men, but I do not believe my mother ever left the ranch except one time during our stay there. There were neither newspapers nor magazines to keep us in touch with the world, no church or Sunday school near.

I wonder how my parents kept track of the days with no calendars. My mother did lose the day once when she did her Saturday cleaning and scrubbing on Sunday, and took a quiet Sabbath rest on Monday. As a rule there was a peaceful calm on Sunday, different from other days, but not always, for at times that was the hardest day in the week, with a crowd of extra men to cook for. Although women were scarce, men were fairly plentiful.

Besides the regular household of fifteen, there were many transient men coming and going. Sometimes they came hunting buffaloes and other game; they did not have to search far for buffaloes as they were seldom out of sight of the house from October to May. At other times they were scouting for Indians who had taken their horses.

The chief recreation for the young men was the hunt and this they thoroughly enjoyed. One noted one while we were at the Stone Ranch was when they went up the river to a place they called Blackjack Thicket, near Fort Phantom Hill, where they had hoped to find some blacktail deer. The common red- and whitetail deer were very plentiful where we lived, but there were no blacktail. I do not remember that they got any deer on this expedition, but they did get a white buffalo which was a very great rarity, this being the first we had ever seen or heard of, and among the many thousands of buffaloes that were killed in this country, I never saw but one other white robe; it was owned by Frank E. Conrad.

Two of my brothers, George and Ben, had a shot at this one, but George being the elder, got the skin. It was given to an army officer at Fort Griffin after the fort was established, to be placed in the Smithsonian Institution at Washington. In my visits to the Capital I have searched diligently in that and other museums and can find no trace of its ever having been placed there. It was there at one time as some of the family saw it, and it does seem as if there would be some record of it. The officials of these institutions have been most kind in assisting me in my search for it.

When summer came my father made his yearly trip to Weatherford for supplies. On this trip my sister and her baby, my brother, Ben, and I were along. The reason for Sister's and my going was mainly to visit with our relatives, the Barbers, and to have some pictures made, little tintypes they were. While we were away the ranch was raided by Indians.

One Sunday morning after most of the men had ridden off leaving only two as guards and the two younger boys, Glenn and Phin, twelve and nine years of age respectively, fourteen Indians, Kiowas and Comanches, charged about the house and fired a few times. Glenn used a gun as well as the two men and the Indians soon left, taking with them five hundred head of cattle that they had rounded up and all the horses they could lay hands on. In those days it was customary for the cattlemen to put the young calves in the pen in order to keep the mothers from straying away too far and to get them located and gentle. (At one time we also had fifty young buffalo calves nursing the cows with the other calves.) There were sometimes a hundred or so calves in the pen. The Indians turned out the calves and rounded in as many of the mothers as they could find, but not all, as some of them were bawling in deep distress for days afterward.

As Indians were not accustomed to seizing cattle, their usual quarry being only horses, some people think these raiders were not Indians, but rather white desperadoes. If they were not Indians, they were artfully disguised in Indian dress, war paint, and feathers, and their war whoops were well simulated, for the family felt certain they were Indians.

Father knew nothing of this incursion until when nearing home he heard that the ranch had been raided by Indians. After this he thought surely the family would return to the fort. Not my little Scotch mother; she was made of more heroic metal. When someone asked her if she had not been terribly frightened, she said, "No, but I was all-fired mad."

The next event of interest happened in April 1867. Some horses had been stolen from settlers east of us and a party of men, riding in hot haste to overtake the Indian marauders, came to our ranch where they were joined by my brothers, George and William, and Si Hough. They overtook the Indians at the Double Mountain Fork of the Brazos, a distance of thirty-five or forty miles from the Stone Ranch. They were loitering here, taking their ease and shooting buffaloes, thinking they were out of the danger zone. They were taken by surprise and only one escaped to tell the tale. They were outnumbered, there being ten white men to seven Indians. One of our men, John Anderson, was shot through the arm, receiving a flesh wound, and a minié ball passed through William's sleeve. Brother George was the only one seriously hurt. He was shot with an arrow that entered his body just above the navel. He was wearing a United States Army belt buckle which was about two inches wide by three long. This buckle, we think, may have saved his life, as the arrow hit the edge of the buckle, breaking the force of the shot to some extent or it would doubtless have gone through his body. These arrows had great force when shot from strong Indian bows. He pulled the shaft out, but the head was left in his body, where it stayed fifteen years. At first they thought it possibly might have dropped in the loose sand when the shaft was taken out and have been covered, but that was not the case, as was proven in after years.

When Si came up and saw George lying there, he swore he would have the scalp of the Indian who shot him. He was not long in getting it. This particular Indian was marked by his gay trappings; his war bonnet of eagle feathers and bridle covered with disks of hammered silver proclaimed him a chieftain, they thought. The silver-studded bridle was given to Brother by Si Hough and is now treasured by William's sons, Brother George having had none to inherit it.

William and John Anderson rode all night to tell the family what had happened. The night before they came, my father had a dream which so impressed him that he told Mother that one of the boys was wounded, and he was walking the yard in distress and looking for a messenger when the two boys came. This premonition seemed almost psychic.

How to get the wounded boy home was a problem. They tied two horses together, heads and tails, and filled in between with their packs. The packs, called kayaks, were made of cowhide and were on the order of old-fashioned saddlebags, only they were much larger and were used to put across a pack horse for carrying provisions for cow hunts and scouts like this one. These were placed across the horses and filled in with bedding, and the wounded man was laid on this improvised bed. A man on each side led the horses as the slow journey home was begun. You can realize that this mode of travel was anything but comfortable for an injured man; it was almost unbearable, but he endured it until nearing home when he asked to be put upon his horse which had an easy gait. He wanted the family to see him sitting his horse! They, of course, did not know that he was still alive. When the scouting party approached the ranch, the younger boys were on top of the smokehouse watching, and when they counted the full number it was a great relief and joy to those at home.

In the meantime, Sam Newcomb was riding night and day to Weatherford, more than a hundred miles away, for a doctor, only stopping for a bite to eat and a fresh horse at the ranches along the way, and he and Dr. James D. Ray of Weatherford rode day and night on the return trip. When the doctor arrived, he probed the wound a little and that ended his treatment. It was all he could do at that time as he did not have the facilities of modern surgery. Strange to say, the wound healed without infection and soon he was going about as usual. However, he suffered a good deal of pain in his body until the arrow was removed, although no one would have suspected this from the active life he led.

The arrow head either went into the muscles of the back at first, or in some manner gradually worked its way to the back. Years afterward there was a knot pushed out near his spine which he suspected was the arrow head coming to the surface, and he was right about it, for in 1882 he went to Kansas City and had it taken out. The following are excerpts from an account in the *Kansas City Journal* of July 18, 1882.

Yesterday afternoon there was removed from the body of George T. Reynolds, a prominent cattleman of Fort Griffin, Texas, an arrow head, two inches long. Mr. Reynolds had carried this head sixteen years, three months and fifteen days.

On Friday last the gentleman came to this city and registered at the

St. James Hotel. His coming was for the purpose of having a surgical operation performed.

Then follows an account of the Indian fight which is omitted here.

On his back opposite the place where the arrow entered his body, he could feel its head. At last he decided to have it cut out and came to Kansas City as mentioned. Scales of rust were removed from the arrow head when it was taken from his body. The point was blunt as if it had been eaten off with rust.

This operation was performed by Drs. Lewis and Griffith, in the presence of Dr. Powell of New York. The gentleman was resting easy last evening and feeling much relieved.

There was no anaesthetic used and before going into the operation he exacted a promise from the doctor that he would stop when asked. Two friends went into the operating room with him to see him through. One of them ran out as soon as the doctor started work. The other, "Shanghai" Pierce, a well known cattleman of South Texas, became so excited when he saw the deep incision that he yelled, "Stop, doctor, you are cutting that man to the hollow." At this my brother called a halt. The cut had missed the arrow head, and had gone down by the side of it. Brother raised himself to a sitting posture and bent forward. The steel arrow head slipped out into the incision.

In addition to the bridle with the silver discs, there were many other trophies of this battle with Indians, bows and quivers full of arrows, beads, earrings, and bracelets by the dozens; and with shame I confess it, there were several scalps, scalps not taken in wanton cruelty, but as a lesson to the Indians. It seemed that by using their own tactics against them, they were more terrified; at least that is what was claimed by the white men.

Before going further, I want to state my sentiments in regard to the Indians. While the pioneers of this country suffered greatly in many ways, not the least being agony of mind as well as body, I do not think the Indians were by any means altogether to blame. The white people came to America as Christians. Did not the Pilgrim fathers come primarily that they might worship God according to the dictates of their own consciences? And they did treat the Indians kindly in the beginning and had a friendly welcome by Massasoit. But this did not continue for long, and as the settling of the country by white people went on, we know there were many who cheated and exploited the Indians in every way possible, and in some instances treated them with ruthless cruelty.

One such incident came under my parents' knowledge while they lived in Shelby County. During the rush to the gold fields of California, a party of young men left their neighborhood to go there. In the party there was one foolhardy fellow who boasted he would shoot the first Indian he saw. The first Indian he saw happened to be a squaw, sitting on a log nursing her baby, and in cold blood he shot her. Could anything have been more dastardly and heartless? They were immediately surrounded by Indians and the man who did the deed was demanded, and it was obvious that if he were not surrendered, they would kill the whole party. So they gave him up and he was deservedly flayed alive. They were merciful not to have killed the whole company; that is what Mr. White Man would have done under like circumstances.

Another incident of cold-blooded cruelty on the part of white men was witnessed by my husband when a young lad. There had been a band of Indians in the country, and a young man, son of Mr. Browning, a prominent citizen, had been killed. A party of men were out scouting for these Indians, or any Indians, when they came upon a lone redskin who apparently was lost. He may have belonged to the band which had killed young Browning, or he may not, for no one knew. When found, he was roasting a skunk for his dinner. The scouts ordered him to march off and he did so, never turning his head. He was shot in the back, and Browning was given the first shot to appease his thirst for vengeance. The young lad mentioned above was in the party and he thought it a shocking display of cowardice on the part of the white men. He says that if they had given the Indian some food and a "plug" of a pony, they would have acted more like Christians and perhaps have served their country better.

Some time during Civil War days, I do not know just what year it was, there was a band of Indians of the Kickapoo tribe passing through this country going across to New Mexico. They were friendly and did not molest anybody or anything. But they were Indians, and that was enough in the minds of some people. When they came to the locality where the city of San Angelo now stands, they saw a body of men and not wanting any trouble they sent one of their men out with a white flag to parley with these white men. The white men wanted no parley, they wanted to fight. They killed this peace messenger and forced an encounter in which the white men were ingloriously whipped. And the Indians went on their way without being further molested.

Now I do not hold any brief for the Indians nor am I posing as a Helen Hunt Jackson, but I do think that our race has much to answer for. How are we going to reconcile that "Trail of Tears" when the Cherokees, a peaceful tribe, were forced to leave their little homes and farms in western Georgia and North Carolina, because, forsooth, the white man wanted the land, therefore the Indian must move on. They were sent into the new country of Oklahoma that the government had provided, and it is a fine country, a rich and beautiful land. But these people did not want to give up their homes where they had spent their lives among familiar surroundings and which they loved perhaps as we love ours. Many of them were old and feeble, and so many died on the way. It is spoken of by those tribes as the "Trail of Tears" to this day.

I think that if they had been treated more humanely from the beginning, there would have been much less rapine and bloodshed. What could we expect of a people that were gradually being driven from their home and country, their hunting grounds being taken without remuneration? When the United States government did set aside certain portions for their exclusive use, did not the white man try in every way to get a share of that? If by no other means, he would take unto himself an Indian wife, and in that way acquire land. If there had been more William Penns, this would have been a more peaceful country in pioneer days. I, for one, believe a good bit in the inherent nobility of the Red Man.

Stephen Crane ———————————————————

Stephen Crane (1871–1900) was sent to Texas by the press syndicate that serialized The Red Badge of Courage, *with instructions to write whatever struck his fancy. Some of his finest stories resulted, rich with the impressionism and symbolism that made him a major force in American letters.*

THE BRIDE COMES TO YELLOW SKY

The great pullman was whirling onward with such dignity of motion that a glance from the window seemed simply to prove that the plains of Texas were pouring eastward. Vast flats of green grass, dull-hued spaces of mesquit and cactus, little groups of frame houses, woods of light and tender trees, all were sweeping into the east, sweeping over the horizon, a precipice.

A newly married pair had boarded this coach at San Antonio. The man's face was reddened from many days in the wind and sun, and a direct result of his new black clothes was that his brick-coloured hands were constantly performing in a most conscious fashion. From time to time he looked down respectfully at his attire. He sat with a hand on each knee, like a man waiting in a barber's shop. The glances he devoted to other passengers were furtive and shy.

The bride was not pretty, nor was she very young. She wore a dress of blue cashmere, with small reservations of velvet here and there, and with steel buttons abounding. She continually twisted her head to regard her puff sleeves, very stiff, straight, and high. They embarrassed her. It was quite apparent that she had cooked, and that she expected to cook, dutifully. The blushes caused by the careless scrutiny of some passengers as she had entered the car were strange to see upon this plain, under-class countenance, which was drawn in placid, almost emotionless lines.

They were evidently very happy. "Ever been in a parlour-car before?" he asked, smiling with delight.

"No," she answered; "I never was. It's fine, ain't it?"

"Great! And then after a while we'll go forward to the diner, and get a big lay-out. Finest meal in the world. Charge a dollar."

"Oh, do they?" cried the bride. "Charge a dollar? Why, that's too much—for us—ain't it, Jack?"

"Not this trip, anyhow," he answered bravely. "We're going to go the whole thing."

Later he explained to her about the trains. "You see, it's a thousand miles from one end of Texas to the other; and this train runs right across it, and never stops but four times." He had the pride of an owner. He pointed out to her the dazzling fittings of the coach; and in truth her eyes opened wider as she contemplated the sea-green figured velvet, the shining brass, silver, and glass, the wood that gleamed as darkly brilliant as the surface of a pool of oil. At one end a bronze figure sturdily held a support for a separated chamber, and at convenient places on the ceiling were frescos in olive and silver.

To the minds of the pair, their surroundings reflected the glory of their marriage that morning in San Antonio; this was the environment of their new estate; and the man's face in particular beamed with an elation that made him appear ridiculous to the negro porter. This individual at times surveyed them from afar with an amused and superior grin. On other occasions he bullied them with skill in ways that did not make it exactly plain to them that they were being bullied. He subtly used all the manners of the most unconquerable kind of snobbery. He oppressed them; but of this oppression they had small knowledge, and they speedily forgot that infrequently a number of travellers covered them with stares of derisive enjoyment. Historically there was supposed to be something infinitely humorous in their situation.

"We are due in Yellow Sky at 3:42," he said, looking tenderly into her eyes.

"Oh, are we?" she said, as if she had not been aware of it. To evince surprise at her husband's statement was part of her wifely amiability. She took from a pocket a little silver watch; and as she held it before her, and stared at it with a frown of attention, the new husband's face shone.

"I bought it in San Anton' from a friend of mine," he told her gleefully.

"It's seventeen minutes past twelve," she said, looking up at him with a kind of shy and clumsy coquetry. A passenger, noting this play, grew excessively sardonic, and winked at himself in one of the numerous mirrors.

At last they went to the dining-car. Two rows of negro waiters, in glowing white suits, surveyed their entrance with the interest, and also the equanimity, of men who had been forewarned. The pair fell to the lot of a waiter who happened to feel pleasure in steering them through their meal. He viewed them with the manner of a fatherly pilot, his countenance radiant with benevolence. The patronage, entwined with the ordinary deference, was not plain to them. And yet, as they returned to their coach, they showed in their faces a sense of escape.

To the left, miles down a long purple slope, was a little ribbon of mist where moved the keening Rio Grande. The train was approaching it at an angle, and the apex was Yellow Sky. Presently it was apparent that, as the distance from Yellow Sky grew shorter, the husband became commensurately restless. His brick-red hands were more insistent in their prominence. Occasionally he was even rather absent-minded and far-away when the bride leaned forward and addressed him.

As a matter of truth, Jack Potter was beginning to find the shadow of a deed weigh upon him like a leaden slab. He, the town marshal of Yellow Sky, a man known, liked, and feared in his corner, a prominent person, had gone to San Antonio to meet a girl he believed he loved, and there, after the usual prayers, had actually induced her to marry him, without consulting Yellow Sky for any part of the transaction. He was now bringing his bride before an innocent and unsuspecting community.

The Bride Comes to Yellow Sky | 145

Of course people in Yellow Sky married as it pleased them, in accordance with a general custom; but such was Potter's thought of his duty to his friends, or of their idea of his duty, or of an unspoken form which does not control men in these matters, that he felt he was heinous. He had committed an extraordinary crime. Face to face with this girl in San Antonio, and spurred by his sharp impulse, he had gone headlong over all the social hedges. At San Antonio he was like a man hidden in the dark. A knife to sever any friendly duty, any form, was easy to his hand in that remote city. But the hour of Yellow Sky—the hour of daylight—was approaching.

He knew full well that his marriage was an important thing to his town. It could only be exceeded by the burning of the new hotel. His friends could not forgive him. Frequently he had reflected on the advisability of telling them by telegraph, but a new cowardice had been upon him. He feared to do it. And now the train was hurrying him toward a scene of amazement, glee, and reproach. He glanced out of the window at the line of haze swinging slowly in toward the train.

Yellow Sky had a kind of brass band, which played painfully, to the delight of the populace. He laughed without heart as he thought of it. If the citizens could dream of his prospective arrival with his bride, they would parade the band at the station, and escort them, amid cheers and laughing congratulations, to his adobe home.

He resolved that he would use all the devices of speed and plainscraft in making the journey from the station to his house. Once within that safe citadel, he could issue some sort of vocal bulletin, and then not go among the citizens until they had time to wear off a little of their enthusiasm.

The bride looked anxiously at him. "What's worrying you, Jack?"

He laughed again. "I'm not worrying, girl; I'm only thinking of Yellow Sky."

She flushed in comprehension.

A sense of mutual guilt invaded their minds and developed a finer tenderness. They looked at each other with eyes softly aglow. But Potter often laughed the same nervous laugh; the flush upon the bride's face seemed quite permanent.

The traitor to the feelings of Yellow Sky narrowly watched the speeding landscape. "We're nearly there," he said.

Presently the porter came and announced the proximity of Potter's home. He held a brush in his hand, and, with all his airy superiority gone, he brushed Potter's new clothes as the latter slowly turned this way and that way. Potter fumbled out a coin and gave it to the porter, as he had seen others do. It was a heavy and muscle-bound business, as that of a man shoeing his first horse.

The porter took their bag, and as the train began to slow they moved forward to the hooded platform of the car. Presently the two engines and their long string of coaches rushed into the station of Yellow Sky.

"They have to take water here," said Potter, from a constricted throat and in mournful cadence, as one announcing death. Before the train stopped his eye had swept the length of the platform, and he was glad and astonished to see there was none upon it but the station-agent, who, with a slightly hurried and anxious air, was walking toward the water-tanks. When the train had halted, the porter alighted first, and placed in position a little temporary step.

"Come on, girl," said Potter, hoarsely. As he helped her down they each laughed on a false note. He took the bag from the negro, and bade his wife cling to his arm. As they slunk rapidly away, his hang-dog glance perceived that they were unloading the two trunks, and also that the station-agent, far ahead near the baggage-car, had turned and was running toward him, making gestures. He laughed, and groaned as he laughed, when he noted the first effect of his marital bliss upon Yellow Sky. He gripped his wife's arm firmly to his side, and they fled. Behind them the porter stood, chuckling fatuously.

II

The California express on the Southern Railway was due at Yellow Sky in twenty-one minutes. There were six men at the bar of the Weary Gentleman saloon. One was a drummer who talked a great deal and rapidly; three were Texans who did not care to talk at that time; and two were Mexican sheep-herders, who did not talk as a general practice in the Weary Gentleman saloon. The barkeeper's dog lay on the board walk that crossed in front of the door. His head was on his paws, and he glanced drowsily here and there with the constant vigilance of a dog that is kicked on occasion. Across the sandy street were some vivid green grass-plots, so wonderful in appearance, amid the sands that burned near them in a blazing sun, that they caused a doubt in the mind. They exactly resembled the grass mats used to represent lawns on the stage. At the cooler end of the railway station, a man without a coat sat in a tilted chair and smoked his pipe. The fresh-cut bank of the Rio Grande circled near the town, and there could be seen beyond it a great plum-coloured plain of mesquit.

Save for the busy drummer and his companions in the saloon, Yellow

Sky was dozing. The new-comer leaned gracefully upon the bar, and recited many tales with the confidence of a bard who has come upon a new field.

"—and at the moment that the old man fell downstairs with the bureau in his arms, the old woman was coming up with two scuttles of coal, and of course—"

The drummer's tale was interrupted by a young man who suddenly appeared in the open door. He cried: "Scratchy Wilson's drunk, and has turned loose with both hands." The two Mexicans at once set down their glasses and faded out of the rear entrance of the saloon.

The drummer, innocent and jocular, answered: "All right, old man. S'pose he has? Come in and have a drink, anyhow."

But the information had made such an obvious cleft in every skull in the room that the drummer was obliged to see its importance. All had become instantly solemn. "Say," said he, mystified, "what is this?" His three companions made the introductory gesture of eloquent speech; but the young man at the door forestalled them.

"It means, my friend," he answered, as he came into the saloon, "that for the next two hours this town won't be a health resort."

The barkeeper went to the door, and locked and barred it; reaching out of the window, he pulled in heavy wooden shutters, and barred them. Immediately a solemn, chapel-like gloom was upon the place. The drummer was looking from one to another.

"But say," he cried, "what is this, anyhow? You don't mean there is going to be a gun-fight?"

"Don't know whether there'll be a fight or not," answered one man, grimly; "but there'll be some shootin'—some good shootin'."

The young man who had warned them waved his hand. "Oh, there'll be a fight fast enough, if any one wants it. Anybody can get a fight out there in the street. There's a fight just waiting."

The drummer seemed to be swayed between the interest of a foreigner and a perception of personal danger.

"What did you say his name was?" he asked.

"Scratchy Wilson," they answered in chorus.

"And will he kill anybody? What are you going to do? Does this happen often? Does he rampage around like this once a week or so? Can he break in that door?"

"No; he can't break down that door," replied the barkeeper. "He's tried it three times. But when he comes you'd better lay down on the floor, stranger. He's dead sure to shoot at it, and a bullet may come through."

Thereafter the drummer kept a strict eye upon the door. The time had not yet been called for him to hug the floor, but, as a minor precaution, he sidled near to the wall. "Will he kill anybody?" he said again.

The men laughed low and scornfully at the question.

"He's out to shoot, and he's out for trouble. Don't see any good in experimentin' with him."

"But what do you do in a case like this? What do you do?"

A man responded: "Why, he and Jack Potter—"

"But," in chorus the other men interrupted, "Jack Potter's in San Anton'."

"Well, who is he? What's he got to do with it?"

"Oh, he's the town marshal. He goes out and fights Scratchy when he gets on one of these tears."

"Wow!" said the drummer, mopping his brow. "Nice job he's got."

The voices had toned away to mere whisperings. The drummer wished to ask further questions, which were born of an increasing anxiety and bewilderment; but when he attempted them, the men merely looked at him in irritation and motioned him to remain silent. A tense waiting hush was upon them. In the deep shadows of the room their eyes shone as they listened for sounds from the street. One man made three gestures at the barkeeper; and the latter, moving like a ghost, handed him a glass and a bottle. The man poured a full glass of whisky, and set down the bottle noiselessly. He gulped the whisky in a swallow, and turned again toward the door in immovable silence. The drummer saw that the barkeeper, without a sound, had taken a Winchester from beneath the bar. Later he saw this individual beckoning to him, so he tiptoed across the room.

"You better come with me back of the bar."

"No, thanks," said the drummer, perspiring; "I'd rather be where I can make a break for the back door."

Whereupon the man of bottles made a kindly but peremptory gesture. The drummer obeyed it, and, finding himself seated on a box with his head below the level of the bar, balm was laid upon his soul at sight of various zinc and copper fittings that bore a resemblance to armour-plate. The barkeeper took a seat comfortably upon an adjacent box.

"You see," he whispered, "this here Scratchy Wilson is a wonder with a gun—a perfect wonder; and when he goes on the war-trail, we hunt our holes—naturally. He's about the last one of the old gang that used to hang out along the river here. He's a terror when he's drunk. When he's sober he's all right—kind of simple—wouldn't hurt a fly— nicest fellow in town. But when he's drunk—whoo!"

There were periods of stillness. "I wish Jack Potter was back from San Anton'," said the barkeeper. "He shot Wilson up once—in the leg—and he would sail in and pull out the kinks in this thing."

Presently they heard from a distance the sound of a shot, followed by three wild yowls. It instantly removed a bond from the men in the darkened saloon. There was a shuffling of feet. They looked at each other. "Here he comes," they said.

III

A man in a maroon-coloured flannel shirt, which had been purchased for purposes of decoration, and made principally by some Jewish women on the East Side of New York, rounded a corner and walked into the middle of the main street of Yellow Sky. In either hand the man held a long, heavy, blue-black revolver. Often he yelled, and these cries rang through a semblance of a deserted village, shrilly flying over the roofs in a volume that seemed to have no relation to the ordinary vocal strength of a man. It was as if the surrounding stillness formed the arch of a tomb over him. These cries of ferocious challenge rang against walls of silence. And his boots had red tops with gilded imprints, of the kind beloved in winter by little sledding boys on the hillsides of New England.

The man's face flamed in a rage begot of whisky. His eyes, rolling, and yet keen for ambush, hunted the still doorways and windows. He walked with the creeping movement of the midnight cat. As it occurred to him, he roared menacing information. The long revolvers in his hands were as easy as straws; they were moved with an electric swiftness. The little fingers of each hand played sometimes in a musician's way. Plain from the low collar of the shirt, the cords of his neck straightened and sank, straightened and sank, as passion moved him. The only sounds were his terrible invitations. The calm adobes preserved their demeanour at the passing of this small thing in the middle of the street.

There was no offer of fight—no offer of fight. The man called to the sky. There were no attractions. He bellowed and fumed and swayed his revolvers here and everywhere.

The dog of the barkeeper of the Weary Gentleman saloon had not appreciated the advance of events. He yet lay dozing in front of his master's door. At sight of the dog, the man paused and raised his revolver humorously. At sight of the man, the dog sprang up and walked diagonally away, with a sullen head, and growling. The man yelled, and the dog broke into a gallop. As it was about to enter an alley, there was a loud noise, a whistling, and something spat the ground directly before it. The dog screamed, and, wheeling in terror, galloped headlong in a new direction. Again there was a noise, a whistling, and sand was kicked viciously before it. Fear-stricken, the dog turned and flurried like an animal in a pen. The man stood laughing, his weapons at his hips.

Ultimately the man was attracted by the closed door of the Weary Gentleman saloon. He went to it and, hammering with a revolver, demanded drink.

The door remaining imperturbable, he picked a bit of paper from the walk, and nailed it to the framework with a knife. He then turned his back contemptuously upon this popular resort and, walking to the opposite side of the street and spinning there on his heel quickly and lithely, fired at the bit of paper. He missed it by a half-inch. He swore at himself, and went away. Later he comfortably fusilladed the windows of his most intimate friend. The man was playing with this town; it was a toy for him.

But still there was no offer of fight. The name of Jack Potter, his ancient antagonist, entered his mind, and he concluded that it would be a glad thing if he should go to Potter's house, and by bombardment induce him to come out and fight. He moved in the direction of his desire, chanting Apache scalp-music.

When he arrived at it, Potter's house presented the same still front as had the other adobes. Taking up a strategic position, the man howled a challenge. But this house regarded him as might a great stone god. It gave no sign. After a decent wait, the man howled further challenges, mingling with them wonderful epithets.

Presently there came the spectacle of a man churning himself into deepest rage over the immobility of a house. He fumed at it as the winter wind attacks a prairie cabin in the North. To the distance there should have gone the sound of a tumult like the fighting of two hundred Mexicans. As necessity bade him, he paused for breath or to reload his revolvers.

IV

Potter and his bride walked sheepishly and with speed. Sometimes they laughed together shamefacedly and low.

"Next corner, dear," he said finally.

They put forth the efforts of a pair walking bowed against a strong wind. Potter was about to raise a finger to point the first appearance of the new home when, as they circled the corner, they came face to face with a man in a maroon-coloured shirt, who was feverishly pushing cartridges into a large revolver. Upon the instant the man dropped his revolver to the ground and, like lightning, whipped another from its holster. The second weapon was aimed at the bridegroom's chest.

There was a silence. Potter's mouth seemed to be merely a grave for his tongue. He exhibited an instinct to at once loosen his arm from the woman's grip, and he dropped the bag to the sand. As for the bride, her face had gone as yellow as old cloth. She was a slave to hideous rites, gazing at the apparitional snake.

The two men faced each other at a distance of three paces. He of the revolver smiled with a new and quiet ferocity.

"Tried to sneak up on me," he said. "Tried to sneak up on me!" His eyes grew more baleful. As Potter made a slight movement, the man thrust his revolver venomously forward. "No; don't you do it, Jack Potter. Don't you move a finger toward a gun just yet. Don't you move an eyelash. The time has come for me to settle with you, and I'm goin' to do it my own way, and loaf along with no interferin'. So if you don't want a gun bent on you, just mind what I tell you."

Potter looked at his enemy. "I ain't got a gun on me Scratchy," he said. "Honest, I ain't." He was stiffening and steadying, but yet somewhere at the back of his mind a vision of the Pullman floated: the sea-green figured velvet, the shining brass, silver, and glass, the wood that gleamed as darkly brilliant as the surface of a pool of oil—all the glory of the marriage, the environment of the new estate. "You know I fight when it comes to fighting, Scratchy Wilson; but I ain't got a gun on me. You'll have to do all the shootin' yourself."

His enemy's face went livid. He stepped forward, and lashed his weapon to and fro before Potter's chest. "Don't you tell me you ain't got no gun on you, you whelp. Don't tell me no lie like that. There ain't a man in Texas ever seen you without no gun. Don't take me for no kid." His eyes blazed with light, and his throat worked like a pump.

"I ain't takin' you for no kid," answered Potter. His heels had not moved an inch backward. "I'm takin' you for a damn fool. I tell you I ain't got a gun, and I ain't. If you're goin' to shoot me up, you better begin now; you'll never get a chance like this again."

So much enforced reasoning had told on Wilson's rage; he was calmer. "If you ain't got a gun, why ain't you got a gun?" he sneered. "Been to Sunday-school?"

"I ain't got a gun because I've just come from San Anton' with my wife. I'm married," said Potter. "And if I'd thought there was going to be any galoots like you prowling around when I brought my wife home, I'd had a gun, and don't you forget it."

"Married!" said Scratchy, not at all comprehending.

"Yes, married. I'm married," said Potter, distinctly.

"Married?" said Scratchy. Seemingly for the first time, he saw the drooping, drowning woman at the other man's side. "No!" he said. He was like a creature allowed a glimpse of another world. He moved a pace backward, and his arm, with the revolver, dropped to his side. "Is this the lady?" he asked.

"Yes; this is the lady," answered Potter.

There was another period of silence.

"Well," said Wilson at last, slowly, "I s'pose it's all off now."

"It's all off if you say so, Scratchy. You know I didn't make the trouble." Potter lifted his valise.

"Well, I 'low it's off, Jack," said Wilson. He was looking at the ground. "Married!" He was not a student of chivalry; it was merely that in the presence of this foreign condition he was a simple child of the earlier plains. He picked up his starboard revolver, and, placing both weapons in their holsters, he went away. His feet made funnel-shaped tracks in the heavy sand.

Katherine Anne Porter

Katherine Anne Porter (1890–1980) was born in Indian Creek near Brownwood and grew up in Texas and Louisiana. A great-grandniece of Daniel Boone and a cousin of O. Henry (Sidney Porter), she is one of the most critically acclaimed writers with Texas roots, combining delicate perceptions with painstaking craftsmanship in creating vivid personalities enduring life's agonies. The setting for the following selection is the rural Texas settled by German Catholic immigrants in the hill country west of San Antonio.

HOLIDAY

At that time I was too young for some of the troubles I was having, and I had not yet learned what to do with them. It no longer can matter what kind of troubles they were, or what finally became of them. It seemed to me then there was nothing to do but run away from them, though all my tradition, background, and training had taught me unanswerably that no one except a coward ever runs away from anything. What nonsense! They should have taught me the difference between courage and foolhardiness, instead of leaving me to find it out for myself. I learned finally that if I still had the sense I was born with, I would take off like a deer at the first warning of certain dangers. But this story I am about to tell you happened before this great truth impressed itself upon me—that we do not run from the troubles and dangers that are truly ours, and it is better to learn what they are earlier than later, and if we don't run from the others, we are fools.

I confided to my friend Louise, a former schoolmate about my own age, not my troubles but my little problem: I wanted to go somewhere for a spring holiday, by myself, to the country, and it should be very simple and nice and, of course, not expensive, and she was not to tell anyone where I had gone; but if she liked, I would send her word now and then, if anything interesting was happening. She said she loved getting letters but hated answering them; and she knew the very place for me, and she would not tell anybody anything. Louise had then—she has it still—something near to genius for making improbable persons, places, and situations sound attractive. She told amusing stories that did not turn grim on you until a little while later, when by chance you saw and heard for yourself. So with this story. Everything was just as Louise had said, if you like, and everything was, at the same time, quite different.

"I know the very place," said Louise, "a family of real old-fashioned German peasants, in the deep blackland Texas farm country, a household in real patriarchal style—the kind of thing you'd hate to live with but is very nice to visit. Old father, God Almighty himself, with whiskers and all; Old mother, matriarch in men's shoes; endless daughters and sons and sons-in-law and fat babies falling about the place; and fat puppies—my favorite was a darling little black thing named Kuno—cows, calves, and sheep and lambs and goats and turkeys and guineas roaming up and down the shallow green hills, ducks and geese on the ponds. I was there in the summer when the peaches and watermelons were in—"

"This is the end of March," I said, doubtfully.

"Spring comes early there," said Louise. "I'll write to the Müllers about you, you just get ready to go."

"Just where is this paradise?"

"Not far from the Louisiana line," said Louise. "I'll ask them to give you my attic—oh, that was a sweet place! It's a big room, with the roof sloping to the floor on each side, and the roof leaks a little when it rains, so the shingles are all stained in beautiful streaks, all black and grey and mossy green, and in one corner there used to be a stack of dime novels, *The Duchess,* Ouida, Mrs. E.D.E.N. Southworth, Ella Wheeler Wilcox's poems—one summer they had a lady boarder who was a great reader, and she went off and left her library. I loved it! And everybody was so healthy and good-hearted, and the weather was perfect. . . . How long do you want to stay?"

I hadn't thought of this, so I said at random, "About a month."

A few days later I found myself tossed off like an express package from a dirty little crawling train onto the sodden platform of a country station, where the stationmaster emerged and locked up the waiting room before the train had got round the bend. As he clumped by me he shifted his wad of tobacco to his cheek and asked, "Where you goin'?"

"To the Müller farm," I said, standing beside my small trunk and suitcase with the bitter wind cutting through my thin coat.

"Anybody meet you?" he asked, not pausing.

"They *said* so."

"All right," he said, and got into his little ragged buckboard with a sway-backed horse and drove away.

I turned my trunk on its side and sat on it facing the wind and the desolate mud-colored shapeless scene and began making up my first letter to Louise. First I was going to tell her that unless she was to be a novelist, there was no excuse for her having so much imagination. In daily life, I was going to tell her, there are also such useful things as the plain facts that should be stuck to, through thick and thin. Anything else led to confusion like this. I was beginning to enjoy my letter to Louise when a sturdy boy about twelve years old crossed the platform. As he neared me, he took off his rough cap and bunched it in his thick hand, dirt-stained at the knuckles. His round cheeks, his round nose, his round chin were a cool, healthy red. In the globe of his face, as neatly circular as if drawn in bright crayon, his narrow, long, tip-tilted eyes, clear as pale-blue water, seemed out of place, as if two incompatible strains had collided in making him. They were beautiful eyes, and the rest of the face was not to be taken seriously. A blue woollen blouse buttoned up to his chin ended abruptly at his waist as if he would outgrow it in another half hour, and his blue drill breeches flapped about his ankles. His old clodhopper shoes were several sizes too big for him. Altogether, it was plain he was not the first one to wear his clothes. He was a cheerful, detached, self-possessed apparition against the tumbled brown earth and ragged dark sky, and I smiled at him as well as I could with a face that felt like wet clay.

He smiled back slightly without meeting my eye, motioning for me to take up my suitcase. He swung my trunk to his head and tottered across the uneven platform, down the steps slippery with mud where I expected to see him crushed beneath his burden like an ant under a stone. He heaved the trunk into the back of his wagon with a fine smash, took my suitcase and tossed it after, then climbed up over one front wheel while I scrambled my way up over the other.

The pony, shaggy as a wintering bear, eased himself into a grudging trot, while the boy, bowed over with his cap pulled down over his ears and eyebrows, held the reins slack and fell into a brown study. I studied the harness, a real mystery. It met and clung in all sorts of unexpected places; it parted company in what appeared to be strategic seats of jointure. It was mended sketchily in risky places with bits of hairy rope. Other seemingly unimportant parts were bound together irrevocably with wire. The bridle was too long for the pony's stocky head, so he had shaken the bit out of his mouth at the start, apparently, and went his own way at his own pace.

Our vehicle was an exhausted specimen of something called a spring wagon, who knows why? There were no springs, and the shallow enclosed platform at the back, suitable for carrying various plunder, was worn away until it barely reached midway of the back wheels, one side of it steadily scraping the iron tire. The wheels themselves spun not dully around and around in the way of common wheels, but elliptically, being loosened at the hubs, so that we proceeded with a drunken, hilarious swagger, like the rolling motion of a small boat on a choppy sea.

The soaked brown fields fell away on either side of the lane, all rough with winter-worn stubble ready to sink and become earth again. The scanty leafless woods ran along an edge of the field nearby. There was nothing beautiful in those woods now except the promise of spring, for I detested bleakness, but it gave me pleasure to think that beyond this there might be something else beautiful in its own being, a river shaped and contained by its banks, or a field stripped down to its true meaning, ploughed and ready for the seed. The road turned abruptly and was almost hidden for a moment, and we were going through the woods. Closer sight of the crooked branches assured me that spring was beginning, if sparely, reluctantly: the leaves were budding in tiny cones of watery green besprinkling all the new shoots; a thin sedate rain began again to fall, not so opaque as a fog, but a mist that merely deepened overhead, and lowered, until the clouds became rain in one swathing, delicate grey.

As we emerged from the woods, the boy roused himself and pointed forward, in silence. We were approaching the farm along the skirts of a fine peach orchard, now faintly colored with young bud, but there was nothing to disguise the gaunt and aching ugliness of the farmhouse itself. In this Texas valley, so gently modulated with small crests and shallows, "rolling country" as the farmers say, the house was set on the peak of the barest rise of ground, as if the most infertile spot had been thriftily chosen for building a shelter. It stood there staring and naked, an intruding stranger, strange even beside the barns ranged generously along the back, low-eaved and weathered to the color of stone.

The narrow windows and the steeply sloping roof oppressed me; I wished to turn away and go back. I had come a long way to be so disappointed, I thought, and yet I must go on, for there could be nothing here for me more painful than what I had left. But as we drew near the house, now hardly visible except for the yellow lamplight in the back, perhaps in the kitchen, my feelings changed again toward warmth and tenderness, or perhaps just an apprehension that I could feel so, maybe, again.

The wagon drew up before the porch, and I started climbing down. No sooner had my foot touched ground than an enormous black dog of the detestable German shepherd breed leaped silently at me, and as silently I covered my face with my arms and leaped back. "Kuno, down!" shouted the boy, lunging at him. The front door flew open and a young girl with yellow hair ran down the steps and seized the ugly beast by the scruff. "He does not mean anything," she said seriously in English. "He is only a dog."

Just Louise's darling little puppy Kuno, I thought, a year or so older. Kuno whined, apologized by bowing and scraping one front paw on the ground, and the girl holding his scruff said, shyly and proudly, "I teach him that. He has always such bad manners, but I teach him!"

I had arrived, it seemed, at the moment when the evening chores were about to begin. The entire Müller household streamed out of the door, each man and woman going about the affairs of the moment. The young girl walked with me up the porch and said, "This is my brother Hans," and a young man paused to shake hands and passed by. "This is my brother Fritz," she said, and Fritz took my hand and dropped it as he went. "My sister Annetje," said the young girl, and a quiet young woman with a baby draped loosely like a scarf over her shoulder smiled and held out her hand. Hand after hand went by, their palms variously younger or older, broad or small, male or female, but all thick hard decent peasant hands, warm and strong. And in every face I saw again the pale, tilted eyes, on every head that taffy-colored hair, as though they might all be brothers and sisters, though Annetje's husband and still another daughter's husband had gone by after greeting me. In the wide hall with a door at front and back, full of cloudy light and the smell of soap, the old mother, also on her way out, stopped to offer her hand. She was a tall strong-looking woman wearing a three-cornered black wool shawl on her head, her skirts looped up over a brown flannel petticoat. Not from her did the young ones get those water-clear eyes. Hers were black and shrewd and searching, a band of hair showed black streaked with grey, her seamed dry face was brown as seasoned bark, and she walked in her rubber boots with the stride of a man. She shook my hand briefly and said in German English that I was welcome, smiling and showing her blackened teeth.

"This is my girl Hatsy," she told me, "and she will show you to your room." Hatsy took my hand as if I were a child needing a guide. I followed her up a flight of steps steep as a ladder, and there we were, in Louise's attic room, with the sloping roof. Yes, the shingles were stained all the colors she had said. There were the dime novels heaped in the corner. For once, Louise had got it straight, and it was homely and familiar, as if I had seen it before. "My mother says we could give you a better place on the downstairs," said Hatsy, in her soft blurred English, "but *she* said in her letter you would like it so." I told her indeed I did like it so. She went down the steep stairs then, and her brother came up as if he were climbing a tree, with the trunk on his head and the suitcase in his right hand, and I could not see what kept the trunk from crashing back to the bottom, as he used the left hand to climb with. I wished to offer help but feared to insult him, having noted well the tremendous ease and style with which he had hurled the luggage around before, a strong man doing his turn before a weakling audience. He put his burden down and straightened up, wriggling his shoulders and panting only a little. I thanked him and he pushed his cap back and pulled it forward again, which I took for some sort of polite response, and clattered out hugely. Looking out of my window a few minutes later, I saw him setting off across the fields carrying a lighted lantern and a large steel trap.

I began changing my first letter to Louise. "I'm going to like it here. I don't quite know why, but it's going to be all right. Maybe I can tell you later——"

The sound of the German speech in the household below was part of the pleasantness, for they were not talking to me and did not expect me to answer. All the German I understood then was contained in five small deadly sentimental songs of Heine's, learned by heart; and this was a very different tongue, Low German corrupted by three generations in a foreign country. A dozen miles away, where Texas and Louisiana melted together in a rotting swamp whose sluggish undertow of decay nourished the roots of pine and cedar, a colony of French emigrants had lived out two hundred years of exile, not wholly incorruptible, but mystically faithful to the marrow of their bones, obstinately speaking their old French by then as strange to the French as it was to the English. I had known many of these families during a certain long summer happily remembered, and here again, listening to another language nobody could understand except those of this small farming community, I knew that I was again in a house of perpetual exile. These were solid, practical, hard-bitten, land-holding German peasants, who struck their mattocks into the earth deep and held fast wherever they were, because to them life and the land were one indivisible thing; but never in any wise did they confuse nationality with habitation.

I liked the thick warm voices, and it was good not to have to understand what they were saying. I loved that silence which means freedom from the constant pressure of other minds and other opinions and other feelings, that freedom to fold up in quiet and go back to my own center, to find out again, for it is always a rediscovery, what kind of creature it is that rules me finally, makes all the decisions no matter who thinks they make them, even I; who little by little takes everything away except the one thing I cannot live without, and who will one day say, "Now I am all you have left—take me." I paused there a good while listening to this muted unknown language which was silence with music in it; I could be moved and touched but not troubled by it, as by the crying of frogs or the wind in the trees.

The catalpa tree at my window would, I noticed, when it came into leaf, shut off my view of the barns and the fields beyond. When in bloom the branches would almost reach through the window. But now they were a thin screen through which the calves, splotchy red and white, moved prettily against the weathered darkness of the sheds. The brown fields would soon be green again; the sheep washed by the rains and become clean grey. All the beauty of the landscape now was in the harmony of the valley rolling fluently away to the wood's edge. It was an inland country, with the forlorn look of all unloved things; winter in this part of the south is a moribund coma, not the northern death sleep with the sure promise of resurrection. But in my south, my loved and never-forgotten country, after her long sickness, with only a slight stirring, an opening of the eyes between one breath and the next, between night and day, the earth revives and bursts into the plenty of spring with fruit and flowers together, spring and summer at once under the hot shimmering blue sky.

The freshening wind promised another light sedate rain to come at evening. The voices below stairs dispersed, rose again, separately calling from the yards and barns. The old woman strode down the path toward the cow sheds, Hatsy running behind her. The woman wore her wooden yoke, with the milking pails covered and closed with iron hasps, slung easily across her shoulders, but her daughter carried two tin milking pails on her arm. When they pushed back the bars of cedar which opened onto the fields, the cows came through lowing and crowding, and the calves scampered each to his own dam with reaching, opened mouths. Then there was the battle of separating the hungry children from their mothers when they had taken their scanty share. The old woman slapped their little haunches with her open palm, Hatsy dragged at their halters, her feet slipping wide in the mud, the cows bellowed and brandished their horns, the calves bawled like rebellious babies. Hatsy's long yellow braids whisked around her shoulders, her laughter was a shrill streak of gaiety above the angry cow voices and the raucous shouting of the old woman.

From the kitchen porch below came the sound of splashing water, the creaking of the pump handle, and the stamping boots of men. I sat in the window watching the darkness come on slowly, while all the lamps were being lighted. My own small lamp had a handle on the oil bowl, like a cup's. There was also a lantern with a frosted chimney hanging by a nail on the wall. A voice called to me from the foot of my stairs and I looked down into the face of a dark-skinned, flaxen-haired young woman, far advanced in pregnancy, and carrying a prosperous year-old boy on her hip, one arm clutching him to her, the other raised above her head so that her lantern shone upon their heads. "The supper is now ready," she said, and waited for me to come down before turning away.

In the large square room the whole family was gathering at a long table covered with a red checkered cotton cloth, with heaped-up platters of steaming food at either end. A crippled and badly deformed servant girl was setting down pitchers of milk. Her face was so bowed over it was almost hidden, and her whole body was maimed in some painful, mysterious way, probably congenital, I supposed, though she seemed wiry and tough. Her knotted hands shook continually, her wagging head kept pace with her restless elbows. She ran unsteadily around the table scattering plates, dodging whoever stood in her way; no one moved aside for her, or spoke to her, or even glanced after her when she vanished into the kitchen.

The men then moved forward to their chairs. Father Müller took his patriarch's place at the head of the table, Mother Müller looming behind him like a dark boulder. The younger men ranged themselves about on one side, the married ones with their wives standing back of their chairs to serve them, for three generations in this country had not made them self-conscious or disturbed their ancient customs. The two sons-in-law and three sons rolled down their shirt sleeves before beginning to eat. Their faces were polished with recent scrubbing and their open collars were damp.

Mother Müller pointed to me, then waved her hand at her household, telling off their names rapidly. I was a stranger and a guest, so was seated on the men's side of the table, and Hatsy, whose real name turned out to be Huldah, the maiden of the family, was seated on the children's side of the board, attending to them and keeping them in order. These infants ranged from two years to ten, five in number—not counting the one still straddling his mother's hip behind his father's chair—divided between the two married daughters. The children ravened and gorged and reached their hands into the sugar bowl to sprinkle sugar on everything they ate, solemnly elated over their food and paying no attention to Hatsy, who struggled with them only a little less energetically than she did with the calves, and ate almost nothing. She was about seventeen years old, pale-lipped and too thin, and her sleek fine butter-yellow hair, streaked light and dark, real German peasant hair, gave her an air of fragility. But she shared the big-boned structure and the enormous energy and animal force that was like a bodily presence itself in the room; and seeing Father Müller's pale-grey deep-set choleric eyes and high cheekbones, it was easy to trace the family resemblance around the table: it was plain that poor Mother Müller had never had a child of her own—black-eyed, black-haired South Germany people. True, she had borne them, but that was all; they belonged to their father. Even the tawny Gretchen, expecting another baby, obviously the pet of the family, with the sly smiling manner of a spoiled child, who wore the contented air of a lazy, healthy young animal, seeming always about to yawn, had hair like pulled taffy and those slanted clear eyes. She stood now easing the weight of her little boy on her husband's chair back, reaching with her left arm over his shoulder to refill his plate from time to time.

Annetje, the eldest daughter, carried her newly born baby over her shoulder, where he drooled comfortably down her back, while she spooned things from platters and bowls for her husband. Whenever their eyes met, they smiled with a gentle, reserved warmth in their eyes, the smile of long and sure friendship.

Father Müller did not in the least believe in his children's marrying and leaving home. Marry, yes, of course; but must that take a son or daughter from him? He always could provide work and a place in the household for his daughters' husbands, and in time he would do the same for his sons' wives. A new room had lately been built on, to the northeast, Annetje explained to me, leaning above her husband's head and talking across the table, for Hatsy to live in when she should be married. Hatsy turned very beautifully pink and ducked her head almost into her plate, then looked up boldly and said, "Jah, jah, I am marrit now soon!" Everybody laughed except Mother Müller, who said in German that girls at home never knew when they were well off—no, they must go bringing in husbands. This remark did not seem to hurt anybody's feelings, and Gretchen said it was nice that I was going to be here for the wedding. This reminded Annetje of something, and she spoke in English to the table at large, saying that the Lutheran pastor had advised her to attend church oftener and put her young ones in Sunday school, so that God would give her a blessing with her fifth child. I counted around again, and sure enough, with Gretchen's unborn, there were eight children at that table under the age of ten; somebody was going to need a blessing in all that crowd, no doubt. Father Müller delivered a short speech to his daughter in German, then turned to me and said, "What I say iss, it iss all craziness to go to church and pay a preacher goot money to talk his nonsense. Say rather that he pay me to come and lissen, then I vill go!" His eyes glared with sudden fierceness above his square speckled grey and yellow beard that sprouted directly out from the high cheekbones. "He thinks, so, that my time maybe costs nothing? That iss goot! Let him pay me!"

Mother Müller snorted and shuffled her feet. "Ach, you talk, you talk. Now you vill make the pastor goot and mad if he hears. Vot ve do, if he vill not chrissen the babies?"

"You give him goot money, he vill chrissen," shouted Father Müller. "You vait und see!"

"Ah sure, dot iss so," agreed Mother Müller. "Only do not let him hear!"

There was a gust of excited talk in German, with much rapping of knife handles on the table. I gave up trying to understand, but watched their faces. It sounded like a pitched battle, but they were agreeing about something. They were united in their tribal skepticisms, as in everything else. I got a powerful impression that they were all, even the sons-in-law, one human being divided into several separate appearances. The crippled servant girl brought in more food and gathered up plates and went away in her limping run, and she seemed to me the only individual in the house. Even I felt divided into many fragments, having left or lost a part of myself in every place I had traveled, in every life mine had touched, above all, in every death of someone near to me that had carried into the grave some part of my living cells. But the servant, she was whole, and belonged nowhere. . . .

The *Turnverein* was an octagonal pavilion set in a cleared space in a patch of woods belonging to Father Müller. The German colony came here to sit about in the cool shade, while a small brass band played cloppity country dances. The girls danced with energy and direction, their starched petticoats rustling like dry leaves. The boys were more awkward, but willing; they clutched their partners' waists and left crumpled sweaty spots where they clutched. Here Mother Müller took her ease after a hard week. Her gaunt limbs would relax, her knees spread squarely apart, and she would gossip over her beer with the women of her own generation. They would cast an occasional caretaking glance at the children playing nearby, allowing the younger mothers freedom to dance or sit in peace with their own friends.

On the other side of the pavilion, Father Müller would sit with the sober grandfathers, their long curved pipes wagging on their chests as they discussed local politics with profound gravity, their hard peasant fatalism tempered only a little by a shrewd worldly distrust of all office holders not personally known to them, all political plans except their own immediate ones. When Father Müller talked, they listened respectfully, with faith in him as a strong man, head of his own house and his community. They nodded slowly whenever he took his pipe from his mouth and gestured, holding it by the bowl as if it were a stone he was getting ready to throw. On our way back from the *Turnverein* one evening, Mother Müller said to me, "Well, now, by the grace of Gott it is all settled between Hatsy and her man. It is next Sunday by this time they will be marrit."

All the folk who usually went to the *Turnverein* on Sundays came instead to the Müller house for the wedding. They brought useful presents, mostly bed linen, pillow covers, a white counterpane, with a few ornaments for the bridal chamber—a home-braided round rug in many colors, a brass-bottomed lamp with a round pink chimney decorated with red roses, a stone china wash-bowl and pitcher also covered with red roses; and the bridegroom's gift to the bride was a necklace, a double string of red coral twigs. Just before the short ceremony began, he slipped the necklace over her head with trembling hands. She smiled up at him shakily and helped him disentangle her short veil from the coral, then they joined hands and turned their faces to the pastor, not letting go until time for the exchange of rings—the widest, thickest, reddest gold bands to be found, no doubt—and at that moment they both stopped smiling and turned a little pale. The groom recovered first, and bent over—he was considerably taller than she—and kissed her on the forehead. His eyes were a deep blue, and his hair not really Müller taffy color, but a light chestnut; a good-looking, gentle-tempered boy, I decided, and he looked at Hatsy as if he liked what he saw. They knelt and clasped hands again for the final prayer, then stood together and exchanged the bridal kiss, a very chaste reserved one, still not on the lips. Then everybody came to shake hands and the men all kissed the bride and the women all kissed the groom. Some of the women whispered in Hatsy's ear, and all burst out laughing except Hatsy, who turned red from her forehead to her throat. She whispered in turn to her husband, who nodded in agreement. She then tried to slip away quietly, but the watchful young girls were after her, and shortly we saw her running through the blossoming orchard, holding up her white ruffled skirts, with all the girls in pursuit, shrieking and calling like excited hunters, for the first to overtake and touch her would be the next bride. They returned, breathless, dragging the lucky one with them, and held her against her ecstatic resistance, while all the young boys kissed her.

The guests stayed on for a huge supper, and Ottilie came in, wearing a fresh blue apron, sweat beaded in the wrinkles of her forehead and around her formless mouth, and passed the food around the table. The men ate first and then Hatsy came in with the women for the first time, still wearing her square little veil of white cotton net bound on her hair with peach blossoms shattered in the bride's race. After supper, one of the girls played waltzes and polkas on the melodeon, and everyone danced. The bridegroom drew gallons of beer from a keg set up in the hall, and at midnight everybody went away, warmly emotional and happy. I went down to the kitchen for a pitcher of hot water. The servant was still setting things to rights, hobbling between table and cupboard. Her face was a brown smudge of anxiety, her eyes were wide and dazed. Her uncertain hands rattled among the pans, but nothing could make her seem real, or in any way connected with the life around her. Yet when I set my pitcher on the stove, she lifted the heavy kettle and poured the scalding water into it without spilling a drop.

The clear honey green of the early morning sky was a mirror of the bright earth. At the edge of the woods there had sprung a reticent blooming of small white and pale-colored flowers. The peach trees were now each a separate nosegay of shell rose and white. I left the house, meaning to take the short path across to the lane of mulberries. The women were deep in the house, the men were away to the fields, the animals were turned into the pastures, and only Ottilie was visible, sitting on the steps of the back porch peeling potatoes. She gazed in my direction with eyes that fell short of me, and seemed to focus on a point midway between us, and gave no sign. Then she dropped her knife and rose, her mouth opened and closed several times, she strained toward me, motioning with her right hand. I went to her, her hands came out and clutched my sleeve, and for a moment I feared to hear her voice. There was no sound from her, but she drew me along after her, full of some mysterious purpose of her own. She opened the door of a dingy bitter-smelling room, windowless, which opened off the kitchen, beside the closet where Hatsy took her baths. A lumpy narrow cot and chest of drawers supporting a blistered looking-glass almost filled the space. Ottilie's lips moved, struggling for speech, as she pulled and tumbled over a heap of rubbish in the top drawer. She took out a photograph and put it in my hands. It was in the old style, faded to a dirty yellow, mounted on cardboard elaborately clipped and gilded at the edges.

I saw a girl child about five years old, a pretty smiling German baby, looking curiously like a slightly elder sister of Annetje's two-year-old, wearing a frilled frock and a prodigious curl of blond hair, called a roach, on the crown of her head. The strong legs, round as sausages, were encased in long white ribbed stockings, and the square firm feet were laced into old-fashioned soft-soled black boots. Ottilie peered over the picture, twisted her neck, and looked up into my face. I saw the slanted water-blue eyes and the high cheekbones of the Müllers again, mutilated, almost destroyed, but unmistakable. This child was what she had been, and she was without doubt the elder sister of Annetje and Gretchen and Hatsy; in urgent pantomime she insisted that this was so—she patted the picture and her own face, and strove terribly to speak. She pointed to the name written carefully on the back, Ottilie, and touched her mouth with her bent knuckles. Her head wagged in her perpetual nod; her shaking hand seemed to flap the photograph at me in a roguish humor. The bit of cardboard connected her at once somehow to the world of human beings I knew; for an instant some filament lighter than cobweb spun itself out between that living center in her and in me, a filament from some center that held us all bound to our unescapable common source, so that her life and mine were kin, even a part of each other, and the painfulness and strangeness of her vanished. She knew well that she had been Ottilie, with those steady legs and watching eyes, and she was Ottilie still within herself. For a moment, being alive, she knew she suffered, for she stood and shook with silent crying, smearing away her tears with the open palm of her hand. Even while her cheeks were wet, her face changed. Her eyes cleared and fixed themselves upon that point in space which seemed for her to contain her unaccountable and terrible troubles. She turned her head as if she had heard a voice and disappeared in her staggering run into the kitchen, leaving the drawer open and the photograph face downward on the chest.

At midday meal she came hurrying and splashing coffee on the white floor, restored to her own secret existence of perpetual amazement, and again I had been a stranger to her like all the rest but she was no stranger to me, and could not be again.

The youngest brother came in, holding up an opossum he had caught in his trap. He swung the furry body from side to side, his eyes fairly narrowed with pride as he showed us the mangled creature. "No, it is cruel, even for the wild animals," said gentle Annetje to me, "but boys love to kill, they love to hurt things. I am always afraid he will trap poor Kuno." I thought privately that Kuno, a wolfish, ungracious beast, might well prove a match for any trap. Annetje was full of silent, tender solicitudes. The kittens, the puppies, the chicks, the lambs and calves were her special care. She was the only one of the women who caressed the weanling calves when she set the pans of milk before them. Her child seemed as much a part of her as if it were not yet born. Still, she seemed to have forgotten that Ottilie was her sister. So had all the others. I remembered how Hatsy had spoken her name but had not said she was her sister. Their silence about her was, I realized, exactly that—simple forgetfulness. She moved among them as invisible to their imaginations as a ghost. Ottilie their sister was something painful that had happened long ago and now was past and done for; they could not live with that memory or its visible reminder—they forgot her in pure self-defense. But I could not forget her. She drifted into my mind like a bit of weed carried in a current and caught there, floating but fixed, refusing to be carried away. I reasoned it out. The Müllers, what else could they have done with Ottilie? By a physical accident in her child-hood she had been stripped of everything but her mere existence. It was not a society or a class that pampered its invalids and the unfit. So long as one lived, one did one's share. This was her place, in this family she had been born and must die; did she suffer? No one asked, no one looked to see. Suffering went with life, suffering and labor. While one lived one worked, that was all, and without complaints, for no one had time to listen, and everybody had his own troubles. So, what else could they have done with Ottilie? As for me, I could do nothing but promise myself that I would forget her, too; and to remember her for the rest of my life.

Sitting at the long table, I would watch Ottilie clattering about in her tormented haste, bringing in that endless food that represented all her life's labors. My mind would follow her into the kitchen where I could see her peering into the great simmering kettles, the crowded oven, her whole body a mere machine of torture. Straight up to the surface of my mind the thought would come urgently, clearly, as if driving time toward the desired event: Let it be now, let it be *now*. Not even tomorrow, no, today. Let her sit down quietly in her rickety chair by the stove and fold those arms, and let us find her there like that, with her head fallen forward on her knees. She will rest then. I would wait, hoping she might not come again, ever again, through that door I gazed at with wincing cycs, as if I might see something unendurable enter through it. Then she would come, and it was only Ottilie, after all, in the bosom of her family, and one of its most useful and competent members; and they with a deep right instinct had learned to live with her disaster on its own terms, and hers; they had accepted and then made use of what was for them only one more painful event in a world full of troubles, many of them much worse than this. So, a step at a time, I followed the Müllers as nearly as I could in their acceptance of Ottilie, and the use they made of her life, for in some way that I could not quite explain to myself, I found great virtue and courage in their steadiness and refusal to feel sorry for anybody, least of all for themselves. . . .

III • OIL AND DUST AND DREAMS OF GLORY

A. C. Greene

A. C. Greene (b. 1923) is widely considered Texas's most influential book critic and reviewer. Among his own writings, A Personal Country—*a book of reflections on life in West Texas—is in its third edition, and demonstrates his writing philosophy: "You have to think you're saying something that never has quite been revealed in quite this fashion about quite this situation. And then you write."*

HOW THE OIL CAME

RANGER TAUGHT US the definition of "boom town." There were oil booms before and booms were to come, but the Ranger boom was the classic, the standard against which the others are measured. By the end of December other oil companies had land men crawling all over the territory signing up mineral rights. As a portent, the old well at Nannie Walker's farm came to life and waked the whole town early New Year's Day, 1918, with an awesome roar as it started blowing millions of cubic feet of gas, then belched strongly a few weeks later and gushed up oil. Before 1918 was out other wells had flowed seven thousand, then eight thousand barrels a day, and finally one hit eleven thousand.

The effect on the countryside was spectacular. Ranger, which had eight hundred persons when the McClesky was drilled, was roiling with thirty thousand a year later and more arriving on the special trains the T&P ran from Fort Worth five times a day. (The railroad's receipts are a good yardstick: $94,000 worth of business in Ranger in 1917 and eighteen months later, $8,146,000 annually.)

Right outside Ranger, along today's Interstate 20, was a gate with a metal sign over it, MERRIMAN CEMETERY. This was the site of the old town of Merriman, Eastland County's first county seat. By the time oil came Merriman had been reduced to a Baptist church and a cemetery. The church turned out to be sitting right over a pool of petroleum and the congregation was offered a goodly sum for the drilling rights on its two acres. But the Baptists formed a drilling company of their own, hit three good wells, and voted to give the Lord eighty-five percent of the money and spend fifteen percent on a new church house.

The Merriman Cemetery made legend. It was reported that the

cemetery association had been offered one million dollars for rights to the graveyard but the members had turned it down because it would disturb their dead. Some semipro bard immediately burst into print in an oil journal with a poem which began, "There's a churchyard down in Ranger . . ." and ending, ". . . standing guard above the gravestones in a lot that's not for sale." (I must have heard the poem given a dozen times in declamation contests during my school days.) Years later the legend was trimmed somewhat more to size when the head of the cemetery group admitted the land had been deeded for burial uses only and reverted to the donors if put to any other purpose.

The town of Ranger became impossible to get to, impossible to walk in, impossible to eat or sleep in. Any kind of flimsy shack was run up and titled a hotel. At least one major West Texas fortune was made when a sharp young country boy from Stephens County listened through the canvas room partition in the hotel where he was staying and overheard a group of investors talking about a big lease killing they were going to bring off next day. He buggied out at dawn (being a farm boy and understanding when a farmer has the most time for business) and sewed the deal up before the outside investors arrived.

Those were the days before oil fields used motor equipment to any extent. Mules and oxen pulled the pipe, cable reels, and boilers. They made loblolly of the streets when it rained. There were men in hip boots at every intersection in Ranger who got two bits a trip for carrying passengers piggyback through the mud. (It cost two dollars a night to sleep in a barber chair.)

Oil, of course, made money, and sin was its invariable companion. Whiskey palaces, gambling halls, and cabarets blazed through the night, waiting to accommodate the oilmen no matter which tower (the oilfield term for a shift) they worked. The names of the cabarets were colorful: Blue Mouse, Palm Island, Grizzly Bear, Old Oklahoma. In one twenty-four-hour period there were five murders in Ranger.

But the lawlessness got to be too much even for roaring Ranger. The Texas Rangers sneaked into town by the back roads one night (the gamblers kept watch at such points as Eastland and Cisco) and captured ninety gamblers and their equipment. A few months later the town's morals got a final jolt from, of all unlikely agencies, the Rotary Club. These gentlemen, joined by the police (who may have had mixed emotions about doing so, since the pay-off was rumored to be astronomical), went down the streets joint by joint, hauling out the wheels, dice tables and boards and smashing the bottles and kegs of outlawed (by prohibition) liquor. By the end of that day the sinners had given up on Ranger.

Within a year the Ranger pool had been proved to stretch from the north end of Stephens County to the south end of Eastland—nearly sixty miles. One field, Breckenridge, was as big as the original and almost as rowdy.

This was a petroleum frontier, an industrial new country in which greed offered the motives which fair play lacked. There was no thought given to conservation. The mechanical and technical equipment was about the same as had been used at Spindletop in 1901—cable-tool drilling rigs that strained to get below three thousand feet; wooden derricks, some as tall as an eight-story building, which had to be constructed by hand; steam boilers for power, fired with wood or by piping crude natural gas directly from the well. The few trucks of a size to haul the cumbersome equipment were less useful than oxen because there were no roads, except dirt tracks, outside the towns.

The main difference between the oil booms of that time and a later day, however, was not so much in the technicians or the equipment they used as in what we might call the philosophy of drilling. Everyone wanted to get rich quick and looked on the chance to do so as one for which he was accountable only to his opportunity and skill. The average oilman of the period, often out of ignorance, nevertheless was totally irresponsible. . . .

Promoters, in fact, liked to let a well "gush" for as long as it would because the spectacular sight of oil roaring up a hundred feet into the air stirred investors like nothing else could.

Today massive drill collars and valves keep this waste of gas and crude from taking place, and stringent regulations concerning well spacing and production days per month are set by the Texas Railroad Commission (which controls the petroleum production industry).

Of the other booms around Ranger, one achieved a legendary status of its own. The field was named for the little village it surrounded, Desdemona, but throughout the oil world it was called Hogtown, because it centered on a marshy trickle known as Hog Creek.

Hogtown, for sheer bad manners, was the worst oil boom in Texas history, according to those myth-making experts who followed the booms. The original city of Desdemona had obtained a post office in 1870 under the name "Desdemonia"—a brave attempt to honor Shakespeare's "white ewe" of Othello. For some reason the post office department didn't get around to changing it to the literary spelling until 1901. Desdemona, fifteen miles south of Ranger, played a hunch. In 1914 all its one hundred citizens met at the Hog Creek school and formed the Hog Creek Oil Company. They felt sure they were sitting on oil. The water wells gave off a substance called damp gas and it smelled exactly like the shallow oil wells at Strawn, according to some citizens who had traveled up there to take a sniff. For another thing, Hog Creek had an oil scum form on its quiet waters now and then. And to top it off, some local scientist had taken a map and drawn a straight line down from Petrolia, the hottest oil site in Oklahoma at the time, through Strawn (whose wells turned out to be minor), and found it extended right through Hogtown. How could nature go against all these signs? (The points were given in a letter a local enthusiast sent to his kinfolks.)

But this faith in signs took a bruising in the next four years. The first well, on a lease owned by the village barber, ran out of funds twice, then was a dry hole at fifteen hundred feet. An Oklahoman was persuaded to bring in his spudder (a drilling rig) but he too ran out of money without any oil on his bits. Fortunately for Hogtown's history, a third attempt got W. E. Wrather (who later became director of the United States Geological Survey) down from Wichita Falls and while exploring a fork of Hog Creek he found an anticline—an upfold of rock which sometimes traps oil. He said it looked promising, so a new Hog Creek Oil Company was formed and a third site picked for drilling. On the night of September 2, 1918, Hogtown finally got oil. The well promptly caught fire from the tool dresser's forge and it took three days of high-pressure steam from four boilers to put out the flames, but it became a two-thousand-barrel-a-day producer. That tilted Eastland County a bit and drained several thousand of the Ranger crowd down to Desdemona-Hogtown.

From the beginning it was a mean, sinful place. Years later I talked to a man who lived through the whole boom, and he mentioned one well-known West Texan who had run a shanty café in Hogtown's palmy days.

"I don't know what happened to us," the man told me. "It seemed like nothing much mattered but 'get that oil out of the ground.' We lost our civilizing. We did things I don't expect anybody anywhere else did and I still can't tell you why. Like Charlie B———. I saw him get so mad once at a big guy who was sleeping with Charlie's girl that he got right down on the ground on the main street and rolled around eating dirt. There must have been a couple hundred people looking. Stuffing his mouth full of dirt and shaking his head and growling like a dog, out in front of that old tent where he run his café. This big guy just stood there watching Charlie eat dirt, laughing at him with an arm around this girl they were sharing."

The women who came in with the Hogtown oil boom were mostly like the one Charlie ate dirt over. They matched the town's nickname. They were brazen like few prostitutes have been in petroleum history, stopping men on the streets at noon to solicit trade and, according to the man who was there, "selling quite a bit of it in broad daylight on the back seat of a Model T touring car."

Squads of the professional ladies would drive out to the wells and offer the crews door-to-door service, day and night. Maybe this sort of thing happened because Hogtown was away from the beaten track, without railroads or nearby cities to civilize it. Maybe the local population was just too small to control the tide of sinful humanity that swept in, and so simply drowned in it.

The Desdemona-Hogtown field was one where the little operator had a chance. In Ranger the major companies controlled most of the producing leases—Humble Oil, then a smaller firm, was bought by Standard so that the big firm could get production in Ranger. But in Desdemona the majors hadn't taken the trouble to lease up the countryside and the Hog Creek Company only had five thousand acres. Many of the other leases, handled by individuals who plunged the family savings into the only size tracts they could afford, were tiny. One lease was for a hundredth of an acre—about the size of a master bedroom. After the Hogtown field had been defined by drilling it could be seen that had either of those first two dry holes been drilled as little as one hundred yards farther north they would have hit oil.

By January 1919, hundreds of wells had been drilled in the compact field, including a famous hole known as the Payne gasser which blew off 40 million cubic feet of gas a day and whose roar could be heard twenty-five miles away. Only a mile from the discovery well the Hogg well flowed fifteen thousand barrels a day to lead the field in production. There just weren't enough pipes, tank wagons, and storage containers to take care of the gushers, and earthen tanks and dirt reservoirs thrown up to catch the overflow were themselves overflowed. Dams were thrown across creeks and gullies, and lakes of crude oil formed behind them. At one time traffic on the road between Hogtown and De Leon (the nearest railroad) was blocked by a river of oil flowing three feet deep over the highway.

The townsite turned out to be the best part of the field and houses, shacks and tents sat amongst the derricks and confusion of the well sites.

Lawlessness of the highjacking and extortion kind became a problem. The "protection" racket was so blatant that men were coming around to the derricks daily to collect from the workers, and some collectors were so cocksure they gave credit between paydays.

But the thug element moved on rather speedily from Hogtown-Desdemona. The Rangers had to come in, but that wasn't the only reason. The field showed its size quickly. It ran only about three miles by three miles and it didn't take long to drill this up. The boom had no place to go, so it left. "Live fast, die young, and make a beautiful corpse" is an old West Texas honky-tonkism, and (aside from the morbid beauty part) that's the way it was with Desdemona. The field output hit 7,375,000 barrels in 1919, dropped to 2,767,000 barrels in 1920 and was making only one-tenth of that by the time the decade was out. Desdemona, from its frantic thousands, settled down to about 150 persons. But, for what that final nicety is worth, it's not called Hogtown any more.

Ranger's peak production year was 1919 when the field averaged 73,000 barrels of oil per day. Then the free-flowing gushers, the unrestrained drilling, took their toll and the field "blew its top," which means it lost its gas pressure. It has been estimated that less than one-third of the oil below Ranger and Desdemona was actually recovered. A multimillion-dollar fortune awaits the invention of an exhaustive recovery system for petroleum. Dozens of schemes have been used, some successful if instituted early enough, but most all marginally successful at best. This waste, because it became economically evident, sobered up some elements of the oil-production business, and common sense, as well as new control machinery, was introduced. Ranger taught the oil world self-control, although it was a decade in coming, and even then the business fought hard against its own best interests. (It was not until the 1950s, for example, that West Texas oilfields quit flaring gas— that is, letting it simply burn off into the air.)

Ranger today has plenty of empty buildings which have grown accustomed to being empty, and people who have grown accustomed to seeing the town's population steadily dwindle. But the romantic aura (and the literal odor) of oil hung over the town for nearly twenty years, and when we traveled through, in the late 1920s, long strings of tank cars were continually lining the T&P. Even in the mid-thirties you drove to Ranger through a modest forest of derricks and pumps.

Maybe someday some engineer will discover a way to go back down into the rock and bring out the rest of Ranger's inheritance and restore history, and life, to the place.

Kathleen McConnell

Kathleen McConnell (b. 1962) grew up in New Jersey and studied engineering at Duke University before hiring on as an oil rig worker in the Gulf of Mexico.

MEMOIRS OF AN OILFIELD SMOOTHNECK

It's my third time on a rig. I'm with another more senior engineer and two operators. One's name is Bubba. Lots of people in the oilfield have that name and I've always instinctively distrusted it. I'm soon to find out why. On this rig, I am unlucky and am sharing a room which doesn't have a private bathroom. What I do have is time to take my first shower on a rig and with Bubba set to guard the door, I'm ready. I enter the bathroom near the galley and find it filthy. The sink is grungy with hair and when I turn on the faucet, I see rusty liquid. My dirtiness overcomes my disgust and I disrobe to get into the shower. Bubba must have wandered toward the galley to sell tickets because, no sooner do I bend over to get my soap, than the door opens and in walks a roughneck in grey coveralls. I'm in a great pose for *Oui* magazine, a popular one out here, and immediately in my mind I am lowered to the level of the women in the pictures. This has nothing to do with what the poor guy must be thinking because he actually looks very embarrassed. He isn't your average rig macho man but that doesn't matter to me. I feel degraded for not being in the place that I, as a "professional woman," should be in. Frustrated to tears, I run around the rig in search of Keith, the other engineer, and to my horror find that the drilling people all look alike in their grey coveralls. Even worse, I am sure that the story is spreading. I plop down in the hallway crying but trying to hide it and be friendly to the many men who stop to chat. Finally I hear the announcement that my boat has arrived and we can leave. As we're leaving, the rig hands clamor to get to the rail to wave good-bye. My crew is laughing and I'm nearly delirious with worry that the story will get out (it did) and that my credibility will suffer because I was seen without my clothes. (It didn't.)

I've settled in at the office and don't feel so awkward. I'm friends with the engineers and have accepted an invitation to go out to the local reggae bar with the guys. All five of us are traveling together on one beeper. I'm glad for the company since I've been offshore for the last week and need some excitement. Since our company hires only the kind of people who can stay up for three nights in a row working *or* partying, I am almost guaranteed a good time with these crazy wildmen. Immediately the beeper goes off and we all tense, wondering who it's gonna be. Turns out it's for Ken who leaves after getting sympathetic back slaps from all. The rest of the gang is looking at chicks (it's hard to have a permanent relationship when you're gone all the time) while I'm figuring out when my last meaningful conversation with another female has been (only fifteen days ago). Any kind of friend is difficult to keep when you are always on call and get tentative days off once or twice a month. My seclusion, then, is not only on the rig but on the shore too.

I guess I'm not being very good company while I'm lost in thought (they all expect me to be their pseudo-girlfriend) and no one is having much luck. I'm blaming myself for their lack of a good time, as if I, as the female, am supposed to keep them entertained and happy. I don't know if I perpetuate this inane role of mine or if they do (or if the whole oil culture does); all I know is that I'm not comfortable trying to fit into these strictly defined behavioral patterns. Steve says, "There aren't *any* girls here!" and I wonder what I am. I should act like a girl but am not treated as one. I crave the acceptance that would come from being in this fraternity of brothers.

We take off for the Cajun bar next door and I get some consolation when every woman in the place turns and looks enviously at me and my entourage. (If only they knew what I had to take.) We bump into my boss and his boss (both drunk) and mine throws out his usual antifemale insults to see what I will do. I shrug them off, giving the impression that they went over my little innocent head. (In fact, they often do.)

My first big trip onto the rig floor is about to take place after having been on a few trips offshore. It's the place where the roughnecks work changing the drill pipe and it's muddy, greasy, and dangerous. I stick out like a sore thumb up there fitting in my coveralls differently (oh, to be flat-chested!) and therefore stand uncomfortably. To get to the rig floor, I have to climb about a million steps and act like I'm not out of breath when I reach the top. Physical strength is one of the qualities I must possess or at least pretend to possess in the man's world of the rig.

As I look out over the rig from my new higher vantage point I have a clear view of objects I have never really seen—the antennae, the legs of the jack-up rig, the heliport. I glance up and notice a slight change on the heliport. All the off-duty men (about seven of them) who have been sunning themselves are mooning me. For some reason, my presence makes otherwise normal men turn into the good ole boys. I'm the seed that the rainmaker pours into the cloud that causes it to rain nuttiness. The other half of the gang, the roughnecks, are looking at me waiting to see my reaction. I swallow hard, resisting my schoolgirl urge to say, "Ew, gross!" Instead I smile a little and pretend that I don't see anything. My first test of professionalism passed.

It's a really special occasion at our office. The "President's Award" is ours after 150,000 accident-free hours and he (my boss's boss's boss's boss) is coming to a gala dinner. I'm excited at the prospect of getting out of my coveralls but my enthusiasm is dimming as the day wears on and my co-workers are teasing me mercilessly. "If I see you in a dress, I'll think you're in drag," Ernie says to me, while the other engineers are mad that I get to leave early to go get my hair done. My ability to play my part well now will determine the ease with which I can progress up the ladder.

I choose a silk dress in hot pink and black which brings out my rosy complexion and shoes that are comfortable yet high enough to make me seem much taller than my five feet. I secretly hope that a little bit of makeup and curls in my long brown hair (usually worn in a braid under my hard hat) will serve my dual purpose of appearing businesslike and yet feminine enough for my co-workers to recognize me as a woman (and a sexy one at that). I am sick of their ignoring my female side, just as I resent my father's repressed desire for me to be a male.

Finally dressed, I arrive with my date, Mike, who is a tall, striking blond. Our entrance causes quite a stir. The guys in my crew rush over with their wives who are eager to meet me since they speak with me so often on the phone at three A.M. They're nice, but I can sense their jealousy and uneasiness. These are the women who get mad at their husbands when I call for them at night (we are on twenty-four-hour call) even though it's only "work" calling. I know that they have nothing to be jealous about since I'm usually so grubby and bitchy from lack of sleep; still, their feelings ring a little bell of hope.

Paul brings me my corsage and asks, "Is that *you*, Kathleen?" Jake, a quiet guy, just keeps staring and eventually tells Mike what a terrific date he has. It's so hard changing roles from male to female all the time.

If I didn't have to worry about fitting in as a woman on a man's rig, I would have more energy to spend on my actual work.

Dinner over, a favorable impression made on the bosses, Mike and I leave, amidst what I sense as astonishment that I could snag one this good. Even with their remarks about how fantastic I look, the men still seem to consider me oilfield trash. We go to see one of our favorite New Wave bands with the usual gang. I change into my pink leopard-print miniskirt, wishing that they could see this oilfield trash now, really getting down on the dance floor. Still, I think, I can show them that I'm just like any other woman, only more so.

A stray rig worker is in the unit talking to me. I had an idea that he liked me when he kept coming in to ask badly camouflaged unnecessary questions. I'd rather be resting or reading now rather than talking to him except that I need all the allies that I can get.

Out here, the drilling company controls the TV, picking the hours and the channels others can watch. The cook rules the galley and woe unto the person who comes in there when the door's closed and he's mopping the floor. The company man runs the whole show and has the right to throw anyone off the rig for any reason, most likely if they either challenge his authority (his manhood) or possibly threaten the system by being different. In this battleground, therefore, many skirmishes are being fought constantly. I become very diplomatic. My "friend" who is sitting with me can be a big help later when we go to work and I need a hand with the heavy pieces.

Just then, the fire alarm sounds. We grab life preservers (way too big for me, of course) and pile into an orange capsule that smells like throw-up though I doubt it's ever been used seriously. I'm not so scared of a fire as I am of a more dangerous blow-out. It's just a drill tonight, though, and afterward I retire to catch two hours of sleep before my work begins.

I've been working with the same crew for a while now: Willie and Nate, two large, muscular black men. When I had to ride in the truck with them because my company car caught on fire, we got lots of stares. A school bus almost had an accident because we were such a sight the day they rode home with me, each wearing a pair of my purple punk sunglasses. Today, my company car dies at home and the dynamic duo are more than happy to leave work and come and get me. On the way to work I need to stop by the dry cleaners. As we drive off, Willie tells me that they made the people at the cleaners nervous and that they had seen a commotion going on in the back. Sure enough, we spot a police car pulling in as we drive away.

I remember an incident at the docks. Nate wanted to ride in my car instead of with Willie in the truck after we'd stopped for Cokes at a 7-Eleven. The doors were locked and as he pounded away at my passenger window a bunch of Texas Ranger-type Marlboro men clambered over to my car to rescue me.

My boss, his boss, and a technical manager are intently listening to me as I begin my eighth and last hour of my oral exams necessary for my promotion. They ask about a new procedure that they'd like to see implemented. They ask what my subordinates will do when I tell them a new way of doing things. How will I handle giving orders, I, a woman two years out of college who's been in the oilfield only a fraction of the time that they have? I answer, "They'll do it and they'll say, 'Yes ma'am'." I've learned my lessons quite well on the rig; guts and glory are everything. The jury here is impressed by my show of strength and gives me the promotion with a bigger raise than many of the male engineers. As my testers leave the room they comment, "That's some woman." Translated, that means, "She's almost a man!"

Looking for my crew in the TV room, I catch a glimpse of a dirty movie and do a quick about-face. Some rigs have rules against them, others show them on occasion. Back in my bunk, where I'm hiding out embarrassed to have disrupted the secret "Elk's meeting," and disgusted at the exploitation of my fellow females, I hear an announcement over the intercom, "Highway to Heaven is on the TV now." I have to chuckle thinking of all those men having to change gears.

The hired drug detectives are at our shop with dogs searching our cars and desks for contraband. They find a bottle of Scotch in my training engineer's desk, a present from the boss at Christmas. It has one shot missing. Since he isn't as clean-cut as the other engineers, having a beard and being a Vietnam vet, a letter goes in his file. Then the real fun begins as we have to give urine samples. A refusal means that you quit your job. Since the lab test doesn't isolate alcohol (unless you've had a drink that hour) and since alcohol is the drug of choice of the good ole boys who stay drunk the majority of the time when on-shore, what the test is doing in effect is weeding out those hippie weirdo freaks who do other drugs not sanctioned by the system. Meantime Joe and Fred, your average rig workers, who leave for the rig with enough alcohol in their blood to keep them pickled at least forty-eight hours offshore, are passed along as fine and upstanding citizens, because theirs is the redneck drug of choice.

The people testing us are real losers, too, submissive types who believe enough in the system to lower themselves to the task of accompanying others to the bathroom and watching them pee. Their counterparts are the Gestapo men who in their younger days were probably Texas cops with mirror sunglasses, crew cuts, "ma'am-ing" you to death as they happily wrote you a speeding ticket while noting that they could have thrown you in jail. Now their power trip consists of sitting at the heliport and dock entrances with half-asleep police dogs—checking your bag for drugs before you go offshore.

I have been awake for fifty-six hours on another rig and finally get some time off to relax. As usual, I am too wired to sleep and have settled into my bunk to write poetry (the only logical thing to do in my stupor). The writing is going well after I get the silly limerick-type verses out of my system and settle into writing a love song. I get stuck on a rhyme and I'm feeling comfortable enough after a week out here to go in search of help. I find Jack, the company man, who has already entertained me with his (joking?) theory that his third wife is trying to kill him for his money and his only safety is offshore. He is joined by Harry, the unusual young, cheery, coherent, tool pusher, and the mud man, an innocuous person whose name I didn't get. They are fairly intent upon some project but notice my arrival. I feel so stupid asking for a dictionary, but do and, unbelievably, they have *two!* Apparently, this is a *word game rig.* Some men on rigs are really into card playing, some fishing, some movies, and some reading magazines; it's remarkable that I'm witnessing a rig involved in so academic a pursuit. They don't have time to help me with my rhyme now because they have been challenged by the roughnecks up on the floor (we can see them on the closed circuit TV monitor) to a contest. Here's an example: Three B M. (Three Blind Mice.) Thirteen L in a B D. (Thirteen Loaves in a Baker's Dozen.) I immediately get their last one, which is standing between them and a case of beer on the bank: One Thousand W T a P P. (One Thousand Words That a Picture Paints.) In the nonphysical world of word games we are on the same level and, as much as I have to stretch it, this experience fits my dream of the way rig life should be for me, all of us working together as equals. I feel satisfied and elated to see a glimpse of how it could be. Even though Jack came across as the typical chauvinist before this, he let down his barriers and opened up the whole rig hierarchy as only he could do with his enormous power. The sissy word game became macho and acceptable and I became an equal all by his decree. I am now offered coffee from Jack's special pot and can sit in his office and read his newspaper, a treat brought by the chopper pilot. The other rig workers are different too and the cook takes enough interest in me to begin sending up vegetarian platters for me, when I have to work through meals. The bet must be a topic of discussion all over the rig and I'm sure the roughnecks are furious that they lost, it all being a matter of manhood. Winning is everything, after all, and even transposed from being the strongest to being the brightest, this is the case. Jack calls a special expensive chopper for us to take back to the docks, saving us the hassle of an eight-hour boat ride, while I'm still glowing that I so easily gained the respect I always craved.

The hierarchy on the rig continues according to the common Southern scheme of submissive female and dominant male. I hate it and feel like an actress in a giant play. The company man and tool pusher, always gruff, are the male leaders, and the nice men who do manage to rise in the ranks are the first to be demoted in a crunch. The female parts are obvious: the cooks and BRs (which stands for bedrooms, the lowest job on the rig, like a maid). Any job which has a woman working it automatically, despite its complexity or respectability among outsiders, becomes a subservient one. Worse than anything is to be called "gay," and even without being a psychologist one can understand why this is so. Anyone a little bit different is threatening to these men who have only their "macho" going for them. Real individuality upsets their fragile control. That's why it perplexes me how my friend, Terry, the vegetarian company man, is able to get respect. He seems the prime target to be labeled gay. What I am, however, is worse than being gay, I'm a lowly woman. What infuriates me is not that I'm asked to do little equivalents to getting the boss a cup of coffee, but that finally I have to stay in my place and not overstep the arbitrary bounds. On one hand the rig system is laughable; on the other, I want to scream.

The hierarchy is a carryover from the Texas mainland generally. All roles are defined in terms of who has the power, and conformity to the rules is mandatory. Male-female, black-white, it's all the same thing. That's why I am always being rescued from Willie and Nate—the poor white damsel and the bad black guys.

Most of the time I would ignore all this so that I could at least function, because I feel as though it is such a losing battle, an uphill struggle with five-hundred-pound weights on my heels and no one to share the burden (at least the black men have company). To combat the odds against me, I use an innocence-deflection technique. On the rig I have to take this to the limit, ignoring the worst comments so well that often my conscious mind doesn't hear them at all. Of course by doing this, I'm playing right into their hands so that the game can continue. I become the sweet little girl who needs to be pampered, whom you can't be too hard on if something goes wrong and whom you amazedly congratulate if all goes well.

The air is heavy on the rig. Heavy with fumes. Heavy with sweat. Heavy with grease. Heavy and stale. The Gulf of Mexico is hot and extra-humid from all the water around. You can see the air rising off the metal of the rig. It's hot enough to worry about my crew getting heat stroke and about how wimpy it would be if I fainted. The grease and grit in the air are magnetically attracted to bodies. My forehead is so uncomfortable from sweat under the plastic band of my hard hat and my hair is thick with humidity and debris from the rig floor. It's so hot the dirty grease the roughnecks use to lubricate the pipe joints is like liquid, making their sculpted muscular arms stand out like those of a body-builder. The mixture of scents from the mud pits, the diesel equipment, the galley (barbecuing fatty steaks), and the multitude of drenched underarms even smells hot as it enters your lungs, which labor mightily to get enough oxygen from the thick noxious cloud. Even inside, where it's over air-conditioned, the feeling of not getting enough air pervades. Cigarette smoke, more galley smells, and odors from people saturated with petroleum mist make the air as oppressive as it is outside. At night, under the big bright rig lights, I can see the hot, fetid air swirling with gnats.

Watching the roughnecks now or sitting with them in the galley as they choke me with their cigarette smoke, I can't help getting a tiny bit sentimental about the whole situation. Once I get to know them, I can see a cute boyishness about them, an unrestrained, untamed reality to them as they are freed to curse, play cards, or whatever they want at night, and be slobs. Silly, I think, to have such a maternal feeling about men who are so much older, but I watch them and laugh inside nonetheless. Other times I get a wistful feeling and experience a bond with the common man. I'd equate this to the way a mother giving birth says that she can relate to all other mothers in an instant. I get a feeling that everyone is equal deep down and feel a sense of camaraderie from being out here together trying to make an honest living by the sweat of our brow.

About my father: He always wanted me to have a major in college that could get me a job. He wasn't especially partial to engineering, but it did satisfy his requirement and so he encouraged (mentally tormented) me to keep on in it even when I found that I didn't like it. Sometimes my father called me his son Kathleen, when he was especially proud. He downplayed the fact that I was making it in a man's world and whenever I had a down day, he'd say that I couldn't hack it because I was a woman. That made me feel a thousand times worse because I think that as a human being I did a great job of dealing with such a hard job, let alone as a woman.

My biggest triumph at my job was that last promotion. All I ever really wanted was some recognition from the company (father?) and in this case I received it. After my oral exams this time, my boss handed me my new business cards, complete with my new title on them.

Part of why my co-workers' criticism bothered me and also why I was in such a dilemma on the rig is that I am so programmed to be pleasing to men. I knew that when salary was brought up and my raises had been higher than some of the guys', I would be threatening to them and have to downplay the disparity. If someone were doing a procedure wrong, I would have to be diplomatic and let my nonassertive self take over so as not to upset the power balance. Every time something like this occurred, I would struggle to project this nonassertive side.

It was grueling having to keep up my guard all the time. When upper management suggested that the engineers wear nicer clothes than coveralls, I refused because I didn't want to stick out any more than necessary. I hated having attention drawn to myself and therefore it was almost the end of the world when that roughneck saw me in the bathroom. That's why I also hated the apparent special privileges I received. I really wanted to be one of the guys and knock down whatever male-female barriers existed. I longed to walk onto the rig and have it just be normal—*truly* normal, not having the cook (the room assigner) scrambling to figure out where to put me or the hands tittering that a "girl" was on board. It never was to be.

Throughout my time in the oilfield, I always knew that I would eventually quit. We all did, actually, and the people that I worked with had marvelous dreams about what they'd do after they had a lot of money. Keith wanted to return to his home in Bermuda and open a sail shop. John wanted some land in Alaska. The only way to stay sane when faced with living this abnormal life was to have these dreams, although few of the men would actually leave. The lure of money was enormous for them, though the idea of having power became of primary importance to me. Being a boss—having the responsibilities of millions of dollars of equipment, and having survived the male chauvinists out there as the last woman offshore in my company in my job—had given me a certain confidence that I had never been able to achieve before.

After two and a half years of work, I developed a health problem which required surgery (probably related to my job stresses, lack of sleep all this time, and breathing of toxic fumes). Suddenly I was faced with the prospect that I could suffer ill health and perhaps even die. I had slowly adjusted to the macho decadence that all the "youngsters" on the rig who continuously abused their bodies had developed. The hospital stay got me thinking more seriously about what I really wanted to do with the rest of my life. Though I'd miss it, I did not want to rot on an oil rig forever, living in a polluted wasteland onshore. So I began to plot my escape in earnest. My dad kept urging me to hang in as long as possible, get my next promotion, hang on and get through the next job. My job became extremely important to him, and since he had just retired my life gave him hours of entertainment in a vicarious kind of way. I felt his pressure intensely and agonized over the decision for weeks until I could not stand it any more.

The night I resigned, after a tearful phone call with my parents (they were tearful, and I think they felt betrayed), I sat down to a bottle of wine alone (I had no friends except through work) and felt a great loss.

Working with the men in such close quarters, I had learned to be empathetic and nonjudgmental. I could identify with my co-workers, who were also oppressed on this rig island with me. Whether one was set apart on an island of sex or color or role or relationship, we were all lonely. As in the great battle of the Alamo, there was no room out here for the weak, the women, the gays, the thinkers, or any other nonmasculine personalities. But in another way, we all became "the women" to be taken care of in this great battle against who knows what. Perhaps the whole thing was a battle against each other, for each other.

Hughes Rudd

Hughes Rudd (b. 1921) was discovered to be a gifted story writer following a career with CBS News that included positions as Moscow bureau chief in the 1960s and "CBS Morning News" anchor in the 1970s. Praised by such authors as William Styron, Thomas Pynchon, and Nelson Algren, Rudd set many of his stories in Texas, including this one about growing up in Waco during the Depression.

THE FISHERS: 1932

After Mr. Fisher lost his job as a brakeman on the Katy he bought a second-hand Chevrolet sedan and drove it as a dime taxi for a while, but there wasn't enough money in it, so he decided he would make pies.

Nobody in the neighborhood knew why he happened to think of pies; nobody asked, and he didn't say. Mr. Fisher wasn't a friendly man. He was big, brakeman-sized, and his neck was red and scaly. It was said he once killed a hobo with the brake club like a baseball bat he used to turn the boxcar brake wheels; he hadn't meant to kill him, but he was loyal to the Katy; he knew his duty.

The Fishers were the only family in the neighborhood which dealt with Sears & Roebuck through the mail. There were three Fisher sons: Homer, seventeen; Weldon, twelve, and Raymond, eight, but the packages were never for them. The first thing Mr. Fisher ordered from the catalogue was a set of cobbler's tools for repairing the family shoes. There were five pairs of iron feet on little columns out in the backyard shed, diminishing in size from Mr. Fisher's mighty sole to Raymond's little one and even after the iron feet were too small for the boys Mr. Fisher still used them. It didn't seem to make much difference.

After the cobbler's tools Mr. Fisher bought a huge steam pressure cooker for Mrs. Fisher to use for canning. It stood in a corner of the screened-in back porch when not in action, like a nickel-plated kettle-drum. And then came a set of barber shears and scissors to cut the family hair and an ugly apparatus of black iron which seized a tire and spread it open so Mr. Fisher could work on the inside of the casing with his repair kit. He bought all these things while he was still a brakeman on the Katy, before times got tough, as though he knew it was going to be like that and was getting ready to hold out as long as he could.

The equipment for the pies was the most elaborate of all. There were four square ovens, with stern, heavy handles on the front like those on a locomotive's firebox door; there were deep metal tubs to do the mixing in, and great steel baking sheets dented to hold dozens of pies. The pies were the nickel size which was very popular at that time. Mr. Fisher fitted the back of the sedan with wooden racks where the finished pies rested in paper plates during delivery, and he was in business.

It was a family undertaking, conceived in silent desperation, and the only one who enjoyed it was Raymond. He was very religious then, a member of the Baptist Young People's Union at the Highland Baptist Church a block away, and he liked carrying the little pies back and forth. He wanted to be a preacher someday.

Homer was the mean one, everybody said: he was always making trouble. He hated the pie-making; he bought a five-dollar guitar and a set of lessons and told everybody he wanted to be a cowboy on the radio. Mr. Fisher didn't like it; he whipped him until he got too big, and after that he would refuse to let Homer into the house some nights when he came home late. They used to wake up the whole neighborhood.

Homer found a job in a poolroom down on the square and in the afternoons, when the pie-making was at its highest pitch, he would open the door of the bedroom where he slept with his brothers and run down the hall and out the back door before his father could catch him. Then he would lean against the screen door while his father tried to push it open, both of them cursing at each other and shouting until you could hear it clear down at Hardin's Grocery. The family never used the front door at all.

After a while Mr. Fisher would have to go back to his pies and Homer would walk around the house and down the driveway to the street, combing his hair, which he greased with Crisco every day. He had a pointed, mean face like a weasel, with beady little eyes like a weasel, and he carried a snap-open knife with a four-inch blade in his pocket. In the summertime the Crisco would start to run before he got to the car line and he would stand there, mopping his forehead with a dirty handkerchief, darting his little eyes around like he was in Chicago or St. Louis, waiting for the streetcar like a weasel in a tight, twelve-dollar suit. He didn't act like a cowboy at all.

Weldon didn't say much; he wanted to be just like Homer. Raymond despaired of him, screamed at him out in the garage as they loaded pies into the sedan, wept over him. There were dozens of empty one-gallon mineral-oil jars stacked around the base of the garage walls and Raymond had to be careful when he was screaming at Weldon or they got knocked over and broken. Mr. and Mrs. Fisher both suffered from chronic constipation; it was their only luxury. They consumed surprising amounts of mineral oil from Sears & Roebuck and every few months Mr. Fisher returned the empties for a refund.

Nobody in the neighborhood ever tasted one of Mr. Fisher's pies. They were never given away nor eaten at home, and people in the neighborhood never went into the places which bought the pies from Mr. Fisher. They were artificial-looking confections, with a broad cone of grainy, hard meringue on top, like plaster. It was impossible to see what was inside, under the meringue, but there were all kinds of fillings: some days it was coconut, other times banana cream or pecan, and always they were a nickel each and quite durable; they held up for days on the counters of the restaurants where Mr. Fisher sold them.

Every day after school Raymond and Weldon worked with their parents, making the pies, but they never ate any. The pies were ammunition, and not to be fired off at random; the enemy was on the porch, fingering the doorknobs; every round must count. After all, Mr. Fisher's pies retailed for a nickel each; he had to sell them for three cents. As the country slowed, grumbled and fell silent, he was out in the sedan all day long, not coming home until nine or ten o'clock at night sometimes, and once he drove clear to Temple, twenty-five miles away, trying to get the bus station there to handle his pies, but they wouldn't do it. And every day Raymond and Weldon would start to work as soon as they got home, mixing, carrying pies to the roaring ovens and from the ovens to the racks, washing the tubs and steel sheets amid clang and clatter. There was always something to do. The light over the back door burned late every night, and the slap-slap of the screen could be heard when others were in bed, for not everyone chose to fight 1932 in this fashion.

When they were finally finished for the night Mr. and Mrs. Fisher would go into their bedroom at the front of the house and Raymond and Weldon would go into their room at the back. Weldon shared a bed with Homer, but he was always asleep by the time the poolhall employee came home. Raymond had a canvas army cot to himself, and after he undressed except for his underwear he would sit on the cot and look at the colored Bible pictures the preacher gave him, talking about them to Weldon, trying to get him interested.

But, "I'm on git me a *git*-tar," Weldon would interrupt in his dull voice, and he would look at Homer's pillow, covered with the dark splotches the Crisco made, and that would make Raymond mad.

"No, you ain't, neither," he would say firmly, pursing his lips and looking at his brother. "You ain't gone do no such a thing." He was eight years old and the preacher had told him that before too long he would become a real member of the church. "We gone buy seeds with that money," he would say, although there was no money, "and one uh them little plows with a wheel on her," for there was a picture of a proud, compact little garden plow in the catalogue and Raymond wanted a garden in the back lot, so they need no longer buy vegetables from Hardin's Grocery. *"He* won't leave you buy no *git*-tar, anyways."

"Mama on make him," Weldon would answer, still looking at the Crisco spots, and Raymond would sigh with exasperation and put his pictures away in a shoebox, then go to bed. It wasn't easy for a BYPU member in this house.

Mrs. Fisher frequently made promises to Weldon and Homer but never to Raymond, since he never asked her for anything. She was a silent woman who never left the house, a small, female version of Homer's weaselness, shuffling from room to room in red felt bedroom slippers. Like her husband, she came from a family of cotton sharecroppers, one of many children born to a dark, brooding couple of no education and apparently less imagination, whose children, the sons and daughters of the pioneers, resembled them exactly. She had never understood town ways and had no curiosity about them, nor had Mr. Fisher, although his work on the Katy and then with the pies took him out into the town every day. They were suspicious of it, not seeing it as merely an extension, a distillation of the cotton farmers who surrounded it, and so Mrs. Fisher never went out into it at all and Mr. Fisher did so narrowly, almost blindly, unaware of gossip or humor or politics, never even reading the paper. People who passed on the sidewalk in front of the house often saw Mrs. Fisher peering at them around the drawn windowshade in her bedroom, and if they were neighbors and went to the back door on some neighbor business she talked to them through the screen, saying as little as was necessary for the business but not unfriendly and even letting them into the house if the business made that necessary, but she never called at the other back doors in the neighborhood. The neighbors did not consider her especially remarkable or eccentric, however; they were accustomed to such people. At that time there were Fishers in every neighborhood, all over the town.

However, in one respect this particular Mr. Fisher, this former brakeman for the Katy railroad, was regarded as strangely out of character, above the normal run of Fishers: he was not a drinking man. The town's Fishers, and certainly the brakemen on the Katy, were whiskey drinkers; it set them apart like their overalls and pointed felt hats, forced into that strange, witches' shape on broom sticks, while the felt was wet. The other people in the town drank home brew which they concocted in their garages. And even that was primarily for summer use, although there were exceptions, of course; but the town's Fishers drank illegal whiskey the whole year 'round; it eased them.

But not the silent, pie-making Mr. Fisher. It was considered odd, a little too respectable; it bordered on sanctimonious display. And yet, Mr. Fisher did not attend the Highland Baptist Church nor any other church. He swore, and violently; he was as vulgar as his antecedents. He broke wind in front of his family or even among the lady shoppers in Hardin's Grocery, if he felt like it; after all, what difference did it make? And always he was dark and sullen, like those violent ancestors, dissatisfied and vaguely resentful, unarmed against his enemy. Not a churchman at all.

But, there it was: he was not a drinking man. He abhorred it. When Homer came home drunk at the age of fourteen his father beat him with his broad, stout belt, a piece of leather as heavy and stiff as harness. After that Homer did not come home drunk; he stayed away until he was sober, vomiting in the distempered men's room of the Phoenix Café on the square.

And women; Mr. Fisher warned Homer about women in such filthy language that it seemed impossible he had ever married, that he had ever brought himself in contact with the diseased, grasping, lying tribe and produced Homer, Weldon and Raymond. When Raymond heard his father lecturing Homer in this way it drove him to furious tears, he would rush out of the house with angry cries and sit in the garage or the shed which joined it, sobbing and promising himself holy vengeance against Mr. Fisher; he prayed that his huge, monstrous parent would be delivered into his hands for righteous, wrathful punishment of the Old Testament variety. And then Mr. Fisher would shout his name and it would be time to start working on the pies and Raymond would go back to his labor, his face stained with tears and dirt and cobwebs. At such times he worked frenziedly, rallying Weldon with fierce shouts, darting from the ovens to the racks in the sedan, scrubbing pans like a small wild man. It seemed that he hoped to outwit his father's vulgarity (although he did not know it as such) with this family labor, this community effort against charity, and in exact proportion to the humbling of his father, to do homage to his mother, that peering, shuffling, weasel-faced woman, member of the caste which Homer was warned to beware. Mother, and little Jesus, and the evil men!

Homer, of course, found girls: a succession of waitresses from the Phoenix Café or others like it, places that were dim, smelling of chili and long-dead grease, with corrugated iron awnings over the sidewalk out front; or girls from the pecan factory, they who worked in stifling heat in summer and not at all in winter since the pecans come in hot weather, girls in loose blue cotton smocks shelling mountains of pecans, carefully picking the meats out whole since broken ones were forfeit in the day's poundage score, their fingers stained a light brown, like Homer's own nicotined fingers. He took them to the Cotton Palace park in summer, and in winter (in the battered, rattling old Ford of a friend) to unpainted farmhouses out in the country, where whiskey was sold. Finally, inevitably, he found one he loved, a Dolores or Rosemary or Dot, and he frequently displayed his four-inch knife in the farmhouse fights, defending the one he had chosen from speech like his own but which was not to be tolerated because it was not his own, and then, equally finally, inevitably, he wanted to bring the girl to the house while Mr. Fisher was away. He told his mother he wanted to have friends at the house for a party.

Mrs. Fisher, not understanding, since this was something she knew nothing of, agreed to plot with him against Mr. Fisher. There was no question of revealing the plan to the husband and father; they refused even to think of such a disaster. Therefore the party must take place in the afternoon, while Mr. Fisher was abroad in town, selling his pies, and must be ended, the guests gone, at a safe hour.

At first Mrs. Fisher was pleasantly stirred by the idea of Homer's party, then frightened. It roused her from the patient, unquestioning gloom in which she unwittingly lived; it was the unknown, the intangible, qualities she perhaps had known in childhood but never since, for in the Fisher household intangibles were not considered, they did not exist in any consciousness save possibly Raymond's nor did any mind other than his dwell on the unknown. Conversation between parents and children was short, monosyllabic, and always of the immediate present. It had been so in the home of her own parents and Mrs. Fisher was not aware that it could or should be otherwise. But now Homer's plan shook her, she felt for the first time that he was "different," that he was moving forward and away from her blood, from something considered normal until now toward something indefinably better, and she was glad he had found his job in the poolroom, among the town people he understood and valued, the restless, active, talky town people. Change (so dreaded, so unwanted, always so near in 1932) must in this matter be good, and her mind moved slowly, unevenly, stiff with disuse, over this aspect of her son and his life in the poolroom on the square, unknown, but so suddenly present and requiring action.

She was not sure what was to make this party but she did not ask Homer. He had told her what he wanted: a party, since other people had them; she had agreed and he had gone off to his poolroom. She might have conceived of it and even tried to form it on some vague remembrance of a country funeral or wedding, with the men in the yard and the women in the kitchen, if Raymond had not sensed her mistake and corrected it.

"You on have ice cream?" he asked, looking up at her. "That's what they have at BYPU parties."

Mrs. Fisher looked down at him with her beady, weasel eyes, duller eyes than Homer's but unmistakably animal-like, wild fear and hate hidden behind the dullness and dumb patience.

"Mm," she said, looking down at her youngest son.

"And one uh them white cakes," Raymond said. "With green ice cream. They can sit in the front room and play the radio."

So it was decided, and on the appointed day Raymond took the limp dollar his mother gave him and walked to Hardin's Grocery, where he bought a white cake packaged in cardboard and cellophane and a quart of lime ice cream. Then he walked home and gave his mother the change from the dollar, put the ice cream in the icebox, the cake on the kitchen table, combed his hair with water and sat down in the kitchen to wait for Homer's party. Weldon stood at a window in the front room and Mrs. Fisher posted herself behind her bedroom windowshade. They peered around the shades, watching for Homer's arrival. Raymond sat in the kitchen, reading his BYPU magazine with thudding heart, longing yet fearful, and Mr. Fisher was in a Mexican café, staring heavily at the counter while he waited for the proprietor to buy or reject his pies, ignoring the rapid, spattering Spanish tongues and the smells of tacos, chili pepper sauce and fried rice, thinking about his old job on the Katy and how well he had performed in it.

Weldon grunted and ran into his mother's bedroom.

"They comin'," he said. "They in a car," raising the shade in front of his mother before she could stop him and she saw a Ford roadster, rakish and battered, turning into the yard.

"Here!" she said, jerking down the shade, and she raised her arm as though she would strike Weldon. She looked at him, then shuffled into the front room and sat down on the sofa, getting up at once to turn on the radio and then return to the sofa. Weldon took the chair by the radio and they sat silently, not moving, not looking at each other, their hands on their thighs as the radio hummed, warming up. They heard the metallic slam of the car doors in the backyard and then the slap of the screen door and voices in the kitchen, coming down the hall, and Homer entered the front room followed by another boy and two girls. The radio hummed powerfully and a man's voice started talking about Purina feeds.

For perhaps ten seconds after the foursome entered the room Mrs. Fisher and Weldon could smell them. There was a stale, rancid odor about them, of grease-impregnated clothing hung too long in a closed closet, the smell of a bed which has not been made for days or weeks, but it faded quickly into the usual close, almost fetid smell of the house and the room's first occupants thought nothing of it. Mrs. Fisher did not look at the young people when she was introduced to them by Homer in a quick, unfinished way, nor did she speak. She continued to sit with her hands on her thighs, her slippered feet close together, gazing steadily and calmly at the wall. She looked small on the bright blue plush of the sofa, and when the girls sat down on each side of her the cushions rose under her, lifting her feet from the floor. She paid no attention. Weldon, following his mother's example or stiff with self-consciousness, sat as he had before, staring straight ahead as though he had been falsely accused of a crime and was not going to talk about it any more. Homer and the other boy leaned against the wall, glowering about them at the furniture, the radio and Weldon. Wooden matchsticks dangled from their lips like gangster cigarettes and their movements were queerly alike; they moved a hand from pocket to matchstick rapidly as it left the pocket then slowed it as it reached the matchstick, slowing it insolently, provocatively, until the fingers took the matchstick delicately and probed the teeth with it. No one spoke. The Purina man talked enthusiastically into the room, his voice rolling jovially, full of promise, over the silent Fishers, the strange boy and the fat-faced, thick-lipped girls, sitting stiffly with their hands holding glittering patent leather purses in their laps.

Then, from nerves or from habit, since it was something she did frequently every day, a symptom, perhaps, of that condition which drove her to such huge, clotted draughts of mineral oil, Mrs. Fisher belched, a rasping, mannish noise which ripped the air like a power saw slicing a plank, and instantly, following immediately in the sound, Weldon, screwed to such high tension as he had never known before and gaseous from the starchy Fisher diet of 1932, broke wind. His face turned scarlet at once but he did not change his position; his expression settled more firmly into that of the badgered, innocent youth, held incommunicado and for no reason whatever in the city jail.

Homer's friend giggled, a wet snicker which seemed to come from his acne-pocked nose, and the girls tittered, but it was plain that all three were laughing kindly and indulgently at Mrs. Fisher's explosion, not Weldon's. They ignored his action, it was not something to laugh at in front of somebody else's mother, whereas the belch was nothing but a comical, ordinary thing, an idiosyncrasy of age; possibly Mrs. Fisher had done it to be entertaining. They chided her gently with their giggles, relieved to find she was human instead of merely Homer's mother, and did not acknowledge Weldon's behavior although in a short time, as soon as they were released from the company and implied influence of another generation, they would speak of it as wonderfully comic while they felt it as a sexual joke, since it reminded them of many things. Thus even Weldon's mishap was not without value and significance. Its implications were deep and exciting; like Homer's pocket-knife, it had an aphrodisiacal quality, although of doubtful necessity, since they already possessed whiskey rights and twenty-five-cent motion pictures.

Mrs. Fisher was uncertain about the actions of Weldon and herself in relation to the strangers, but she didn't dwell on it. She felt the need for conversation rather than thought, the need to impress directly upon these visitors the warning that she was a being, Homer's mother, in fact, and so she turned to him.

"He'll whup you to death when he finds out," she said in a flat, matter-of-fact tone.

Homer looked startled; for an instant he imagined something had gone wrong, that his father had learned of the party and forced the complicity of Mrs. Fisher, Weldon and Raymond in setting a dreadful trap for him. He pictured Mr. Fisher lurking in the garage or the shed, big, solid and dangerous in his blue overalls, biding his time. But the vision and the fear passed quickly; he realized his mother's intent, that of self-assertion in the only way she knew: the threat, the hint of a catastrophe in which she would not be implicated and on which she would not bother to pass judgment (although in this case she was certain to be involved in any mischance, she would stand or fall with Homer whether she willed it or not, since she was now hopelessly committed) and he understood it, because he used the device himself.

"Oh, yeah?" he said, curling his lips around the matchstick. "He ain't never gone touch *me* no more," and he glared at his friends, as though it were they who threatened him. He narrowed his eyes and twisted his lips painfully farther, he hunched his shoulders up and forward in a gesture of aggressive defense; he tried very hard to look as he felt a young man with a four-inch blade in his pocket should look.

"*That* old fool," he said.

"You hush your mouth now," said Mrs. Fisher, but she had lost interest; her eyes turned from Homer back to the wall. Her old feeling of numbness, of dumb, undirected patience was settling back on her, there seemed no reason to impress these people with her existence after all; she had established her familiar relationship with Homer and that was enough. Her excitement about the party ebbed away quickly, since the level it had reached on the flat beach of her consciousness had been only relatively high; she sank back into stagnancy and the room was silent against the jangling cries of the hillbilly band which had replaced the Purina man at his insistence.

"Hev yuh evah bin bahlooHOO," the radio mournfully sang, "Hev yuh evah bin loHONEly, hev yuh evah bin bahloo . . ."

"Say!" said Homer's male friend, and in a falsetto, sad and thin, he whined, "Aw haw!" and snapped his fingers in admiration, nodding at the radio. Homer glared at him.

"I'n play that," he said. "Come on," and he walked out of the room into the hall, followed by the other boy and, without having spoken a word, the two girls. They went down the hall and entered the bedroom Homer shared with his brothers. The door closed behind them and in a moment Mrs. Fisher and Weldon heard the twang of Homer's guitar and the angry whine of his voice.

"Hev yuh evah bin loHONEly, hev yuh evah bin bahlooHOO," he sang, sounding almost exactly like the man on the radio, striving, it seemed, for the coyote's piercing wail of longing and lone, barren desire.

Mrs. Fisher and Weldon sat in the front room, unmoving, as stolid and controlled as a pair of Al Capones, their eyes calm, almost lifeless. Mrs. Fisher felt the situation had altered and probably in the wrong direction, if it had any good or bad characteristics at all, but she was uncertain about it. Drugged with inertia, she allowed the fact, "they in the bedroom," to appear before her without any sentiment attached to it whatever. Weldon's thoughts were more active. He wondered what they were doing in there. They listened to Homer's voice and the primitive guitar for several minutes, and then the sounds stopped.

"Every penny counts nowadays," the man on the radio said. "Increase the output of your hens with Purina egg mash. Don't delay, do it today, with the red and white checkered Purina."

The hillbilly band started again and a thin, cowpuncher voice sang of the Alamo and a Comanche maiden in the moonlight.

"He'll kill him," Mrs. Fisher said. "That's what he'll do, he'll just kill him."

"What?" Raymond stood in the doorway with a saucer of ice cream and cake in each hand. "What is it, Mama?"

Mrs. Fisher did not look at him.

"Where they got to now?" said Raymond, standing there with the saucers. "Here I done dished up the party stuff and they ain't here."

He sat down next to his mother and looked from her to Weldon. His brother, still holding his position of outraged dignity, turned his head toward him.

"They in the bedroom," he said.

"The bedroom?" Raymond sounded disgusted. "What for? They can't hear no radio in there," and he put the saucers down on the floor. "What you sittin' there so funny for?" he asked his brother. "What the matter with you, anyway?"

"Hush up, now," said Mrs. Fisher, and she rose from the sofa and shuffled down the hall to the bedroom door, facing it, bent forward slightly.

"Homer!" she cried. "I know you in there!"

There was no sound from the bedroom.

"I'll get a stick!" Mrs. Fisher said, but she did not try to open the door. She waited a moment, then called. 'The ice cream's meltin'."

"Lemme take 'em a saucer," Raymond said. He stood at her side, looking up at her with a happy smile, proud of the ice cream and cake, eager to make friends with Homer's guests.

"Git!" said Mrs. Fisher, and she slapped him.

Raymond stood there for a moment, eight years old, a BYPU member, unable to believe what had happened. Then the sting spread from his face over his body and he was suddenly unbearably ashamed of the day, the house and everybody in it, including himself.

"Wah!" he screamed, running down the hall toward the back porch. "I never done nothing!" and as he rushed for the screen door he met his father, coming in.

Mr. Fisher was not a good salesman; the light did not burn within him and this was a fatal darkness. His heaviness, his lowering offer of his wares was noticed even in the Mexican restaurants, or perhaps especially there, and on the day of Homer's party he had canvassed the Mexican section of town, exhibiting his cement-like pies indifferently, brooding about the Katy railroad until he could stand it no longer. He went home earlier than usual.

When he turned into the driveway and saw the Ford roadster

parked there, the whorish, insolent little car in his yard, he knew instantly what had happened and at once began cursing and shouting threats. He jumped from the sedan before it stopped and was on the back porch, thrusting Raymond aside, before the car ran up against the garage and halted with a sound of splintering wood.

"Where is he!" roared Mr. Fisher, rushing up the hall to his wife, undoing his belt as he went. "Where is that drunkard, that whoremonger!"

Mrs. Fisher stood in front of the bedroom door, still holding her slight stooping position. She looked calmly and absolutely unbelievingly at her husband and might have remained there indefinitely if Homer had not jerked the door open and jumped into the hall, wearing nothing but his underwear shorts.

During the blink of an eyelid the trio stood bunched up in front of the open door, then Mr. Fisher's arm rose with the belt and Homer leaped back into the room, slamming the door behind him. Mr. Fisher immediately launched himself against it.

"Now you listen!" Homer cried from the other side. "These here is high-class people, Daddy!"

"Ah!" grunted Mr. Fisher, crashing rhythmically against the door. "Ah! Ah!"

Mrs. Fisher turned and shuffled unhurriedly back to the front room. She pushed Weldon aside as she entered and reseated herself on the sofa. Weldon went back to his chair by the radio and they sat as they had before, but breathing heavily this time.

From the hallway came the steady thudding sounds of Mr. Fisher's body against the door and Homer's muffled shouts from the bedroom, mingled with other, foreign cries, treble wails made by the girls as they dressed themselves and crawled out a window, followed by Homer's boy friend. Mrs. Fisher and Weldon heard the Ford start, backfire, and roar in reverse down the driveway and into the street, but they did not get up to look outside. That part of the day, of life, was finished; it held no interest for them any longer. At the same time the activity at the bedroom door was hardly mysterious; they were not titillated by that, either. They sat on in the front room in vegetable, breathing stillness, waiting.

After his father crashed past him Raymond continued his flight from the house, screaming with outrage and shame. He ran into the shed and clambered wildly about over barrels and boxes, then settled down in a corner behind the broken remains of a rabbit hutch, relic of one of Mr. Fisher's earlier, less frantic attempts at self-sufficiency.

"I never done a single thing!" he said to the boxes and barrels, and tears streamed down his cheeks as he thought of the slap, the entrance of his father and the abrupt disintegration of Homer's party or what had been intended as Homer's party since for Raymond it had never begun. The sponge white cake in its neat cardboard package, and the green ice cream! All lost now, scattered and smashed like all dreams of good things.

"I'm on show him some day," muttered Raymond, clenching his fists. "He ain't even a Christian daddy at all," and he imagined the triumph of love and God, the gentle, childish triumvirate of Father, Son and Holy Ghost ruling in this house, washing all sins away.

If only I done turned the other cheek, he thought, if only I remembered to do that. Next time I will, and he felt better, a soft, forgiving smile parted his wet lips and he squatted farther down behind the rabbit hutch, waiting for Homer's punishment to begin and then end, while in the house Mr. Fisher, in the agony of 1932, crashed rhythmically against the bedroom door.

Woody Guthrie

Woody (Woodrow Wilson) Guthrie (1912–1967) expressed in story and song the struggles of poor people of the Southwest in the Dust Bowl and the Depression. James Dickey said of him: "As we freefall through the Industrial Age, we clutch at the kind of folk hero that Woody Guthrie was, and is. He is by far the most gifted of all the earth-poets." Following his father into the oilfield towns of Texas gave him experiences like the one recounted in this passage from his autobiography, Bound for Glory.

BOY IN SEARCH OF SOMETHING

I was thirteen when I went to live with a family of thirteen people in a two-room house. I was going on fifteen when I got me a job shining shoes, washing spittoons, meeting the night trains in a hotel up in town. I was a little past sixteen when I first hit the highway and took a trip down around the Gulf of Mexico, hoeing figs, watering strawberries, picking mustang grapes, helping carpenters and well drillers, cleaning yards, chopping weeds, and moving garbage cans. Then I got tired of being a stranger, so I stuck my thumb in the air again and landed back in the old home town, Okemah.

I found me a job at five dollars a week in a push-button service station. I got a letter twice a week as regular as a clock from Papa out on the Texas plains. I told him everything I thought and he told me everything he was hoping. Then, one day, he wrote that his burns had healed up enough for him to go to work, and he'd got him a job managing a whole block of property in Pampa, Texas.

In three days I was standing in the little office shaking his hand, talking old times, and all about my job with him as general handyman around the property. I was just past my seventeenth birthday.

Pampa was a Texas oil boom town and wilder than a woodchuck. It traveled fast and traveled light. Oil boom towns come that way and they go that way. Houses aren't built to last very long, because the big majority of the working folks will walk into town, work like a horse for a while, put the oil wells in, drill the holes down fifteen thousand feet, bring in the black gushers, case off the hot flow, cap the high pressure, put valves on them, get the oil to flowing steady and easy into the rich people's tanks, and then the field, a big thick forest of drilling rigs, just sets there pumping oil all over the world to run limousines, factories, war machines, and fast trains. There's not much work left to do in the oilfields once the boys have developed it by hard work and hot sweat, and so they move along down the road, as broke, as down and out, as tough, as hard hitting, as hard working, as the day they come to town.

The town was mainly a scattering of little old shacks. They was built to last a few months; built out of old rotten boards, flattened oil barrels, buckets, sheet iron, crates of all kinds, and gunny sacks. Some were lucky enough to have a floor, others just the dusty old dirt. The rent was high on these shacks. A common price was five dollars a week for a three roomer. That meant one room cut three ways.

Women folks worked hard trying to make their little shacks look like something, but with the dry weather, hot sun, high wind, and the dust piling in, they could clean and wipe and mop and scrub their shanty twenty-four hours a day and never get caught up. Their floors always was warped and crooked. The old linoleum rugs had raised six families and put eighteen kids through school. The walls were made out thin boards, one inch thick and covered over with whatever the women could nail on them: old blue wallpaper, wrapping paper from the boxcars along the tracks, once in a while a layer of beaver board painted with whitewash, or some haywire color ranging from deep-sea blue through all of the midnight blues to a blazing red that would drive a Jersey bull crazy. Each family usually nailed together some sort of a chair or bench out of junk materials and left it in the house when they moved away, so that after an even thirty-five cents worth of hand-made wash benches, or an old chair, or table had been left behind, the landlord hired a sign painter to write the word "Furnished" on the "For Rent" sign.

Lots of folks in the oil fields come in from the country. They heard about the high wages and the great number of jobs. The old farm has dried up and blowed away. The chickens are gone dry and the cows have quit laying. The wind has got high and the sky is black with dust. Blow flies are taking the place over, licking off the milk pails, falling into the cream, getting hung up in the molasses. Besides that, they ain't no more work to do on the farm; can't buy no seed for planting, nor feed for the horses and cows.

Hell, I can work. I like to work. Born working. Raised working. Married working. What kind of work do they want done in this oil boom town? If work is what they want done, plowing or digging or carrying something, I can do that. If they want a cellar dug or some dirt moved, I can do that. If they want some rock hauled and some cement shoveled, I can do that. If they want some boards sawed and some nails drove, hell's bells, I can do that. If they want a tank truck drove, I can do that, too, or if they want some steel towers bolted up, give me a day's practice, and I can do that. I could get pretty good at it. And I wouldn't quit. Even if I could, I wouldn't want to.

Hell with this whole dam layout! I'm a-gonna git up an' hump up, an' walk off of this cussed dam place! Farm, toodle-do. Here I come, oil town! Hundred mile down that big wide road.

Papa's new job was the handling of an old ramshackle rooming house, right on the main street, built out of corrugated iron on a framework of two-by-four scantlings, and cut up into little stalls called rooms. You couldn't hardly lay down to sleep in your room without your head scraping the wall at one end and your feet sticking out in the hall. You could hear what was taking place in the six stalls all around you, and it was a pretty hard matter to keep your mind on your own business for trying to listen in on the rooms on each side of you. The beds made so much racket it sounded like some kind of a factory screaking. But there was a rhythm and a song in the scraping and the oil boom chasers called it "the rusty bedspring blues." I got so good at this particular song that

I could rent a flop in a boom-town hotel, and go to my room and just set there and listen a minute, and then guess within three pounds of the other roomers' weight, just by the squeek of the springs.

My dad run one of these houses. He tended to a block of property where girls rented rooms: the girls that follow the booms. They'd come in to look for work, and they'd hit the rooming house so as to set up a home, and straighten out their citizenship papers with the pimps, the McGimps, the other girls, and the old satchels that acted as mothers of the flock. One of Papa's boarders, for instance, was an old lady with gray hair dyed as red as the side of a brick barn, and her name was Old Rose. Only there never was a rose that old. She'd been in all of the booms, Smackover, Arkansas, Cromwell, Oklahoma, Bristow, Drumright, Sand Springs, Bow Legs, and on to East Texas, Kilgore, Longview, Henderson, then west to Burke-Burnett, Wichita Falls, Electra, and farther west, out on the windy plains, around Panhandle, Amarillo, and Pampa. It was a thriving business, boom chasing; and this old rusty sheet-iron rooming house could have been in any of these towns, and so could Old Rose.

Come to think of it, I've been in every one of these towns. I might of slept in this old rooming house a dozen times around over the country, and it was awful high-priced sleeping. I might of paid out a lot of them sheets of iron. And the girls that stayed here, they might of paid out a truck load or two of them two-by-fours. The usual price is about five dollars a week. If a girl is working, that is not so much, but if she's out of job, it's a lot of money. She knows that the officers might grab her by the arm any time for "Vag," for it's a jail house offense to be a-loafing in a boom town.

I remember one little girl that come in from the country. She blowed into town one day from some thriving little church community, and she wasn't what you'd call a good-looking girl, but she wasn't ugly. Sort of plump, but she wasn't a bit fat. She'd worked hard at washing milk buckets, doing housework, washing the family's clothes. She could milk an old Jersey cow. Her face and her hands looked like work. Her room in the rooming house wasn't big enough to spank a cat in. She moved in, straightened it up, and gave it a sweeping and a dusting that is headline news in a oil boom town. Then she washed the old faded window curtains, changed the bed and dresser around every way to see how it looked best, and tacked pretty pictures on her wall.

She didn't have any extra clothes with her. I wondered why; something went haywire at home, maybe. Maybe she left home in a hurry. Guess that's what she done. She just thought she'd come into town and go to work in a café or hotel or in somebody's house, and then when she got her first week's pay, she'd get what things she needed, and add to them as she went along. She wasn't a town girl. You could tell that. Everything about her looked like the farm, and the outhouses and barns, and the pastures, and wide-open spaces, and the cattle grazing, and the herds of sheep, or like looking out across the plains and seeing a hard-working cowhand rolling down across the country on a fat bay mare. Some way or another, her way of talking and the words that she knew just didn't seem to connect up with this oil-smeared, gasoline-soaked, whiskey-flavored, wild and fast-moving boom town. No cattle; no milk buckets. Nothing about raising an early garden, or putting on a big-brim straw hat and driving a speckled mare and a black hoss to a hay rake. I guess she was just a little bit lost. The other girls flocked in to see her, walking on high-heel shoes, with a bottle or two of fingernail paint, some cigarettes, different flavors of lipstick, and a half a pint of pale corn whiskey. They jabbered and talked a blue streak. They giggled and snickered, and hollered. Oh, Kid, this, and Oh, Kid, that. Everything they said was funny and new, and she would set, listen, soak it all in, but she didn't talk much. She didn't know much to talk about. Didn't smoke, and didn't know how to use that fingernail paint. Hadn't seen the picture show lately. Once in a great while she'd get up and walk across the floor and straighten up something that had got pushed over, or remark that she had to scrape the grease and dirt off of her two-burner hot plate.

When the girls had gone off to their rooms, she'd take a good look around over her room to see if it was neat enough, and if it was she'd sometimes take a little walk down the old dark hall, out into the back yard that stood about ankle deep in junk and garbage. You'd run onto her every once in a while out there. You'd catch her with a handful of old sacks and papers, carrying them in a high north wind out to the alley to put them in the trash box. Sometimes she'd smile at you and say, "I just thought I'd pick up a few of these papers."

She's thinking it's over a week now since I paid my room rent. Wonder what the landlord will do? Wonder if I'd grab the broom and pitch in and sweep out the hall, and go and carry a few buckets of water and mop it, wonder if he'd care? Maybe it'll get under his skin, and he might give me a job of keeping it up.

She'd come to the office where Papa was, and she'd set down and turn through the magazines and papers, looking at all of the pictures. She liked to look at pictures of the mountains. Sometimes she'd look at a picture for two or three minutes. And then she'd say, "I'd like to be there."

She'd stand up and look out the window. The building was just one story. It was all right down on the ground. The sidewalk went past the door, and all of the oilfield boys would crowd up and down the street, talking, staggering, in their work clothes, khaki pants and shirts smeared with crude oil, blue overhalls soaked with grease and covered with thick dust, salted and flavored with sweat. They made good money. The drillers drawed as high as twenty-five dollars a day. Boy, that was a lot of money. They wasted most of it. Whooped it off on slot machines and whiskey. Fights broke out every few minutes up and down the street. She could see the mob gang up. She could see a couple of heads bobbing up and down and going around in the middle. Pretty soon everybody would be beating the hound out of everybody else, choked, wet with blood and hot sweat. You could hear them breathing and cussing a block away. Then the fight would bust up and the men would come down the sidewalk, their clothes tore all to pieces, hats lost, hair full of mud and dirt, whiskey broke.

She was new in town, I knew that because she held back a little when a fist fight broke out. She just didn't much want to jump into that crazy river of oilfield fist fighters. She might have liked it if she'd known the people better, but she didn't know anybody well enough to call them friend. It was plumb dangerous for a strange girl even to go from one joint to the other looking for a job, so she waited till her money was all gone and her room rent was about two weeks behind. Then she went to a few places and asked for work. They didn't need her. She wasn't experienced. She went back several times. They still didn't need her. She was flat.

She got acquainted with a one-eyed girl. The one-eyed girl introduced her to a truck driver. The truck driver said he might find her a job. He would come in every day from the fields with a yarn about a job that he was trying to get her. The first few days they usually met in the office or hall and he would tell her all about it. But he'd have to wait another day or two to see for sure. The day come along when they didn't happen to meet in the office or hall, so he had to go to her room to tell her about something else that looked like a job for her. He made this a regular habit for about a week and she turned up at the office one day with seven dollars and fifty cents to pay on her rent. This was a big surprise to my dad, so he got curious. In fact he stayed curious. So he thought he would do a little eavesdropping around over the hotel to see what was going on. One day he saw her go off uptown with the one-eyed girl. In about an hour they come back with their hats in their hands, brushing their hair back out of their eyes, talking and saying that they was awful tired. The one-eyed girl took her down the hall and they went into a room. Papa tiptoed down to the door and looked through the keyhole. He could see everything that was going on. The one-eyed girl took out a teaspoon and put something in it. He knew then what it was. The girl struck a match and held it under the spoon, and heated it real hot. That's one way of fixing a shot of dope—morphine. Sometimes you use a needle, sometimes you sniff it, sometimes you eat it, sometimes you drink it. The main idea seems to be any old way to get it into your system.

He pushed the door open and run in while they was trying to take the dope. He grabbed the works away from the one-eyed girl and bawled both of them out good and proper, telling how terrible it was to get on the stuff. They cried and bawled and talked like a couple of little babies, and swore up and down that neither of them used it regular, they didn't have the habit. They just bought it for fun. They didn't know. The girl from the country never tasted it. She swore that she never would. They all talked and cried some more and promised never to touch the junk again.

But I stayed around there. I noticed how that girl with the one eye would come and go, and come and go, feeling one minute like she was the queen of the whole wide world, all smiles, laughing and joking; and then she'd go and come again, and she'd be all fagged out, tired and footsore, broke, hungry, lonesome, blue, and her eye sunk way back, her hair tangled. This kept up after Dad took away her morphine apparatus, and after all of her big promises to lay off the stuff. The farm girl never showed the least signs of being on dope, but the truck driver brought a little bottle of whiskey along with him after he got to knowing her better, and through the partition I heard them drinking.

Mister truck driver ate his meals in a little greasy wall restaurant right next door. He introduced her to the boss of the joint, a man with TB, about six foot four inches tall, skinny and humped as a spider. He had studied to be a preacher, read most of the books on the subject, and was bootlegging liquor in his eating place.

He gave the girl a job in the kitchen of this place, where she done all of her work, his work, and run over two or three swampers and helpers trying to keep the place from falling down, and all of the boards on the roof, and all of the meals cooked and served. It was so hot I don't see how she stood it. I more or less went into and out of these places because Papa was looking after them. Personally, I never have been able to figure out how anybody ate, slept, or lived around in this whole firetrap.

He give her one dollar a day to hang around there. He didn't call it a job, so he didn't have to pay her much. But he said if she wanted to hang around, he'd pitch her a dollar every night just to show her that his heart was on the right side.

The whole rooming house had been added onto a little at a time by moving old odd shacks onto the lot, till it had about fifty stalls. None of them were ever painted. Like a bunch of matchboxes strung along; and some of them housed whole families with gangs of kids, and others sheltered several men in one room where there was fifteen or twenty cots in a one-bed space, dirty, bed-buggy, slick, slimy, and otherwise not fit to live in or around.

It was my job to show folks to their rooms, and show the rooms to the people, and try to convince them that they was really rooms. One day when I was out bungling around with a mattress and a set of rusty bed springs, I chanced to hear a couple having more or less of a two-cylinder celebration in one of the rooms. I knew that the room was supposed to be vacant. Nobody was registered in there. The door was shut and the thumb-latch was throwed. I had a sneaking idea of what was up.

Through a knothole in the shack, I saw a half a pint of hot whiskey setting up on the old dirty dresser, and it was about eighty-nine percent drunk up. The bed didn't have a sheet on it, or any kind of covers, just the bare mattress. It was a faded pink mixed with a running brownish green, trimmed around with a bed-bug tan color soaked into the cloth. The TB boss of the little café and bootleg store was setting on the side of the bed with the country girl. Both of them had had a few out of the bottle. He was talking to her, and what he said had been said too often before by other men like him to put into quotes. You've had lots of trouble lately, haven't you? You look kinda sad. Even when you smile or laugh, it stays in your eyes. It never goes away. I've noticed it a lot since you've been around me lately. You're a good girl. I've read lots of books and studied about people. I know.

She said she liked to work.

He told her that she had a pretty face.

You got pretty eyes, even if they are sad. They're blue. Sad and blue.

She said she wasn't feeling so bad now since she had a job.

He said he wished that he could pay her more than a dollar. He said she made a good hand. He didn't feel like working very hard. It was too hot for him in his condition with the low roof.

I could hear him breathe and could hear the rattling in his lungs. His face was pale and when he rubbed his hand over his chin the red blood would show through his skin. He said, I feel better when I got you around.

She said that she was going to buy a few little things.

Where do your folks live at? Must have run away from home once. Tell me what caused it.

Her family lived thirty-five miles away in Mobeetie. Thirty-five or forty miles. She never did know just how far. Times got hard. And the farm gets awful lonesome when the sun comes up or when it goes down. A family argument got started and she got mad at her folks. So she bought a bus ticket. Hit the oilfields. Heard lots about oilfields. Said they paid good wages and always was needing somebody to work in them.

You've got a job right where you are. Just as long as you want it. I know you'll learn as you keep working. I don't think my dollar is entirely wasted. This fall is going to be good, and you'll know my business better, and I'll pay you better. We'll get an old man to be dishwasher. It's too much for you when business get rushing.

Her hand was resting on the mattress and he looked down at it and said, It looks nice and clean, and I don't want the strong lye soap and the hot dishwater to make it all red and dry the skin out. Cause it to chap. Break open. Bleed. He put his hand on hers and give it a good friendly squeeze. He rubbed real slow up and down her arm with the back of his hand just barely touching her skin, and they stopped talking. Then he took her hand and folded his fingers between hers and pulled her hand from the mattress and took the weight from her arm in such a way that she fell back across the bed. He held her hand and he bent over and kissed her. And then he kissed her again. They kept their mouths together for a long time. He rolled over against her, and she rolled up against him. She had good firm muscles on her shoulders and her back, and he felt each one of them, going from one to the other. Her green café uniform was fresh washed and ironed so that it shined where the light struck it, and where it curved to fit her body. Several times he rubbed across the belt that tied in a big bow knot above her hips and he pulled the sash and the knot came loose. The uniform started coming open a little at the front and by the touch of his hand he laid it half open almost without her knowing about it. His hands was long and his fingers was slim and he'd turned the pages of lots of books, and he took the first two long fingers of his right hand and caught the thickness of the uniform between them, and with a twist of his wrist he turned the rest of the dress back. He played and felt of both of her breasts, his fingers walking from first one and then the other like some kind of a big white spider. His TB caused him to make a loud spitty noise when he breathed in and out, and he was breathing faster all of the time.

I heard the sound of somebody's feet walking down the old boardwalk, and I took a quick glance down and out of the door, and saw somebody's shadow coming. I was standing on the steel frame of an iron folding cot, and I jumped down from my lookout for a minute. It was my dad. He said he had to go to the bank and for me to come and watch the office. There was a couple there to look at a room and the room had to be fixed up before they moved in. Needed linens. I stood there for about ten seconds not saying a thing. My dad looked sort of funny at me. I didn't let on. Just stood there straining my ears through that wall, and wondering what I was a-missing. But, shucks, I knew. Yeah, I knew, it was just exactly like all of the rest of them, and I wasn't a-missing out on nothing.

John Henry Faulk

John Henry Faulk (b. 1913) turned the art of storytelling into a means of expressing his own populist political philosophy. He became a CBS radio and TV host in the 1950s until, during the McCarthy years, he was accused of pro-Communist activities by the watchdog group Aware, Inc. After losing his job, he sued Aware and eventually won one of the largest libel suits in history (recounted in his best-selling Fear on Trial*). He returned to national prominence as a folklorist and storyteller featured on the syndicated TV program "Hee-Haw."*

A GLORIOUS FOURTH

Me and Earl was invited over to Turk and Eller's place for the Fourth of July. Eller's my sister. Her and her husband Turk sort of took me over after Mama died. They never liked Earl much. They blamed him for getting me to drop out of high school and move in with him at his rooming house. But they was wrong. Earl never had to get me to do it. I was tired of being broke all the time and never gittin' to go nowhere. So when Earl told me I could share them two rooms with him, I jumped at the chance. Then, 'course, he got me a job there at the filling station, working nights. That made it 'bout perfect.

Turk and Eller never hold nothing against a person long. So when she stopped by the filling station to invite me over to eat with them on the Fourth, she told me to bring Earl, too.

Turk got us into a game of horseshoes before we got good set down. He beat both of us about five straight games. Earl said, "Hell, Turk, you too good. Let's set up there on the porch where there's some shade. Play dominoes. Too damn hot out here in the sun."

Turk shook his head. "I'm in that mill all day ever' day. I git a chance to git out in the air, I ain't going to pass it up." He just went on pitching horseshoes at the posts, like he was playing somebody. Me and Earl went up and sat down in the porch swing.

The sun was really pouring it on. You could see the heat waves shimmerin' along the top of the fence. Everything in the neighborhood was takin' it easy. The only sounds you could hear, besides Turk a-gittin' ringers, was Ella fixin' dinner in the kitchen and a couple of hens cacklin' over in Mrs. Musset's barn. Even the locusts had stopped singing out. There weren't enough breeze to stir the long moss on the oak trees over there at the Baptist Church.

We heard a car coming up the road from towards the mill. Earl, he knows cars. He always says he's goin' to be a mechanic one of these days. He cocked his ear. "Bet you four bits that's Raymond Cannon's Chevy. I kin tell by the way the engine's missin' out." Sure enough, in a minute ol' Raymond come a-steaming around the bend in that '29 Chevy of his. He pulled up at the gate. Turk called, "Howdy Ray. Git out and come in. I was just a-hopin' that somebody would come along and play me a game of horseshoes. Alvin and Earl's skeered."

Raymond jumped out of his car. "Horseshoes, hell. Ain't you heard? Nigger stabbed Deppity Sheriff Ross this morning down at Patton's Corners. Sheriff Hicks wants us all up at the courthouse right away. Wants us to help round up that nigger. Come on. Bring your guns if you got twelve gauges. Sheriff's got buckshot."

Me and Earl was done up and ready. Turk just stood there holding the horseshoes. He don't hurry about nothin' like that.

Raymond asked if he had a drink in the house. Turk shook his head. "We don't keep none, Ray. Reckin the boys and me better not go along. Eller's fixin' a big dinner for us. Been cookin' all morning. She wouldn't want us runnin' off." Turk never did have no appetite for gitting mixed up in trouble.

Raymond spit, "Why, goddam, Turk, you ain't going to let a bad nigger run loose, are you? Sheriff ain't going to like it if you don't come. He said get every white man I could find. Hit ain't goin' to take us long to search Cow Flats. Sheriff says that's where the nigger's hidin'." Cow Flats is the colored section of town. I don't know how it got that name. But it's always been called Cow Flats.

Turk just stood there shaking his head no. "They don't need us, Raymond. That's business for police. That boy'll probably give hisself up to the law."

Me and Earl was anxious. Earl started in the house. "I'll tell Eller that we got business to do—she kin hold off dinner a while." Raymond was waiting. He called, "Tell her you'll be back in a couple of hours. Hellfire, Turk. This here's the Fourth of July. Don't you want to celebrate the Fourth?" Turk shook his head. "Not that way, I don't."

I went in the kitchen. Earl was funnin' Ella, tellin' her we had to go save the country. Ella didn't like our going off. She hadn't started fryin' the chicken, but she said, "Y'all ain't got no business runnin' off like this. I been over this hot cook stove all mornin'. My head's jest splittin' and my throat's hurtin' right where Mama's hurt." Ella's always skeered she's got cancer of the throat like Mama had.

Earl kept on a jollyin' her, "Aw, Eller, ain't you heared of the Glorious Fourth? Folks s'pose' to celebrate. Me and Alvin will clean up everythin' after dinner, I swear." Earl can talk a woman into anything. Ella was pouting, but she give in. "Well, if y'all ain't back in two hours, everythin' is goin' to be cold." We got Turk's shotgun out of the closet and went out in the front yard. Turk said he reckoned if we was goin' he had better go along, too. We all climbed into Raymond's car and took off.

On the way up to the courthouse, Raymond told us what had happened at Patton's Corners. He said Deputy Ross had come down there to arrest some colored crapshooters, and one of the boys had run up and stabbed him in the back. The deputy went down and the boy run.

It bein' a holiday, most of the men around Pineville was off work. There must of been twenty fellows standing and squattin' around in the shade. Most of them had shotguns or rifles. Sheriff Hicks was standin' under one of them big magnolia trees near the courthouse steps. I could tell he was madder'n all git-out. He was stomping around and he was whupping the leaves off of the low branches of the tree with his cane. Earl nudged me. "Ol' High Sheriff's mad, all right. Look at him." Raymond peeled back his lips in that sideways grin of his. "He's got a right to be mad! Niggers out stabbin' his deputies all the time."

Earl laughed, "Yeah, but he better not let Miss Elsie Patton ketch him tearin' up that magnolier tree that-away. She'll make him fergit all about his depitties and cuttin' niggers." I said, "That's right. Papa used to say that Elsie Patton counted every leaf on them trees. Thought more of them than she did of human beings." Miss Elsie Patton is a old maid that sort of runs the town. Her folks used to own about everything in these parts. She planted them magnolia trees long before I was born. Named one "Mother" and the other one "Father." Reckin them's the only trees with names in Texas.

Sheriff Hicks called us all together. He can sure look mean when he wants to. He started out in that bullfrog voice of his. "Boys, you all know what happened. I just want to say that my deputy, Ross, might die. Doctor's still working on him. But I ain't goin' to have no nigger cutting up my boys. We got word that that boy that done the cuttin' is hiding out there in Cow Flats. I'm deputizing all of you, till we bring him in. I want Raymond Cannon to take half of you and go up to the north end of Cow Flats. I want Dick Scantling to take the rest of you down to the south end. I want you to check every shack and shed and corncrib out there. I don't want no showin' off and hell raisin'. I want that boy." He passed out buckshot to them with shotguns.

A bunch of us piled into Ray's car with four or five hanging on the running boards. I'd done got so worked up that I even forgot how hot it was. We was all laughin' and jokin' like we was on our way to a Sunday school picnic.

Except Turk. He didn't say a word. Just set there between me and Raymond in the front seat and looked straight ahead. But Archer was following along behind us with some fellows in his Ford coupe. It's a '28, but he's always hurrahing Raymond about his Ford, old as it is, being better than Raymond's Chevy. He would keep honkin' and pullin' up behind Raymond like he was tryin' to pass us. Raymond was cussin' mad. He don't like for nobody to crowd him like that.

We stopped by Wendy's store. It sits right at the north end of the road that runs up through Cow Flats. I call it a road. Some folks call it a street, but it ain't nothing but a sandy lane, really. The colored folks' houses, or shacks, are scattered along each side for about a half mile. When we got out of the cars, we could see the people sittin' on their front porches and kids playin' 'round in the yards. They was most of them off for the day, even if it wasn't their Fourth. When they seen us startin' down the road with guns, they started fading into their houses in a hurry, calling to the kids to git in, too.

By the time we started into the first shack, you couldn't see a colored person stirrin' nowheres. They are skittish that way. I couldn't help feelin' kind of important.

When we would come up to a place, we'd have to go in. We couldn't get them out. Raymond would cuss and yell, "Open her up, or we'll kick the goddam door in." And he'd hurl off and kick the door durn near off the hinges. Or he would threaten to just start shootin' into the house.

Most of the shacks didn't have but two or three rooms, so it didn't take long to search them. The colored folks would back up in a corner and wall their eyes. In a couple of places they pretended that they were sick, and laid in bed with the covers over them. Raymond would jerk the quilts off and they would just lay there, with all their clothes on.

In one shack there was a old woman and her three kids. One was a girl about sixteen, I reckon. She was light brown, and a pretty good looker for a colored girl. She and the old lady and the other two kids was pushed up agin the wall, plumb wide-eyed scaired. Raymond walked over to her and winked, "Gal, you shore you ain't hiding that boy up under your dress?" She shook her head, and looked like she didn't understand. "She deef," the old woman sort of stuttered out. Raymond grinned and motioned for her to pull up her dress.

Turk hadn't said nothin' since we had left home. He looked right at Raymond, "Come on, Ray, that ain't what we come here for. Let's git out of here! Right now!"

We got out in a hurry. Raymond come out. He was peeved at Turk, but he tried to joke it off, "Hellfar, Turk, you ain't got no sense of humor. I wasn't goin' to hurt that girl." Turk didn't say nothin', but I knowed he wasn't enjoyin' the business.

We would see colored people tryin' to sneak out the back of their shacks and run for the woods. Raymond would yell, "Stop where you're at or I'll shoot." They would stop. One old man, called Pegleg on account of he had a peg leg, was hobblin' out of his place when we came around the corner of his shack. Raymond hollered and the old man throwed both hands up in the air. He's kind of touched in the head. Raymond said, "Peg, goddammit, what do you mean by tryin' to sneak off? How in the hell you think you goin' to git away on that peg leg?" The old fellow didn't look 'round. Just kept his hands up. Raymond winked at us, and said, "You know better 'n to sneak off from the law. I ought to kill you where you stand, you old devil. But I'm goin' to give you a chance. If you can make it to them bushes before I count ten, I won't shoot you. Now git." It was near fifty yards to the woods, but old Pegleg took off like a cripple turkey. Raymond let him git about half way, then he pointed his gun straight up in the air and shot. Pegleg thought he was killed for sure. He fell on the ground headfirst and just laid there.

I started to laugh but looked at Turk and decided not to. Raymond called out, "You'll have to git somebody else to bury you, Peg. We're in a hurry." And we started to the next shack. Peg hadn't started gettin' up when I looked back.

We could see Buck Scantling and his bunch down at the far end. They was goin' in and out of houses. Raymond started hurryin' us up. I didn't know why at first. I asked Earl why Raymond was gittin' such a move on. He nodded his head towards a house a little ways down the road. "Ray wants to git to Arthur Franklin's place before Buck gits there. He's been layin' for old Franklin a long time."

Arthur Franklin is the colored school superintendent. He ain't exactly uppity, but he sort of give hisself airs sometimes. Him and his wife come here about five years ago when the county commissioners decided to put in a superintendent for the colored schools. He called hisself Professor Franklin. Drives a durn good car, too. Nineteen thirty-five Buick. He keeps it just as shiny as the day he got it. He used to drive into Raymond's filling station with his wife and just sit there, waiting for Raymond to take care of him. Old Raymond did it a couple of times, but one time he told Raymond to check his tires and put water in the radiator. That done it. Raymond backed off and give him a cussin' and told him he didn't want his business.

There was a white picket fence around Franklin's yard and all sorts of flowers planted. The house was new-lookin' white and yellow. If it hadn't been in Cow Flats, you would never know colored people lived there. Raymond told a couple of the boys to go around in back in case Franklin tried to run. Turk stopped in the road. He looked at Raymond hard. "Ray, you know that Franklin wouldn't hide nobody in his place." Raymond grinned and kicked the gate open. He motioned for us to go in. He said, "You heered what the sheriff said, Turk. Search ever' place. That's what I aim to do. Come on."

Me and Earl was sort of anxious to git into Franklin's house. We had heard all sorts of tales about how fine it was inside. Folks said he had 'lectric iceboxes, big pianos, and all sorts of stuff in there.

We walked up on the porch and Raymond banged on the door with the butt of his gun. Franklin opened it and we could tell that he had been expectin' us. But he didn't make a move to let us in. Just stood there. He was scared. But he didn't move. Raymond said, "We're here in the name of the law. Sheriff ordered us to search this house." Franklin didn't move and his face didn't change. He said polite-like, "You're welcome to search my home. Do you have a search warrant?" That stopped Raymond flat. We hadn't even thought of no search warrant. Nobody else had asked us for one. Raymond's face was twisted and his teeth was showin'. He turned plumb red in the face. He said, sort of lame-like, "We're all deputized. We don't need no warrant. We're here under orders from Sheriff Hicks." Franklin still didn't move. He nodded, "This is a private home. It's illegal to enter this house without a search warrant." Turk had come up. He said, "He's right Ray. We ain't got no right in his house without no search warrant. We better get one before we make trouble." Just for a minute Franklin looked at Turk, nodding. Then he grunted, "By God, here's our warrant," and he brung the butt of his gun up under Franklin's chin. It made a crunching pop, Franklin's head snapped back and his glasses flew off. He fell like a sack of cow feed. His wife had been standin' a little behind him. She let out a scream and jumped at Raymond. He let her have it across the head with the barrel of his gun and down she went, out cold. Raymond stepped over them and called, "All right, boys, search the house. And search it good." We poured in after him. It was a clean place, but nothin' special. We didn't see no 'lectric icebox, but they did have a piano and a lot of Sears Roebuck furniture, that overstuffed kind. We knew we wasn't going to find that boy there. But we acted like we was looking. Old Raymond was havin' hisself a time. He was pullin' down pictures and turnin' over furniture and tearin' up the bed. "Never kin tell where that boy might hide," he said. After a little he called to us, "Ain't here, boys. Let's get goin'."

As we was goin' out, we stopped to look at Franklin and his wife. He was sitting up, holdin' his head, still dazed. She was layin' where she fell, moanin' and cryin'. One of the fellows asked Raymond, "Reckon they need some help, Ray?"

Raymond kept walkin'. "Hell, no. They ain't hurt bad. Cain't hurt no nigger hittin' him in the head. Got to hit 'em on the heel to kill 'em. That's where their brains is." We all walked out into the road. Turk hadn't gone in the house. He was waitin' for us out there. We seen Sheriff Hicks comin' up the road in his Ford. He called out to us, "We got him, boys. He give hisself up at the courthouse. Come on down to my office. Got sodywater for the boys and something stronger for the men." A couple of fellows rode back with him and the rest of us started up through Cow Flats to our cars. The colored folks were still layin' low. Not a sign of them outside. The sun was right straight up over us, and it was blisterin' hot. As we walked past the shacks, Raymond would sing out, "You folks can come out. Celebration's over."

When we started back toward town in the car, Turk said, "You better take us on home, Ray. Eller'll be waiting dinner on us." Raymond grinned and looked at Turk out of the corner of his eye. "You don't need no dinner bad as you need a drink, Turk. Come on down and have jest one drink for the Fourth of July." Turk shook his head. "No, Ray, I don't want no drink for the Fourth of nothin'. Take us by home."

Me and Earl wanted to go down to the courthouse, but when Turk talks that way there ain't no arguing with him. Raymond joked about this and that, but he took us on home. We was gettin' out of the car and Raymond said, "Wish you would come along, boys. Turk, if you ain't keerful, folks are going to be saying you ain't got no patriotism." Turk never answered him. We went in and Ella was waitin' for us. Turk never ate much, said the heat must of got him. But me and Earl made up for him. We was hungry as starved dogs.

Larry L. King

Larry L. King (b. 1929) became celebrated as the author and later playwright of The Best Little Whorehouse in Texas. *But the Putnam-born author, who has been a Nieman Fellow at Harvard and a visiting professor at Duke and Princeton, is at his spicy best telling stories with a political angle, honed during his experiences on the Kennedy-Johnson campaign team, on the staff of Congressman (now House Speaker) Jim Wright, and as former editor of the* Texas Observer.

THE AMERICAN REDNECK

The maddest I remember being at my late wife (a Yankee lady, of Greek extraction and mercurial moods) was when she shouted, during a quarrel the origins of which are long lost, that I was "a dumb Redneck." My heart dangerously palpitated; my eyes bugged; I ran in tight circles and howled inarticulate general profanities until, yes . . . my neck turned red. Literally. I felt the betraying hot flush as real as a cornfield tan. My wife collapsed in a mirthful heap, little knowing how truly close I felt to righteous killing.

Being called dumb wasn't what had excited me. No, for I judged myself ignorant only to the extent that mankind is and knew I was no special klutz. But being called a Redneck, now, especially when you know in your genes and in the dirty back roads of your mind that you *are* one—despite having spent years trying not to be—well, when that happens, all fair has gone out of the fight. I do not cherish Rednecks, which means I dislike certain persistent old parts of myself.

Of late the Redneck has been wildly romanticized; somehow he threatens to become a cultural hero. Perhaps this is because heroes are in short supply—we seem to burn them up faster nowadays—or maybe it's a manifestation of our urge to return to simpler times: to be free of computers, pollution, the urban tangle, shortages of energy or materials or elbow room. Even George Wallace is "respectable" now, having been semimartyred by gunfire and defanged by defeat. Since 'Necks have long been identified with overt racism, we may be embracing them because we long ago tired of bad niggers who spooked and threatened us; perhaps the revival is a backlash against hairy hippies, peaceniks, weirdos of all stripes. Or the recent worship of Redneckism may be no more than the clever manipulations of music and movie czars, ever on the lookout for profitable new crazes. Anyway, a lot of foolishness disguised as noble folklore is going down as the 'Neck is praised in song and story.

There are "good" people, yes, who might properly answer to the appellation "Redneck": people who operate mom-and-pop stores or their lathes, dutifully pay their taxes, lend a helping hand to neighbors, love their country and their God and their dogs. But even among a high percentage of these salts-of-the-earth lives a terrible reluctance toward even modest passes at social justice, a suspicious regard of the mind as an instrument of worth, a view of the world extending little farther than the ends of their noses, and only vague notions that they are small quills writing a large, if indifferent, history.

Not that these are always mindless. Some value "common sense" or "horse sense" and in the basics may be less foolish than certain determined rote sophisticates and any number of pompous academicians. Some few may read Plato or Camus or otherwise astonish; it does not necessarily follow that he who is poor knows nothing or cares little. On the other hand, you can make boatloads of money and still be a Redneck in your bones, values, and attitudes. But largely, I think—even at the risk of being accused of elitism or class prejudice—the worse components of 'Neckery are found among the unlettered poor.

Attempts to deify the Redneck, to represent his life-style as close to that of the noble savage are, at best, unreal and naïve. For all their native wit—and sometimes they have keen senses of the absurd as applied to their daily lives—Rednecks generally comprise a sad lot.

They flounder in perilous financial waters and are mired in the socio-political shallows. Their lives are hard: long on work and short on money; full of vile bossmen, hounding creditors, debilitating quarrels, routine disappointments, confrontations, ignorance, a treadmill hopelessness. It may sound good on a country-western record when Tom T. Hall and Waylon Jennings lift their voices, baby, but it neither sounds nor feels good when life is real and the alarm clock's jarring jangle soon must be followed by the time clock's tuneless bells.

Now, the Rednecks I'm talking about are not those counterfeit numbers who hang around Austin digging the Cosmic Cowboy scene, sucking up to Jerry Jeff Walker and Willie Nelson, wearing bleached color-patched overalls, and rolling their own dope, saying how they hanker to go live off the land and then winging off to stay six weeks in a Taos commune before flying back on Daddy's credit card. May such toy Rednecks choke on their own romantic pretensions.

No, and I'm not talking about Good Ol' Boys. Do not, please, confuse the two; so many have. A Good Ol' Boy is a Redneck who has acquired a smidgen or much more of polish; I could call him a "former Redneck" except that there ain't no such when you bore bone-deep. One born a 'Neck of the true plastic-Jesus-on-the-dashboard and pink-rubber-hair-curlers-in-the-supermarket variety can no more shuck his condition than may the Baptist who, once saved, becomes doctrinarily incapable of talking his way into hell.

The Good Ol' Boy may or may not have been refurbished by college. But bet your ass he's a climber, an achiever, a con man looking for the edge and the hedge. He'll lay a lot of semi-smarmy charm on you, and bullshit grading from middling to high. He acts dumber than he is when he knows something and smarter than he is when he doesn't. He would be dangerous game to hunt. Such parts of his Redneck heritage as may be judged eccentric or humorous enough to be useful will be retained in his mildly self-deprecating stories and may come in handy while he's working up to relieving you of your billfold or your panties. Such Redneck parts as no longer serve him, he attempts to bury in the mute and dead past. And he becomes maniacal when, say, a domestic quarrel causes him to blow his cool enough that those old red bones briefly rise from their interment so that others may glimpse them.

A Good Ol' Boy turns his radio down at red lights so that other drivers won't observe him enjoying Kitty Wells singing through her nose. He carefully says "Negro," though it slips to "Nigra" with a shade much Scotch, or even—under stress, or for purposes of humor among close associates—slides all the way down to "nigger." He does not dip snuff or chaw tobacco, preferring cigarettes or cigars or perhaps an occasional sly hip toke of pot. He has forgotten, or tells himself he has forgotten, the daily fear of being truly ragged and dirt poor—and, perhaps, how to ride a horse, or the cruel tug of the cotton sack, or the strength of the laborer's sun. He may belong to a civic club, play golf, travel, own his own shop, or run somebody else's. For a long time he's been running uphill; sometimes he doesn't know when he's reached level ground and keeps on struggling. Having fought and sweated for his toehold, he'll likely be quick to kick those who attempt to climb along behind him.

While all Good Ol' Boys have been at least fringe Rednecks, not nearly all Rednecks rise to be Good Ol' Boys. No. Their gizzards don't harbor enough of something—grit, ambition, good fortune, con, education, flint, self-propellants, saddle burrs, chickenshit, opportunity, whatever—and so they continue to breed and largely perpetuate themselves in place, defanged Snopeses never to attain, accumulate, bite the propertied gentry, or smite their tormentors. These are no radicals; though the resentful juices of revolution may ache their bloodstreams, they remain—with rare, crazed exceptions—amazingly docile. They simply can't find the handles of things and drop more than they can pick up.

Though broad generalities deserve their dangerous reputation, one hazards the judgment that always such unreconstructed Rednecks shall vote to the last in number for the George Wallaces or Lester Maddoxes or other dark ogres of their time; will fear God at least in the abstract and Authority and Change even more; will become shade-tree mechanics, factory robots, salesmen of small parts, peacetime soldiers or sailors; random serfs. (Yes, good neighbors, do you know what it is to envy the man who no longer carries the dinner bucket, and hope someday you'll reach his plateau: maybe shill for Allstate?) The women of such men are beauticians and waitresses and laundry workers and notions-counter clerks and generally pregnant. Their children may be hauled in joust-about pickup trucks or an old Ford dangling baby booties, giant furry dice, toy lions, nodding doggies and plastered with downhome bumper stickers: HONK IF YOU LOVE JESUS, maybe, or GOAT ROPERS NEED LOVE TOO. Almost certainly it's got a steady mortgage against it, and at least one impatient lien.

We are talking, good buddies, about America's white niggers: the left behind, the luckless, the doomed. It is these we explore: my clay, native roots, mutha culture. . . .

*　　*　　*

I didn't know I was a Redneck as a kid. The Housenwrights were Rednecks, I knew—even though I was ignorant of the term; couldn't have defined it had I heard it—and so were the Spagles and certain branches of the Halls, the Peoples, the Conines, the many broods of Hawks. These were the raggedest of the ragged in a time when even FDR judged one-third of a nation to be out-at-elbows. There was a hopelessness about them, a feckless wildness possible only in the truly surrendered, a community sense that their daddies didn't try as hard as some or, simply, had been born to such ill luck, silly judgments, whiskey thirsts, or general rowdiness as to preclude twitches of upward mobility. Such families were less likely than others to seek church; their breadwinners idled more; their children came barefoot to the rural school even in winter. They were more likely to produce domestic violence, blood feuds, boys who fought their teachers. They no longer cared and, not caring, might cheerfully flatten you or stab you in a playground fight or at one of the Saturday-night country dances held in rude plank homes along the creek banks. Shiftless badasses. Poor tacky peckerwoods who did us the favor of providing somebody to look down on. For this service we children of the "better" homes rewarded them with rock fights or other torments: "Dessie Hall, Dessie Hall / Haw Haw Haw / Your Daddy Never Bathes / But He's Cleaner Than Your Maw."

Ours was a reluctant civilization. Eastland County, Texas, had its share of certified illiterates in the 1930s and later, people who could no more read a Clabber Girl Baking Powder billboard than they could translate from the French. I recall witnessing old nesters who made their laborious "marks" should documents require signatures. A neighboring farmer in middle age boasted that his sons had taught him simple long division; on Saturdays he presided from the wooden veranda of Morgan Brothers General Store in Scranton, demonstrating on a brown paper sack exactly how many times 13 went into 39, while whiskered old farmers gathered for their small commerce looked on as if he might be revealing the internal rules of heaven.

We lived in one of the more remote nooks of Eastland County, in cotton and goober and scrub-oak country. There were no paved roads and precious few tractors among that settlement of marginal farms populated by snuff dippers, their sunbonneted women, and broods of jittery shy kids who might regard unexpected visitors from concealment. We were broken-plow farmers, holding it all together with baling wire, habit, curses, and prayers. Most families were on FDR's relief agency rolls; county agriculture agents taught our parents to card their cotton by hand so they might stuff homemade mattresses. They had less success in teaching crop rotation, farmers feeling that the plot where Daddy and Granddaddy had grown cotton remained a logical place for cotton still. There were many who literally believed in a flat earth and the haunting presence of ghosts; if the community contained any individual who failed to believe that eternal damnation was a fair reward for the sinner, he never came forward to declare it.

Churches grew in wild profusion. Proud backwoodsmen, their best doctrines disputed by fellow parishioners, were quick to establish their rival rump churches under brush arbors or tabernacles or in plank cracker boxes. One need have no formal training to preach; the Call was enough, a personal conviction that God had beckoned one from a hot cornfield or cattle pen to spread the Word; this was easy enough for God to do, He being everywhere and so little inclined toward snobbery that He frequently visited the lowliest Eastland County dirt farmer for consultations. Converts were baptized in muddy creeks or stock tanks, some flocks—in the words of the late Governor Earl Long of Louisiana—"chunking snakes and catching fevers."

It was not uncommon, when my father was a young man, for righteous vigilantes to pay nocturnal calls on erring wife beaters or general ne'er-do-wells, flogging them with whips and Scriptures while demanding their immediate improvement. Such godly posses did not seek to punish those who lived outside the law, however, should commerce be involved; when times were hard, so were the people. Bootleggers flourished in those woods in my youth, and it was not our responsibility to reveal them. Even cattle thieves were ignored so long as they traveled safe distances to improve their small herds.

My father's house was poor but proud: law-abiding, church-ridden, hardworking, pin-neat; innocent, it seems in retrospect, of conscious evil, and innocent, even, of the modern world. Certainly we had good opinions of ourselves and a worthy community standing. And yet even in that "good" family of work-worn, self-starting, self-designated country aristocrats there were tragedies and explosions as raw as the land we inhabited: My paternal grandfather was shot to death by a neighbor; an uncle went to the pen for carnal knowledge of an underaged girl; my father's fists variously laid out a farmer who had the temerity to cut in front of his wagon in the cotton-gin line, a ranch hand who'd reneged on a promise to pay out of his next wages for having his horse shod, a kinsman who threatened to embarrass the clan by running unsuccessfully for county commissioner a ninth straight time. My father was the family enforcer, handing out summary judgments and corporal punishments to any in the bloodline whose follies he judged trashy or a source of community scorn or ridicule. It was most tribal: Walking Bear has disgraced the Sioux; very well, off with Walking Bear's head.

So while we may have had no more money than others, no more of education or raw opportunity, I came to believe that the Kings were somehow special and that my mother's people, the proud and clannish Clarks, were more special still. A certain deference was paid my parents in their rural domain; they gave advice, helped shape community affairs, were arbiters and unofficial judges. I became a "leader" at the country school and in Bethel Methodist Church, where we took pride in worships free of snake handling or foot washings—although it was proper to occasionally talk in tongues or grovel at the mourners' bench.

I strutted when my older brother, Weldon, returned in his second-hand Model A Ford to visit from Midland, a huge metropolis of nine thousand noblemen in oil, cowboy, and rattlesnake country more than two hundred miles to the west. I imagined him a leading citizen there; he had found Success as manager of the lunch counter and fountain at Piggly Wiggly's and announced cowpoke melodies part time over the facilities of radio station KCRS. More, he was a hot-fielding second baseman with the semiprofessional Midland Cowboys baseball team. Any day I expected the New York Yankees to call him up and wondered when they did not.

Weldon epitomized sophistication in my young mind; he wore smart two-toned shoes with air holes allowing his feet to breathe, oceans of Red Rose hair oil, and a thin go-to-hell mustache. In the jargon of the time and the place he was "a jellybean." Where rustics rolled their own from nickel bags of Duke's Mixture or Country Gentlemen, my brother puffed luxurious "ready rolls." When he walked among local stay-at-homes on his rare visits, he turned the heads of milkmaids and drew the dark envied stares of male contemporaries who labored on their fathers' farms or, if especially enterprising, had found jobs at the broom factory in Cisco. He was walking proof of the family's industry and ambition, and he reinforced my own dreams of escape to bigger things.

Imagine my shocked surprise, then, when—in my early teens—I accompanied my family in its move to Midland City, there to discover that *I* was the Redneck: the bumpkin, the new boy with feedlot dung on his shoes and the funny homemade haircuts. Nobody in Midland had heard of the Kings or even of the Clarks; nobody rushed to embrace us. Where in the rural consolidated school I had boasted a grade average in the high nineties, in Midland the mysteries of algebra, geometry, and biology kept me clinging by my nails to scholastic survival. Where I had captained teams, I now stood uninvited on the fringes of playground games. My clothes, as good as most and better than some in Eastland County, now betrayed me as a poor clod.

I withdrew to the company of other misfits who lived in clapboard shacks or tents on the jerry-built South Side, wore tattered time-faded jeans and stained teeth, cursed, fought, swigged beer, and skipped school to hang around South Main Street pool halls or domino parlors. These were East Texans, Okies, and Arkies whose parents—like mine—had starved off their native acres and had followed the war boom west. Our drawls and twangs and marginal grammar had more of the dirt farmer or drifting fruit picker in them than of the cattleman or small merchant; our homes utilized large lard buckets as stools or chairs and such paltry art as adorned the wall likely showed Jesus on the cross suffering pain and a Woolworth's framing job; at least one member of almost every family boasted its musician: guitar or banjo or mandolin pickers who cried the old songs while their instruments whined or wailed of griefs and losses in places dimly remembered.

We hated the Townies who catcalled us as shitkickers ... plowboys ... Luke Plukes. We were a sneering lot, victims of cultural shock, defensive and dangerous as only the cornered can be. If you were a Townie, you very much wished not to encounter us unless you had the strength of numbers; we would whip your ass and take your money, pledging worse punishments should the authorities be notified. We hated niggers and meskins almost as much as we hated the white Townies, though it would be years before I knew how desperately we hated ourselves.

In time, deposits of ambition, snobbery, and pride caused me to work exceedingly hard at rising above common Redneckery. Not being able to beat the Townies, I opted to join them through pathways opened by athletics, debating, drama productions. It was simply better to be in than out, even if one must desert his own kind. I had discovered, simply, that nothing much on the bottom was worth having.

I began avoiding my Redneck companions at school and dodging their invitations to hillbilly jam sessions, pool hall recreations, forays into the scabbier honky-tonks. The truth is, the Rednecks had come to depress me. Knowing they were losers, they acted as such. No matter their tough exteriors when tormenting Townies, they privately whined and sniveled and raged. The deeper their alienations, the smaller they seemed to become physically; excepting an occasional natural jug-butted Ol' Boy, Rednecks appeared somehow to be stringier, knottier, more shriveled than others. They hacked the coughs of old men and moved about in old men's motions somehow furtive and fugitive. I did not want to be like them.

Nor did I want to imitate their older brothers or fathers, with whom I worked in the oilfields during summers and on weekends. They lived nomadic lives, following booms and rumors and their restless, unguided hearts. It puzzled me that they failed to seek better and more far-flung adventures, break with the old ways and start anew; I was very young then and understood less than all the realities. Their abodes were tin-topped old hotels in McCamey, gasping-hot tents perched on the desert floor near Crane, a crummy tourist court outside Sundown, any number of peeled fading houses decorating Wink, Odessa, Monahans. Such places smelled of sweat, fried foods, dirty socks, the bottoms of the barrel, too much sorry history.

By day we dug sump pits, pissanted heavy lengths of pipe, mixed cement and pushed it in iron wheelbarrows ("wheelbars"), chemically blistered our skins while hot-doping new pipeline, swabbed oil storage tanks, grubbed mesquite or other prickly desert growths to make way for new pump stations. We worked ten hours; the pay ranged from seventy to ninety-four cents for each of them, and we strangely disbelieved in labor unions.

There was a certain camaraderie, yes, a brotherhood of the lower rungs; kidding could be rough, raw, personal. Often, however, the day's sun combined with the evening's beer or liquor to produce a special craziness. Then fights erupted, on the job or in beer joints or among roommates in their quarters. Few rules burdened such fights, and the gentle or unwary could suffer real damage. Such people frightened me. They frighten me now, when I encounter them on visits to West Texas beer joints or lolling about a truckstop café. If you permit them to know it, however, your life will become a special long-running hell: *Grady, let's me and you whup that booger's ass for him again.* Often, in the oil patch, one had to act much tougher than the stuff he knew to be in his bones. It helped to pick a fight occasionally and to put the boots to your adversary once you got him down. Fear and rage being first cousins, you could do it if you had to.

But I can't tell you what it's really like, day to day, being a Redneck: not in the cool language of one whom time has refurbished a bit or by analytical uses of whatever sensibilities may have been superimposed through the years. That approach can hint at it in a general way, knock the rough edges off. But it isn't raw enough to put you down in the pit: let you smell the blood, know the bone dread, the debts, the random confrontations, the pointless migrations, or purposeless days. I must speak to you from an earlier time, bring it up from the gut. Somehow fiction is more suited to that.

Bill Brett learned about killings as a deputy sheriff and deputy constable ("I never had to kill anybody; stopped a few fights in the jail, though"). He started writing sixteen years ago, basing several stories on actual happenings in the Piney Woods counties of Liberty, Hardin, and Jefferson. Brett has published three volumes of stories.

THE KILLINGS

Oh, sure, there's been lots of killings in this country. Especially during the oil-boom days at Batson and Saratoga. Old Milvid and Mary C. and the other logging camps had their share during their heyday, too. I don't recollect but three, maybe four, right here at home, though.

Let's see, now, Dan Thomas killed a feller, a Mexican. I heard his name at the time but I've forgot it. Mr. Kroger killed Dr. Banning. Fletcher Morrow killed a feller name of Baines, and Mr. George Redding killed O. R. Manning. Them four is all I remember offhand.

There wasn't none of them killings done during no shoot-out. I never heard of one in this country. These was more or less executions. Seemed like around here when a man figured another one needed killing he went at it like any other job, picked the best tool for it and got it over with.

Dr. Banning and Baines was both killed with the same ol' double-barrel Remington ten-gauge. I think maybe some of the Krogers still own it. George Redding used a old Winchester lever-action ten-gauge on Mr. Manning. Papa said it was the best shooting shotgun he'd ever seen and had killed a million ducks and geese when Mr. Redding was market-hunting. I don't know what ever happened to it.

Dan Thomas killed the Mexican with a old .41 single-action Colt pistol. It was more or less a case of have to, and Dan would have got out of it if he could have. He was constable in this precinct then, he weren't no gun-toter like some lawmen, just farmed and worked out when he could, like most folks. He only run for the job because the county paid five dollars a month regular and fees for serving papers and such.

That shooting come about when the police at Houston sent Dan a telegram that this Mexican feller had knifed a man and was on a freight train heading this way. Dan had the station agent flag the train and was searching it when the Mexican made at him with that knife, and Dan put a ball in his forehead. I 'spect that shot was an accident. Dan didn't shoot that much.

Fletch Morrow claimed at his trial he'd killed Baines because he'd feared for his life. Told on the stand that they'd had words over some of Baines's hogs tearing in his field, and Baines said next time he seen him he was going to kill him if he got life in the pen for it. Two or three days after they'd had the words, Fletcher seen him pass on the road to town and was behind a tree waiting for him when he come back. One of the Carr kids was coming from the gristmill and seen it, and he said Fletcher shot Baines once while he was walking and again before he hit the ground.

Old man Kroger set in a saloon and waited for Dr. Banning and shot him when he stepped in the door. I heard several tales, but it was four or five years before I heard the straight of the matter, and then I wished I hadn't. It was personal between the two men and none of my business. Nor yours. They've both still got folks living around here.

I knowed a little more than just second- or thirdhand talk about Mr. Redding killing Mr. Manning. They was both close neighbors of ours. Papa had a place then about seven miles out of Liberty on the old Nacogdoches stage road, and Mr. Redding lived about half a mile below us, what they call the Bob Ray place now. Mr. Manning was farming the Hardin place on up above us about a mile.

Well, their falling out was about a dog and come up this way. Papa and Mr. Manning went one morning to George Redding's to help butcher hogs, and when they started into the yard one of Mr. Redding's dogs bit Mr. Manning. Papa said since they were expected, neither one of them had hollered hello nor spoke to the dog before they opened the gate, so he kinda figured the dog was in the right.

After dinner Mr. Manning was cutting up a hog—they was working in the backyard so's the well was handy—and the old dog came in under the table and bit him again. Papa said he could tell it really set him afire that time, but he just said if he had a biting dog he'd break his damn jaw, and kept on a-working.

A few days later the dog come in home with his bottom jaw busted in three or four places. Not being able to eat or drink, 'course he didn't pull through. Mr. Redding was sure mad and looking for somebody to put the blame on, and the upshot was he accused Mr. Manning of killing his dog. Mr. Manning denied it, and one word led to another, and they was both pretty hot before it was over.

Now, you understand, this weren't just no pet dog. This was a cur dog like most folks in this country kept and as necessary as a plow or axe or any other tool. There just weren't no way a feller could tend to hogs or gather cattle in this Big Thicket country without dogs, and can't till yet.

A man's got a natural feeling for his own dog anyhow, and when it's a using dog and they work together a few years, he also develops a kind of respect for the dog and don't like to have him bad-mouthed and ain't going to have him hurt or abused. I've always figured Mr. Redding felt that way about his old dog.

Well, things rocked on a while, and ever'body got busy putting their crops in, and it looked like it had blowed over about the dog till along in June.

A feller had moved in on the Christian place that winter, about three miles east of us, and had got in twelve or fifteen acres of corn and a patch of sweet taters and then got down with recurrent fever. It was really malaria, but we didn't know it as such at that time. Anyway, Mama heard at church one Sunday that folks was going to work his crop Tuesday, if it didn't rain.

Well, the weather stayed clear and we was pretty well out of the grass at home, so Tuesday morning me and Papa loaded up some plow tools on the wagon and got ourself over there about sunup. There was about nine or ten men showed up. Mr. Redding and Mr. Manning both come, and maybe as many boys.

Mr. Will Martin, this feller's closest neighbor, kinda took over and sorted ever'body out as to what to do. (I thought that feller's name would come to me in a minute, but I be dang if I can recollect it.) Well, anyway, the feller's woodpile was so low his wife was picking up chips, so Mr. Will told off three or four men and some boys to tend to wood-getting and put the rest of us to hoeing or plowing.

Papa got out some coffee Mama had ground and sent by us, and the man's wife built a fire around her washpot in the backyard and kept hot coffee for us all day. She'd of fed us, too, such as they had, but we'd all brought a lunch, mostly biscuits and bacon and syrup or jelly, packed in a syrup bucket to keep out dirt and ants and such.

'Long about the middle of the day the fellers getting wood come in with a couple of good loads of blocks, and we all spread our grub out along the edge of the back porch and got some of that hot coffee and had us a syrup-bucket banquet. 'Course we insisted the feller's wife and kids eat something. The lady just eat a few bites here and there, just enough so she could say how good it tasted and how well it was cooked, but them three little young'uns didn't just nibble. They'd been on sawmill gravy and cornbread and garden sass so long they sure did wade into them biscuits and sweet'nin' and sidemeat. After they ate till their navels was sticking out like a pot leg, I seen Mr. Redding open his syrup bucket and take out a piece of cake he'd saved back and go divide it amongst the three. Time we went back to work, their ma had throwed a quilt down in the dog trot where it was cool, and them little fellers was piled up like puppies and dead to the world.

Shorty Lloyd was there a-helping that day. Shorty was the kind of feller that always had a funny story to tell. Whilst we was eating he got to telling us about a Watkins Products peddler walking into old Mrs. Smith's yard and before she could get to the door and holler one of her dogs took a britches leg off for him. Said the peddler told him he believed the dog would have got the other one, but he kept dodging and kicking till he got in a good lick and knocked him down.

Mr. Manning spoke up and said he'd of stomped his damn head off while he had him down. When he said that, I seen George Redding wheel and give him a hard look, and I knowed then things hadn't blowed over as much as I thought.

Well, we'd got through hoeing that morning, so us that'd been at that helped split and stack the wood and the men got back to plowing, and by three or four o'clock we was all finished, loaded up, and ready to go home.

To show you how folks neighbored them days, Mr. Will Martin had broke a plow handle that morning and the rest of the day he'd used a old Georgia Stock that belonged to the feller where we was working. (What in the hell was that feller's name? All I can think of is Jackson, and I know dang well that ain't it.) Well, anyway, this feller couldn't get out of bed, but Mr. Will made it a point to go in ever' once in a while and ask about something or get his advice about what we was doing and ever' time he did he'd brag on that old plow. Easiest running plow he'd ever seen and the best handling and I don't know what all. That evening he told the feller he was going to butcher a beef the next day, and if he could spare that Georgia Stock, he'd swap him a forequarter for it. 'Course, they both knowed that old plow wasn't worth half what the beef was, but Mr. Will knowed the feller wouldn't take the beef as a outright gift, bad as he needed it. By swapping this way, it was changed from just plain charity and he got to keep a little pride and got the beef for his family too.

After the kids went to sleep, the lady—(that feller's name was Grayson, Albert Gray—no, Elbert Grayson. I knowed I'd recollect it after a while).

Well, as I was saying, after the kids went to sleep Mrs. Grayson had went and gathered a bunch of garden sass and had it all washed and cleaned, and after we was loaded up and ready to go, she invited the men to help themselves, if they needed any of it. 'Course they had plenty of such at home, but they all picked out a mess of something and made over it and said how nice the stuff was. Papa took a bunch of mustard greens and said he was proud to get them, that the lice had took ours, which was a lie, and Shorty Lloyd took a big handful of radishes and said he was glad to get the damn things, that he believed ever' damn radish his wife had planted the whole damn year had been pithy by the time they come up, and he hadn't had a decent damn radish for two damn months. Shorty was good-hearted but had been knowed to cuss. Mr. Manning took some tomatoes and said theirs was late and they hadn't had one all spring the worms hadn't been at, and thanked her two or three times, and the rest done about the same.

I 'spect the lady knew they had plenty of such truck at home, but it was all she had to offer for what we'd done and them men weren't about to shame her by belittling it. Helping folks when they need it is fine and is highly spoke of in the Good Book, but if it ain't done in such a way that they can hold their heads up afterward it's best not done at all.

You could tell ever'body felt good about the day's work from the way they was laughing and joshing when we pulled out for home. They also knowed their neighboring would be paid back if they ever needed it.

Papa and me went by Mr. Manning's and helped him block his wagon up so's he could pull the wheels and grease the spindles. Whilst we was at it, I heard him tell Papa he was going to meet the road gang at Woods Spring the next morning and finish working out his road tax. Back then you could pay it in money or work it out three days a year.

The next morning a little after good daylight, me and Papa had finished feeding and was going to the house after more coffee when Mr. Manning passed and waved at us. He was riding at a lope, and Papa remarked he'd got off late.

About the time Mama brought our coffee out on the front porch, we heard a shot, and in a minute or two another one. We could tell they was about at Mr. Redding's, and in just another minute or two we heard Mrs. Redding scream, just as clear. Me and Mama and Papa all three started running that way hard as we could. I wouldn't have believed it, but Papa outrun me and met Mrs. Redding first, about halfway to their place, and shook her till she quit screaming and told him George had killed Mr. Manning. When I got to them, he told me to take her back to meet Mama and help get her to our house and then catch my saddle horse and meet him at Redding's, that I'd have to go to Liberty for the sheriff.

Mr. Redding had stood at his front gate with that old ten-gauge and shot Mr. Manning off his horse and then walked out to the road and shot him again point-blank.

Papa always said them two was the best men he'd ever neighbored with.

James A. Michener ———————————

James A. Michener (b. 1907) found triumphant success with his first book, a collection of short stories, Tales of the South Pacific, *which won the Pulitzer Prize in 1947 and became the basis for the immortal Rodgers and Hammerstein musical. He has written twenty nonfiction works on the arts and politics, but it is his fourteen novels that have made him a major influence in fiction—the master of the sweeping plot that details the clash and intertwining of cultures through telescoped historical episodes. This selection from* Texas *depicts a small town reeling from the Ku Klux Klan and oil speculators.*

THE TOWN

The scandal in Waxahachie over the dancing Sunday School girls was an amusing diversion which might have happened in any Texas town of this period and which could be forgiven as misguided religiosity. But the much more serious madness that gripped Larkin at about the same time was an aberration which could not be laughed away, for it came closer to threatening the stability of the entire state.

Precisely when it started no one could recall. One man said: "It was patriotism, nothing more. I saw them boys come marchin' home from the war and I asked myself: 'What can I do to preserve our freedoms?' That's how it started, best motives in the world."

Others argued that it had been triggered by that rip-roaring revival staged in Larkin by the ranting Fort Worth evangelist J. Frank Norris, a type much different from the spiritual Elder Fry. Norris was an aggressive man who thundered sulphurous diatribes against saloon keepers, race-track addicts, liberal professors, and women who wore bobbed hair or skirts above the ankle. He was especially opposed to dancing, which, he claimed, "scarlet women use to tempt men."

His anathema, however, was the Roman Catholic church, which he lambasted in wild and colorful accusation: "It's the darkest, bloodiest ecclesiastical machine that has ever been known in the annals of time. It's the enemy of home, of marriage and of every decent human emotion. The Pope has a plan for capturing Texas, and I have a plan for defeating him."

He was most effective when he moved nervously from one side of the pulpit to the other, extending his hands and crying: "I speak for all you humble, God-fearing folks from the forks of the creek. You know what's right and wrong, better than any professors at Baylor or SMU. It's on you that God relies for the salvation of our state."

One man, not especially religious, testified: "When J. Frank Norris shouted 'I need the help of you little folks from the forks of the creek,' I knowed he was speakin' direct to me, and that's when I got all fired up. I saw myself as the right arm of God holdin' a sword ready to strike."

A University of Texas historian later published documents proving that in Larkin, at least, it had originated not with Norris but with the arrival of three quite different outsiders who had not known one another but who did later act in concert. The earliest newcomer was a man from Georgia who told exciting yarns of what his group had accomplished. The next was a man from Mississippi who assured the Larkin people that his state was taking things in hand. But the greatest influence seemed to have been the third man, a salesman of farm machinery who drifted in from Indiana with startling news: "Up there our boys are pretty well takin' over the state."

From such evidence it would be difficult to assess the role played by religion, for while very few ministers actually participated, almost every man who did become involved was a devout member of one Protestant church or another, and the movement strenuously supported religion, with the popular symbols of Christianity featured in the group's rituals.

Whatever the cause, by early December 1919 men began appearing throughout Larkin County dressed in long white robes, masks and, sometimes, tall conical hats. The Ku Klux Klan, born after the Civil War, had begun its tempestuous resurrection.

In Larkin it was not a general reign of terror, and nobody ever claimed it was. The local Klan conducted no hangings, no burnings at the stake and only a few necessary floggings. It was best understood as a group of unquestioned patriots, all of them believing Christians, who yearned to see the historic virtues of 1836 and 1861 restored. It was a movement of men who resented industrial change, shifting moral values and disturbed allegiances; they were determined to preserve and restore what they identified as the best features of American life, and in their meetings and their publications they reassured one another that these were their only aims.

Nor was the Larkin Klan simply a rebellion against blacks, for after the first few days there were no blacks left in town. At the beginning there had been two families, offspring of those black cavalrymen who had stayed behind when the 10th Cavalry rode out of Fort Garner for the last time. At first these two men had kept an Indian woman between them, but later on they had acquired a wandering white woman, so that the present generation was pretty well mixed.

They were one of the first problems addressed by the Ku Kluxers after the organization was securely launched. A committee of four, in full regalia, moved through the town one December night and met with the black families. There was no violence, simply the statement: "We don't cotton to havin' your type in this town." It was suggested that the blacks move on to Fort Griffin, where anybody was accepted, and a purse of twenty-six dollars was given them to help with the expense of moving.

One family left town the next morning; the other, named Jaxifer, decided to stay, but when a midnight cross blazed at the front door, the Jaxifers lit out for Fort Griffin, and there was no more of that kind of trouble in Larkin. The Klan did, however, commission four big well-lettered signs, which were posted at the entrances to the town:

NIGGER!
DO NOT LET THE SETTING SUN
FIND YOU IN THIS TOWN.
WARNING!

Thereafter it was the boast of Larkin that "no goddamned nigger ever slept overnight in this town."

Nor did the Klan stress its opposition to Jews. Banker Weatherby, an old man now who had been among the first to join the Klan, simply informed three Jewish storekeepers in town that "our loan committee no longer wishes to finance your business, and we all think it would be better if you moved along." They did.

The strong opposition to Catholicism presented more complex problems, because the county did contain a rather substantial scattering of this proscribed sect, and whereas some of the more vocal Klansmen wanted to "throw ever' goddamned mackerel snatcher out of Texas," others pointed out that even in as well-organized a town as Larkin, more had drifted in than they thought. They had not been welcomed and their mysterious behavior was carefully watched, but at least they weren't black, or Indian, or Jewish, so they were partially acceptable.

The Larkin Klan never made a public announcement that Catholics would be allowed to stay, and at even the slightest infraction of the Klan's self-formulated rules, anyone with an Irish-sounding name was visited, and warned he would be beaten up if he persisted in any un-Christian deportment.

When the town was finally cleaned up and inhabited by only white members of the major Protestant religions, plus the well-behaved Catholics, it was conceded that Larkin was one of the finest towns in Texas. Its men had a commitment to economic prosperity. Its women attended church faithfully. And its crime rate was so low that it barely merited mention. There was some truth to the next signs the Klansmen erected in 1920:

LARKIN

BEST LITTLE TOWN IN TEXAS

WATCH US GROW

If the Klan avoided violence against blacks or Jews or Catholics, who were its targets? An event in the spring of 1921 best illustrates its preoccupations, for then it confronted a rather worthless man of fifty who had been working in the town's livery stable when Larkin still had horses. He now served as janitor and polishing man at the Chevrolet garage, but he had also been living for many years with a shiftless woman named Nora as his housekeeper; few titles in town were less deserved than hers, for she was totally incapable of keeping even a dog kennel, let alone a house. Jake and Nora lived in chaos and in sin, and the upright men of the Klan felt it was high time this ungodly conduct be stopped.

In orderly fashion, which marked all their actions, they appeared at Jake's cabin one Tuesday night carrying a lighted torch, which all could see, and in their clean white robes, their faces hidden by masks, they handed down the law: "All this immoral sort of thing is gonna stop in Larkin. Marry this woman by Friday sundown or suffer the consequences."

Jake and Nora had no need of marriage or any understanding of how to participate in one had they wanted to. By hit-and-miss they had worked out a pattern of living which suited them and which produced far fewer family brawls than some of the more traditional arrangements in town. The Klansmen were right that no one would want a lot of such establishments in a community, but Jake felt there ought to be leeway for the accommodation of one or two, especially if they worked well and produced neither scandal nor a horde of unruly children.

On Wednesday the Klansmen who had handed Jake and Nora their ultimatum watched to see what corrective steps the couple proposed taking, and when nothing seemed to have been done, two of the more responsible Klansmen decided to visit the couple again on Thursday night, and this they did in friendly fashion: "Jake, you don't seem to understand. If you don't marry this woman . . ."

"Who are y'all? Behind them masks? What right . . . ?"

"We're the conscience of this community. We're determined to wipe out immoral behavior."

"Leave us alone. What about Mr. Henderson and his secretary?"

The boldness of this question stunned the two Klansmen, each of whom knew about Mr. Henderson and his secretary. But it was not people like Henderson whom the Klan policed, and for someone like Jake to bring such a name into discussion was abhorrent. Now the tenor of the conversation grew more ominous: "Jake, Nora, you get married by tomorrow night or suffer the consequences."

Jake was prepared to brazen the thing out, but Nora asked in real confusion: "How could we get married?" and the two hooded visitors turned their attention to her: "We'll take you to the justice of the peace tomorrow morning, or if you prefer a church wedding, Reverend Hislop has said he'd do it for us."

"Get out of here!" Jake shouted, and the two men withdrew.

The next day passed, with Jake sweeping at the Chevrolet garage and showing no sign of remorse for his immoral persistence. Those Klansmen in the know watched his house—or was it Nora's house?—

and saw that nothing was happening there, either, so at eight that Friday evening seven Ku Kluxers met with the salesman from Indiana, and after praying that they might act with justice, charity and restraint, marched with a burning cross to Jake's place. Planting the cross before the front door, they summoned the two miscreants.

As soon as Jake appeared he was grabbed, not hurtfully, and stripped of his shirt. Tar was applied liberally across his back, and then a Klansman with a bag of feathers slapped handfuls onto the tar. He was then hoisted onto a stout beam, which four other Klansmen carried, and there he was held, feet tied together beneath the beam, while the moral custodians tended to the slut Nora.

Around the world, in all times and in all places, whenever men go on an ethical rampage they feel that they must discipline women: "Your dresses are too short." "You tempt men." "Your behavior is salacious." "You must be put in your proper place." This stems, of course, from the inherent mystery of women, their capacity to survive, their ability to bear children, the universal suspicion that they possess some arcane knowledge not available to men. Women are dangerous, and men pass laws to keep them under restraint. All religions, which also deal in mysteries, know this, and that is why the Muslim, the Jewish, the Catholic and the Mormon faiths proscribed women so severely and why other churches ran into trouble when they tried belatedly to ordain women as ministers.

The men of the Ku Klux Klan were as bewildered by sex as any of their reforming predecessors, and on this dark night they had to look upon Nora-with-three-teeth-missing-in-front as a temptress who had seduced Jake into his immoral life. But what to do with her? There was no inclination at all to strip her, but there was a burning desire to punish her, so two men dragged her out beside the flaming cross and tarred her whole dress, fore and aft, scattering feathers liberally upon her.

She then was lifted onto the rail, behind her man, whereupon two additional men supported it, and in this formation the hooded Klansmen paraded through the streets of Larkin behind a sign which proclaimed:

EMORALITY IN LARKIN
WILL STOP

Jake and Nora did not respond as the Klansmen had hoped. They did not marry, and when the long parade was over they returned home, scraped off the tar, and said "nothin' to nobody." Early Saturday morning Jake was at the garage, sweeping as usual and saying hello to any who passed. He had no idea who had disciplined him, and at noon he walked home as usual for his lunch. Nora went to the store late Saturday for her weekend supplies, and on Sunday, Jake fished as always, up at the tank, which contained some good-sized bass, while Nora sat on her front lawn where scars from the burned cross still showed.

Such behavior infuriated the Klansmen, who convened after church on Sunday a special meeting at which it was discussed with some heat as to whether the two should be flogged. The Indiana man was all for a public whipping in the courthouse square, but the Georgia man argued against it: "We found it does no good. Creates sympathy. And it scares the womenfolk."

Instead, the men found an old wagon and a worthless horse, and these they drove to Jake's place on Monday evening. Throwing the two adulterers into the back, they piled the wagon with as many of their household goods as possible, then drove west of town till they were beyond sight of the beautiful courthouse tower which bespoke order and justice for this part of Texas. There the Klansmen plopped Jake onto the driver's bench and gave him the reins: "Straight down this road is Fort Griffin. They'll accept anybody."

The hooded posse returned to Larkin after sunset, and two hours later Jake and Nora, driving the old horse that Jake had often tended in the livery stable, came back to town. With no fanfare they rode down familiar streets to their home, unpacked their belongings, and went to bed.

That was Monday. On Wednesday night Jake was found behind the garage, shot to death.

No charges were ever filed against the Klansmen, and for the very good reason that no one knew for sure who they were, or even if they had done it. At least, that was the legal contention. Of course, everyone knew that Floyd Rusk—who could not hide his size even under a bed-sheet—was one of the leaders, perhaps *the* leader, because he was obvious at all the marches and the cross burnings, but no one could be found who could swear that yes, he had seen Floyd Rusk tarring Jake.

It was also known that Clyde Weatherby was an active member, as were the hardware merchant, the doctor, the schoolteacher and the druggist. Some four dozen other men, the best in the community, joined later. With an equal mix of patriotism and religion, these men of good intention began to inspect all aspects of life in Larkin, for they were determined to keep their little town in the mainstream of American life as they perceived it.

They forced six men to marry their housekeepers. They lectured, in an almost fatherly manner, two teen-aged girls who seemed likely to become promiscuous, and they positively shut down a grocer against whom several housewives had complained. They did not tar-and-feather him, nor did they horsewhip him; those punishments were reserved for sexual infractions, but they did ride him out of town, telling him to transfer his shop to Fort Griffin, where honesty of trade was not so severely supervised.

By the beginning of 1922 these men had Larkin in the shape they wanted; even some of the Catholics, fearing that reprisals would next be directed at them, had moved away, making the town about as homogeneous as one could have found in all of Texas. It was a community of Protestant Christians in which the rules were understood and in which infractions were severely punished. Almost none of the excesses connected with the Klan in other parts of the nation were condoned here, and after two years of intense effort the Klansmen, when they met at night, could justifiably claim that they had cleaned up Larkin. With this victory under their belt, they intended moving against Texas as a whole, and then, all of the United States.

In 1922 they got well started by electing their man, Earle B. Mayfield, a Tyler grocer, to the United States Senate, but this triumph had a bitter aftermath, because for two years that august body refused to seat a man accused of Klan membership, and when it did finally accept him, he was denied reelection. The Larkin members assuaged their disappointment by achieving a notorious victory in the local high school, where the principal, an enthusiastic Klansman, inserted in the school yearbook a well-drawn full-page depiction of a nightrider in his regalia of bedsheet, mask and pointed hat astride a white stallion under a halo composed of the words GOD, COUNTRY, PROTESTANTISM, SUPREMACY. At the bottom of the page, in a neatly lettered panel, stood the exhortation LIKE THE KLAN, LARKIN HIGH WILL TRIUMPH IN FOOTBALL.

In the growing town, however, the Klan suffered other frustrations. The editor of the *Defender,* an effeminate young man from Arkansas, had the temerity to editorialize against them, and in a series of articles he explained why he opposed what he called "midnight terrorism." This unlucky phrase infuriated the Klansmen: "We have to guard the morals of Larkin at night because during the day we have to run our businesses. Terrorism is shooting innocent people, and no man can claim we ever done that, and live."

They handled the newspaper with restraint. First they approached the editor, in masks, and explained their lofty motives, pointing out the many good things they had done for Larkin, like eliminating vice and increasing church membership, but they made little impression on the young man.

Next they threatened him. Three Klansmen, including one of enormous bulk, visited him at his home at two in the morning, warning him that he must halt all comment on the Klan "or our next visit is gonna be more serious."

The young editor, despite his appearance, was apparently cut from a robust Arkansas stock, because he ignored the threats, whereupon the governing committee of the Klan met to discuss what next to try. The meeting was held in the bank, after hours and without masks. Nine men, clean-shaven, well-dressed, giving every evidence of prosperity and right living, met solemnly to discuss their options: "We can tar-and-feather him. We can whip him publicly. Or we can shoot him. But one way or another, we are going to silence that bastard."

There was support for each of these choices, but after additional discussion, the majority seemed to settle upon a good horsewhipping on the courthouse steps, but then Floyd Rusk, huffing and puffing, introduced a note of reason: "Men, in this country you learn never to bust the nose of the press. If you flog that editor publicly, or even privately, the entire press of Texas and the United States is goin' to descend upon this town. And if you shoot him, the federal government will have the marshals in here."

"What can we do?" the banker asked.

"You have the solution," Rusk said.

"Which is what?"

"Buy the paper. Throw him out." When this evoked discussion, Rusk listened, judged the weight of various opinions, and said: "It's quick, it's effective, and it's legal."

So without even donning their hooded costumes, the leading members of the Klan accumulated a fund and bought the paper, then, avoiding scandal, quietly drove the young editor out of town. That source of criticism was silenced, because before hiring a new editor, also a young man but this time from Dallas, the leading Klansmen satisfied themselves that he was a supporter of their movement and had been a member in the larger city.

The second problem was not so easily handled. Reverend Hislop was no irritating liberal like the editor from Arkansas, for he was against everything the Klan was against—immorality, adultery, drunkenness, shady business practice, the excesses of youth, such as blatant dancing—but he taught that these evils could best be opposed through an orderly church; he suspected that Jesus would not have approved of nightriders or flaming crosses, for the latter symbol was too precious to be so abused. Hislop was not a social hero; he kept his suspicions to himself, but as in all such situations wherein a man of good intention tries to hide, the facts had a tendency to uncover him, and that is what happened.

The Klansmen, eager to adopt a procedure which had proved effective in many small towns across the state, initiated the policy of having a committee of six members dress in full regalia each Sunday morning and march as a unit to either the Baptist or Methodist church, timing their arrival to coincide with the collection. Silently, and with impressive dignity, they entered at the rear, strode up the middle aisle in formation, and placed upon the altar an envelope containing a substantial cash contribution. "For God's work," the leader would cry in a loud voice, whereupon the six would turn on their heels and march out.

Such pageantry impressed the citizens, gaining the Klan much popular support, especially when the amount of the contribution was magnified in the telling: "They give two hunnerd big ones for the poor and needy of this community." Many believed that God had selected them as His right arm, and the moral intention of most of their public acts supported this view. Some thoughtful men came to believe that soon the Klan would assume responsibility for all of Texas, and that when that happened, a new day of justice and honest living would result.

Reverend Hislop did not see it this way. As a devout Southerner and a strong defender of the Confederacy, he understood the emotions which had called forth the original Klan back in the dark days after 1865, and supposed that had he lived then, he would have been a Klansman, because, as he said, "some kind of corrective action was needed." But he was not so sure about the motives of this revived Klan of the 1920s: "They stand for all that's good, that I must confess. And they also support the programs of the church. They're against sin, and that puts them on my side. But decisions of punishment should be made by courts of law. In the long range of human history, there is no alternative to that. When the church dispensed justice in Spain and New England, it did a bad job. When these good men dispense their midnight justice at the country crossroads, they do an equally imperfect job. Martha, I cannot accept their Sunday contributions any longer."

The decision had been reached painfully, but it was set in rock. However, Hislop was not the kind of man to create a public scandal; that would have been most repugnant. So on Sunday, when the six hooded Klansmen marched into his church, their polished boots clicking, he accepted their offering, but that very afternoon he summoned Floyd Rusk and the Indiana salesman to his parsonage, where he told them: "It is improper for you to invade the House of the Lord. It's improper for you to assume the duties of the church."

"Why do you tell me this?" Rusk asked, and Reverend Hislop pointed a finger at the rancher's enormous belly: "Do you think you can hide that behind a costume?"

"But why do you oppose the Klan?" Rusk asked. "Surely it supports God's will."

"I am sometimes confused as to what God's will really is."

"Are you talkin' atheism?" Rusk demanded.

"I'm saying that I'm not sure what is accomplished by tarring a silly woman like Nora."

"Surely she was an evil influence."

"They thought that in Salem, when old women muttered. They hanged them. What are you going to do to Nora now?"

"Nora has nothing to do with this. We're turning Larkin into a Christian town."

"In some things, yes. Mr. Rusk, don't you realize that for every wayward person you correct, there are six others in our town who cheat their customers, who misappropriate funds . . . Life goes on here much as it does in Chicago or Atlanta, but you focus only on the little sinners."

"You do talk atheism, Reverend Hislop. You better be careful."

"I am being careful, Mr. Rusk, and I'm asking you politely, as a fellow Christian who approves of much that you do, not to enter my church any more with your offerings. The money I need, and it can be delivered in the plate like the other offerings, but the display I do not need."

On Sunday the six Klansmen in full regalia entered the church as usual. Led by a portly figure, they marched to the altar, where the large one said in a loud voice: "For God's work."

Before they could click their heels and retreat, Reverend Hislop said quietly: "Gentlemen, God thanks you for your offering. His work needs all the support it can get. But you must not enter His church in disguise.

You must not associate God with your endeavors, worthy though they sometimes are. Please take your offering out with you."

No Klansman spoke. At the big man's signal they tramped down the aisle and out the door, leaving their money where they had placed it.

On previous Sundays the deacons who passed the collection plates and then marched to the altar, where the offerings were blessed, had rather grandiloquently lifted the Klan donation and placed it atop the lesser offerings, but on this day Reverend Hislop asked them not to do this. To his astonishment, one of the deacons who was a member of the Klan ostentatiously took the envelope from where Rusk had left it and placed it once more atop all the offerings, as if it took precedence because of the Klan's power in that town and in that church.

The battle lines were drawn, with a good eighty percent of the church members siding with the Klan rather than with their pastor. On the next Sunday the same three characters played the same charade. Floyd Rusk in his bedsheet made the donation; Reverend Hislop rejected it; and the deacon accepted it.

On the following Tuesday the church elders met with Reverend Hislop, a quiet-mannered man who deplored controversy, and informed him that his services were no longer required in Larkin. "You've lost the confidence of your people," the banker explained. "And when that happens, the minister has to go."

"You're the elders," Hislop said.

"But we want to make it easy for you," the man from Indiana said. "There's a Methodist church in Waynesboro, Pennsylvania, lovely town among the hills. It needs a pastor, and the bishop in those parts has indicated that he would look kindly upon your removal there."

Like the purchase of the newspaper and elimination of its editor, the Larkin Methodist Church was purified without public scandal. Reverend Hislop preached on Sunday; he rejected the Klan offering; the deacons accepted it; and on Thursday he quietly disappeared.

The Klan now ruled the little town. All blacks were gone; all Jews were gone; no Mexicans were allowed within the town limits; and the lower class of Catholics had been eased out. It was a town of order, limited prosperity, and Christian decency. All voices of protest had been effectively silenced. Of course, as Reverend Hislop had pointed out, the same amount of acceptable crime prevailed as in any American town: some lawyers diverted public moneys into their own pockets; some doctors performed abortions; some politicians contrived election results to suit their purposes; and a good many deacons from all the churches drank moderately and played an occasional game of poker. There was a fair amount of adultery and not a little juggling of account books, but the conspicuous social crimes which offended the middle-class morality of the district, like open cohabitation or lascivious dancing, had been brought under control.

Then, just as the Ku Kluxers were congratulating themselves, a small, dirty, sharp-eyed man named Dewey Kimbro slipped into town, bringing an irresistible alternative to the Klan, and everything blew apart.

He first appeared as a man of mystery, under thirty, with sandy red hair and a slight stoop even though he was short. He would often ride his horse far into the countryside and tell nobody anything about it. He spoke little, in fact, and when he did his words fell into two sharply defined patterns, for sometimes he sounded like a college professor, at other times like the roughest cowboy, and what his inherited vocabulary had been, no one could guess.

He attracted the attention of the Klansmen, who were not happy with strangers moving about their domain, and several extended discussions were held concerning him, with Floyd Rusk leading the attack: "I don't want him prowling my ranchland." To Rusk's surprise, the banker said: "When he transferred his funds to us, he asked about you, Floyd."

"He did? He better lay off."

Things remained in this uncertain state, with Kimbro attracting increased attention by his excursions, now here, now there, until the day when Rusk demanded that his Klansmen take action: "I say we run him out of town. No place here for a man like him." But the others pointed out that he had transferred into the Larkin bank nearly a thousand dollars, and that amount of money commanded respect.

"What do we know about him?" Rusk asked with that canny rural capacity for identifying trouble.

"He boards with Nora."

"The woman we tarred-and-feathered?"

"The same."

"Well," announced a third man, "he sure as hell ain't havin' sex with someone like her."

"But it don't look good," Rusk said. "We got to keep watchin'."

Then Kimbro made his big mistake. From Jacksboro he imported on the Reo bus, which ran between the two towns, a twenty-year-old beauty named Esther, with painted cheeks and a flowery outfit she could not have paid for with her clerk's wages. Kimbro moved her right into Nora's place, and on her third night of residence the couple was visited by the hooded Klan.

"Are you two married?"

"Whose business?" Kimbro asked the question, but it could just as well have come from Esther.

"It's our business. We don't allow your kind in this town."

"I'm here. And so is she."

"And do you think you'll be allowed to stay here?"

"I sure intend to. Till I get my work done."

"And what is your work?" a masked figure asked.

"That's my business."

"Enough of this," a very fat Klansman broke in. "Kimbro, if that's your real name, you got till Thursday night to get out of town. And, miss, you by God better be goin' with him."

On Tuesday and Wednesday, Dewey Kimbro, named after the Hero of Manila and just as taciturn, rode out of town on his speckled horse. Spies followed him for a while, but could only report that he rode a while, stopped a while, dismounted occasionally, then rode on. He met no one, did nothing conspicuous, and toward dusk rode back into town, where Esther and Nora had supper waiting.

The three had gone to bed—Kimbro and the girl in one room—when four hooded figures bearing whips appeared, banging on the door and calling for Kimbro to come out. Under the hoods were Lew and Les Tumlinson, twin brothers who ran the coal and lumber business, Ed Boatright, who had the Chevrolet agency where the dead Jake had worked, and Floyd Rusk, the big rancher.

When Kimbro refused to appear, the Tumlinson twins kicked in the door, stormed into Nora's small house, and rampaged through the rooms till they found Kimbro and his whore in bed. Pulling him from under the covers, they dragged his small body along the hallway and through the front door. On the lawn, in about the same position as when Jake and Nora were tarred, Rusk and Boatright had erected a cross, and were in the process of igniting it when the twins shouted: "We got him!" When the cross lit up the sky, a horde of onlookers ran up, and there was so much calling back and forth among the hooded figures that the crowd knew who the four avengers were: "That's Lew Tumlinson for sure, and if he's here, so's his brother. The fat one we know, and I think the other has got to be Ed Boatright."

Dewey Kimbro, who never missed anything, even when he was about to be thrashed, heard the names. He also heard the fat man say:

"Strip him!" and when the nightshirt was torn away and he stood naked, he heard the same man shout: "Lay it on. Good."

He refused to faint. He refused to cry out. In the glare of the flaming cross, he bore the first twenty-odd slashes of the three whips, but then he lost count, and finally he did faint.

At nine o'clock next morning he barged into Floyd Rusk's kitchen, and the fat man, who was an expert with revolvers from an early age, anticipated trouble and whipped out one of his big six-shooters, but before he could get it into position, he glared into the barrel of a small yet deadly German pistol pointed straight at a spot between his eyes.

For a long, tense moment the two men retained their positions, Rusk almost ready to fire his huge revolver, Kimbro prepared to fire first with his smaller gun. Finally Rusk dropped his, at which Kimbro said: "Place it right here where I can watch it," and Floyd did, sweating heavily.

"Now let's sit down here, Mr. Rusk, and talk sense." When the big man took his place at the kitchen table, with his gun in reach not of himself but of Kimbro, a conversation began which modified the history of Larkin County.

"Mr. Rusk, you whipped me last night—"

"Now wait!"

"You're right. You never laid a rawhide on me. But you ordered the Tumlinson twins and Ed Boatright . . ." Rusk's glistening of sweat became a small torrent. "I ought to kill you for that, and maybe later on I will. But right now you and I need each other, and you're far more valuable to me alive than dead."

"Why?"

"I have a secret, Mr. Rusk. I've had it since I was eleven years old. Do you remember Mrs. Jackson who ran the little store?"

"Yes, I believe I do."

"You wouldn't remember a boy from East Texas who spent one summer with her?"

"Are you that boy?"

"I am."

"And what secret did you discover?"

"On your land . . . out by the tank . . ."

"That's not my land. My father gave it to the Yeagers."

"I know. Your father promised it in the 1870s. You formalized it in 1909."

"So it's not my land."

Kimbro shifted in his chair, for the pain from his whipping was intense. He had a most important statement to make, and he wanted to be in complete control when he made it, but just as he was prepared to disclose the purpose of his visit, Molly Rusk came into the kitchen, a big blowzy woman who, against all the rules of nature, was pregnant. She had a round, happy face made even more placid by the miracle of her condition, and with the simplicity that marked most of her actions, she took one look at Kimbro and asked: "Aren't you the man they whipped last night?" and he said: "I am."

She was about to ask why he was sitting in her kitchen this morning, when Rusk said respectfully: "You better leave us alone, Molly," and she retired with apologies, but she had barely closed the door when she returned: "There's coffee on the stove." Then she added: "Floyd, don't do anything brutal with that gun."

"True, the land is no longer yours, Mr. Rusk," Kimbro said quietly. "Your daddy promised it to Yeager, but when you transferred it legally, you were clever enough to retain the mineral rights."

Rusk leaned far back in his chair. Then he placed his pudgy hands on the edge of the table, and from this position he sat staring at the little stranger. Finally, in an awed voice he asked: "You mean . . ."

Kimbro nodded, and after readjusting his painful back, he said: "When I stayed here that summer I did a lot of tramping about. Always have."

"And what did you find at the tank?"

"A small rise that everyone else had overlooked. When I kicked rocks aside, I came upon . . . guess what?"

"Gold?"

"Much better. Coal."

"Coal?"

"Yep. Sneaked some home and it burned a glowing red. Kept on burning. So I kept on exploring . . ."

"And you located a coal mine?"

"Nope. The strain was trivial, played out fast. But I covered the spot, piled rocks over it, and if you and I go out there this morning, we'll find a slight trace of coal hiding where it's always been."

"And what does this mean?"

"You don't know? I knew when I was ten. Read it in a book." He shifted again. "I read a lot, Mr. Rusk."

"And what did you read, at ten?"

Kimbro hesitated, then changed the subject entirely: "Mr. Rusk, I want you to enter into a deal with me, right now. Word of a gentleman. We're partners, seventy-five to you, twenty-five to me."

"What the hell kind of offer is that? I don't even know what we're talkin' about."

"You will. In two minutes, if you make the deal."

"You'd trust me, after last night?"

"I have to." Kimbro banged the table. "And by God, you have to trust me, too."

"Is it worth my while? I have a lot of cattle, you know."

"And you're losing your ass on them, aren't you?"

"Well, the market . . ."

"Seventy-five, twenty-five for my secret and the know-how to develop it."

Again Rusk leaned back: "What do you know about me, personally I mean?"

"That you're a bastard, through and through. But once you give your word, you stick to it."

"I do. You know, Kimbro, when I was fourteen or thereabouts I rode to Dodge City with a—"

"You went to Dodge City?"

"I did, with the greatest trail driver Texas ever produced, R. J. Poteet. He tried to make a man of me, but I wouldn't allow it. At Dodge, I killed two men, yep, age fifteen I think I was. Poteet's two point men spirited me out of town. Just ahead of the sheriff. But on the ride back to Texas he and his men held a kangaroo court because they knew damned well I hadn't shot in self-defense. Found me guilty and strung me up. I thought sure as hell . . ." He was sweating so profusely that he asked: "Can I get that towel?"

"Stay away from the gun."

"They slapped the horse I was sitting on, I fell, I felt the rope bite into my neck. And then Poteet caught me. He lectured me about my wrong ways, and I spat in his face." He laughed nervously. "I was scared to death, really petrified, but I wouldn't show it. Poteet went for his gun, then brushed me aside."

He rocked back and forth on the kitchen chair, an immensely fat man of forty-seven. Replacing his hands on the table, he said: "That hanging was the making of me, Kimbro. Taught me two things. You've uncovered one of them. I am a man of my word, hell or high water. And I have never since then been afraid to use my gun when it had to be used. If you're partners with me, be damned careful."

"That's why I brought this," Kimbro said, indicating the gun which he had kept trained on the fat man during their discussion.

"So what did you learn?" Rusk asked.

"Partners?" Kimbro asked, and the two shook hands, after which the little fellow delivered his momentous information: "At ten I knew that coal and petroleum are the same substance, in different form."

Rusk gasped: "You mean oil?" The word echoed through the quiet kitchen as if a bomb had exploded, for the wild discoveries in East Texas had alerted the entire state to the possibilities of this fantastic substance which made farmers multimillionaires.

"At fourteen," Kimbro continued, "I studied all the chemistry and physics our little school allowed, and at seventeen I enrolled at Texas A&M."

"You a college graduate?"

"Three years only. By that time I knew more about petroleum than the professors. Got a job with Humble, then Gulf. Field man. Sort of an informal geologist. Worked the rigs too, so I know what drilling is. Mr. Rusk, I'm a complete oilman, but what I really am is maybe the world's greatest creekologist."

"What's that?"

"A contemptuous name the professors give practical men like me. We study the way creeks run, the rise and fall of land forms, and we guess like hell." He slammed the table. "But by God, we find oil. It's downright infuriating to the college people how we find oil."

"And you think you've found some on my land?"

"From the run of the creeks and the rise in your field, I'm satisfied that we're sitting near the middle of a substantial field."

"You mean real oil?"

"I do. Not a bunch of spectacular gushers like Spindletop. But good, dependable oil trapped in the rocks below us."

"If you're right, could we make some real money?"

"A fortune, if we handle it right."

"And what would right be?"

"How much of this land around here do you own?"

"I'm sure you've checked at the courthouse. Well over seven thousand acres."

"Where does it lie, relation to the tank?"

"South and some across Bear Creek to the west."

"I'm glad you can tell the truth. But if I'm right, the field runs north and east of the tank. Could you buy any of that land?"

"Look, I don't have much ready cash."

"Could you lease the mineral rights? I mean right now. Not tomorrow, now."

"Is speed so necessary?"

"The minute anyone suspects what we're up to . . . if they even guess that I'm a creekologist . . . Then it's too late."

"How does an oil lease work?"

Kimbro had to rise, adjust his scarred back, and sit gingerly on the edge of the chair: "There can be three conditions of ownership. First, you own your seven thousand acres and all mineral rights under them. Second, Yeager owns the good land we want, the surface, that is, but he owns nothing underneath. Tough on him, good for us."

"Yes, but do we have the right to invade his property in order to sink our well?"

"We do, if we don't ruin his surface. And if we do ruin it, we pay him damages, and he can't do a damned thing about it."

"He won't like it."

"They never do, but that's the law. Now, the third situation is the one that operates mostly. Farmer Kline owns a big chunk of land, say three thousand acres. He also owns the mineral rights. So we go to him and say: 'Mr. Kline, we want to lease the mineral rights to your land. For ten years. And we'll give you fifty cents an acre year after year for ten years. A lot of money.' "

"What rights do we get?"

"The right to drill, anyplace on the farm, as many holes as we want, for ten years."

"And what does he get?"

"Fifteen hundred dollars a year, hard cash, year after year, even if we do nothing."

"And if we strike oil?"

"He gets a solid one-eighth of everything we make, for as long as that well produces. To eternity, if he and it last that long."

"Who gets the other seven-eighths?"

"We do."

"Is it a good deal . . . for all of us, I mean?"

"For Farmer Kline, it's a very fair deal. He gets an oil well without taking any risk. For you and me, the deal with Kline is about the best we can do, fair to both sides. It's his oil but we take all the risks."

"And between you and me—seventy-five, twenty-five?"

"Tell you the truth, Rusk, with some men like me you could get an eighty, twenty deal, but nine out of ten such men would never find a bucket of oil. I know where the oil is. For you, it's a very good deal. As for me, if I had the land or the money, I wouldn't say hello to you. But I don't have either."

"So what should we do?" Rusk asked permission to pour some coffee, whereupon Kimbro pushed the big revolver across the table to him.

"I trust you, Rusk. I have to. We're partners."

Robert Caro

Robert Caro began a projected three-volume study of Lyndon Johnson after winning a Pulitzer Prize for his biography of Robert Moses in 1975. The selection titled "The Sad Irons" offers a revelation of how a personality like Johnson could come to political power by bringing electrical power to the rural poor of the Texas Hill Country. In describing with painful lyricism the plight of Hill Country farm women, Caro credits his wife Ina's interviews with over fifty farm women around Johnson City, and quotes Stella Glidden, editor of the Johnson City weekly paper: "Without understanding what it means to grow up in a place like this, no one will ever understand LBJ."

THE SAD IRONS

Without electricity, even boiling water was work.

Anything which required the use of water was work. Windmills (which could, acting like a pump, bring water out of a well into a storage tank) were very rare in the Hill Country; their cost—almost four hundred dollars in 1937—was out of the reach of most families in that cash-poor region, and the few that had been built proved of little use in a region where winds were always uncertain and, during a drought, nonexistent, for days, or weeks, on end. And without electricity to work a pump, there was only one way to obtain water: by hand.

The source of water could be either a stream or a well. If the source was a stream, water had to be carried from it to the house, and since, in a country subject to constant flooding, houses were built well away from the streams, it had to be carried a long way. If the source was a well, it had to be lifted to the surface—a bucket at a time. It had to be lifted quite a long way: while the average depth of a well was about fifty feet in the valleys of the Hill Country, in the hills it was a hundred feet or more.

And so much water was needed! A federal study of nearly half a million farm families even then being conducted would show that, on the average, a person living on a farm used 40 gallons of water every day. Since the average farm family was five persons, the family used 200 gallons, or four-fifths of a ton, of water each day—73,000 gallons, or almost three hundred tons, in a year. The study showed that, on the average, the well was located 253 feet from the house—and that to pump by hand and carry to the house 73,000 gallons of water a year would require someone to put in during that year sixty-three eight-hour days, and walk 1,750 miles.

A farmer would do as much of this pumping and hauling as possible himself, and try to have his sons do as much of the rest as possible (it was Lyndon Johnson's adamant refusal to help his mother with the pumping and hauling that touched off the most bitter of the flareups with his father during his youth). As soon as a Hill Country youth got big enough to carry the water buckets (which held about four gallons, or thirty-two pounds, of water apiece), he was assigned the job of filling his mother's wash pots before he left for school or the field. Curtis Cox still recalls today that from the age of nine or ten, he would, every morning throughout the rest of his boyhood, make about seven trips between his house and the well, which were about three hundred feet apart, on each of these trips carrying two large buckets, or more than sixty pounds, of water. "I felt tired," he says. "It was a lot of water." But the water the children carried would be used up long before noon, and the children would be away—at school or in the fields—and most of the hauling of water was, therefore, done by women. "I would," recalls Curtis's mother, Mary Cox, "have to get it, too—more than once a day, more than twice; oh, I don't know how many times. I needed water to wash my floors, water to wash my clothes, water to cook. . . . It was hard work. I was always packing [carrying] water." Carrying it—after she had wrestled off the heavy wooden lid which kept the rats and squirrels out of the well; after she had cranked the bucket up to the surface (and cranking—lifting thirty pounds fifty feet or more—was very hard for most women even with a pulley; most would pull the rope hand over hand, as if they were climbing it, to get their body weight into the effort; they couldn't do it with their arms alone). Some Hill Country women make wry jokes about getting water. Says Mrs. Brian Smith of Blanco:

"Yes, we had running water. I always said we had running water because I grabbed those two buckets up and ran the two hundred yards to the house with them." But the joking fades away as the memories sharpen. An interviewer from the city is struck by the fact that Hill Country women of the older generation are noticeably stooped, much more so than city women of the same age. Without his asking for an explanation, it is given to him. More than once, and more than twice, a stooped and bent Hill Country farm wife says, "You see how round-shouldered I am? Well, that's from hauling the water." And, she will often add, "I was round-shouldered like this well before my time, when I was still a young woman. My back got bent from hauling the water, and it got bent when I was still young."

The Hill Country farm wife had to haul water, and she had to haul wood.

Because there was no electricity, Hill Country stoves were wood stoves. The spread of the cedar brakes had given the area a plentiful supply of wood, but cedar seared bone-dry by the Hill Country sun burned so fast that the stoves seemed to devour it. A farmer would try to keep a supply of wood in the house, or, if he had sons old enough, would assign the task to them. (Lyndon Johnson's refusal to chop wood for his mother was another source of the tension between him and Sam.) They would cut down the trees, and chop them into four-foot lengths that could be stacked in cords. When wood was needed in the house, they would cut it into shorter lengths and split the pieces so they could fit into the stoves. But as with the water, these chores often fell to the women.

The necessity of hauling the wood was not, however, the principal reason so many farm wives hated their wood stoves. In part, they hated these stoves because they were so hard to "start up." The damper that opened into the firebox created only a small draft even on a breezy day, and on a windless day, there was no draft—because there was no electricity, of course, there was no fan to move the air in the kitchen—and a fire would flicker out time after time. "With an electric stove, you just turn on a switch and you have heat," says Lucille O'Donnell, but with a wood stove, a woman might have to stuff kindling and wood into the firebox over and over again. And even after the fire was lit, the stove "didn't heat up in a minute, you know," Lucille O'Donnell says—it might in fact take an hour. In part, farm wives hated wood stoves because they were so dirty, because the smoke from the wood blackened walls and ceilings, and ashes were always escaping through the grating, and the ash box had to be emptied twice a day—a dirty job and dirtier if, while the ashes were being carried outside, a gust of wind scattered them around inside the house. They hated the stoves because they could not be left unattended. Without devices to regulate the heat and keep the temperature steady, when the stove was being used for baking or some other cooking in which an even temperature was important, a woman would have to keep a constant watch on the fire, thrusting logs—or corncobs, which ignited quickly—into the firebox every time the heat slackened.

Most of all, they hated them because they were so hot.

When the big iron stove was lit, logs blazing in its firebox, flames licking at the gratings that held the pots, the whole huge mass of metal so hot that it was almost glowing, the air in the kitchen shimmered with the heat pouring out of it. In the winter the heat was welcome, and in spring and fall it was bearable, but in the Hill Country, summer would often last five months. Some time in June the temperature might climb to near ninety degrees, and would stay there, day after day, week after week, through the end of September. Day after day, week after week, the sky would be mostly empty, without a cloud as a shield from the blazing sun that beat down on the Hill Country, and on the sheet-iron or corrugated tin roofs of the boxlike kitchens in the little dog-run homes that dotted its hills and valleys. No matter how hot the day, the stove had to be lit much of the time, because it had to be lit not only for meals but for baking; Hill Country wives, unable to afford store-bought bread, baked their own, an all-day task. (As Mrs. O'Donnell points out, "We didn't have refrigerators, you know, and without refrigerators, you just about have to start every meal from scratch.") In the Hill Country, moreover, summer was harvest time, when a farm wife would have to cook not just for her family but for a harvesting crew—twenty or thirty men, who, working from sun to sun, expected three meals a day.

Harvest time, and canning time.

In the Hill Country, canning was required for a family's very survival. Too poor to buy food, most Hill Country families lived through the winter largely on the vegetables and fruit picked in the summer and preserved in jars.

Since—because there was no electricity—there were no refrigerators in the Hill Country, vegetables or fruit had to be canned the very day they came ripe. And, from June through September, something was coming ripe almost every day, it seemed; on a single peach tree, the fruit on different branches would come ripe on different days. In a single orchard, the peaches might be reaching ripeness over a span as long as two weeks; "You'd be in the kitchen with the peaches for two weeks," Hill Country wives recall. And after the peaches, the strawberries would begin coming ripe, and then the gooseberries, and then the blueberries. The tomatoes would become ripe before the okra, the okra before the zucchini, the zucchini before the corn. So the canning would go on with only brief intervals—all summer.

Canning required constant attendance on the stove. Since boiling water was essential, the fire in the stove had to be kept roaring hot, so logs had to be continually put into the firebox. At least twice during a day's canning, moreover—probably three or four times—a woman would have to empty the ash container, which meant wrestling the heavy, unwieldy device out from under the firebox. And when the housewife wasn't bending down to the flames, she was standing over them. In canning fruit, for example, first sugar was dropped into the huge iron canning pot, and watched carefully and stirred constantly, so that it would not become lumpy, until it was completely dissolved. Then the fruit—perhaps peaches, which would have been peeled earlier—was put in the pot, and boiled until it turned into a soft and mushy jam that would be packed into jars (which would have been boiling—to sterilize them—in another pot) and sealed with wax. Boiling the peaches would take more than an hour, and during that time they had to be stirred constantly so that they would not stick to the pot. And when one load of peaches was finished, another load would be put in, and another. Canning was an all-day job. So when a woman was canning, she would have to spend all day in a little room with a tin or sheet-iron roof on which a blazing sun was beating down without mercy, standing in front of the iron stove and the wood fire within it. And every time the heat in that stove died down even a bit, she would have to make it hotter again.

"You'd have to can in the summer when it was hot," says Kitty Clyde Ross Leonard, who had been Johnson's first girlfriend. "You'd have to cook for hours. Oh, that was a terrible thing. You wore as little as you could. I wore loose clothing so that it wouldn't stick to me. But the perspiration would just pour down my face. I remember the perspiration pouring down my mother's face, and when I grew up and had my own family, it poured down mine. That stove was so hot. But you had to stir, especially when you were making jelly. So you had to stand over that stove." Says Bernice Snodgrass of Wimberley: "You got so hot that you couldn't stay in the house. You ran out and sat under the trees. I couldn't stand it to stay in the house. Terrible. Really terrible. But you couldn't stay out of the house long. You had to stir. You had to watch the fire. So you had to go back into the house."

And there was no respite. If a bunch of peaches came ripe a certain day, that was the day they had to be canned—no matter how the housewife might feel that day. Because in that fierce Hill Country heat, fruit and vegetables spoiled very quickly. And once the canning process was begun, it could not stop. "If you peeled six dozen peaches, and then, later that day, you felt sick," you couldn't stop, says Gay Harris. "Because you can't can something if it's rotten. The job has to be done the same day, no matter what." Sick or not, in the Hill Country, when it was time to can, a woman canned, standing hour after hour, trapped between a blazing sun and a blazing wood fire. "We had no choice, you see," Mrs. Harris says.

Every week, every week all year long—every week without fail—there was washday.

The wash was done outside. A huge vat of boiling water would be suspended over a larger, roaring fire and near it three large "Number Three" zinc washtubs and a dishpan would be placed on a bench.

The clothes would be scrubbed in the first of the zinc tubs, scrubbed on a washboard by a woman bending over the tub. The soap, since she couldn't afford store-bought soap, was soap she had made from lye, soap that was not very effective, and the water was hard. Getting farm dirt out of clothes required hard scrubbing.

Then the farm wife would wring out each piece of clothing to remove from it as much as possible of the dirty water, and put it in the big vat of boiling water. Since the scrubbing would not have removed all of the dirt, she would try to get the rest out by "punching" the clothes in the vat—standing over the boiling water and using a wooden paddle or, more often, a broomstick, to stir the clothes and swish them through the water and press them against the bottom or sides, moving the broom handle up and down and around as hard as she could for ten or fifteen minutes in a human imitation of the agitator of an automatic—electric—washing machine.

The next step was to transfer the clothes from the boiling water to the second of the three zinc washtubs: the "rinse tub." The clothes were lifted out of the big vat on the end of the broomstick, and held up on the end of the stick for a few minutes while the dirty water dripped out.

When the clothes were in the rinse tub, the woman bent over the tub and rinsed them, by swishing each individual item through the water. Then she wrung out the clothes, to get as much of the dirty water out as possible, and placed the clothes in the third tub, which contained bluing, and swished them around in *it*—this time to get the bluing all through the garment and make it white—and then repeated the same movements in the dishpan, which was filled with starch.

At this point, one load of wash would be done. A week's wash took at least four loads: one of sheets, one of shirts and other white clothing, one of colored clothes, and one of dish towels. But for the typical, large, Hill Country farm family, two loads of each of these categories would be required, so the procedure would have to be repeated eight times.

For each load, moreover, the water in each of the three washtubs would have to be changed. A washtub held about eight gallons. Since the water had to be warm, the woman would fill each tub half with boiling water from the big pot and half with cold water. She did the filling with a bucket which held three or four gallons—twenty-five or thirty pounds. For the first load or two of wash, the water would have been provided by her husband or her sons. But after this water had been used up, part of washday was walking—over and over—that long walk to the spring or well, hauling up the water, hand over laborious hand, and carrying those heavy buckets back.* Another part of washday was also a physical effort: the "punching" of the clothes in the big vat. "You had to do it as hard as you could—swish those clothes around and around and around. They never seemed to get clean. And those clothes were heavy in the water, and it was hot outside, and you'd be standing over that boiling water and that big fire—you felt like you were being roasted alive." Lifting the clothes out of the vat was an effort, too. A dripping mass of soggy clothes was heavy, and it felt heavier when it had to be lifted out of that vat and held up for minutes at a time so that the dirty water could drip out, and then swung over to the rinsing tub. Soon, if her children weren't around to hear her, a woman would be grunting with the effort. Even the wringing was, after a few hours, an effort. "I mean, wringing clothes might not seem hard," Mrs. Harris says. "But you have to wring every piece so many times—you wring it after you take it out of the scrub tub, and you wring it after you take it out of the rinse tub, and after you take it out of the bluing. Your arms got tired." And her hands—from scrubbing with lye soap and wringing—were raw and swollen. Of course, there was also the bending—

*Because so much water was required in washing, the introduction of a gas-operated washing machine by the Maytag Company in 1935 did not help the farm wife much, even if she could afford to buy it, which most Hill Country wives could not: she still had to fill and refill the machine with water.

hours of bending—over the rub boards. "By the time you got done washing, your back was broke," Ava Cox says. "I'll tell you—of the things of my life that I will never forget, I will never forget how much my back hurt on washdays." Hauling the water, scrubbing, punching, rinsing: a Hill Country farm wife did this for hours on end—while a city wife did it by pressing the button on her electric washing machine.

Washday was Monday. Tuesday was for ironing.

Says Mary Cox, in words echoed by all elderly Hill Country farm wives: "Washing was hard work, but ironing was the worst. Nothing could ever be as hard as ironing."

The Department of Agriculture finds that "Young women today are not aware of the origin of the word 'iron,' as they press clothes with lightweight appliances of aluminum or hollow stainless steel." In the Hill Country, in the 1930s an iron was *iron*—a six- or seven-pound wedge of iron. The irons used in the Hill Country had to be heated on the wood stove, and they would retain their heat for only a few minutes—a man's shirt generally required two irons; a farm wife would own three or four of them, so that several could be heating while one was working. An iron with a wooden handle cost two dollars more than one without the handle, so Hill Country wives did their weekly loads of ironing—huge loads because, as Mary Cox puts it, "in those days you were expected to starch and iron almost everything"—with irons without handles. They would either transfer a separate wooden handle from one iron to another, or they would protect their hands with a thick potholder.

Since burning wood generates soot, the irons became dirty as they sat heating on the stove. Or, if any moisture was left on an iron from the sprinkled clothes on which it had just been used, even the thinnest smoke from the stove created a muddy film on the bottom. The irons had to be cleaned frequently, therefore, by scrubbing them with a rag that had been dipped in salt, and if the soot was too thick, they had to be sanded and scraped. And no matter how carefully you checked the bottom of the irons, and sanded and scraped them, there would often remain some little spot of soot—as you would discover when you rubbed it over a clean white shirt or dress. Then you had to wash that item of clothing over again.

Nevertheless, the irons would burn a woman's hand. The wooden handle or the potholder would slip, and she would have searing metal against her flesh; by noon, she might have blister atop blister—on hands that had to handle the rag that had been dipped in salt. Ironing always took a full day—often it went on into Tuesday evening—and a full day of lifting and carrying six- or seven-pound loads was hard on even these hardy Hill Country women. "It would hurt so bad between the shoulders," Elsie Beck remembers. But again the worst aspect of ironing was the heat. On ironing day, a fire would have to be blazing in the wood stove all day, filling the kitchen, hour after hour, with heat and smoke. Ironing had to be done not only in the winter but in the summer—when the temperature outside the kitchen might be ninety or ninety-five or one hundred, and inside the kitchen would be considerably higher, and because there was no electricity, there was no fan to so much as stir the air. In a speech in Congress some years later, Representative John E. Rankin described the "drudgery" a typical farm wife endured, "burning up in a hot kitchen and bowing down over the washtub or boiling the clothes over a flaming fire in the summer heat." He himself remembered, he said, "seeing his mother lean over that hot iron hour after hour until it seemed she was tired enough to drop." Rankin was from Mississippi, but his description would have been familiar to the mothers of the Edwards Plateau. The women of the Hill Country never called the instruments they used every Tuesday "irons," they called them "sad irons."

Washing, ironing—those were chores that were performed every week. Then, of course, there were special occasions—harvest time and threshing time, when a woman had to cook not just for her family but for a crew of twenty or thirty men; the shearing, when, because there was no electricity and her husband had to work the shears, she had to crank the shearing machine, pedaling as if she were pumping a bicycle up a steep hill, pedaling, with only brief pauses, hour after hour; "He was always yelling 'Faster, faster,' " Mrs. Walter Yett of Blanco recalls. "I could hardly get up the next morning, I was so tired after that." Washing, ironing, cooking, canning, shearing, helping with the plowing and the picking and the sowing, and, every day, carrying the water and the wood, and because there was no electricity, having to do everything by hand by the same methods that had been employed by her mother and grandmother and great-great-great-grandmother before her— "They wear these farm women out pretty fast," wrote one observer. In the Hill Country, as many outside observers noted, the one almost universal characteristic of the women was that they were worn out before their time, that they were old beyond their years, old at forty, old at thirty-five, bent and stooped and tired.

A Hill Country farm wife had to do her chores even if she was ill—no matter how ill. Because Hill Country women were too poor to afford proper medical care, they often suffered perineal tears in childbirth. During the 1930s, the federal government sent physicians to examine a sampling of Hill Country women. The doctors found that, out of 275 women, 158 had perineal tears. Many of them, the team of gynecologists reported, were third-degree tears, "tears so bad that it is difficult to see how they stand on their feet." But they *were* standing on their feet, and doing all the chores that Hill Country wives had always done—hauling the water, hauling the wood, canning, washing, ironing, helping with the shearing, the plowing, and the picking.

Because there was no electricity.

Billy Lee Brammer

Billy Lee Brammer (1930–1978) is widely acclaimed as Texas's best writer of political fiction. Brammer used his experiences as a Senate press aide to Lyndon Johnson in his best-selling novel, The Gay Place, *set in 1950s Texas.*

THE GAY PLACE

The country is most barbarously large and final. It is too much country—boondock country—alternately drab and dazzling, spectral and remote. It is so wrongfully muddled and various that it is difficult to conceive of it as all of a piece. Though it begins simply enough, as a part of the other.

It begins, very like the other, in an ancient backwash of old dead seas and lambent estuaries, around which rise cypress and cedar and pine thickets hung with spiked vines and the cheerless festoons of Spanish moss. Farther on, the earth firms: stagnant pools are stirred by the rumble of living river, and the mild ferment of bottom land dissolves as the country begins to reveal itself in the vast hallucination of salt dome and cotton row, tree farm and rice field and irrigated pasture and the flawed dream of the cities. And away and beyond, even farther, the land continues to rise, as on a counterbalance with the water tables, and then the first faint range of the West comes into view: a great serpentine escarpment, changing colors with the hours, with the seasons, hummocky and soft-shaped at one end, rude and wind-blasted at the other, blue and green, green and gray and dune-colored, a staggered faultline extending hundreds of miles north and south.

This range is not so high as it is sudden and aberrant, a disorder in the even westerly roll of the land. One could not call it mountain, but it is a considerable hill, or set of hills, and here again the country is transformed. The land rises steeply beyond the first escarpment and everything is changed: texture, configuration, blistered façade, all of it warped and ruptured and bruise-colored. The few rivers run deep, like old wounds, boiling round the fractures and revealing folds of slate and shell and glittering blue limestone, spilling back and across and out of the hills toward the lower country.

The city lies against and below two short spiny ribs of hill. One of the little rivers runs round and about, and from the hills it is possible to view the city overall and draw therefrom an impression of sweet curving streets and graceful sweeping lawns and the unequivocally happy sound of children always at play. Closer on, the feeling is only partly confirmed, though it should seem enough to have even a part. It is a pleasant city, clean and quiet, with wide rambling walks and elaborate public gardens and elegant old homes faintly ruined in the shadow of arching poplars. Occasionally through the trees, and always from a point of higher ground, one can see the college tower and the capitol building. On brilliant mornings the white sandstone of the tower and the capitol's granite dome are joined for an instant, all pink and cream, catching the first light.

On a midsummer morning not very long ago the sun advanced on the city and lit the topmost spines of hill, painting the olive drab slopes in crazy new colors, like the drawing of a spangled veil. Then the light came closer, touching the tall buildings and the fresh-washed streets. The nearly full-blown heat came with it, quick and palpitant. It was close to being desert heat: sudden, emphatic, dissolving chill and outdistancing rain . . .

It was neither first light nor early heat that caused the two politicians to come struggling up from sleep at that hour, but an old truck carrying migratory cotton pickers.

The younger of the two politicians was named Roy Sherwood, and he lay twisted sideways in the front seat of an automobile that was parked out front of an all-night supermarket. Arthur Fenstemaker, the other one, the older one, floundered in his bedcovers a few blocks distant in the governor's mansion.

The old truck banged along the streets, past dazzling store fronts and the Juicy Pig Stand and the marble façades of small banks in which deposits were insured to ten thousand dollars. The dozen children in the back of the truck had been first to come awake. They pulled aside the canvas flaps and peered out at the city, talking excitedly, whooping and hee-hawing as the old truck rolled north, straining, toward the capitol grounds and the governor's mansion, where Arthur Fenstemaker slept, and the supermarket where Roy Sherwood's car was parked.

The truck came to a sudden stop and began, with a terrible moaning of gears and transmission, to back into a parking space next to Roy Sherwood's car.

Roy heard the commotion and blinked his sore eyes in the early light. He struggled to untangle his long legs from between the steering wheel and seat cushion, and he was able, finally, to sit up and examine the truck. He unrolled a window and leaned his head out, taking deep breaths, blinking his eyes. The children in the truck watched him gravely for a moment and then began to giggle. Their laughter subsided abruptly when Roy called out to them: *"Buena día . . ."*

There was silence and then a small voice answered back: ". . . *día* . . ."

Roy smiled and opened the car door. He stood on the cool pavement for a moment, weaving slightly, trying to hold his balance. He was dizzy with fatigue and an hour's poor sleep and possibly a hangover. "One hell of an awful *día,"* he muttered under his breath. The children were laughing again, and fairly soon he began to feel better. The driver of the truck climbed down and came round to Roy's side to stare at him. The fellow had a murderous look—a bandit's look. He was wearing a wrinkled double-breasted suit coat over what appeared to be a polo shirt and uncommonly dirty and outsized denim slacks. He stared at Roy with his bandit's eyes until Roy lifted his hand in a vague salute. Then the Mexican smiled, showing hilarious buck teeth, lifted his arm in the same indecisive gesture and almost immediately turned and walked toward the supermarket, flapping his feet in gray tennis shoes.

The children attempted to engage Roy in conversation. Roy came closer to the back of the truck, trying to understand some of it, cocking his head and listening carefully and interrupting now and then: *"Qué? . . . Cómo? . . . Despacio,* for chrissake, *despacio . . ."* The children giggled hysterically; two or three adults in the front cab stared at him, looking uneasy, and finally Roy gave it up and waved good-bye and wandered into the supermarket.

The inside of the store was aglow with yellow light. Everything was gorgeous and brightly packaged. Only the people—the cashier and the Mexican gathering breakfast staples and Roy himself—seemed out of phase with the predominating illusion. Roy looked all around, examining the market with as much wonder and concentration as might have been demonstrated in viewing Indian cave mosaics or a thousand-year-old cathedral. He stared all around and then he uncapped a bottle of milk and tore open a bag of cinnamon buns. He wandered over the market eating and drinking, pausing occasionally to stare enraptured at a prime cut of beef or a phonograph album or a frozen pizza or a stack of small redwood picnic tables. There seemed no limit to what the market might conceivably have in stock. Roy decided the pussy willow cuttings were his favorite; they were a little fantastic: out of season, out of habitat . . . He wondered if the pussy willow had been shipped fresh-frozen from the East, like oysters or cheese blintzes. He moved on; he had something else in mind.

He located this other without difficulty—a tall pasteboard box containing twenty-four ice cream cones, maple flavored. The box of cones was part of it; the plastic scoop stapled to the outside of the box solved the next most immediate problem. He carried the cones and the scoop to the cashier and then went back to pick up two half-gallon cartons of ice cream.

Outside again, at the back end of the truck, the children and two or three of the older Mexicans crowded round to watch. Roy left off serving after a while, letting one of the older girls take his place. There were a few accented whoops of *Ize-Cream . . . Aze Creeem,* but the children were unusually quiet for the most part, sweetly, deliriously happy waiting in line to be served. Presently, he returned to his car and sat in the driver's seat to watch. One hell of a crazy *día,* he reminded himself. Not to mention the *día* before and the night or the goddam *noche* in between.

He turned now and looked in the back seat. It was all there . . . All of it . . . All his art objects purchased during his twelve hours travel on the day before: the button-on shoes, the iron stewpot, the corset model, the portrait of President Coolidge, the Orange Crush dispenser with its rusted spigot, part of an old upright piano. Everything except . . . But he remembered now. The television set, one of the earliest models, big as a draft animal, with a seven-inch picture tube . . . He'd left it in knee-high Johnsongrass fifty miles outside town. He grunted to himself, thinking of the television set: it was a terrible loss; he'd been blinded by the wine on the day before and thoughtlessly left the television behind. He grunted again and reexamined his treasure in the back seat.

The Mexican children were finished with their ice cream, and he could hear their singsong voices rising in volume. The elder, the old bandit in gray tennis shoes, came out of the supermarket carrying his grocery sack. He moved past Roy, nodding, showing his wonderful teeth.

"You need a stewpot?" Roy said suddenly.

The Mexican was jerked back as if suspended by a coil spring. His face twitched, but he managed to smile and mumble an incomprehensible something in Spanish.

"Stew pot," Roy repeated. "Fine piece of workmanship . . . You need one? For free . . . *por nada . . . Tiene usted una stew pot-to?*"

The old Mexican gasped in alarm, altogether mystified. Roy climbed out of the car and opened the back door, pointing to the soot-covered vessel. It was very much like the ones in which neighborhood washerwomen had boiled clothes during his childhood. He loved the stewpot. But now he knew he must *make the gesture*. It was part of being a public figure. He addressed the Mexican: "Here . . . You want it? Desire you the stew pot?"

Roy struggled with the pot; it was big as a washtub. The old man accepted it on faith, smiling as if vastly pleased. He bowed politely and turned toward the truck, carrying the stewpot with great dignity. The children in back greeted him with strident questions. Roy sat in the front seat of the car and watched, wondering if he ought to make a speech. They'd never understand a word, but he could make pleasant sounds. It was no matter. His Mexicans back home never understood anything, either. You just paid their poll taxes and showed them where to mark ballots when election time came round. He'd made a speech the night before. One of his best. Parked alongside a narrow river, he and the girl had lain on a picnic blanket and finished the last of the wine and the chicken. Then he had climbed a huge magnolia tree and plucked a great white bloom from the top, before descending to one of the lower limbs to make the presentation speech. He'd never been in better form. Though there had been some difficulty about addressing the girl. Using her name seemed to take all the fire out of the occasion. "Ladies . . ." he had said in the beginning, but it wasn't quite right. Nor "Fellow ladies . . ." He'd made a number of attempts: "Dear Lady" and "Most High and Mighty Ouida, Bride of My Youth, My Rock, My Fortress, My Deliverance, Horn of My Salvation and My High

Tower . . ." But that had been too excessive for what, basically, was meant to be a ceremony of some dignity and restraint. He'd finally called her "My Dear Miss Lady Love . . ."

He thought he might step outside the car and possibly stand on the Orange Crush dispenser, addressing the Mexican children briefly, but after a moment the truck started up with a great thrashing sound and began backing out of the driveway. Roy sat for a moment, rubbing his eyes, and then he got his own car started and proceeded slowly down the main street of the city behind the truck carrying the cotton pickers. After a block or so, he grew impatient with the business of waving at the children, and nodding, and blinking his lights, and waving again; and finally he raced the car's engine and passed them by. A noisy, high-pitched cry came from the children; their flapping arms caught his vision briefly through the side windows. He grinned oafishly, studying his face in the mirror. "I have a way with crowds," he said aloud to himself. "I have gifts of rare personal magnetism . . ." He listened to the dying cheers from in back, and he thought he detected a clanging in the midst of it, a series of bell tones, deep and dull and flattish, metal on metal. My old iron stewpot, he thought . . .

Arthur Fenstemaker heard the cheers and the children's laughter and the groan of the truck's motor blended with the blows struck on the stewpot. He lay in his bed on the second floor of the governor's mansion and listened thoughtfully. He was reminded for a moment of an old International he'd driven in the oilfields years before. The Mexicans were blocks away now, and he opened his eyes, still wondering over the sound from the street below. He reached for cigarettes and matches. After a moment he lay back in the bed, gasping for breath. He left the cigarette burning in a tray and pulled himself closer to Sweet Mama Fenstemaker. His right arm was pressed under his own huge weight, but he did not want to turn away just yet. Sweet Mama smelled goddam good; she nearly always perfumed herself at bedtime.

The governor lay like that for several minutes, listening for sounds in the house or from the street, pressing his big nose against his wife's skin, until the kitchen help began to arrive downstairs. Then he rolled off the bed and went to the bathroom. He brushed his teeth and smoked another cigarette; he swallowed pills and massaged his scalp and began to stalk about the second floor of the mansion. He looked in on his brother: Hoot Gibson Fenstemaker lay sleeping quietly, knotted in bedclothes. The governor turned back to his dressing room and stared at himself in a full-length mirror, sucking in his stomach, shifting from side to side. He slipped on gartered hose and shoes and a robe, and again stood listening, leaning over a stairwell and cocking his head. Soon he could hear the limousine being eased into position on the concrete drive. Fenstemaker strode down to the end of the hall and opened a casement window. A highway patrolman circled the car, examining tires, polishing chrome. The governor put his head through the window and yelled: "Hidy!"

The patrolman looked up, squinting against the sun, trying to smile.

"Hah'r yew, Mist' Fenstemaker," he said.

"Nice mornin'," the governor said, looking around.

"Hassah!" the patrolman said.

The patrolman stood on the concrete apron, gazing up at the governor. He kicked a tire with the heel of his shoe; he patted a fender of the car. He stared at the governor, and finally added, ". . . Sure nice one . . ."

Fenstemaker turned his head, looking over the city from the second-story window. The mansion was constructed along Georgian lines and was situated on a small rise that placed it nearly level with the capitol dome and some of the office buildings downtown. Mist blurred the hilltops to the west, and occasionally, a mile or more away, lake water flashed in the sun. The smell of flowers, blooming in profusion in the backyard garden, was fused with the harsh bouquet of compost heaps and kitchen coffee. Fenstemaker pinched his big nose and took deep breaths. The patrolman continued to gawk at him.

"I'm not goin' anywhere right off," Fenstemaker said.

He pulled his head back inside and rang for his coffee. He sat at a desk in his study and shuffled through papers. The butler arrived with a small coffeepot, dry toast, juice, and a half dozen newspapers.

"You had your breakfast?" Fenstemaker said. "You had your coffee?"

"Yessir," the butler said.

Fenstemaker sipped his coffee and shuffled papers.

"I hope it was better than this" he said. "Siddown and have some more."

The butler poured himself a cup and stood blowing on it, waiting.

"Siddown for Christ's sake," Fenstemaker said.

"Yes sir."

"Goddam."

"Sir?"

"I'm just goddammin'."

"Yes sir."

"Let's get a new brand of coffee," Fenstemaker said. He made a face. "I'll tell the cook."

"Nothin' tastes like it used to," Fenstemaker said. "Not even vegetables."

"Sweet potatoes especially," the butler said.

"Not even goddam sweet potatoes," Fenstemaker said.

The two of them sipped coffee. The governor turned through the newspapers, talking but not looking up. "You think it's gettin' better?"

"What's that?"

"Bein' a colored man. You think it's any better?"

The butler looked at him desperately. "I got a good job," he said.

The governor did not seem to pay attention. He went on talking and turning pages. "Maybe little better, I guess . . . Discussions goin' on. . . . Least *that's* not like it used to be. Hell! I remember old Pitchfork Ben Tillman—the things he said . . ." Fenstemaker broke off momentarily, peering at the newsprint, then went on: "Of course bein' better still don't make it very good. I was thinkin' yesterday, signin' my mail, how I'd feel if I wrote a public official about, you know, my rights? I was lookin' over what I'd been sayin'. 'Well now this sure is a problem, involvin' grave emotional questions, and we can't tolerate havin' second-class citizens in this free country and I'm sure gonna do what I can . . . Try to make reasonable progress toward a solution . . . Sure keep your views in mind . . .' Why *God damn!* Some cornpone Buddha say that to *me*, I'd set a bomb off under him."

The butler grinned. "I think most colored people vote for you," he said. "Even when you don't say things exact . . ." He began gathering cups and saucers.

"I'm a damned good politician," Fenstemaker said. "I know how good I am and I ain't doin' much, so what about the others not so good? Goddam and hell!"

"You want another pot?" the butler said.

"Yes," the governor said. "Switch to that ersatz stuff—I think it's probably better than this . . . And some fruit. They got any watermelon down there?"

"I'll see," the butler said. "They don't, we get you some."

The governor's brother, Hoot Gibson Fenstemaker, appeared at the door. He rubbed his eyes and smiled, looking deranged. "You get me some coffee, Jimmy?" he said. The butler nodded, carrying the tray. Hoot Gibson stepped inside.

"Mornin' Arthur."

"You enjoy that party last night?" the governor said.

"Sure did. I like parties here."

"I think you danced with every lady."

"I think I did," Hoot Gibson said. "I liked that orchestra, too. It was like Wayne King."

"I remember at college you had some Wayne King records," the governor said, looking up from the papers. "And Henry Busse. What in hell ever happened to Henry Busse?"

"He dead?" Hoot Gibson said. He thought a moment. *Hot Lips!* I booked old Henry Busse once for the gymnasium. A dance. Made two hundred dollars promoting old Henry Busse . . ." Hoot Gibson's eyes went cloudy, thinking about Henry Busse. He sipped from his brother's coffee cup.

Fenstemaker looked up patiently. "Don't make that noise," he said. Hoot Gibson gripped the cup with both hands and stared at the coffee. The governor read the papers. Hoot Gibson picked up one of the sheets and glanced over the headlines. "I think I got a hangover," he said.

The governor cleared his throat but did not comment.

"I might go back to bed a while," Hoot Gibson said.

"Take some aspirin and sleep another hour," the governor said.

Hoot Gibson stood and stretched and scratched himself. He loosened the drawstring on his pajamas and retied it. "I think I'll do that," he said. ". . . You got anything for me today?"

The governor looked up and said: "You remember that fellow talkin' to me and Jay last night? Up here—out on the screen porch?"

"That new lobbyist?"

"That's the one."

"I know him. He's workin' the capitol nearly every day now."

"Well suppose you keep an eye on him," the governor said. "Follow him around. Or get someone to do it for you. Find out where he goes, who he's seein'. Do that today and tonight. Maybe tomorrow. Don't for God's sake let him know he's bein' watched. Give me a report—and don't come around *tellin'* me about it. Write it up."

Hoot Gibson looked vastly pleased. He vanished down the hall, humming to himself.

The governor signed some papers. He looked at the clock—it was nearly seven; nearly nine in the East. He reached for the phone and got the long distance operator, making notes of persons he could call in the Eastern time zone. He talked with an economist in New York. They discussed investments; Fenstemaker asked questions about the stockmarket; he complained that none of the big investors seemed interested in municipal bonds. "I got some mayors in trouble," he said. "They need help. You got any ideas?" He listened to the economist's ideas. They complained to each other about the goddam Republican high interest rates.

Fenstemaker rang off and placed more calls; he talked with his two senators, a union official in Philadelphia, a college professor in Boston. The professor was a nephew whom he'd put through college a half-dozen years before. "Listen," the governor said, "those are wonderful speeches you been sendin' down—especially if I was runnin' in Oyster Bay or Newport. But I'm not, happily. Try to remember I'm way the hell down here in coonass country . . . You forget your beginnin's? You need a little trip home? Might do you good . . . I need some ideas . . . You got good ideas . . . But I want 'em in speeches that sound like Arthur Fenstemaker and not some New goddam England squire . . ."

He completed the calls and turned back to the papers on his desk. An assistant had left him a note attached to a handwritten letter: *"This may interest you, though I advise against reading it when you're trying to shake off a low mood. It is very sad."*

He read the letter attached:

Sirs:

We the people of the 9th grade Civics class at Hopkinsville feel that you the people of the Government should try to conquer the world here before you try to conquer outer space. We feel that there may be some kind of gas on the moon that is under the surface and if a rocket hit it, it may open the surface of the moon and these gases may escape and get into our own environment and kill us. So we feel that you should leave well-enough alone. We feel that if the Good Lord had wanted us to conquer outer space he would have put here on earth instruments in-stead of people. We would like to know what you think about this issue.

Sincerely,
THE 9TH GRADE CLASS

Fenstemaker rubbed the back of his neck and pulled on his nose and sat staring at the names of the ninth grade class at Hopkinsville. He put the letter down and reached for the phone.

"Jay . . ."

Jay McGown's voice came to him feebly; then it got stronger. There was music being played on the radio in Jay's room. The music ended and an announcer talked about a cure for piles.

"Sir?" Jay was saying. ". . . Sir?"

"What in hell's goin' on there?"

"Sir?"

"You think we got a chance on that school bill?"

"School bill? Sure we got a chance," Jay said.

"I got your note and that letter," the governor said.

"Ah."

"Let's take a run with that bill this week," Fenstemaker said.

"You think this week's really the best time?" Jay said. "Old Hoffman's still in the hospital. We'd need him. He wrote the damn thing.
At least his name's on it."

"Who's that? Who wrote it, then?"

"A lobbyist for the schoolteachers. A lawyer from the education
agency."

"Who else?"

"Me."

"Well let's take a run with it," Fenstemaker said.

"Who'll we get to floor-manage?"

"Who's on the committee?" the governor said.

"You know that committee better than I do," Jay said.

"Name some," Fenstemaker said. "I forget."

"Who you want me to name?"

"Name some."

Jay named some of the members.

"They don't sound so good to me," the governor said.

"They aren't," Jay said. "We'd probably end up with half a bill. Old
Hoffman's not much, but he won't lose us any votes. He knows how to
manage a bill."

"How 'bout Roy Sherwood?" Fenstemaker said.

"Roy's a good friend of mine," Jay said.

"So?"

"But he's not exactly one of our boys."

"Maybe he just never got invited in," the governor said.

"He's pretty damned independent," Jay said. "And lazy. That's a bad
combination."

Chimes from the college signaled the half hour. The highway patrolman polished the limousine on the side drive. The butler came into the
room with an enormous slice of watermelon. Fenstemaker broke off a
piece with his hand and began to eat. There was a silence on the phone
while the governor ate watermelon. Then he said: "He help write that
bill? He do anything at all?"

There was another silence before Jay began to answer: "That's right.
He helped a lot. Fact is, he was the only one on that lousy committee
who gave a damn. With Hoffman gone."

"Well old Hoff got it reported out for us before he went to the hospital," Fenstemaker said.

"How'd you know about Roy?"

"It just sort of came to me in the night," the governor said.

"Well I thought you might disapprove. My getting him to help us. He's a friend of mine, like I said, and we needed some help from someone on the committee. Desperately."

"All right," the governor said. "That's just fine. I'm delighted. You think he could carry it?"

"I don't know. I really don't. He's never worked a bill in three terms here. I'm not even sure he'd accept the job."

"Well I'll just ask him and see."

"You think he could hold the votes we've got? He might scare some off."

"See about that, too," the governor said. He paused, and then added: "He ain't worn himself out on Earle Fielding's wife, has he?"

There was a pause before Jay answered: "That piece of information just come to you in the night, too?"

"Everything does," the governor said, his voice warm with pleasure. "Borne on the wind. Like a cherub. It do fly . . . Listen . . . We'll just see how old Roy reacts. Okay? Take a little run. Pull out all the stops and try to get this thing through. Maybe tomorrow. We can't afford to wait much longer. They'll be building up opposition soon's it appears Hoffman's well. We put off any time, we lose votes and we lose hard cash in that bill . . . You want some cash for Hopkinsville, don't you? We'll just have to get that goddam thing through in a hurry. Can't afford to have any great debates . . ."

Jay was silent on the other end of the line while Fenstemaker talked. Then the governor rang off without formality. He dialed another number on the phone and waited during the six or seven rings. He pressed the disconnect and dialed again. After another interval, Roy Sherwood answered.

"What're you doin'?" Fenstemaker boomed.

"Sleeping," Roy Sherwood said. "Real good, too."

"Hell of a note," Fenstemaker said. "World's cavin' in all round us; rocket ships blastin' off to the moon; poisonous gas in our environment . . . Sinful goddam nation . . . laden with iniquity, offspring of evildoers. My princes are rebels and companions of thieves . . ."

"*What?*"

". . . A horror and a hissing . . ."

"Who the hell is this?"

"Isaiah," Fenstemaker said. "The Prophet Isaiah."

"I'm going to hang up in just about three seconds," Roy said, "but first I'd really like to know who the hell this is?"

"Arthur goddam Fenstemaker. Hah yew?"

"I think it really is," Roy said after a moment. "Governor? That you?"

"Come over the mansion and see," Fenstemaker said. "You like watermelon? I got some damn good watermelon. You come over here and we'll break watermelon together."

Roy's response was plaintive but respectful: "It's awful early in the morning for breakfast."

"Nearly eight."

"I know," Roy said. "That gives me nearly three hours sleep."

"Well, you're a young man. I needed five."

Roy was silent.

"You come over and talk to me about this bill?" Fenstemaker said.

"What bill's that?"

"That school thing you did for Jay. Damn good job."

"Thanks. I appreciate it. But what do you want to talk about?"

"About when you're gonna get off your ass and pass it for me."

"*Pass* it. Hell, I'm just the ghost writer. Passin' it is your—"

"I mean take charge in that madhouse."

"Hah?"

"I mean floor-manage for me."

"You sure you got the right man, Governor? I never in my life—"

"I got you, all right," the governor said. "Roy Emerson Sherwood. Nonpracticin' lawyer. Family's got cattle, little cotton. Never struck no oil, though. Elected Sixty-third Legislature. Reelected without opposition to Sixty-fourth, Sixty-fifth. Never did goddam thing here till you wrote that bill the other day . . ."

"You got the right man, I guess," Roy said.

"You help me with that bill on the floor?"

"When you plan to bring it up?"

"Tomorrow."

"*Tomorrow!* Godalmighty—"

"Day after, maybe. Come on over here."

"Governor, I couldn't learn the *number* that bill, condition I'm in right now. Let me sleep a little. Just a little. Let me think about it."

"*Sinful* goddam nation . . . Laden with iniquity . . . My princes are—"

"All right," Roy said wearily.

"How you like your goddam eggs?" the governor said.

Frederick Barthelme

Frederick Barthelme (b. 1943) grew up in Houston along with his older brother Donald. Their father's architectural gifts were passed to the younger brother in both painting and writing, where the quotidian affairs of suburban life appear with humor and precision, detachment and deep affection. "Trip" is a typically bizarre encounter between strangers, told with a warmth and a spareness that is both satisfying and troubling.

TRIP

Harry Lang's company Chevrolet breaks down on the highway fifteen miles outside of Dallas. He gets the car to a small old town called Cummings, leaves it at the gas station, and calls Fay, a woman he met at a corporate sensitivity workshop in San Antonio last year and the reason for his trip. They have spent the last six months having long and wistful and detailed telephone conversations on the company WATS line, talking about everything that they can think of, even business, and sometimes nothing at all, just sitting on opposite ends of the line, allowing the delicate contact between them a few extra minutes; finally, they agreed that he should come for a visit.

Now, from the garage in Cummings, he tells her that he will not get into town until the next day, because of his car. Two hours later he's at the Starlight Motor Hotel watching television when there's a knock on the door. It's Fay, standing on the other side of the screen, fidgeting with her shirt cuffs. "May I come in?" she says.

He pushes open the screen and steps back so she can enter the room, which is small, paneled, dark. It's dusk; the only lights outside are the star-shaped motel sign and the yellow neon ringing the eaves of the buildings.

Fay sits on the bed. "It's real clammy in here."

He clicks on the table lamp. The base of the lamp is a bronze cowgirl on horseback twirling a lariat. "You look wonderful," he says. "How'd you get away?"

"Easy," she says. "I can't leave you alone. After an hour I decided I should come to you. You got a Bufferin?" She looks around the room. "What's that music?"

He listens, but doesn't hear any music. Fay is thirty-five, small, and pretty. She's wearing white shorts, a Polo dress shirt with a tiny round-tipped collar, and brown-striped espadrilles. She bounces on the bed, testing it.

Harry opens his suitcase, brings out a bottle of Anacin. "Will these do?"

She picks two pills out of his palm and points toward the open bathroom door. "Use your water?"

He tucks in his shirttail and uses the window as a mirror to fix his hair. When she comes out of the bath, she's patting her face with a small coral towel that has "Starlight" stitched into it in awkward brown script. "You want to eat something?" she says.

They go in her car to the Spur station to check on his Chevrolet. The station owner, a mechanic named Gorky, is on his back under the car. "Lucky you don't live out here," he says. "Toss me a five-eighths. Second drawer."

Harry finds the socket the mechanic wants and drops it into his palm.

"Don't get into Dallas much," Gorky says. "I don't mind, though. We got fishing and women. It doesn't matter really—for an old son like me the fish don't bite and the women don't either. You see a lock washer out there somewhere, about so big?" Again the hand shoots out from under the car, thumb and forefinger spread.

Harry hands him a washer, but the mechanic drops it; when he tries to turn over onto his stomach, he can't make it because the Malibu's not jacked up enough. Finally, he says, "Crap," and rolls out from under the car. He sits up, his back against the door, and wipes his hands on a red rag, then rubs the rag around on his puffed, stubble-covered face.

"So, what do you think?" Harry asks. "About the car?"

"I'm happy you're spending the night is what I think." Gorky tells a kid who looks like a young TV actor to watch the gas islands, then motions toward a primered GMC pickup with a bed full of tractor tires. "I can let you borrow this one, but maybe you don't need it since you got this woman here."

"He hasn't got me yet," Fay says. She loosens her thin leather belt, then refastens it, taking it up a notch and centering the buckle above her fly.

The mechanic stares at her for a minute, then laughs. "Anyway, I'll have yours tomorrow. Maybe one or so, huh?"

"Fine," Harry says.

"Go to Nick's if you want to eat." Gorky scrubs at his palm with the rag. "I mean, if you don't go in town. It's just up here a mile. Good chow. Dottie get you set?"

Dottie is Mrs. Kiwi, the owner of the Starlight, a tiny woman with a barrel chest and a dwarf's face. This afternoon she was wearing a fuchsia muscle shirt.

"I got a nice room," Harry says. "Thanks."

"I told her about you," Gorky says, waving a hand at a circling bug. "Me and her's kinda, you know"—he takes a long time thinking of the word, getting it right—"acquainted."

At Nick's Sandwich Shop Harry orders a Kingburger and Fay has a salad with Green Goddess dressing. Afterward they go to the Odeon Theater to see the movie. There's a crowd of a dozen people out front, but there's no one in the box office. Harry stares at Fay's eyes, which are mismatched in a becoming way. Two teenagers in line behind them are talking about a girl named Rose Ann they both seem to be in love with.

"I saw my neighbors making it in the driveway," Fay says, bending to look past him at the teenagers. "I watched out the bedroom window."

Harry sticks his hands in his pants pockets, then brings them out again and folds his arms, admiring the crispness and neatness of Fay's clothes.

"This woman does the dishes in a bikini, you know what I mean? Then she's out in the driveway moaning like a cow. I envied her."

The kids are listening; they've gotten very quiet. Fay points a finger at him. "I wear a fair bikini myself"—she pauses for emphasis, wagging the finger—"but mostly on the beach."

Two teenage couples join the line. Harry says. "Uh-huh."

Fay puts her hand on his side, on his ribs. "Last Christmas I helped Melody—that's her name—last year I helped her build shelves in the downstairs bath, a couple of little four-inch shelves, nothing big. Then, in June, what do you think I found in there?" She pauses and looks at him triumphantly, as if he'll never guess. "It was the saw, the electric saw, tucked in alongside the toilet. If it was me, I'd have had the thing back in its place before it stopped turning."

He folds one hand inside the other and starts to crack the knuckles, but she frowns, anticipating the sound. "Oh, sorry," he says, and puts the hands back into his pockets.

"No," she says. "I want to hear them. Go on."

"I don't think so," he says, shaking his head.

"She plays this music all the time. You're trying to sleep, or read, or sit in the tub—sometimes I spend a whole afternoon in the tub—and here comes Nat King Cole into your life."

The kids have started their conversation again. They're brothers, and they're trying to be sensible about this thing with Rose Ann, but they're having trouble deciding who's going to get her.

"I like music," Fay says. "Don't get me wrong. I even like Nat King Cole, once every forty years or so." She digs into her boxy purse and then turns around holding a Polaroid snapshot of a man in a bathing suit. "This is my husband, Tim. I thought you ought to see him." She pokes the picture at Harry. "Take a look."

The man in the picture is overweight. He doesn't have much hair, and his legs are peculiarly thin for the rest of his body. He's standing alongside a Buick sedan holding a hose with water running out the end. Behind him in the picture there's a two-car garage and, off to the extreme left, the shoulder and leg of another man, also in bathing trunks.

"He looks fine to me," Harry says, handing the snapshot back to her. "He's a good-looking man."

She takes the picture and holds it very close to her face. "You think so?" She moves the picture up and down, examining her husband. "He docs have eyes," she says, snapping open the purse and dropping the photograph inside. "I think I married the eyes, really. That's the first thing I noticed about you—eyes."

A kid on a girl's bicycle rides up beside them. "You all on line?" he asks. When Fay says they are, the kid says, "You want to give me a cut? I'm only ten."

Fay nods, so the kid gets off the bike, puts it down on the sidewalk where he's standing, and gets into line.

"I love kids, don't you?" she whispers. "I don't like to think about not having any. I suppose it's my fault. You don't mind me talking, do you?"

"I guess not," Harry says.

In the flickering light of the theater marquee Fay's face is all white planes and sharp shadows; she looks like somebody vulnerable in a forties movie poster. Her hair is tight to her scalp in dark knots.

"Maybe you should call the police or something," Harry says. "About this woman."

"Not on your life, buster." She pulls a thread away from one of the belt loops of her shorts. "Melody's one of the highlights of my life. A role model for me." She snaps the thread off her waist. "Besides, she's gorgeous to look at. The husband ain't bad either."

Harry reaches for the thread, which she has rolled into a tiny ball between her fingers.

"He runs the Bonanza out by us. He likes me, but I don't have the guts to sleep with him. I guess I don't want to."

One of the brothers has bumped Harry several times trying to hear Fay's story. He says something to the other one and the brothers both laugh.

Fay glances at the boy. "He's a handsome kid, isn't he?" she says, loud enough for the boy to hear. "Maybe he needs some attention."

"Excuse me?" the boy says. "Were you talking to me?"

"What?" she says, as if she's been interrupted. "Oh. No, I was talking to Harry—this is Harry."

"Howdy," Harry says.

"Howdy?" the brothers say to each other, exchanging silly looks.

She twists back toward the ticket booth. Looking over her shoulder, she says, "Rose Ann probably loves you both, you're so cute." She pulls Harry forward in line. "Howdy? Oh, never mind. Let's talk about something else—are you hot?"

"No, I'm okay."

"I perspire," she says, opening her arms and glancing at her chest. "I admit it, Harry. And I won't wear those teeny satin tops, those thin ones you see everywhere." She sighs, then smiles and straightens her blouse.

"I don't think we'll ever get in here," Harry says.

"I mean, I could if I wanted to. And plum lips and metallic underpants—you interested?" She laughs and fingers some of the curls over her ear. "It's not that I wasn't trained, you know. I was trained just like everybody else. I can do the business—here, I'll show you." She wraps an arm around his neck, moistens her lips with her tongue, then tightens her grip and pulls his face close to hers, her eyes flashing.

"Hey," Harry says, tugging free. "That's pretty good."

The line is moving. They're halfway to the ticket window. Three boys with big portable radios go by, heading for the box office. The radios are tuned to the same station and the area in front of the theater is suddenly full of Mexican polka music. "What are you guys doing?" Fay shouts. "The line's back here."

*   *   *

At the Starlight after the movie Fay gets into Harry's bed. "I'm going to stay all night, okay?" She twists around under the spread for a minute and produces her shorts and sandals, which she deposits on the floor by the telephone. "I think I'll keep this on for now," she says, pinching her shirt and tugging it a couple of times.

"Great," he says.

Harry's up first, at noon. He takes a shower in the metal stall, being as quiet as he can, but when he comes out Fay is gone and Mrs. Kiwi is banging on the screen. "What do you people think I'm running here, a bordello?"

Harry jumps. "Just a minute, I'm coming."

He just gets his pants on before she's in the open door brandishing her passkey. Her muscle shirt is cranberry this time.

She sighs and rolls the key between her fingers. "I've been running the Starlight twenty-two years and I've seen it all. Her creeping out of here like that—you should be ashamed."

He points toward the parking lot. "We're together."

Mrs. Kiwi pockets the key in the stretch trousers she's wearing. "Yes. I see that." She nods gravely, then puts on a grin and pats Harry's arm. "I understand perfectly, Mr. Lang."

"We work together. I mean, she works here in Dallas, and I work in Louisiana, but for the same company."

"Sure," Mrs. Kiwi says, patting more solicitously than before. She makes a sucking noise between her teeth, then laughs. "There's a lot of that around is what I understand. More and more." She shades her eyes and stares through the white dust at her office, then puts her fists on her hips and looks at his bare feet.

Fay pulls the screen door open. "Harry? What's going on?"

"Nothing, darling," Mrs. Kiwi says, shooing Fay with the backs of her hands. "You go on outside before the Baptists see you. Maybe we all ought to go outside." She turns back to Harry. "I was a girl myself— fourteen brothers. You don't get so many families like that any more, what with the economy and the state of things. All of them died, too. One after another. I had dead brothers all over this country for a while. I would've had a big family if Mr. Kiwi, God rest his soul, hadn't passed on so sudden. That's a long time ago now, forty years." She snorts and does a little twist with her head, then says, "Well, now, that's about enough of that." She reaches into her pocket and gets a folded piece of note paper. "A. D. called earlier on and said the car's gonna be late. I've got the number here if you want to dial him up."

She shakes the paper at Harry. There's a telephone number in blue ballpoint in one corner, but the rest of the sheet is covered with foreign words and phrases. The words *buena* and *bueno* appear repeatedly in block letters at the center of the sheet. "Maybe I'll give him a call," Harry says.

Mrs. Kiwi wipes at the perspiration stuck in her eyebrows, then looks at her fingers. "I think you kids better come on for some lunch—I mean, once you get straightened away." She points over her shoulder with a thumb.

"Let me check with her," Harry says. "Okay?"

She nods and turns to look at a passing long-haul truck that has huge limes painted on its side. "But you're welcome." She nods several more times, her crinkled gray hair springing in the noon sun, then abruptly starts off toward the office, kicking up dust. "Got biscuits," she says over her shoulder. "Plenty of biscuits."

Fay brings a slimline briefcase when she comes back to the room. She undresses and quickly showers, then puts on a slip and a white shirtwaist dress that clings to her legs when she moves. Walking back and forth at the foot of the bed, she says, "I think I'd better call Tim soon." She looks at the nails on her left hand, holding the hand very close to her face and popping the tips of the fingers out from under her thumb. The nails are the flat orange of flesh-colored stockings. "I don't want him to think I had a wreck and died on the highway. I want him to know where I am." She sits on the bed, keeping the telephone between them. Her hair's wet. "I mean, he still likes me and everything."

"He should," Harry says.

"Damn right," she says. "I like him, don't I?"

Harry goes into the bathroom while she calls Tim. The conversation is quick; Fay's part is full of half sentences and short silences in which he can hear her flicking her fingers.

When they drive out, Mrs. Kiwi is behind her counter, and Gorky is there too, playing with some kind of phonograph record, spinning it on a pencil. He waves. His GMC is parked up close to the back of the office, mostly out of sight.

"I feel like going somewhere," Fay says. "Somewhere pretty. I wonder if they have a zoo out here. We could get hot dogs—you like hot dogs? We could feed the seals."

Harry points out the car window at a one-story shack that has a dozen glittery brown vinyl booths piled up on the porch and PEACOCK CAFE stenciled in silver on the door. "We could go there."

"I don't want to go there, Harry. I want to go somewhere where there are seals, but I guess there aren't any seals out here. I probably should've waited for you in town. You don't seem to be working at this."

He taps on the dashboard and looks at the scenery for a minute; the road is lined with empty lots full of tires, hundreds of automobile tires. "I agree," he finally says.

"What do you agree?" The dress is pulled over her knees, bunched at her thighs, fanned awkwardly around her on the seat.

"Why don't we just get a burger?"

She steers the car into a gas station where a guy in a business suit is looking at a small John Deere tractor. Fay smiles and says, "Excuse me," out the car window to the guy, and he has to step up on the pump island to let her through. "Looks like he sells rats, doesn't he?" she whispers.

They go back to Nick's. She wants to sit at the counter, so they get stools between a huge man wearing bib-style overalls and a kid who's picking his teeth while he waits for food. The big guy takes a look at them when they sit down, then goes back to his smothered chicken.

Nick's is sixty feet deep and twenty feet wide. On one side it's a low counter and a kitchen, on the other a row of wooden booths. In between are a few school cafeteria tables.

"Well, so tell me about yourself," Fay says after they've ordered hamburgers. "You eat here often?"

"Here come the burgers," he says, pointing at the cook who's slipping meat patties on two fat buns.

There's a whine from the doorway, and a girl in an electric wheelchair comes in. Everyone seems to know her. She slaps left hands with some of the customers as she steers herself to the back. She has shoulder-length hair, dark skin, puffy lips, big eyes. She's wearing a soft-blue pullover. The waiters, kids in jeans and short-sleeved shirts, dote on her, bring silverware and napkins and water, and stay to talk. She teases them with sexy laughs and white smiles. The waiters stand by her table, straddle the oak chairs. Harry catches the girl's eyes once, between the turned backs, and she stares at him as if they were old, loving friends.

"Okay," Fay says. "This isn't so marvelous. No more burger for me."

She drops her hamburger on the paper plate and shoves it away from her, accidentally knocking it off the counter.

The big guy next to Harry says, "Jesus." He pushes himself up on the counter and peers behind it to see where the hamburger landed. "Hey, Manny. Take a look." He points toward the floor.

The old man doing the cooking shuffles over, picks up the hamburger, and stands right in front of Harry. "What's wrong here? You get a bad one?"

"It's fine," Fay says. "It really is good, but we've got an emergency." She pushes off the stool and opens her purse.

"Look, lady. If it's bad, just say so. We get a bad one now and again."

She puts a five-dollar bill on the counter. "No," she says, smiling. "It's good. You ready, Harry?"

Manny picks up the five and holds it out to Harry. "Take it," he says, waving the hamburger back and forth between Fay and himself. "I can understand this. Take the money."

The guy in the overalls wipes his face on the sleeve of his T-shirt, leaving a strip of coleslaw like a green worm on his shoulder. He and Harry slide off their stools at the same time and the guy is at least half a foot taller. He looks at Fay, then plucks the bill out of Manny's hand and puts it in hers. "You heard the man," he says.

Outside, Fay goes straight for her car. They drive to the Starlight without talking. She looks determined and lovely steering with one hand, propping her head on the other. Mrs. Kiwi is on her knees in the tiny horseshoe-shaped flower bed by the office; she goes up like a squirrel in the foot-high tulips and waves as Fay and Harry go under the portico.

The bed in Harry's room has been made and there are new towels in the bath; the air conditioner, which he left running, has been turned off, so the room is stuffy. Fay stands in front of the open door, her legs dark against the light fabric of the skirt; she's fiddling with her pale sunglasses. Harry sits on the edge of the bed and looks at the knees of his pants. She opens her purse, looks inside, closes it again, then comes away from the door and stands in front of him.

"I don't know how to explain all this," he says, smoothing the skirt at her hip with his fingers. Mrs. Kiwi is coming across the oyster-shell lot swinging a plastic bag full of biscuits.

Fay slips her glasses into place. "When's your birthday?" she says. "I want to get you something nice for your birthday."

Frank X. Tolbert

Frank X. (Francis Xavier) Tolbert (1912–1984) wrote a daily column in the Dallas Morning News *for twenty-three years and a weekly column for seven years thereafter, perfecting the form of "informal history." He was at his best evoking a much-taken-for-granted part of the Texas landscape (he invented the Texas chili cook-off). His sketch of Texas blues singer Mance Lipscomb matches two of the state's most vital natural resources.*

A MOJO HAND

When I first knew Mance Lipscomb he was seventy years old and a sharecropper farmer. Only, as he explained it: "With me it was more croppin' and less sharin'."

"Then I got me a good Mojo Hand," he said.

For the last decade of his life Mance was a nationally recognized extraordinaire, a singer with a saxophone sound in his throat, a master guitarist, and a composer of the blues, or of what he called "sinful songs."

He made frequent appearances, along with his friend, Sam (Lightnin') Hopkins of Houston, at blues festivals all over the United States. Mance and Lightnin' could draw crowds on a college campus like a winning football team. Mance told me: "Old fellows like me and Lightnin' is about the onliest ones left keeping our style of music in rotation."

One time in the Navasota river bottoms near the town of Navasota, Mance and I were following his rabbit hounds. The dogs were hitting cold trails, and they made harsh music of frustration. It began to rain. Mance called up the dogs and they leaped in the cargo box of the pickup truck. And we drove to the Lipscomb family place on the outskirts of Navasota.

Mance lived in an old frame cottage with his wife of more than fifty years, Elnora, and a dozen or so "grands," as the Lipscombs called grandchildren.

Elnora and a half dozen of the grands were watching television. So Mance and I sat out on the front gallery on hide-bottomed chairs, and we watched the rain come down, and my host hit a few chords on a guitar every now and then.

Mance and his friend Lightnin' Hopkins were disciples of one of the greatest of blues singers and composers, the late Blind Lemon Jefferson.

"I just knew Blind Lemon at the Buffalo Association," said Lipscomb, speaking of an annual musical gathering of black religionists at Buffalo, Texas. "Lightnin' was about raised by Blind Lemon. Lightnin' ran off with Blind Lemon when he was just a shirttail kid and stayed with Blind Lemon for several years."

Not many of Lipscomb's neighbors along Carlos Road seemed to know that he was a celebrity who drew big crowds to his "gigs" from Boston to Berkeley. His music was appreciated locally except by some "church people," his wife included. She objected to his compositions described as "sinful songs."

Mance didn't say he composed a song, though. He "estimated" a song. He never used the word "composed."

Lipscomb made strange and lovely sounds with his guitar, what he proudly called "my bottomless sound." He fretted the strings with the hasp of a flat, old pocketknife.

"A steel pick or a bottleneck don't fret as pretty as a pocketknife hasp," explained the old man. "Me and Lightnin', and before us old Hudie Ledbetter, is the last of the real guitar pickers. The rest is just thumpers." By "Hudie Ledbetter" he meant the master of the 12-string guitar, Hudie (Lead Belly) Ledbetter.

That time on the porch with the rain coming down he got in a kind of sad mood. He said he had been "estimating" a sad song for an album to be called *Evil Blues*. The lyrics included:

> Early morning blues sitting by my bed.
> And when I want to eat breakfast
> Blues jump right out of my bread . . .

He said one of Elnora's brothers had helped him with the words for a song called "Shake, Mamma, Shake."

"Only brother-in-law done turned preacher and he say he ain't estimating no more of my sinful songs."

Mance said his long years as a tenant farmer weren't all bad. "Sometime I got to play my box (guitar) at church house parties and common school closings (he meant school commencement exercises), and in beer joints.

"Maybe I was lucky I didn't get to go to gigs in the air force (he meant airlines) all over the country until I got a lot of age and caution on me. Some of my friends were mighty famous when they was young. And some of them died young.

"Take Sonny Boy Williams. They never was nobody who could play the blues on a harmonica like Sonny Boy. But he got to be a big man up in New York City and he was stobbed four times until he died. And Blind Lemon. No one could sing like Blind Lemon. He got mighty famous and sold hundreds of thousands of records through those Victrola people, and he influenced a lot of people besides me and Lightnin'. Blind Lemon left his friends and somebody caught him on a dark street at night in Chicago and knocked him in the head and took his poke and left him to freeze to death."

Mance plays the guitar from top to bottom. And while he sang one of Blind Lemon's songs he played both the bass and the lead on the guitar. This Blind Lemon song started out:

> Mamma tole me, and Papa too:
> 'Whiskey and women gonna be the death of you . . .'

Blind Lemon was buried in an unmarked grave in a cemetery on the edge of Wortham, Texas. In the 1960s, though, the people of Wortham took up a collection and put a historical marker over Jefferson's grave.

Lightnin' Hopkins was in Europe at the time and couldn't come to the dedication at Wortham. Mance was there, though, and so were five white musicians from New York City who went through some sort of mumbo jumbo involving sticking brooms in the earth around the grave.

"I didn't give no mind to those broomstickers," said Mance. "I sang a mournful song over Blind Lemon's grave. I sang one he wrote. It's called 'One Kind Favor' or 'Please See to My Grave Kept Clean.'"

Then there on the porch Mance began to play the blues and in his brittle but pleasant baritone he sang Blind Lemon's dirge, starting with:

> Dig me a grave, oooh wide and deep,
> Put tombstones at my head and feet . . .

After that Lipscomb made it seem that two guitars were going instead of just one as he played a song he said was one of his own, "Mamma Let Me Lay It on You." He explained: "I estimated this song a long time ago on this same porch. A white singer named Bob Dylan must have liked this song. He followed me around to gigs for two years, to places like Berkeley and Los Angeles and he wrote a song to the same music called 'Follow Me Down,' only he changed the words. He mentioned me on the album, I understand."

Lipscomb had an esoteric language of his own. Sometimes he would say he "predicted a song." By this he meant he heard a "field song and kept it from being lost to recollection." He mentioned a sort of a sequel to the old "Easy Rider" folk song called "Wonder Where My Easy Rider Gone?"

"I predicted this song a long time ago. Heard an old, old man singing it in the fields when we was working. Easy Rider is a woman in the song, you know."

"Wonder Where My Easy Rider Gone" was strictly guitar, but next Lipscomb did one with lyrics. "This kind of a sinful song and I wrote it with no help from my preacher brother-in-law. This is a song about a big, mean fellow and his friend girl."

First he sang the role of the "big, mean fellow" in a deep voice:

> Blues in the bottle, stopper in the hand,
> If you want to be my woman you gotta heed my command.

Mance then explained: "This kind of a sassy woman, the big, mean fellow's friend girl. She rise up in the bed and she sass him good." In a falsetto tone, Mance sang the sassy girl's role, first speaking of her bedmate as if he weren't there:

> Mistreatin' Daddy wake me up 'bout two A.M.
> Try to make me swear I got no man but him.

Mance next explains that the girl has turned over in bed and addressed the big, mean man this way:

> Daddy, listen, and don't raise no san',
> I won't as' you 'bout no woman
> If you won't as' me 'bout no man!

After that Lipscomb spoke of his recent trip to Los Angeles: "I'm mighty glad to get back on the Nava-sot with Elnora and my grands and my hound dogs. I sell a few of my albums, mostly to college kids. They listen close to my records and try to estimate my style. Only it don't do them a doggone bit of good unless ear music is in them.

"I found one white boy in California who could almost get on my side and find my bottomless sound. Only he was kind of twistified. Almost everyone in Los Angeles is twistified. If you twistified they ain't much you can do except get you a good Mojo Hand. And they ain't no better Mojo Hand than a sparkle stick, you know a limb off a farkleberry tree. The Indian people down in Polk County put a lot of store in the power of the sparkle stick. They say it's a Mojo Hand that can change your person and give you good luck."

I knew a little about Mojo. There is a high school football team in Odessa, Texas, with the nickname of the Mojos, and they are a good-luck, winning bunch. But I don't think they use farkleberry sticks for their Mojo Hands. I asked Lipscomb for his definition of a Mojo Hand, and he said:

"Well, it's a way of getting something or getting something done or influencin' someone, only you got no hope of getting anything done unless you got a good Mojo Hand—like a sparkle stick from a farkle-berry tree limb."

Mance said he had a feeling he was going to have "a bad sickness and have to go to the horse-pital." He played and sang Lightnin' Hopkins's version of a Mojo Hand song, and it suggested that the Mojo doesn't always work on some people:

I'm goin' to Louisiana to get me a good Mojo Hand
To try and stop my woman from foolin' 'round with another man . . .

And this was the end of the song:

I got me a Mojo Hand working but it won't work on you,
'cause you won't do nothin' I tole you to do . . .

The rain had stopped. A white man drove up. He said his father was a lifelong friend of Mance's. His father was about to die and he wanted to hear Lipscomb play and sing for the last time.

Mance went off with the man. And I never saw him again. He died a few weeks later.

Elnora spoke a fine tribute. She said: "Mance and me never had much money, but we never had any unshared money."

Larry McMurtry

Larry McMurtry (b. 1936) is known by millions who've never read any of his ten novels for the films made from them: Hud, The Last Picture Show, Lovin' Molly, *and* Terms of Endearment, *the latter the Academy Award winner for Best Picture in 1983. McMurtry won the Pulitzer Prize in 1986 for* Lonesome Dove. *Outspoken in support of using regional themes in fiction, he says of Texas as a source of ideas: "The material is here, and it has barely been touched. If this is truly the era of the Absurd, then all the better for the Texas writer."*

THE LAST PICTURE SHOW

A week before the picture show closed down Duane came home from boot camp. He drove in on Sunday morning and word soon got around that he was leaving for Korea in a week's time. Sonny learned that he was home Sunday night, when he and Billy were having a cheeseburger in the café.

"Wonder where he is?" he asked. "He hasn't been to the poolhall."

"I kinda doubt he'll come," Genevieve said, frowning. "His conscience is hurting him too much about your eye. I think he's gonna stay at the rooming house this week."

"Well, maybe he'll come in," Sonny said. "There ain't much to do in this town. I couldn't live in it a week without going to the poolhall, I know that."

"I think it's all silly," Genevieve said. "Why don't you go see him? Be a shame if he goes to Korea without you all seein' one another."

Sonny thought so too, but he was nervous about going to see Duane. He kept hoping Duane would show up at the poolhall and save him having to make a decision; but Duane didn't. So far as anyone knew, he spent the whole week watching television at his mother's house. A couple of boys saw him out washing his Mercury one afternoon, but he never came to town.

As the week went by, Sonny got more and more nervous. Several times he was on the verge of picking up the phone and calling—once he did pick it up, but his nerve failed him and he put it back down. If Duane didn't want to be bothered there was no point in bothering.

Friday night there was a football game in Henrietta, but Sonny didn't go. He heard the next morning that Duane had been there drunk. All day he considered the problem and finally decided that he would go see Duane at the rooming house and let the chips fall where they may—it couldn't hurt much to try. If Duane didn't want to see him all he had to do was say so.

About five thirty, as it was beginning to grow dark, Sonny got in the pickup and drove to the rooming house. Duane's red Mercury was parked out front. A norther had struck that afternoon and sheets of cold air rushed through the town, shaking the leafless mesquite and rattling the dry stems of Old Lady Malone's flowers. Sonny rang the doorbell and then stuffed his hands in his pockets to keep them warm.

"H'lo, Mrs. Malone," he said, when the old lady opened the inside door. The screen door was latched, as always. "Duane here?"

"That's his car, ain't it?" she said, edging behind the door so the wind wouldn't hit anything but her nose and her forehead. "He's here if he ain't walked off."

She shut the door and went to get Duane. Sonny shuffled nervously on the porch. In a minute, Duane opened the door and stepped outside.

"Hi," Sonny said, finding it hard to get his breath because of the wind. "Thought I'd better come by and see you before you got off."

"Glad you did," Duane said. He was nervous, but he did look sort of glad. He was wearing Levi's and a western shirt.

"Want to go eat a bite?" Sonny suggested.

"Yeah, let me get my jacket."

He got his football jacket, the one from the year when the two of them had been co-captains, they got in the warm pickup, and drove to the café. Conversation was slow in coming until Sonny thought to ask about the army, but then Duane loosened up and told one army story after another while they ate their hamburger steaks. It was pretty much like old times. Penny waited on them—she had twin girls during the winter, put on twenty-five pounds, and was experimenting that night with purple lipstick. Old Marston had died in February of pneumonia— he had gone to sleep in a bar ditch in the wrong season. Genevieve had hired a friendly young widow woman to do the cooking.

"Guess we ought to take in the picture show," Sonny said. "Tonight's the last night."

"A good thing, too," Penny said, overhearing him. "Picture show's been gettin' more sinful all the time, if you ask me. Them movie stars lettin' their titties hang out—I never seen the like. The last time I went I told my old man he could just take me home, I wasn't sittin' still for that kind of goings on."

The Last Picture Show | 285

"Yeah, we might as well go," Duane said, ignoring her. "Hate to miss the last night."

They went to the poolhall and Sonny got his football jacket too. Then they angled across the square to the picture show and bought their tickets. A few grade-school kids were going in. The picture was an Audie Murphy movie called *The Kid From Texas,* with Gale Storm.

"Why hello, Duane," Miss Mosey said. "I thought you was done overseas. Hope you all like the show."

The boys planned to, but somehow the occasion just didn't work out. Audie Murphy was a scrapper as usual, but it didn't help. It would have taken *Winchester '73* or *Red River* or some big movie like that to have crowded out the memories the boys kept having. They had been at the picture show so often with Jacy that it was hard to keep from thinking of her, lithely stretching herself in the back row after an hour of kissing and cuddling. Such thoughts were dangerous to both of them.

"Hell, this here's a dog," Duane said.

Sonny agreed. "Why don't we run down to Fort Worth, drink a little beer?" he asked.

"My bus leaves at six thirty in the mornin'," Duane said. "Reckon we could make it to Forth Worth and back by six thirty?"

"Easy."

Miss Mosey was distressed to see them leaving so soon. She tried to give them their money back, but they wouldn't take it. She was scraping out the popcorn machine, almost in tears. "If Sam had lived, I believe we could have kept it goin'," she said, "but me and Jimmy just didn't have the know-how. Duane, you watch out now, overseas." Outside the wind was so cold it made their eyes water.

Sonny insisted they go in the pickup. He knew Duane would go to sleep on the way back and he didn't want the responsibility of driving the Mercury. The wind shoved the pickup all over the road, but the road was still a lot better for their spirits than the picture show had been. Rattling out of Thalia reminded them a little of the time—it seemed years before—when they had gone to Matamoros. As soon as they reached a wet county they stopped and bought two six-packs of beer. The cans spewed when they were opened and the smell of beer filled the cab.

By the time they crossed the Lake Worth bridge they had gone through a six-pack and a half and were feeling okay. Soon they came to the Jacksboro highway bars and Sonny pulled off at a place called the Red Dot Tavern. Inside, a lot of tough-looking boys with ducktails were playing the shuffleboard, and a couple of women with dyed hair were sitting at the bar with their middle-aged sweethearts. The ducktails looked at the boys beligerently, but no direct challenges were offered.

"All we can do here is get drunk and get whipped," Duane said. "Let's see what the prospects are on South Main."

They drove slowly around the courthouse—the only courthouse they knew that had a neon American flag on top—and parked far down Main Street, where the bars were. The wind whipped around the big granite courthouse and cut right down the street, as cold as it had been in Thalia. The boys went in a hash house and had some chili and crackers to fortify themselves, then let the wind blow them down the street to a bar called the Cozy Inn, where a three-piece hillbilly band was whomping away. One middle-aged couple was dancing, and a few more were sitting in the booths or at the bar. The barmaid, a friendly old woman in her mid-fifties, wiped off their table with the end of her apron and then brought them some beer.

"Where you boys from?" she asked. "Thalia? Ain't it windy up there? I wouldn't live that close to the plains for nothin'. My oldest sister lives out in Floydada."

In a few minutes the band ended its set and the three young musicians straggled off to the rest room to relieve themselves.

"Maggie, you sing us a couple," one of the older customers said.

The barmaid didn't much want to, but the other couples took up the cry and finally she went over and picked up a guitar, shaking her head and deprecating herself.

"I ain't much of a singer," she said, but she strummed a minute or two and sang "Your Cheatin' Heart." Everyone thought she was real good, the boys included. Her voice was rough but strong—it filled the Cozy Inn better than the three sideburned young honky-tonkers had. She sang like she meant every word; it was not hard to believe that she had run afoul of a cheating heart or two somewhere in her life. After that she sang "Making Believe," and would have put the guitar down and gone back to the bar if Duane hadn't gone up and stopped her. He liked her singing.

"I'm goin' off to Korea tomorrow, ain't no tellin' when I'll get to Fort Worth agin," he said. "Sing one more."

"Why sure, if that's the case," the woman said. "Both my boys was in the service. I was right proud of 'em."

"These is for the soldier boys," she announced, not wanting the rest of the crowd to think she was singing out of vanity. She sang "Filipino Baby" and everyone applauded loudly; encouraged, she finished with "Peace in the Valley" and went back to the bar to draw someone a

Pearl. Sonny felt suddenly depressed. The old barmaid had reminded him that he wasn't in the army. It seemed a fine thing to be going off to Korea and Sonny wished very badly that he could go. When the band came back the boys left and stood on the cold street a minute, both slightly wobbly from the beer.

"We sure ain't findin' no women," Duane said. "Want to look some more or do you want to take the easy out?"

"It's too cold to prowl much," Sonny said.

With no more ado they turned up the street toward the easy out, a whorehouse called the New Deal Hotel. It was about the nicest whorehouse in that part of the country, but a little expensive on that account. Since it was Duane's last night the boys decided to splurge. When they got to the hotel a bunch of high school boys from Seymour were standing on the sidewalk shivering, trying to get up the nerve to go inside. It was easy to tell they were from Seymour because of their football jackets.

"Yep, it's a whorehouse all right," Duane said. "You boys coming up?"

"How much do they charge?" one boy asked, his teeth chattering. "We're afraid to go up for fear we ain't got the money."

"They start at about ten bucks," Duane said, and the boys' faces fell. They had been hoping for five.

Sonny and Duane went on in and up the green-carpeted stairs, leaving the Seymour boys to count their money. The madame was a quiet, polite woman who looked and dressed like the saleswomen in a Wichita Falls department store. Sonny's girl was a polite, thin-nosed brunette from Corsicana, named Pauline. Everything was splendidly comfortable in the New Deal: the rooms were warm, the beds wide and clean, the carpets good. The girls were pleasant, but so efficient that afterward it seemed to Sonny that he and the girl had barely touched. Before he was even thawed out he and Duane were going back down the green stairs, each ten dollars poorer and neither much less horny.

The Seymour boys were all gone, the streets almost empty. While they were walking back to their pickup the city streetsweeper chugged by and Sonny remembered Billy and hoped Miss Mosey had seen he got home out of the cold.

"Well, I guess the next piece I get will be yellow," Duane said philosophically.

By the time they got back to the Lake Worth bridge, he was asleep. Sonny didn't care—he enjoyed the drive, and was in no hurry. With the wind blowing against him he couldn't make much time, but he didn't need to. North of Jacksboro he stopped the pickup and got out to take a leak, and Duane woke up and followed suit. It was about five o'clock when they pulled into Thalia. The posterboards in front of the picture show were naked. It seemed to Sonny it would have been better to have left *some* posters up, even the posters to *The Texas Kid.*

"Got about two hours till bus time," he said, when they were at the rooming house. "Want to go down and have some coffee?"

"Yeah," Duane said. "Wait till I go in and get my gear."

In his uniform Duane looked a lot different. When he got back in the pickup he casually handed Sonny the keys to the Mercury. "Here," he said. "Why don't you look after that car for me?"

Sonny took the keys, embarrassed. "Your Ma don't need it?" he asked.

"I wouldn't want her drivin' it, no better than she can drive. You might help her run the groceries home, if you have time."

Sonny didn't know what else to say. In the warm café they both got a little sleepy and ended up playing the jukebox to keep awake. Genevieve wasn't there. Her husband had gone back to work in August and she had hired a girl named Etta May to work the night shift.

When the bus pulled up out front, both boys were glad. Sitting and waiting was hard on the nerves. The bus driver came in to have a cup of coffee and Sonny and Duane walked across the street to the yellow Continental Trailways bus. The wind made their eyes water, and took their breath—they had to turn their backs to it. Duane leaned his dufflebag against the front of the bus.

"Hear anything from Jacy?" he asked suddenly, since there was just two minutes left to talk.

"No, not a thing. She hasn't been back to town since August. I guess she just stays in Dallas all the time."

"I ain't over her yet," Duane said. "It's the damnedest thing. I ain't over her yet. That's the only reason me and you got into it, that night. Reckon she likes it down in Dallas?"

"It's hard to say," Sonny said. "Maybe she does. Reckon you and her would have got it all straightened out if I hadn't butted in?"

"Aw no," Duane said. "They would have annulled me too, even if we had. You all never even got to the motel?"

"No," Sonny said.

The bus driver came out of the café and hurried across the street, tucking his chin into his shoulder so his face would be out of the wind. Duane picked up the dufflebag and he and Sonny shook hands awkwardly.

"Duane, be careful," Sonny said. "I'll take care of that Mercury."

"Okay," Duane said. "See you in a year or two, if I don't get shot."

He got on and waved quickly from the window as the bus started up. A ragweed skated across the dusty street and the bus ran over it. Sonny put his hands in his pockets and walked back across the street to the pickup, not feeling too good. It was another one of those mornings when no one was there.

William C. Martin

William C. Martin (b. 1937) became the nation's only columnist to review church services the way others review the arts, for Texas Monthly *magazine. Chairman of the sociology department at Rice University, and frequent contributor to* Harper's, The Atlantic, *and* Esquire, *he grew up on a farm between Devine and Big Foot.*

GIFTS FROM MY FATHER

About eighteen months ago, my father learned he had a rare kidney disease that would progressively, inevitably so wreck the various organs of his body that one of them—heart, liver, lungs, brain, blood vessels, skin, the kidneys themselves—would fail, and he would die. Intellectually, he accepted the fact he was going to die. He did not rage against the dying of the light—rage is not his style—but neither did he offer to help reduce the wattage. He prepared for death in a way I found completely characteristic. He seemed to take some pleasure in the fact that only two other people in South Texas had his disease, and that the doctors had told him it was completely unrelated to the two packs of cigarettes he had smoked every day for fifty-seven years. The powerful combination of drugs he took every morning made him feel, by his own account, like he had "just drunk a quart of cheap whiskey and was trying to drive uphill on a bad road in an overloaded Model T truck with no muffler." Still, he kept on driving. By summer he had a little collection of adding-machine tapes indicating how much and how long the payments would be for the sale of his business, how much various men owed him, what the interest ought to be on his certificates of deposit, how much stock he had in the Tri-County Farmer's Co-Op, and how much it would be worth when he died.

All his life he had driven modest cars, lest he offend the farmers with whom he had worked. Now, he drove to San Antonio and paid cash for a fully equipped, top-of-the-line maroon Lincoln Continental. A few days later, when I rushed to his hospital bed to be present when he died, wondering what blessing he would bestow upon me, what his last words of advice or caution or love might be, he opened his eyes and said, each word slow, labored, and barely audible, "Did . . . you . . . see . . . my . . . car?"

I spent much of the next several weeks with him in that hospital room, thinking about what it means to have a parent die. I realized, as I had at the birth of my oldest child, that it was not the first time this had happened, which diminished its importance just a bit. But I also knew I was experiencing the universal, which ennobled the event immeasurably.

I thought about what it had meant to be his son. I don't know whether our relationship was anything extraordinary or not. I remember wishing he would play with me more, much as I suppose my children wish I had played with them more. He always worked hard, but sometimes in the summer he took me on business trips and, after a day of sitting in a sweltering car or a cluttered, dusty office in a grain mill or a warehouse or a fertilizer plant, he would buy me a hot roast beef sandwich and take me to see a movie starring Francis the Talking Mule or Eddie Bracken or Leo Gorcey and the Bowery Boys. In the fall, we always managed to see several Southwest Conference football games, and at least twice he took me to the State Fair. He made me believe it was important to shake hands firmly, to remember names, and to look people in the eye when I talked to them. He tried to make me believe it was important to wear a hat and lace-up shoes. I knew he was smart and honest, and it pleased me that, when it came time to build a new high school or recruit a new doctor for the town, he was always one of the three or four men everybody knew would have to be in on it. Not everything I heard or knew about him was good, but the balance was clearly in that direction.

I was pretty sure he was proud of me, but learned not to expect him to say much about it. I was also pretty sure he thought it was something of a waste of talent for me to become a preacher or a teacher or a writer instead of going into a field with more substance to it—like the agriculture business. As recently as three years ago he suggested I come to Pearsall for a couple of months and learn about what he did, in case I ever had to take over. When I suggested he come to Houston for a couple of months and explain it to me, he was incredulous; after all, he had a regular job. On the other hand, when I overheard him talking about "that boy of mine that went to Harvard and teaches over at Rice," or when I met someone whose only impression of me had come through him, I could tell he wasn't entirely disappointed.

It was not a simple matter to fasten these strands of memory that trailed across my mind to this deteriorating figure in a hospital bed. The legs that had stepped off fields in a strong, measured stride were now white and hairless and thin, except for water-filled knees. The wrinkled feet were like balloons that had been inflated to capacity and allowed to go down. The swollen stomach summoned images of starving children. The organ that had propelled half of me into existence and that had first represented "man genitals" to me was now virtually useless even for its most basic task, unable to contain the involuntary flow. To compound the sense of strangeness, his charts and name tags listed his first name as "Lowell," and the doctors and nurses called him that, even though an injury he had sustained as a teenager left him a nickname— "Peggie" (short for "peg leg")—that was as permanent and natural as his slight limp and as unfeminine as his Stetsons.

As I looked at him for days, it became more difficult to remember how he had looked when he was well than to imagine how he would look when he was dead. Still, he was not dead, and even in this most extreme of living states, he maintained the tough, ironic Texas grit that marked his whole life. When the nurse asked if he could roll over to allow her to change his sheets, he said, "I can do anything once and several things twice." When she complimented him on the good amount of urine he had voided, he said it was nothing compared to what he could do on a heavy dose of diuretics. When she told him she was going to measure it and pack it in some ice, he said that was fine with him, but he thought they'd have a hard time selling it. Once, a nurse looked at him and declared him comatose. He registered not a flicker of protest for two hours, then said, in weak indignation, "Comatose! . . . I've . . . got . . . as . . . much . . . sense . . . as . . . I've . . . ever . . . had!"

It should be no surprise that a man who claims to have lived just about every day of his life the way he wanted did not take well to life in a single bed. He despised his oxygen mask and sought constantly to pull it off; finally, he had to be restrained by cuffs tied to the side bars of the bed. It is not easy to tie one's father to a bed, but I got better at it. Dozens, no, hundreds of times, he begged me to untie him. When he saw that begging would not help, he resorted to a technique he had practiced all his life: making a deal. "There's a pocketknife in my trousers," he said. "If you'll get it and cut me loose, I'll give you the knife."

"I can't do that," I told him. "If I cut you loose, you'll take off the oxygen mask and you'll have a heart attack and die. I can't do that."

He thought about it, then looked at me and said, "It's a seven-dollar-and-fifty-cent knife."

Like Jacob with the angel, I wanted to wrestle with that old man's soul and not let go until he promised me a blessing. But my determination to concentrate as closely as possible on that spark that refused to go out was consistently thwarted by a great cloud of witnesses. People I had not seen in years or, worse, had never seen came to pay their respects. My mother not only appreciated the company, but kept score. I suffered moderate ambivalence. My father was terminally exhausted and did not need or want visitors. One Saturday afternoon, when no fewer than twelve people crowded into the room, chattering and watching the ball game and using the telephone and nibbling on a cake roll filled with Cool Whip, I noticed he was trying to say something and moved to the edge of his bed. He forced out only two words, but they were apt: "Ringling Brothers." At times like that—and there were others—I wanted everybody to clear out and leave us alone, but eventually I realized my possessiveness was inappropriate. I was there because about forty years and nine months earlier my number came up in the ultimate roulette game. Most of them had earned the right to be there, and the kind of love and respect they showed extended my understanding of family.

Brother and Sister Harrell and Brother and Sister Caddel and Brother and Sister Danchak, church folk from Devine and Pearsall, came by several times and said they'd be glad to do anything they could. Brother Swim, who used to drive down from San Antonio to preach for us, stopped by nearly every day to check up and lead us in "a word of prayer for Brother Peggie." Temo Hernandez, one of my dad's most valued employees in recent years, apologized for breaking into tears but explained that "Mr. Martin was like a second father." Temo's wife left a long letter thanking him for helping them get through some difficult times and told how their children thought of him as a grandfather. Odis Doyal, who worked for him thirty years, said. "You know, your dad is sort of like an older brother to me." To Elmer Stehle, a thin, leather-faced workingman I have known all my life, he was more like an uncle. Henry Brigman, who has, according to my mother, "made a good little preacher," said, "You all are sort of like kinfolks." Anaceto Cortez, a small, wrinkled man in khaki trousers and purple shirt, put his hand on my shoulder and said, "He's my good, good amigo. I know him for a long time. He's sure a good man." Jesse Alvarado, a former employee and old friend, said through tears, "He always called me 'Mexican,' but he treated me like a white man." One banker gave my mother a check for several thousand dollars and told her there would be no interest. Another made sure she knew where to come in case she needed any more. And an apparently endless procession of men in Western pants and boots and short-sleeved shirts, with creases in their oiled hair that fairly pled to have the respectfully removed hats returned to their natural places, stood around and said things like, "Your dad did us a lot of favors." I was beginning to see that he had done me some, too.

As he sank lower and lower, our lives organized themselves around death. I flew back and forth between Houston and San Antonio every few days and held reservations on a lot of flights I didn't take. In addition to his primary ailment and long-standing emphysema, he developed pneumonia and tuberculosis, his liver multiplied in size, his heart and kidneys began to fail, his skin leaked water and blood, and—what we had all dreaded most—he lost his mind, except for rare lucid moments. As every vital sign got worse, the doctors said they did not recommend "heroic measures," since the only kind of life these might sustain would be so severely reduced as to be worse than death for such a man as this. I had seen a television program about Karen Ann Quinlan a few nights before and found it ironic that my mother and sister and I had just stood in the hall and agreed to let a life end with as much dignity as was still possible. No controversy, no trial, no headlines. We just talked about it and cried a little bit and that was that.

Mama told me who would speak at the funeral and who would be the pallbearers, and explained that, even though she and Daddy had always said they weren't going to spend a lot of money on a casket, she had changed her mind, because Pearsall is a high-class town and people would remember it if she put him away in something cheap. I drove over to the Wonderland Mall and bought a new white shirt to bury him in and thanked the salesgirl when she told me to have a nice day.

A few days later, about two in the morning, a nurse said, "He's going. His eyes have begun to set. He probably won't last more than an hour now." My mother, whose life had been bound up with this man for nearly half a century, squeezed his hand and said, "Don't leave me, honey." Somehow, he heard her and had strength enough to answer. He said, "I'm not."

And he didn't. From that moment, he began to get better—just a little, but better. After a couple of weeks, the doctors said maybe he could die at home if he could survive the seventy-mile trip in an automobile. He survived, but his mind was still gone and we were apprehensive of my mother's ability to care for this wasted but familiar body now inhabited by a demented, sometimes irascible stranger. For two weeks, he said little that made sense. Then one night my mother heard a loud bump and woke up to find him sitting on the floor. Neither of them can figure out how he got out of bed, but they don't ponder that mystery too much. More significant is that he began then, and has continued, to think and speak in a completely normal manner. His explanation is probably as good as any: "I fell flat on my butt and I've been fine ever since. I just gave myself a good chiropractic adjustment."

As I am writing this, eight months after his fall, he is still alive and interested in reading what I might have to say about him. He walks with a cane and he drives his new Lincoln. As a matter of fact, he had a wreck trying to gun it out of a parking lot in front of a lesser vehicle. He enjoys having people tell him what a fine car it is, and he likes for you to notice how good it rides out on the highway. He stays in touch with the doctors, but has worked out his own regimen, taking pills in the dosages that make him feel better rather than those prescribed. When his skin began to itch terribly, an apparent side effect of the medicine, he cured it by rubbing himself with Pine-O-Pine for a couple of weeks. And to make sure he doesn't lose his mind again, he goes to the chiropractor every so often.

It seems to be working. He looks bad and he knows it. He laughs about the time he saw an old man coming out of the post office and thought he'd rather die than be that feeble, then realized he was seeing his own reflection in the mirrored door and changed his mind, on the spot. When I first see him, I am always taken aback at how worn and small and bent he looks, but then he starts talking—about the church's new bus ministry or some article he has read or some story he thinks I might like to hear. I may be wrong, but I think he is making a conscious effort to pass on the oral tradition. In the last few months, he has told me wonderful stories I had never heard before, stories about driving a wagon to the gin when he was six or selling watermelons in Waco when he was twenty, stories filled with every detail that is pertinent and a good many that aren't. And when he talks a while, he seems to straighten up and fill out and his skin gets smooth and he is young and strong again, like a man about forty.

He spends most of his time nowadays working in his yard, an avocation to which he turned only in retirement. He putters and plants and pulls nut grass for several hours a day, sometimes sitting so long on a low stool that he can barely get up. He's had a fence put up and a sprinkler system installed, and the last time I saw him he had ordered some cuttings that were supposed to grow into giant shade trees in less than two years. When he opened the package and found three or four little pieces of root that looked like rotted grapevine, I think he suspected it had not been one of his wisest purchases. But, as I have indicated, he doesn't give up easily. He looked them over, twirled them between his fingers, then said, "Better go get me a ladder. I'd hate to get trapped up in one of these things in case I don't get out of the way fast enough."

I finally got up the nerve to tell him how much I appreciated the way he had maintained the integrity of his personality all the way to what I had thought was the end. He said, "I'm glad that's the way it was and I'm glad you noticed. Some people are full of fear. They are afraid to live and afraid to die. As long as you have that attitude, you are half whipped to start with. I heard people saying I was going to die, but I never really thought I would. I felt sort of like I was falling off a tall building and somebody was going to come along and put a mattress out for me. I wasn't ready, but if it was time, I wasn't going to panic. I guess I inherited that from Mama and Papa."

He explained how matter-of-factly both his parents had faced death and how he had admired that. I understood what he was saying. I told him, "It's hard to give your children a greater gift than that." He said something like "Wellsir," and, typical of the way he has always dealt with conversations that get too close to the core, started talking about a helicopter that was flying over the house. Later, as I prepared to leave—knowing then, knowing now, that any such leave-taking might be the last—he said, "I'm glad we had that little talk." I told him I wished I could do something to make him well. Since I couldn't, I would try to be the best man I knew how to be. He squeezed my hand. I think he understood what I was saying. I hope I did.

L. C. "Peggie" Martin died August 13, 1978, after a brief period of hospitalization. He was seventy-three years old. At his well-attended funeral, his grandsons served as pallbearers, his friends sang "Amazing Grace" and "I Come to the Garden Alone," and, in keeping with his precise instructions, no one read the Twenty-third Psalm. Five men who had known him well spoke with reasonable accuracy of his work, his character, and his personality. More than once, the burden of sorrow was lightened by laughter at the memory of an uncommon man. Adapting the words of the Apostle Paul to the audience and the occasion, the last speaker closed his remarks by saying, "Peggie Martin fought the good fight; he finished the course; he kept the faith; and he hoed his row to the end."

William C. Gruben

William C. Gruben (b. 1943) has family roots in Spur and lived in Bilene, Houston, and San Antonio before settling in Dallas. He has written comedy and gags for several Hollywood entertainers. This essay first appeared in The Atlantic *magazine for September 1985.*

THE LAST HISTORY EVER OF FATIGUE IN TEXAS

The reader is advised to pay close attention to this history, because no others on the subject will ever be written. While this is not the writer's decision, he agrees that it is all for the best. Nevertheless, it is a sad state of affairs when so modest a summary must be the final statement on fatigue in Texas.

Like oil, fatigue existed in Texas long before its commercial possibilities were appreciated. The Tejas Indians had seven different words for *tired,* and the Lipan Apaches had twenty-two, not counting words used only in secret ceremonies. These last will never be known. Some Indians had no actual words for *tired* but did have as many as forty-one different ways to look tired.

The early Spaniards brought to Texas a large vocabulary of words for *tired*. Later they invented new phrases to describe varieties of fatigue not experienced in the old country, such as "tired of mountain lions and bears," "tired of rattlesnakes," and "generally tired of Texas."

The Anglo-Saxon settlers also devised new phrases to describe the peculiarities of exhaustion in Texas. In addition, they worked out a series of hand gestures, signs, and finger movements that allowed them to depict fatigue at times when they were too tired to talk about it. A proficient settler could close his mouth, close his eyes, lie flat on his back, and still tell his friends that he was tired, through the judicious use of just one finger. Modern Texans have been unable to improve upon this mode of communication, although it was developed more than a hundred and fifty years ago.

The Anglo-Saxon settlers greatly increased fatigue in Texas, however, because they prevented Indians from getting a good night's sleep. The Indians responded in kind. Sometimes one of these groups would be up all night making loud noises, as revenge for what the other had done the night before. The Indians improvised percussion instruments from hollow logs and would work in shifts to keep the settlers awake. The Anglo-Saxon settlers organized all-night watches, during which they fired rifles into the air. The women would strike ladles and spoons against stewpots in order to do their part.

These mutual antagonisms sometimes erupted in violence that was later regretted by both sides. In one particularly sordid incident a group of settlers gave neighboring Indians several jars of peach preserves laced with a virus that caused sleeping sickness. The Indians retaliated by burning the bedrooms of several settlers' log cabins.

After Texas became an independent nation, a Treaty of Silence was signed with the Indians. According to this compact, everyone agreed to stop making loud noises and go home and go to bed.

On the great Texas cattle drives the invention of the swing shift resulted in many sleepless nights and led to the state's first fatigue-related commercial enterprise—the fatigue market. The market began informally. Someone who had got, say, twelve hours of sleep the night before would trade a few of his hours for a jackrabbit stew and some homemade liquor.

As the market developed, traveling "rest merchants" began to buy sleep in towns with an excess supply and sell it in towns with a shortage. An efficient rest merchant could put together enough sleep from differnet people to package an entire night's shut eye. He would then sell it to a cowboy who had been up all night directing a stampede. For a while everyone was happy. Someone with nothing better to do could make a good income just by sleeping late on Sunday mornings. Before long, however, unscrupulous businessmen began to smuggle in poor-quality sleep from foreign countries and even to steal sleep from drunks who had passed out. Cowboys who bought sleep from rest merchants started to complain of frequent headaches. When federal agents realized that some of the contaminated sleep was crossing state lines, they stepped in and shut down the market forever.

At the turn of the century the oil boom brought fatigue to Texas in epidemic proportions. After fourteen hours on a drilling rig many oil-field roughnecks suffered from insomnia. The price of a sleeping pill jumped to ten dollars, and a glass of water to wash it down cost three dollars. Some roughnecks would pool their money, break up a pill, and just get drowsy together. Others got religion. Denominations with long sermons on biblical minutiae were popular among roughnecks who otherwise would have had to count sheep.

These measures did not work for everyone, though, and not a few roughnecks took to drinking all night and shooting each other with horse pistols. In response one town council secretly legalized the eighty-minute hour and hired Pinkerton detectives to break into homes and adjust watches and clocks to comply with the law. The idea was that if roughnecks worked fourteen eighty-minute hours, they would have to go right back to work as soon as they got off, and couldn't cause any mischief. The ruse was discovered the next morning, however, when the sun came up at three A.M.

The roughnecks retaliated by hiring the same Pinkerton men to adjust the town's clocks to a forty-minute hour and a twenty-three-hour day. The Greenwich International Dateline and Hour Commission soon learned of the misdeeds, as it always does, and the guilty roughnecks were arrested.

While insomnia and insufficient sleep time were plaguing oilfield workers and cowboys, Texas farmers were suffering from too much sleep. After their first views of West Texas's unrelievedly flat terrain, newly arrived farmers would sometimes go to sleep for days, only to wake up and, seeing the same thing all over again, go right back to sleep. Realizing that cotton would never be king at this rate, the governor authorized emergency shipments of hot coffee in tank cars. Soft-drink manufacturers were ordered to include stimulants in their formulas. These efforts proved fruitless.

Soon, however, oil and cattle were discovered in West Texas, and roughnecks and cowboys moved in to drink and fight all night. Farmers woke up with a start, and the cotton crop was saved. The roughnecks were all given official pardons for their earlier shenanigans with the clocks.

An outbreak of bedding-related violence occurred in 1914 with the onset of the so-called Bandit Wars. Overtired Mexican revolutionaries often invaded Texas on foraging expeditions and were not shy about taking mattresses by force. To get a decent night's rest, many South Texas ranchers had to take their bedding to urban centers and sleep in town. Others placed mattresses on buckboards and hired teamsters to drive them around all night. This discouraged bandits from creeping up and yanking mattresses out from under unwary sleepers and then running away, but the expense was prohibitive for all except the well-to-do. In spite of these safeguards the bandit-revolutionaries were able to steal many mattresses and destroy even more. On some nights the border skies were black with the smoke of burning bedding. Many Texans were forced to sleep in hammocks. Finally U.S. National Guardsmen were called up and stationed along the border, and the ranchers went back to bed.

Today subtler influences have replaced armed conflict and bedding sabotage as major causes of exhaustion in Texas. The increasing complexity of city life has resulted in much confusion that leads to fatigue. Faced with a myriad of urban pressures, many Texans now get so mixed up that they forget to go to bed until eight or nine in the morning. Soon they lose their jobs and live in the streets as "fatigue derelicts," begging for "your old pajamas" or panhandling money for pillow rental. Others turn to crime. All too often an urban Texan will come out in the morning to his car, only to discover that it has been broken into and slept in.

The future of Texan fatigue is uncertain, but some researchers believe that much of the damage will be self-inflicted. It has long been known, even among the ancient Indian tribes of Texas, that fatigue is an altered state of consciousness. Through the improper use of history books Texas teenagers have found out about this. As a result some young people are wearing themselves out just to "get a buzz" and because it is "something different." Police officers are even beginning to see young children who refuse to go to bed or, worse, secretly stay awake under the covers, until they "get wasted." Because of this abuse of history a new state law forbids any mention of fatigue in print. The discussion you are reading is the last reference to fatigue that will ever be allowed in the state. Although it is sad that no one will ever again learn about the fatigue problems of the early settlers and Indians, it is a small price to pay to stop all this.

IV • JUST AS IT IS

Willie Morris

Willie Morris (b. 1934) crafted an indelible sketch of intellectual coming of age in the Texas of the 1950s in his autobiography North Toward Home, *especially in the sections dealing with his time as a student at the University of Texas and as editor of the* Texas Observer. *His gifts for making his experiences reflect a larger national sensibility led to his being named editor-in-chief of* Harper's *(1967–71) and to several books on Southern and Southwestern themes.*

NORTH TOWARD HOME

What strikes me most in reading books like Alfred Kazin's haunting poetic reminiscences of boyhood in an immigrant Jewish neighborhood in the East, is the vast gulf which separates that kind of growing up and the childhood and adolescence of those of us who came out of the towns of the American South and Southwest a generation later. With the Eastern Jewish intellectuals who play such a substantial part in American cultural life, perhaps in the late 1960s a dominant part, the struggle as they grew up in the 1930s was for one set of ideas over others, for a fierce acceptance or rejection of one man's theories or another man's poetry—and with all this a driving determination to master the language which had not been their parents' and to find a place in a culture not quite theirs. For other Eastern intellectuals and writers whom I later was to know, going to the Ivy League schools involved, if not a finishing, then a deepening of perceptions, or of learning, or of culture.

But for so many of us who converged on Austin, Texas, in the early 1950s, from places like Karnes City or Big Spring or Abilene or Rockdale or Yazoo City, the awakening we were to experience, or to have jolted into us, or to undergo by some more subtle chemistry, did not mean a mere finishing or deepening, and most emphatically did not imply the victory of one set of ideologies over another, one way of viewing literature or politics over another, but something more basic and simple. This was the acceptance of ideas themselves as something worth living by. It was a matter, at the age of eighteen or nineteen, not of discovering *certain* books, but the simple *presence* of books, not the nuances of idea and feeling, but idea and feeling on their own terms. It is this late coming to this kind of awareness that still gives the intellectuals from the small towns of our region a hungry, naïve quality, as opposed to the sharp-elbowed overintellectuality of some Easterners, as if those from down there who made it were lucky, or chosen, out of all the disastrous alternatives of their isolated lower- or middle-class upbringings, to enjoy and benefit from the fruits of simply being educated and liberal-minded.

What we brought to the University of Texas in the 1950s, to an enormous, only partially formed state university, was a great awe before the splendid quotations on its buildings and the walls of its libraries, along with an absolutely prodigious insensitivity as to what they implied beyond decoration. Minds awakened slowly, painfully, and with pretentious and damaging inner searches. Where an Alfred Kazin at the age of nineteen might become aroused in the subway by reading a review by John Chamberlain in *The New York Times* and rush to his office to complain, we at eighteen or nineteen were only barely beginning to learn that there *were* ideas, much less ideas to arouse one from one's self. If places like City College or Columbia galvanized the young New York intellectuals already drenched in literature and polemics, the University of Texas had, in its halting, unsure, and often frivolous way, to teach those of us with good minds and small-town high school diplomas that we were intelligent human beings, with minds and hearts of our own that we might learn to call our own, that there were some things, many things—ideas, values, choices of action—worth committing one's self to and fighting for, that a man in some instances might become morally committed to honoring every manifestation of individual conscience and courage. Yet the hardest task at the University of Texas, as many of us were to learn, was to separate all the extraneous and empty things that can drown a young person there, as all big universities can drown its young people, from the few simple things that are worth living a life by. Without wishing to sound histrionic, I believe I am thinking of something approaching the Western cultural tradition; yet if someone had suggested that to me that September night in 1952, as I stepped off the bus in Austin to be greeted by three fraternity men anxious to look me over, I would have thought him either a fool or a con man.

I emerged from that bus frightened and tired, after having come five hundred miles nonstop over the red hills of Louisiana and the pine forests of East Texas. The three men who met me—appalled, I was told later, by my green trousers and the National Honor Society medal on my gold-plated watch chain—were the kind that I briefly liked and admired, for their facility at small talk, their clothes, their manner, but whom I soon grew to deplore and finally to be bored by. They were the kind who made fraternities tick, the favorites of the Dean of Men at the time, respectable B or C-plus students, tolerable athletes, good with the Thetas or the Pi Phis; but one would find later, lurking there inside of them despite—or maybe because of—their good fun and jollity, the ideals of the insurance salesman and an aggressive distrust of anything approaching thought. One of them later told me, with the seriousness of an early disciple, that my table manners had become a source of acute embarrassment to all of them. That night they drove me around the campus, and they were impressed that I knew from my map-reading where the University library was, for two of them were not sure. . . .

The student newspaper, *The Daily Texan,* turned out to be one of the two or three best college dailies in America, with an old and honorable tradition. It was housed in a brand-new building in the middle of the campus, and its physical setup was impressive; there were individual offices for the important editors, a "city room" with a big copy desk and two wire-service tickers, and a chute to drop the copy down to a modern composing room below. I felt good just walking into those offices, for it was obvious they were designed for professionals.

In its finest moments, and they had been often, *The Daily Texan* had defended the spirit of a free university even when the University of Texas itself was unable or unwilling to do so, and in these periods it had reached an eloquence and displayed a courage that would have challenged the mature profession. The tolerant seniors who ran it were bemused enough to give me a weekly column in my first semester, to report on the hundred or more college papers I was assigned to read every week. Here I began to read about strange ideas like integration, and issues of academic freedom, and observations that Dwight D. Eisenhower might be something of a bore. This was heady stuff indeed. On some nights I would stay up until three or four in the morning in my dormitory room, with the newspapers scattered on the tables and floors, trying to understand the incomprehensible goings-on in Berkeley or Ann Arbor or Colorado Springs or Chapel Hill. I gradually began to see the differences in all these papers; the ones from Harvard or Yale and a few big state universities were almost daringly outspoken, and kept talking about "conformity" and "self-satisfaction" in a way that both mystified and aroused me, but the great majority which poured in from all over America spoke a tongueless idiom, imploring students to turn over a new leaf at the start of each semester, give blood to a blood drive, collect wood for a bonfire, or use their leisure time more wisely. Something was out of order here, but I did not know quite what or why. I also wrote sports, covering the minor stories that would be given to me, and came under the blunt criticism of hard-headed types who may have been turning out the best sentences on the campus in those days. Once I wrote two thousand words on a baseball game; the six veteran sports writers, gleeful, pejorative, and smelling of Lone Star beer, pointed out for me that the only thing I had neglected to provide was the score.

It is my painful duty to describe myself one night, carrying two dozen signs saying, BE SURE TO VOTE NEXT TUESDAY IN THE STUDENT ELECTIONS, trying to hammer them into the frozen ground at strategic points on the campus, and finally, secretly and in despair, throwing the whole batch of them into a sewer. I returned to my dormitory one afternoon from a meeting of the student government committee on public relations. One of the catchers on the baseball team, who had been drunk since just after breakfast, asked me where I had been, and I made the mistake of telling him. He was enraged, went into a frenzy, and tried to throw me out of the fourth-floor window. Some of the poker players, not wishing tragedy or scandal to befall the dormitory, came to my assistance, and the fight for better public relations at the University of Texas was allowed to survive.

Once I was invited to the apartment of a young graduate student and his wife. The walls of their apartment were lined with books, more books than I had ever seen before in a private dwelling—books everywhere and on everything. I was astonished; I tried to talk with those people, but I was unaccountably shy, and I kept looking at their books out of the corner of my eye, and wondering if I should *say* something about them, or ask perhaps if they were for sale or if they formed some kind of special exhibit. It is a rare experience for certain young people to see great quantities of books in a private habitat for the first time, and to hear ideas talked about seriously in the off-hours. Good God, they were doing it for pleasure, or so it seemed. The wife, who was also a graduate student, asked me what I wanted to do with myself when I graduated from college. "I want to be a writer," I said, but not even thinking about it until the words were out; my reply surprised me most of all, but it was much more appropriate in those surroundings to have said that instead of "sports announcer," which probably constituted my first choice. "What do you want to write about?" she persisted. "Just

. . . things," I said, turning red. That night, stirred by the conversation and by all the books I had seen, I went to the library, promising myself to read every important book that had ever been written. I was at a loss, because I did not have the faintest notion where to start. I picked out the most imposing volumes I could find—Lord Bryce on the American Commonwealth, which put me to sleep for ten nights in a row. But once this fire is lit, to consume and to know, it can burn on and on. I kept going back to the library, taking out tall stacks of books and reading them in a great undigested fury: Hemingway, Faulkner, Wolfe, Dreiser, anything in the American literature and American history shelves that looked promising. I started buying Modern Library books with the money I made writing for the newspaper, and I pledged to myself, as Marilyn Monroe had, that I would read them all, and in alphabetical order.

I believe now that the University of Texas was somehow beginning to give me an interest and a curiosity in something outside my own parochial ego. It was beginning to suggest the power not merely of language, but the whole unfamiliar world of experience and evocation which language served. That world was new, and the recognition of its existence was slow, uncertain, and immature. Books and literature, I was beginning to see, were not for getting a grade, not for the utilitarian purpose of being considered a nice and versatile boy, not just for casual pleasure, but subversive as Socrates and expressions of man's soul. It took me years to understand that words are often as important as experience, because words make experience last, but here, in the spring of my freshman year, there were men who were teaching me these things, perhaps with very little hope that anyone in their classrooms remotely cared, and I think perhaps I may have been listening. Freshman English was the first step; it was often the first and last time that many young people, headed in a state like Texas for insurance or business or the Junior League, might have had for a kind of small internal salvation.

For freshman English there was Frank Lyell, a fellow Mississippian, and it was his high values, giving my outrageous themes D's and C's when I had expected A's as something of a birthright, which first suggested that the editorial texture I had given the Yazoo High *Flashlight* would hardly serve in a world where English was master tongue. This was not merely a matter of syntax, discipline, and unheard-of-words. There came an awareness that loose, insensitive, and poorly formed language belie a loose, insensitive, and poorly formed mind. Lyell assigned a two-thousand-word autobiography, which I began with a description of the fading lonely sunlight outside Brackenridge Hall, went back through seventeen years of baseball, religion, and small-town hopes, and ended up in a volley of rhetoric in the same place six hours later. One sentence read: "My dog Skip and I wandered the woods and swamplands of our Mississippi home shooting rabbits and squirrels." To which the professor appended the comment: "Who was the better shot, you or the dog?" I was enraged. I can remember one morning the teacher reading a passage from a novel and asking "Isn't that marvelous?" The sorority girls sat there taking down everything he said, while in the back of the room I could see three or four ranch boys, who always sat there in a self-contained group, nudging each other and snickering over the teacher's unusual recommendations.

Yet there *was* loneliness in those fading Sunday afternoons, and madness in the meaningless activities that served to make one versatile and well rounded. The editors of the campus humor magazine, a cynical and knowing lot, must have recognized this. In May one of them told me to be sure and read the next issue; there was to be an article on me. It turned out to be a burlesque of a young campus character named Willie X, who had joined everything and wanted to know everything. Late one night he was walking down the University "Drag" reading a pamphlet, and as he crossed Twenty-fourth Street something fortunate occurred for the University of Texas. He was run over by a two-ton truck.

That whole first year was also one peregrination after another between Texas and Mississippi and Mississippi and Texas. At holidays there was the long bus ride through the lonely little Texas towns—Round Rock and Carthage, Jacksonville and Tyler and Kilgore, through the pine forests in the moonlight into Shreveport—the layover in the station there for another bus, then on through Ruston and Monroe to the big bridge and Vicksburg. The two places, Mississippi and Texas, were already beginning gradually to exist in separate realities for me, one meaning one thing, one another, and I was as ambivalent as my sense of place. Yet by the end of that first year I believe I already had had an unusual glimpse of this state university in the beginnings of the Eisenhower age: its ambiguity, its complexity, its promise.

In the early 1950s the University of Texas was trying desperately to come up in the world. The vast holdings the state had given it in the late nineteenth century, when it was mainly a collection of wooden shacks on a hill, had turned out to be rich in oil; its reputation had suffered from the egregious Texas myth. The school had never enjoyed the steady blessing of influential public support which had made the four or five great American state universities preeminent. It had had to struggle hard against the aggressive philistinism of its old agrarian culture, and time and again it had been hurt badly by ruddy nabobs and crossroads potentates who were suspicious of its very existence. As early as 1917, when Governor "Pa" Ferguson warned the people of the state that it was a nesting place for sinners and profligates, the university was having political troubles. The state legislature, quartered those few blocks down the street, had investigated the campus on several occasions, and once, when the university bought a $20,000 collection of Byron, Shelley, Tennyson, Browning, and Lamb, the lower house had protested that all these writers were "obscene or atheistic."

Some kind of turning point for the place occurred in the 1940s, when it suffered a series of blows that might have killed most struggling colleges. The firing of President Homer Rainey was something of a legend in American higher education. Rainey became president in 1939, and was confronted by a board of regents increasingly dominated by appointees of Governor "Pappy" O'Daniel, the flour salesman and radio entertainer who was himself a tool of some of the most uncivilized wealth known to man. The clash between O'Daniel's men and Rainey had been direct and brutal; professors were fired, books blacklisted, and a state which had contributed Martin Dies to national politics was clearly not ready to support a university with pretensions toward independence. When Rainey was fired, the American Association of University Professors after a three-year investigation censured the regents' "systematic, persistent, and continuous attempts by a politically dominant group to impose its social and educational views on the University." The place was deeply damaged, and after that the only thing to do was forget.

The 1950s were a quiescent time at the university, just as they were not a very poetic time in America. There were no student protests, no sit-ins and stand-ins such as were to occur in the more activist sixties. There was as much, probably more to dissent from then, but I am convinced that the softening of disaffection on most campuses was an accurate reflection of the somnolence of our national life. The fire seemed to have gone out of many of the more rebellious old-timers, as if courage had been the victim of its own strength. The Rainey episode, which had split the campus in two, when five thousand students could march to the state capitol to dispute the latest barbarisms, carrying a black-draped coffin labeled "academic freedom," was still sensitive in many minds—and in none more so than the people who called the shots. The AAUP blacklist, if one mentioned it in the environs of the main building, provoked mild attacks of administrative epilepsy, and there were enough administrators over there to carry an epidemic a long way.

Texas itself, its chronic xenophobias fed by the passions of the McCarthy period, was not an entirely pleasant place in those years. There was a venom in its politics and a smugness in its attitude to outsiders and to itself. Democratic Party conservatism in the state was infinitely less sophisticated, cruder and more corrupting than its counterpart would be in the 1960s. Businessmen, Texas-style—promoters, a lot of Snopeses—were firmly in power in the statehouse, just as they controlled the university. In my senior year every member of the board of regents was an appointee of Governor Allan Shivers, a strong follower of McCarthy. In the prevailing ethic, education was where it belonged: in the hands of oil and gas men, corporation lawyers, cattle ranchers, and experienced old wildcatters. Texas reformers in that day were much like the old American mugwumps of the last century, and their antagonists resembled the industrialists of the 1880s, who were similarly held to be—in Richard Hofstadter's words—"uneducated and uncultivated, irresponsible, rootless and corrupt, devoid of refinement or of any sense of noblesse." With rare exceptions among these people in Texas in the 1950s, there was not even yet the argument that higher education was good for attracting industry. The dominant attitude was that higher education attracted other, less desirable, elements and was to be handled warily, and, when the occasion demanded it, with all the old and tested dogmatisms. Varsity football stirred up the only undiluted enthusiasm among them. There was one student protest meeting in these years over McCarthy, where most of the speakers prefaced their remarks by tracing their loyal ancestry back to Sam Houston, Davy Crockett, or the Alamo, and if possible to Queen Elizabeth and King Alfred.

In this context it was not difficult to see the problems that Logan Wilson, the president of the University, was up against. He was a highly capable if somewhat frosty administrator who added new dimensions to aloofness. If the mood were on him he would have thought nothing of condescending to the Virgin Mary during silent meditations. His aim was to heal the wounds of the calamitous Rainey era with analgesic balm and periodic injections of Novocain, and at the same time, in these years of spiritual drought, to build a better financial base for the University of Texas while praying for rain. The challenge, politically and for the school's position in a conservative state, was to keep the lid on. For this reason Wilson's tenure may have been something of a bridge from more disastrous years to the 1960s, when the University of Texas would come alive again. But then it was a stolid and unimaginative time, and few were those to take a dare.

As for me, I slowly began to see many of these things, but mainly through a prism. It was only later that I directly faced these aspects of Texas society and found them tawdry and suffocating. What I mainly noticed then were the boorish remarks of regents, who could make the most reflective and charitable monk in the most isolated cloister want to bite back, the mindless self-satisfactions of most of the students, and, politically, the general hardening of the arteries after the Supreme Court decision of 1954. It was also during this time, as a foretaste of later years, that a second-team halfback named Duke Washington broke away on a touchdown for Washington State against Texas. A large part of the Texas student section, myself included, stood up to applaud the first Negro ever to play in Texas Memorial Stadium.

I suppose it was the students, and the life they and their adult counselors had devised for themselves, that I was noticing most, as always. Led by the organized structure of the fraternities and sororities, the great hotbed of philistinism in the 1950s, this campus, as others surely did, reached unprecedented heights of carefully planned frivolity—parades with homemade floats, sing-songs, carnivals—anything, in fact, to do something meaningless with all that energy. It was the era of the beauty queens, bless their souls and bodies, and they decorated the front pages of *The Daily Texan* and inspired their own mystique, like Hollywood starlets tied down unfairly by classes and lectures. They were Edna and Mary Lou and Lee, Sara Sue and Jimmy and Debbie, and in Brackenridge Dormitory their relative virtues would be discussed philosophically, though always graphically. It was also the period of "retreats," when organizations, accompanied by deans, sub-deans, assistant deans, deans emeritus, and various other spiritual, marital, social, medical, and inspirational advisors, would isolate themselves at some dude ranch out in the hills. Here they would sit around in circles talking into the weary night about the virtues of greater campus "service" and all the nuances of human sincerity. My experience with one of them, with the deans leading the prayers at the beginning and end, brought back to me the religious youth meetings at the country churches in Yazoo County, except that these in Texas were much blander, devoid of exuberance, and somehow lacking *possibility*. If a new idea was ever unloosed by these strange semi-evangelical institutions it has yet to be reported, but may be hemmed in by the statute of limitations.

There was a core of serious, rather independent souls gathered around an institution called the Christian Faith and Life Community, one of those robust experiments in community intellectual living that was in such stark contrast to the comfortable campus life of the 1950s. Despite the incomprehensible language they spoke, existential with a thin overlay of Calvin, which discouraged outsiders without training in structural linguistics or those who could not afford an interpreter, they kept their directions inside (sometimes, perhaps, *too* south-southwest of the inner light). The Y was a haven for other serious students, and as a forerunner to the flowering of the ecumenical movement encouraged controversial seminars and lectures on questions that usually mattered. These groups, and they were good people, were the repositories of whatever liberalism existed on a conscious level at the University of Texas at the time.

From all these things I had, by my junior year, become strangely removed, both intellectually and emotionally. I had ceased to be the torrid activist I had been before, and I was chiefly interested in the panorama. I knew so many different people—lonely twenty-year-old-failures who drank coffee and ate cheesecake at one A.M. in the Snak Shak, suave leaders of clubs and committees, janitors, sorority girls, campus cops, lady booksalesmen, ranch boys from West Texas, grubby graduate students, and an occasional beauty queen—one in particular, though she was a Phi Beta Kappa. They are now lawyers, politicians, manufacturers of toilet seats and garbage-can lids, Junior Leaguers, schoolteachers, members of the John Birch Society, doubles in Hollywood westerns, and wives of New York editors.

The beauty queen with the Phi Beta Kappa key was the one who would endure. Her name was Celia. She had come as an honor student from the most proper high school in Houston, a frenetically social institution on the fringes of that rich man's paradise called River Oaks, yet her own social instincts were decidedly on the wane. She lived in a palatial sorority house, but her elders berated her for carrying laundry out the front door, and she drank wine on the sly in her room and read Sartre and Tillich and Fromm and books on Renaissance art. She went to every "retreat" and spiritual seminar she could get her hands on, but finally they lost their steam for her; unlike many of the students of that day she spoke plain English, and took her existentialism with a healthy and detached curiosity. She began to shun all the beauty-queen elections with an honest, though complicated, disdain, but they still kept *electing* her. She was so beautiful, in the wholesome American way, that those elections were foregone conclusions. What could she do? she asked. She couldn't *resign*. With this contorted attitude she ended up being elected the official Sweetheart of the University of Texas, and five thousand people sang "The Eyes of Texas" to her in the gymnasium, although Sartre, Tillich, and Fromm were not present. We would walk around the campus talking about Hemingway in the sunshine, or the Romantic poets, and we gave each other books with florid personal inscriptions from the Transcendentalists. We parked in borrowed cars out by one of Lyndon Johnson's lakes, or in front of the sorority house where couples loved and petted each night on public exhibit. When I turned twenty, one cold November night, we drank a quart of California wine, and for a birthday present she gave me a book of Victorian poetry, and with an unsteady hand and a big laugh she wrote on the flyleaf, "Grow old along with me, the best is yet to be, the last of life, for which the first was made." The laugh was to be on her.

Al Reinert

Al Reinert's articles on Texas sports and popular culture appear in many national and regional publications. He is a contributing editor to Texas Monthly *magazine, with numerous investigative and feature articles in national publications.*

THE RITES OF FALL

"I started playing football as a kid in Hernando, Mississippi. I remember talking to the coach standing there on the street in front of the bank one day. Told him I was interested in coming out and playing football. He said, 'We'll be glad to have you.' That was his very words, and it was very impressive to me then as a young man. 'We'll be glad to have you.'

"Now I had played baseball and I wasn't too enthused about that. I had played in the band, too. But I had some cousins who played football, and I thought it must be the greatest thing in the world to get out there and be a football player. There was something different and appealing about it that was very strong. Seeing people out there hitting and running over each other, and going after each other and *yet*, nobody getting mad or losing friendships over it.

"Now I'm forty-three years old and I been in the business of coaching and teaching for nineteen years. But I can't put my heart into teaching, only coaching. Right here, in football, I can say, 'Now, son, this is *life*. We're gonna go out there today and this is your assignment. And if you don't survive it today you're gonna get fired and lose your position. But if you do survive it, you're a starter. You're on your way.' That kid comes out here at two-thirty after classes. He's tired, drowsy. I feel like if I can teach him to reach down and give me some real go-get-um then he's got a chance. He's learned something he can use all his life. I teach him to keep challenging. If some kid knocks him on his butt, he can't *accept* it. He's got to learn to get up and go at him again. And again. That's football and that's life. I got kids come out and can't cut it. We all have 'em. And I can tell you from experience what'll happen to 'em. They'll be hauling pulpwood like their daddy. Or be working all their life as a laborer. They gonna be satisfied to go right back to doing that. But I have other kids I can teach to challenge, to keep coming back, and they are the kids that're gonna go somewhere.

"I remember when I was playing high school football, and I was running in the backfield, my coach called me in one day and said, I was gonna have to be doin' a little bit better if I wanted to keep my first-string position. Well, that bothered me, of course, because I was being told I needed to improve. But he did it in a way that I kept my pride and went on to improve. In the past I'd been told, 'You can't do that. Get over here. Let a man do that.' You know, my daddy dealing with me as a kid. But the coach told me the situation man to man.

"Like when he said, *'We'll* be glad to have ya. *We'll* be glad to have ya. We start to work out August first. Come on up there and get your stuff.' And right then it was just like a fella telling me, 'Well, pardner, you can be part of our organization.' And I don't know of any coach that don't do that with a kid and I think it's the greatest thing in the world.

"My dad, when I told him I was going to Hernando to play football, he said, 'You get killed playing that damn game, and I ain't coming to your funeral.' And I'm telling you, my dad never saw me play a game in my life. My mother did. But he thought it was crazy. I could be earning money and I was risking my neck getting broke. A lotta pressure gets put on kids that way, and it's not fair. A kid should be able to make his decision to play or not to play. To belong. It makes a kid feel special. He belongs to a good program with a good purpose in life.

"Nowadays I go to a football game and you know what I think about? Gladiators. I don't see a football game at all. I picture myself out there in a toga, and everybody's shouting 'Kill the bum! Kill him!' Right here tonight, you watch what happens. These fans go crazy. And yet, it's the one time in life for that little hometown kid that he'll ever be known. He'll strut out there with that jersey and helmet on like a damn racehorse coming to run. The band's striking up and he's ready to go. God, it's the greatest thing in the world. He couldn't fight his way outta a wet popcorn bag, but I guarandamtee you right then he can whip anybody. His momma is up in the stands clapping and yelling for her boy, and soon as he gets a good lick he comes alimping off showing his battle scars.

"You ask that kid why he likes the game and he says, 'I don't know, just like it.' But it's so clear, so plain to see. We all want to be out there facing the challenge for our town, for our people. We'll never get that chance again. And if we get whipped five times in a row, we learn that you don't necessarily get whipped six. We learn to face the challenges one at a time. I mean that kid might get hit and rolled up like a nickel window shade. But he learns that if he keeps getting up he'll be admired, he'll be loved, he'll be a man, by god. It's something he may not get at home, and for sure not in the classroom."

—Jim Norman, head coach, Big Sandy School

"I grew up in a small town in East Texas, a 2A town where we usually had a real good football team. From the time I can remember my dad was the football coach. He was baseball and basketball and track coach, too, but that was sort of on the side. He was the football coach mainly. I learned to play when I was only about six or seven years old, going with Dad to the team practices. Even for my age I was very small, but I was quick and fast, and I loved competing with guys much bigger than me. I loved the physical contact, too. There was something about football—the *hitting*, and being hit—that appealed to me. I also developed very good coordination when I was very young. I guess it was mostly because Dad paid me in the summers and after school to go into the gym and shoot basketball, or hit baseballs, or throw a football. He said it would be worth it in the long run—to him and to me—for him to pay me to do that, rather than me being paid by somebody else to work for them at some meaningless job.

"By the time I was ten, I could outrun a lot of the guys on the varsity football team, which they didn't like very much because if I outran them in the wind sprints, then Dad made them do laps. I was called 'the Rabbit' back then because I was so little and so fast. But by the time I was a freshman in high school I thought I was ready to be the starting varsity quarterback. But there was a senior who had played two years and he started the first two games of the season, which we won because we had a very good team that year. The third game of the year we were playing the district champions and we were behind three to nothing in the last quarter. We hadn't been able to move the ball at all. Time was running out, and the fans—and I mean the whole town was there—were getting fed up with our team. I wanted in the game so bad I was about to go nuts, but I knew Dad wouldn't put me in until *he* thought the time was right. With about two minutes left in the game, we got the ball on our own ten-yard line, just about where we'd had it all night. Dad looked around and said, 'Where's that damn Rabbit? Get in there. This is it. Run that option right. And don't look back.'

"I remember that I wasn't a bit nervous, like I thought I'd be. I took the option right and I didn't look back. All I remember is running down that sideline as fast as I could go and hearing a voice right behind me. It was yelling, seemed like right in my ear, 'Run, you little son of a bitch, RUN!' I tried to outrun him, but he stayed with me, seemed like one step behind me, yelling 'RUN, you little son of a bitch, RUN!' When I crossed the goal line for a touchdown the crowd was going crazy. Then I saw Dad, red in the face, huffing and puffing. He had chased me the last sixty yards down the sideline, right behind me, yelling in my ear.

"That was the greatest moment in my life, I guess. At least I remember it best. The whole town standing on its feet, cheering for me, and our team carried me off the field. We missed the extra point, but we won the game, and I was the starting quarterback from then on.

"I've always had a lot of confidence in myself, especially since that first varsity play. That's the biggest difference maybe between me and some other guys. When the chips are down, when it's third and long, *I* want the ball. I'll give it to someone else, of course, if it seems like the best thing to do. But I'm hoping it's me that gets it, because I always believe I can make the first down. Always. And I usually do."

—Les Koenig, Jr., former quarterback,
Hamshire-Fannett High School and Memorial
High School, Houston

Don Meredith ─────────────────────

*Don Meredith is a native of Mount Vernon, Texas, and was an
all-American quarterback for Southern Methodist University in
Dallas, then starred for the Dallas Cowboys 1962–68 before his
career as a commentator for "ABC Monday Night Football."*

DON MEREDITH REMEMBERS

There is something special about high school football in Texas, something that makes it different from high school football in other states,
and I think it's because Texas itself is so different. This was something
I sort of felt even when I was playing in high school, but I didn't
understand it then. I'm not sure I understand it now. After I went to
college and then into professional football, though, and traveled around
the country and visited with people from other states, I began to realize
what a significant part high school football plays in Texas: it does sym-
bolize something the state represents.

I guess it's probably several things, but number one is that it's a
physical concept, a physical confrontation of one against another. I
think football has that attraction for everyone to some extent, but particularly for Texans. Whether it's true or not, the image of Texas and
the setting of Texas is that it was done by rugged individuals who would
physically stand their ground, who would *physically* settle an area.
Football, one town against another, became a great outlet for Texans,
a way of saying this is what makes us best. But of course you don't realize
any of this when you're growing up in Texas, I know I certainly didn't.
Football was just part of the school structure you grew up with: you just
sort of accepted it. You just went out and played.

Mt. Vernon was just a little Northeast Texas town, basically a farming community of about fifteen hundred people. There were maybe two hundred kids in the high school, and some of them came a pretty good ways to get there. We lived a block from the school, a block from church. My dad owned a dry goods store that sold a combination of work clothes, Wolverine work shoes, Big Smith overalls, yellow dent corn, with a part in the back where he sold seeds. He always had those posters up back there that gave the football team schedule, and he'd write in the scores after every game. Dad was on the school board. And I have a brother, Billy Jack, who's five and a half years older than me, and he had always played ball.

We played against towns like Sulphur Springs, Mt. Pleasant, Pittsburg, Gilmer, Atlanta, and all these towns are bigger than Mt. Vernon. It was the smallest town in the 2A district but we had always had a reputation for having good athletic teams. Back in 1948 they won state in football *and* basketball, went undefeated in both sports, and it was mostly the same kids playing on both teams. So that kind of tradition was there when I was growing up; you were just expected to play ball. It wasn't really a pressure thing—it had already gone past pressure.

I started playing football when I was in the second grade. I was on the eighth-grade team and the only kid below the fifth grade, I believe, who played that year. I was seven years old. That didn't seem unusual to me or anybody else; it was just a natural flow of consequences from the games and things I had always done. I played basketball, too, twelve months a year; to me it was just as much fun as football. The sense of play was what I really loved. I believe that the guys who play football well for a long time, who go on to be successful in professional football, have somehow maintained that sense of play in their minds or they wouldn't have been able to do it. If your first experiences in football are really fun for you, then hopefully you can carry that over for the rest of your football career—however long it turns out to be—and hopefully into the rest of your life as well.

I can honestly say that football was always fun for me; I really did enjoy it. Partly it was that physical thing, of course, learning to do something well with your body, learning *about* your body. This is especially true for young kids. There's a kind of sensuous pleasure in being able to do something that is physically coordinated, that is totally in synch, when the flow of your body becomes a movement. That part is really so special, I think it's something that kids can feel instinctively.

Then as I got older and started playing high school ball I bumped into new emotional things, too, feelings I'd never run into before and don't know if I'd have found some other way or not. Like when you're fourteen or fifteen years old and you start to eat on Friday—you're going to play that night—and by this time you realize it's a game and it's very competitive and your stomach starts turning around, maybe even a little diarrhea slips in. And you get up to go to the bathroom and you pee so many times you can't believe it. All these things are building up and because they're new sensations they're kind of exciting, they're kind of a high. Those were early thrills for me.

Then you realize that it's become much more than that, it's bigger than that, it becomes a communal thing. In a small town everybody sort of gets involved some way or another, and you see all these supporters— the townsfolk—and whether you know them well or not you still know who they are. I think it's the first time that a young kid feels all the different responsibilities of belonging to a group, being a real member of his community. That's when it becomes a rather heavy trip. You say to yourself, 'uh-oh,' and you get that identification everybody kind of strives for by pleasing other people. Unfortunately this can carry over for a long time and you spend your whole life trying to please somebody else.

The most important thing about playing in high school is that you learn to deal with all these new emotions and sensations. Like getting out in front of all those people, for instance. I saw a survey a while ago that listed the various things that most people are afraid of. Snakes were number two. The number one thing that most people feared was getting up in front of a group of other people. Through athletics you're more or less pushed out there and it helps to eliminate some of that fear, you realize it doesn't hurt. It's a way of learning something about yourself, learning to be proud of yourself.

I remember we had a graduating class of thirty-five kids my senior year (class of '56), and about seventeen of us were boys. Out of that seventeen I'd guess maybe twelve played football, and the other five were exempt for obvious reasons: just a little bit too small, glasses too thick, or lived too far out of town. If you were able to play football, you did, it was as simple as that. I was the tallest kid in the school, six-three my senior year, so I played center on the basketball team. In football I was quarterback on offense and middle linebacker on defense.

The name of our team was the Mt. Vernon Purple & White Tigers. I don't know why we were called that, I've never heard of a purple-and-white tiger. The one moment I remember best was during my junior year. We were playing against Sulphur Springs and they were the big powerhouse that year. It was our homecoming game, I think, and I wanted to play really well because it was the first game that my brother had come back to see me play in. He was the quarterback for Texas Christian University, and I sure did want to look good for him.

And I sure had the chance. Sulphur Springs ran a single wing and was real strong on the ground, so we put in a new defense that was basically a ten-man line with me playing linebacker and the whole secondary, since they didn't throw very much. It was a pretty weird defense. Then on offense we ran kind of a spread with me at quarterback. So it was a deal where I had the chance to either really do something wonderful or else get ripped apart. I guess I ran with the ball almost every play on offense and made almost every tackle on defense.

I think it was probably the best game, physically, I ever played. I was so tired—by the last quarter I was just exhausted. Then on one play I got tackled and was hit in the groin somehow, and it made me sick to my stomach. I knew I was going to throw up. We used an inverted huddle where ten guys line up while the quarterback stands in front calling the plays, and I remember wondering why the other ten guys wouldn't come into the huddle. I was throwing up and yet at the same time I couldn't figure out why the rest of my team didn't gather around me. So I was just standing there in the middle of the field all by myself, throwing up.

It was a kind of a combination of an embarrassing moment and yet at the same time it was—I don't know how to explain it. It was almost like I knew at that moment that I'd given everything I had to give, total commitment. Not holding back anything. Like being truly clean and truly free as far as maximum effort. It's an emotional feeling, an emotional high that is basically unparalleled. Once you've had that experience I believe it's something you keep looking for the rest of your life in whatever you do.

You can have it in other things besides athletics, of course, that feeling of, you know, that's *it*, you've got my best shot. This is my best lick. It's that feeling that gives you self-respect—in the long run it's much more important than whether you win or lose or whatever. Our game with Sulphur Springs was maybe the game I'm proudest of in my whole career. If you can walk away from something like that and still hold your head up, it's a nice feeling. Maybe the best feeling there is. Well, the second best feeling there is.

Dan Rather

Dan Rather (b. 1931) seems to follow in a Texas-rooted CBS connection that includes not only John Henry Faulk and Hughes Rudd, but Walter Cronkite, Bob Schieffer, and Linda Ellerbee, among others. In his 1977 autobiography The Camera Never Blinks: Adventures of a TV Journalist *(with Mickey Herskowitz), Rather recounts the start of his reporting career under the guidance of a salty veteran teacher at Sam Houston State Teachers College.*

A LITTLE LEARNING

The dream begins, most of the time, with a teacher who believes in you, who tugs and pushes and leads you on to the next plateau, sometimes poking you with a sharp stick called truth.

Mine was named Hugh Cunningham and he taught journalism in 1950 at Sam Houston State Teachers College. With an enrollment sometimes as low as seven hundred and no pretensions, Sam Houston blended quietly into the red clay and piney woods of East Texas. Traces of the Old South still existed in that part of the state, where cotton, though never king, was about all anyone had. Cotton, lumber, and a few scraggly cattle.

With a population of five thousand, Huntsville had grown up around the school, a lean, scenic town with a colorful history. General Sam Houston had built a cabin there and came back to it to die. So the school was named after the liberator of Texas, the hero of San Jacinto and the first elected president of the Lone Star Republic.

For whatever interest it may hold for historians, until the 1920s the official name of the college was the Sam Houston Institute of Teaching. When freshmen started wearing sweatshirts with the school's initials the state legislature hastily passed an act and renamed it.

How Hugh Cunningham happened to wind up there, with a master's degree from the Missouri School of Journalism, young, with a mind that could light up a room, I do not know. But it was a break for me. Otherwise I would not have lasted in college longer than three weeks and most likely would not have gone on to whatever career I have had. That may be putting too much on one man's conscience, but I owe a debt to Hugh Cunningham.

Actually, my ticket to college was to have been football. Based on

A Little Learning | 321

my size (I weighed 150), and my talent, which was marginal, there was no reason, other than my own ignorance, for me to think that the gridiron would become my salvation. But I had started at end in my senior year at Reagan High School in Houston and I had shown I could catch a pass. There was nothing to indicate I was a gifted athlete, nothing to feed the hope that it would pay my way through college, except that it was the only hope I had.

So near the end of my last high school year I dropped by the gymnasium to see the coach, a man named Lamar Camp. Football coaches tend to be a major influence on a young man's life. Coach Camp had kept me in school when I wanted to drop out and get a job, the choice people in my neighborhood often faced around the tenth grade.

"I want to start looking for a college," I told him.

"That's fine," he said. Coach Camp was a taciturn man.

"It occurs to me that it might help if I had a letter from you," I replied.

He stared at me for several moments. I thought he hadn't understood what I meant. Finally he just said, "Look, you're not going to play college football. You're not big enough. You're not fast enough. You're not good enough."

There was no misunderstanding what *he* meant and I was absolutely crushed by it. I went home, in a daze, to decide if college was so important after all. Neither of my parents had finished high school. My father, Irvin Rather—known to his friends as Rags—had worked as a pipeliner for twenty years, which meant that he dug ditches for a fair amount of his lifetime. He met my mother, Byrl, at the Travelers' Hotel in Victoria, where she worked as a waitress, fresh off the farm, sending money back home every week to help her family through the Depression.

Mother later passed a high school equivalency test and took a few night classes at a junior college. But, basically, they were not people who understood what a college education represented, other than as something a lucky few people strived for, a goal. Their immediate concern was to feed and clothe three kids. I was the oldest, born on the last day of October 1931, at Wharton. Then came Don and Patricia, six and eight years younger.

I don't intend for this to sound like another version of Up from Poor. We were not poverty-stricken, but money was always tight. My father felt that if I finished high school that would be achievement enough, as indeed in the 1940s it was. As far back as our heirloom Bibles recorded, no one on either side of our family had ever attended college.

Yet, in a curious way, I developed my passion to become a reporter through my father. That was all I could ever remember wanting to do, to work for a newspaper. I never thought of broadcasting as a career until I was nearly out of college. But radio did intrigue me. As a boy in Houston I listened to the broadcasts of the roller derby at the City Coliseum. Sometimes as I walked to school I would reconstruct in my mind my own roller derby play-by-play. I was, vicariously, the greatest roller derby describer who ever lived.

At home I was surrounded by newspapers. My father was an impulse subscriber, a voracious reader, and a man of sudden angers who would leap from his chair and cancel whichever paper had offended him. We went through every newspaper in town, the *Post*, the *Chronicle*, and the *Press*, which was part of the Scripps-Howard chain and known locally for its muckraking policies. There was a constant harangue about newspapers in our house. My father would read something in the *Press* that riled him and he would shout, "Mother, cancel the *Press*. We're through with that paper forever. I don't want to ever see it in here again."

At one point we were down to the *Christian Science Monitor* and the *St. Louis Post-Dispatch*, which arrived in the mail, usually a week late.

Out of that cycle, somehow, grew my interest in the news, how it was gathered and reported and in what form it reached our home. I had always written for the school papers, usually on sports, and in the summer of 1948 had worked at the *Press* as a gofer. That, of course, was just below a copyboy. I'd go for coffee or cigars or egg rolls, or whatever the reporters needed.

I was still determined to get to college and my mother, bless her, was adamant that I should make the attempt. I considered myself fairly street-smart. I had been to sea briefly one summer, at sixteen, worked on an oil rig, and dug pipeline ditches. But no money had been set aside for my schooling. It was that way with most families.

So I picked out the nearest small school with a full, four-year enrollment, and that happened to be Sam Houston State, seventy-five miles northeast of Houston. I knew nothing else about it, but I hitchhiked to Huntsville and asked around for the football coach. I found him in the basketball gym, a little crackerbox the students used to call the Tarpaper Tabernacle. He was watching a game, his head swiveling from side to side, and the entire time I talked to him he never once looked me in the eye.

I said, "Coach, I'm Dan Rather. I'm from Houston, Reagan High School, and I'm a football player."

He said, "Uh-huh," and in a very fishlike way he shook my hand.

This meeting was my introduction to Puny Wilson, who had been a great football player at Texas A&M in the days when the All-American selectors did their picking from the Ivy League. According to local legend, Puny Wilson also had the distinction of being the only football coach in the nation who actually, honestly, had a degree in basket weaving.

When he was in college peach growing was the rage in East Texas towns eager for new income. The peach crops created a demand for baskets in which to ship the fruit. So the Agricultural and Mechanical College of Texas offered an undergraduate certificate in basket weaving, and Coach Puny had one.

He was a disillusioned man long before that day in 1950 when I approached him in the gym. Fourteen straight losing seasons will do that to a coach.

My conversation with him was painful, punctuated by long silences. I explained to him that I would graduate at midterm and could enroll for the next semester, which was to begin the fifteenth of February.

He said, "Well, spring training starts March sixth and I'd be glad to have you come out."

That was all I needed to hear. It was an invitation to try out for the team and, in my mind, that was tantamount to a scholarship. I was ecstatic as I hitchhiked the seventy-five miles to Houston. When I told my mother the news she was jubilant. Then my dad came home and he thought it was madness. One, there was no money to cover my living expenses. Two, my football tryout did not sound like a very solid arrangement to him. And, three, there was a lapse of maybe three weeks between the start of classes and spring training.

The final jolt came when I informed my father I intended to major in journalism. That was not a word he could define and it was never clear to him how I thought I could make a living at it. He understood newspapers. But if one was going to college, it was to become a teacher or an engineer or a lawyer.

The days passed very quickly, and what my mother instinctively knew was that if I didn't go off to school immediately, I would never get there. She was simply very determined about it. She had never been on a university campus, but her feeling was that once I enrolled something would work out.

In February 1950, Mother took me to Huntsville on the Greyhound bus. We had a car, a 1938 Oldsmobile, but there was some doubt as to whether it would hold together, so we rode the bus. In my lifetime I have not made many more exciting trips than that one. We went first to the office of the dean of men, where I mentioned, proudly, that I was a candidate for the football team.

The dean replied that he didn't know anything about that, but registration ended that week and I needed twenty-five dollars to enroll and fifteen dollars for student fees. My mother had brought along two twenty-five-dollar U.S. Savings Bonds—bought during the war and not yet worth their full value—and while I waited in the dean's office she went into town and cashed them.

There was just enough money to cover all the fees, and when I was enrolled I could only guess what my mother felt. I don't know if anyone who didn't live or grow up during the war will understand what my mother had done. But a family paid $18.75 for a savings bond and waited ten years for it to mature and pay back $25. You cashed one only in an emergency.

Again, this isn't meant as Humble Beginnings nostalgia. That was simply the way it was. Next I found a boarding house a block from the campus and the manager agreed to give me a month's credit.

I had a great sense of satisfaction about the whole process. Really, I was very little different from the farmers' sons and daughters who were enrolling that day, the youngsters who had been valedictorians in Roans Prairie and Sundown and North Zulch, who carried whatever they owned in cardboard boxes wrapped with rope. Or the workmen's kids from Beaumont and Dallas and Houston, who lacked the money or the grades to get into the bigger universities. I felt at home, walking the grounds in my blue jeans, open-neck white shirt, and tennis shoes.

Later, when I signed up for classes, I paid my first visit to the young journalism professor, Hugh Cunningham. He had started the department and only had five or six students enrolled. That suited him fine. His idea was to work with a small number of young people and turn out a handcrafted product.

Where journalism was concerned he had a jealous nature. "Why are you here?" he demanded. "Do you know why you want to major in journalism?"

I said, "It's the only thing I've ever wanted to do."

He said, "What makes you think you can do it?"

I kind of bristled. "Well, I *know* I can."

With that reply, he barked out a half dozen facts and he had me sit down and write a news story for him. Now that I think about it, I was in the odd position of having to try out for the journalism department even before the football team.

From that moment Cunningham took me under his wing. When he heard about my football plans he threw up his hands.

"That's crazy," he said. "You don't want to be a football player. You'll get killed."

"There's no other way I can stay in school," I said. "This way I'll get a scholarship."

He laughed out loud. But he didn't push me about it. Possibly he knew it would do no good. Sometimes we ought not to be talked out of our mistakes. But I had to survive the next three weeks before the football practices started, and during that time Cunningham literally fed me out of his own pocket. In the meantime he kept lining up part-time jobs for me. I became a correspondent for the local Huntsville *Item,* which neither then nor now would be mistaken for one of America's distinguished newspapers. I was to string for the wire services—calling in basketball scores, mostly—and I also received ten dollars a month for cranking out publicity about the college. He had put together a package that would allow me at least to tread water.

In addition, I held a series of odd jobs, none of which lasted very long: I waited tables, pumped gas, worked at the Zesto Tastee-Freez stand. It was a dollar here and a dollar there and then it was time to report for football. Just as Cunningham had warned, I damned near got killed. To begin with, we had played two-platoon football in high school and I knew nothing about defense. Beyond that I lacked speed and couldn't block.

As if my other handicaps were not enough, Puny Wilson had a fearful prejudice toward city boys. He was a big, rawboned ol' country boy himself and he typed me—this was laughable—as just another pampered, big-city dude. His idea of a gut check, of putting a youngster to the test, was to stick the candidate at defensive end and run one power sweep after another in his direction. In the first two weeks of practice I did not distinguish myself. Cunningham used to drop by the practice field, a cow pasture rally, and he would stand there, shake his head, and cover his eyes when the herd rumbled over my body.

Finally it dawned on me that Coach Puny was trying to make me quit. One afternoon as I limped toward the showers he ambled over, dressed as usual in a T-shirt, football pants, and army surplus boots. He splattered a missile of tobacco juice amid the sand and cockleburs, rubbed the stubble of his beard, then put his arm around me. It was the first human gesture he had shown me.

"Son," he said, "I watched ya out thar the whole time t'day. And I wanna tell ya sumptun' I hope'll stay with ya the rest of your life. You're little." Pause. "And you're *yellow!*"

Well, I set about trying to prove he had at least the last part of it wrong. The proof was to be that I wouldn't quit. I played day after day, getting my bones smashed. Finally I went to see him and asked about my scholarship. Coach Puny was a tough, no-nonsense man, about fifty, and this time he didn't try to belittle me. I think he sensed that I really wanted to stay in school and that I needed help. For all I know, Cunningham may have put the fix in. Anyway, Puny said, "There's no way you can get a scholarship. But if you want to come back out in the fall, practice starts August fifteenth." (This was the same routine we had gone through before, but I accepted it, again, as an invitation.)

But I realized he had a heart when he told me I could drop around to the Bearcat Den—that was where they fed the football team—and take my meals on weekends. Coach Puny knew the boarding house, where I was eating on credit, closed its kitchen on the weekend.

I struggled through that spring and, in spite of everything, the odd jobs and the strange meal arrangements, Hugh Cunningham managed to capture and hold my attention. He was about five nine, slight, with dark hair combed straight back. An intensity poured out of him like water from a fire hose.

His idea of teaching journalism was to get you away from the classroom. He didn't believe the reporter's craft could be taught in school, and when he did, it was only because the state required it. The college had to have a curriculum. There had to be a Journalism 101. But Hugh Cunningham didn't really give a damn about any of that. He wanted us out in the field. "Write stories," he kept hammering at us. "Go interview the college horticulturist. Go downtown. Hang around the courthouse. Ride with the police. I don't want to see you the rest of the afternoon."

I learned long ago that the term *a good teacher* is redundant. While the phrase *a bad teacher* is a contradiction in terms. Rare is the teacher who fully understands what a tremendous difference he or she can make, but Cunningham was one of them. He picked the courses his students needed to get a degree, and he set their standards. Often he lectured me: "Coming out of a school this size, with no reputation at all, your only chance is to make virtually straight A's."

That admonition I took to heart. I studied as hard as I could without actually feeling pain. Before breakfast, in the afternoons, and at night I worked at money-paying jobs. Classes were crammed into the morning hours. Homework was done in snatches of time during the day and after midnight. In between and all about was the school paper. With Cunningham and Cecil Tuck, we put out the *Houstonian* twice a week. Tuck was another of Cunningham's prize students. He eventually went to Hollywood and has done well writing for television. He helped to discover and promote Glen Campbell, among others. Cecil was in much the same financial shape as I was, maybe worse. He stayed in school that semester by writing bad checks and then scrambling to cover them. Truth to tell, we often covered for one another with criss-crossing hot checks. We always paid our bills, but some semesters it took longer than others.

Meanwhile, Cunningham kept preaching experience to us, that you learned to write by writing. Cecil and I would compose stories and mail them to the *Houston Post.* Heaven knows, most of the time no response came and none was really expected. We would just send them off into this great vacuum. We'd do a feature story on a football player, or a teacher, or some campus character. Once, we sent out a piece on the lady who maintained Sam Houston's home. That was the big bone. The story was published and we were very proud. (You could get that feature printed almost every year. Even today. There is something about Sam Houston still having a housekeeper that seems to impress big city editors.)

Cecil was a major presence at the college. He was sloppy and fun and we hit it off from the beginning. He came from a sawmill town near Jasper and for that place, and for those times, he was an authentic free spirit. I believe he still holds the Lone Star Conference record for gin consumed by a third-string linebacker. He would occasionally show up for football practice under the influence, as they say, and he did not take many things seriously, including Cunningham.

Hugh was always torn. He knew he was a gifted teacher, knew how much of himself he was putting into us. But at the same time he wanted to be on the cutting edge of journalism. He was always taking summer jobs at newspapers like the *Atlanta Constitution.* He saw things in us and tried to express them in the way a father would, but he finally gave up trying to convince Cecil.

He couldn't talk to Tuck the way he could to me. Cecil would fall asleep or say, "Aw, come off that shit." So Cunningham would say to me, with a wrenching earnestness, "You can do it, Dan. You can go all the way." Keep in mind that for Hugh Cunningham, getting a job with the *Houston Post* was going all the way. A byline in the *Houston Chronicle* would have given him raptures. That was going all the way.

Cecil Tuck was country down to his toes. I never knew how or why he wanted to be a reporter. But we came along at the same time, and for the next three and a half years Cunningham tutored and pushed us. It was a fine relationship. I cannot imagine any student, anywhere, having a more meaningful one.

All that summer of my freshman year my major concern was winning a football scholarship in the fall of 1950. I still saw no way to stay in school without it. I landed a job during the summer working on a pipeline gang, digging ditches, as my father had done for so many years. I was able to save almost two hundred dollars and that relieved some of the pressure.

Still, it wasn't enough to get me through the school year. The money I had earned only meant that I could pay my bill at the boarding house and not mooch off Cunningham. So when football practice started in the fall I was there, drawing a uniform. The coaches looked at me with a weary respect. I was like a bastard cat you keep throwing off the end of the dock, and by the time you drive home he's waiting on the doorstep. But I stuck it out, long after all the others who didn't have scholarships had quit, and one or two more had given theirs back.

Before the first game I went to Coach Puny again and asked him where I stood. I think he may have been getting used to me. He still wouldn't give me a scholarship, he said, but I could suit out for the games if I wanted. I believe part of him wanted me to make it. We had a fine passer that year named Cotton Gottlob, and he knew I could catch the ball. There was always the possibility that the eight ends ahead of me might get hurt.

I worked out every day, letting the power sweep roll over me in waves, and I suited out for the first three games. Finally, in a fit of conscience, Coach Puny Wilson called me in and said, "Son, take my advice, give it up. It's useless for you." And that was it. I can remember walking out of his office and into the rain. Tears streamed down my face. It was one of the few times in my life I can remember crying.

My pride was involved. I had put so much of myself, emotionally, into it. And there was the feeling that I wouldn't last through the school year. All of that just came down on me.

Hugh Cunningham picked me right up. "It's the best thing that ever happened to you," he said. "You'd have wound up coaching or crippled or both. You don't know how lucky you are."

The next thing I knew he had obtained a job for me at the radio station in Huntsville, KSAM. It was Kay Sam to all who knew the station, what was known in the trade as a teakettle. Kay Sam had an operating power of 250 watts, the lowest allowed by the FCC. It was a three-room shack with a tower in the back, an oversized outhouse with an antenna sticking out the top. Our signal did not even carry to the city limits of Huntsville. We used to sell advertising to merchants over in Madisonville, fifteen miles away, and nobody in Madisonville could hear the station after six o'clock.

Kay Sam was basic, good ol' boy radio. We used to sell time on the pitch of a dollar a holler—the idea being that advertising spots cost a dollar each—but we often cut the price to forty cents.

The station was owned and managed by a Baptist minister known as Pastor Lott, Ted Lott. He was a journalist at heart. He loved the stories, the newscasting. He took a genuine liking to me, but I also filled a need for the station. He wanted to know if I had ever done any play-by-play of football games, and I said no, but I was sure I could.

He said, "Well, let me hear you. Go ahead, do some."

So I sat there and made up a game in my head, using the players from Sam Houston and a mythical opposing team. Altogether I did five or six minutes, and it wasn't difficult. It was not unlike the times I had invented a broadcast of the roller derby on the way to school or other occasions when I would amuse myself with the play-by-play of an imaginary football game in which I would be the hero with two seconds left on the clock.

When I walked out of the station Cunningham was gleeful. "Now that does it," he said. "If you really do a job for him, that's going to keep you in school and you'll have no more worries."

Kay Sam became my scholarship. Almost as important, it was the kind of place where you could make a lot of mistakes. At one point, in the same week, I was broadcasting the junior high, high school, college, and black high school games. I did not lack for air time. I also put together the newscasts and on occasion covered executions at the state prison for the wire services. The town was so small then that a myth had grown up around the executions. You were supposed to be able to tell when they threw the switch to the electric chair because all the lights in Huntsville would dim for a few seconds. I have never been certain that was so, but it was pretty romantic stuff, and I must say I believed it at the time.

By now I was knocking down seven dollars a month acting as sports information director for the college and forty cents an hour at KSAM, plus a talent fee for the football games, usually ten dollars. I actually came out of Sam Houston State with a little money squirreled away.

Pastor and Mrs. Lott became major influences on my life with their many kindnesses and, of course, by continuing to provide my best-paying job.

My survival was due to Cunningham, and he would not sit still for a thank-you. He was like a man cleaning out an attic so he could see what was there. He wanted you to get on with your future, go to class, make your grades, and, when you had the time, read the Chicago Great Books series. Hugh wouldn't classify himself as an intellectual, not then and I suppose not now. He probably would have laughed at the idea. But he had a restless mind and a decency impossible to overstate.

He was also a very tough editor. He would keep kicking material back to his students. It was not uncommon to have to rewrite a story as many as a dozen times before it suited him. And when it came to the student paper he was a lion defending the cubs. Once, an executive whose company published a house organ walked through the journalism offices. Cunningham instantly indexed this outlet as a job resource, a place where one of his graduates might break in, writing for the company publication.

The visitor was politically conservative and he questioned Hugh about a couple of items in that week's student paper. Looking back, it was ridiculous, but he wondered if these stories didn't smack of left-wing socialism. Now, communism might have been big in the eastern academic circles, but it hadn't reached Huntsville yet. Socialism was still our big threat.

Cunningham simply threw him out. No fuss, no ceremony. And Hugh himself was by no stretch of the imagination a liberal. But this was ground where strangers were not welcome. He cared so much about news gathering, and the integrity of it, that he would tolerate no compromises. Later Hugh's principles would lead him into difficulty with the college.

Cunningham's practices might strike someone at Columbia University, or Northwestern, as quaint, but each semester when we returned to school he required us, in class, to repeat out loud the journalist's creed: "A public journal is a public trust . . ." It was like the Boy Scout oath and he took it seriously. In a way it was beautiful. Not very sophisticated, perhaps, but then he was not dealing with sophisticated minds.

Without my really being aware, I had the best of two worlds. On the one hand, I had Cunningham drilling into me the fundamentals—who, what, when, where, why, and how. Get it, get it right, get it fast. Over and over again. "I want to know *exactly* what was said," he told us. "Treat it fairly. Write it fast." He often emphasized the need for quality writing, but he knew that reality was a city desk clamoring to meet a deadline, caring less if you made the language pretty.

That approach, I would learn in time, was tailor-made for broadcasting. Meanwhile I was working at a radio station where nothing was closed to me. I could do anything I was big enough to try. This led to some comic crises, but it was the richest kind of training.

One of Pastor Lott's best clients, and one of my major assignments, was the "Gospel Hour" from eight to nine at night, with the air time bought and filled by the local black funeral home. This period usually served as my break time, with the exception of those nights when the "Gospel Hour" 's anchorman failed to appear and I had to fill in, faking a deep, East Texas black accent, or what I thought was one. I owed much to the early work of Amos 'n' Andy.

I would also sing occasionally on the air, although I no longer remember whether I did so for my own amusement or because of a sponsor's requirement. But for the most part it was lonely work and at night I usually had the station to myself. I put in a lot of hours there, studying in between records and newscasts and commercials. Once in a while one of the co-eds from the school would drop by during the "Gospel Hour"—the only show that ever allowed me an hour of privacy—and we would slip out to the back room and go off to paradise.

Youth will have its way, but I am here to tell you that you have never tried to make out until you have known passion in the back of the Huntsville radio shack while the "Gospel Hour" was on the air. You have to know that I calculated my break time with great care. A lot of disc jockeys can dredge such memories from their small-town days. If you ever worked nights at a one-man radio station, you needed a diversion to pass the time. That *was* the standard diversion, but with the "Gospel Hour" pouring out of the speakers, a new dimension was added.

In truth, KSAM was a one-man operation simply because you could not operate the station with less. On the weekend I put us on the air at six in the morning and kept the broadcast going until midnight. I answered the phone, repaired the equipment, mowed the lawn, and painted the tower.

Long-playing records—those of one artist in particular—were all that saved me from working nineteen hours without food. The artist was Pastor Lott's brother, in spirit if not in fact, who sold Bibles out of Del Rio, Texas. The pastor's brother had recorded several religious albums featuring such favorites as "The Old Rugged Cross." He would pick a guitar and preach a little between songs.

At six P.M. each Saturday and Sunday I would put on one of those records, hop into the "Mobile News Unit" (a 1937 Plymouth pickup truck), and drive to the Dairy Bar two miles away. There I would order two hamburgers to go and get back to the station before the record had stopped playing.

One night I decided to alter the routine a little. I listened to a few bars of the opening hymn, hustled into the truck, and headed for the Dairy Bar. A new waitress, a freshman at the college, had started working there and I noticed she had nice legs. So I said to myself, well, it doesn't matter much whether you take the hamburgers back or eat them here, so long as you get back to the station before six thirty. I sat there, made small talk with the girl, and watched the big diesel trucks roll by on Highway 75 to Dallas.

I had been at the Dairy Bar about twenty minutes when the phone rang.

"It's Pastor Lott," she said, handing me the phone across the counter. The pastor was in a very unpastoral mood.

"Young man," he roared, "have you heard my radio station any time lately?"

"No, sir. You see . . . well, I got detained here."

"Well, you get your butt where you can hear it. Then you get back to the station . . . fix it . . . and you're fired."

Click.

I rushed out to the truck and turned on the radio. The voice of Pastor Lott's brother came through loud and clear. "GO TO HELL!" he thundered. "GO TO HELL . . . GO TO HELL . . ." And he had been thundering it for about twenty minutes.

The record was stuck.

Anyone who has ever lived in a small town can appreciate the impact of twenty solid minutes of "Go to hell" on the local radio station. Especially when the station is owned by "a man of the cloth," as some of the townspeople referred to Pastor Lott.

Luckily for me, the Christian ethic prevailed. Pastor Lott found it in his heart to forgive me, especially after Hugh Cunningham reminded him that finding dependable help for forty cents an hour wasn't easy, not even in Huntsville.

I could not foresee that there was another ordeal yet to come. It would involve, of all people, Fulton Lewis, Jr., whose nightly broadcast from Washington in the 1950s was carried by more than three hundred stations, many of them in small towns. A lot of people thought it was less a newscast than a platform for Lewis's right-wing political views.

Believe me, you could sell time in Huntsville, Texas, for Fulton Lewis. It was a participating program; that is, the network (Mutual) took the first position and the local station could sell the next two. Three times during each ten-minute broadcast Lewis would say, "I'll be back after these important words," and take a one-minute break. There was a two-beat pause. Then I would cut away for our own commercial message: "The Huntsville National Bank is proud to present Fulton Lewis, Jr. Put your money in a local account, don't go to the big city of Conroe . . . etc., etc. Now, here again is Fulton Lewis, Jr."

We had sold one of the spots. For the other, if you didn't cut away after the two-beat pause, the staff announcer in Washington would read a sustaining spot, a plug for the Red Cross, or whatever. That night I ran our one local spot, and was off in the back filing records when I heard Lewis say, "I'll have more news after these important words."

And the next important word anyone heard was *"Horseshit."*

I thought to myself, holy smoke, what's this? I raced into the control room, not believing what I had just heard and wondering if the obscenity had gone out over the air.

Immediately, the phones started ringing off the wall. In a small town everyone knows everyone else, and people were calling in to say, "Dan Rather, I am mortified at you for using such language on the air." Fortunately for me, Pastor Lott couldn't get through because the phones were jammed. He decided to drive to the station, but by the time he got there the network was already carrying a brief apology. What had happened was that Lewis or someone at his side had thrown the switch before his announcer had the copy ready, and when the announcer said "horseshit" he didn't know his microphone was on.

Of course, a good many people in town refused to believe that explanation. Over the next few weeks it became a mini-scandal locally, with people arguing over whether Rather had said it or Pastor Lott, and had we tried to cover up by blaming poor Fulton Lewis. The funny thing was, Pastor Lott would never use such language, not even if he had to describe what came out of the rear end of a horse.

Thanks in part to such incidents, Cecil Tuck and I came to be considered a little avant-garde around the college. For one thing, we made our own way. A lot of students did that, of course, and there was no particular credit in it. But the school paper gave us certain entrées, and Cecil even ran for the student council. We roomed together after our freshman year off campus, which required special permission, and we had such good times, such a sense of joie de vivre, that it spilled over into occasional fistfights. All part of the image.

You have to understand how small the school was; how small the town. One summer we had five hundred students and I knew nearly every one of them by name and hometown.

There was no social life as such. The Sans Souci of Huntsville was the Texas Café. If you took a date to the Texas Café and ordered the chicken-fried steak, well, you were a man of means. Few students owned cars. Nobody owned a new one with the exception of a wealthy girl from Beaumont, who was a sensation on campus.

In our senior year Cecil and I bought a 1939 Ford for sixty dollars. After a good deal of tinkering we sometimes were able to get the heap to run, after a fashion, but that really wasn't why we bought it. We figured if we could just get the car to the dormitory, we'd have a place to bring a girl after the movie. That old Ford didn't have to run.

Once, I did get it cranked up, which turned out to be a near disaster. We had driven off to Elkins Lake to count the stars and now I was returning my date to Elliott Hall, which was at the foot of a hill. The car had no brakes and there was no tread on the tires, but we would use the clutch for slowing down. Coming down the hill this night, the clutch went out. I couldn't get the gears to work. We were gaining speed.

The women students had an eleven o'clock curfew, and at three minutes to eleven the lights outside the dorm would start blinking to signal that their time was up. Couples would straggle out of the brush, and they would appear in various stages of dishevelment. That was the scene as my car came careening down the hill. My whole life, such as it was at twenty-one, flashed before my eyes. My only hope, I decided, was to jump the curb and ram into the low stone wall that encircled the campus. Just kamikaze right into the damned wall.

At the last minute my headlights picked up the fact that there were still a dozen or so couples clustered in front of the wall, stealing one last goodnight kiss. I hit the curb, veered away, knocked over a fireplug and came to a halt against the front of the dormitory. Water sprayed everywhere. It was a miracle that no one got splattered against the building like some kind of bug. My date wasn't even hurt.

There followed a long session about that incident with the dean, who tried to impress me with how dangerous the situation had been. I agreed wholeheartedly, while pointing out that it was unavoidable. I could not be held responsible for students necking against a wall.

The wonder was that I ever finished school. The Weeper—that was Cecil's nickname—did not. He was sort of handsome, in a chunky way, but he could give you an expression so sad he would touch the heart of a Greek statue. Tuck was always in financial hot water and he was forced to drop out with one semester to go. I knew it was coming the day Cecil climbed to the top of the water tower.

Huntsville, like Rome, was built on a series of hills. There was a water tower, eighty feet high, down by the gymnasium, and one night a girl came running from that direction to get me. "Dan, Dan," she squealed, "you gotta come. Cecil's on the water tower. And he's drunk and he doesn't have his clothes on."

You have to get this picture. Huntsville was a small town that hadn't changed in character since the days of the Republic of Texas. Here was a crowd gathered down below while my friend, Cecil Tuck, stood on top of the tower and shouted, "PISS ON THE WORLD." And, sure enough, he did.

I climbed those eighty feet to the top of the tower to coax him down. Over the years I have thought many times about that moment, and Cecil. As his talent grew and he became respectable, I always hoped that he would not lose that nerve or spirit. Many do. He never did.

Between us, I regret to say, we were responsible, at least indirectly, for Cunningham's leaving Sam Houston State. By 1953 the McCarthy era was in full swing, and the Korean War had almost devastated the campus of able-bodied males. The administration hurriedly arranged for the formation of an ROTC unit, which provided a shelter of sorts for those students who needed, or wanted, to avoid the draft. They drilled in makeshift uniforms, in shirts that didn't match their pants. Cecil and I wrote pieces in the student paper poking fun at the ROTC's ragtag army. I must say that Cecil's stories were much funnier than mine. He was always much better when a story called for a light touch. This was a comical subject, in some ways, but the humor was lost on the school's officials, who had gone to considerable lengths to bring in the ROTC, and, really, for good reasons.

Now here was the school newspaper making fun of what the college had done. So Cunningham was called on the carpet, a form of bullying that he took badly. He was told to exercise more control over his department. He said it was a matter of principle with him to teach his people independence. "I give them guidance," Hugh said, "and help them with their writing and editing, but they decide what goes into the paper. I don't decide that for them."

This may have been very small potatoes in the context of where we were and the times we were in. But Cunningham did not take the scolding lightly. Not long afterward he left. He wasn't around when I graduated, but he had given Sam Houston State a journalism school, against what odds only Cecil Tuck and I could fully appreciate. He had said to us several times, almost in despair, "You know, I feel guilty because I really should be encouraging you to go to Texas. It's the only university in the state with a journalism department worthy of the name, and you are good enough to make it there."

I never felt that I suffered for having attended Sam Houston. Among other reasons, I had opportunities that would not have been available at a larger school. One of them was the closeness that could develop with a professor like Hugh Cunningham. He stayed in teaching—it was and is his life—and has taught for years at the University of Florida. He encouraged us to think, and read, and form opinions.

On our own time he had us reading the work of people such as Elmer Davis. Then he would grill us with questions in that Gatling-gun style of his. "For the working reporter," he demanded, "what's the most important thing Elmer Davis said?"

There was silence in the room. None of us knew.

"Don't let the bastards scare you," he said.

Shelby Hearon

Shelby Hearon (b. 1931) has set several of her novels in Texas, often featuring, as does this selection from A Prince of a Fellow, *strong female protagonists and a powerful sense of place and flow of time, vividly portrayed.*

A PRINCE OF A FELLOW

I am a frizzy-haired, washed-out princess looking for a prince. Some ordinary prince on a limping horse, to carry me off to his leaking, rented castle, to share his beans and salt pork and lie beside him in his bed. No one special; after all, I am nothing fancy. At thirty I have never established residence with a man, and those I have rubbed bellies with have been no better than I was willing to settle for. Concerned as I am with reality, I don't get my hopes too high; just a third son of a minor king.

Which search is the reason I had this morning in my radio station still another prospect, this one a writer down from Connecticut, here on a grant at the historic J. Frank Dobie Ranch. Which meant that for shelter he got an old farmhouse and for inspiration a field, a creek, and a view of the neighbor's cows.

I love to interview writers, as they are not fettered by facts. Thrusting characters and parrying plots spin from their fingers onto the yellow pad as slickly as spider webs. Silently inside their heads herds thunder and doors slam with a reverberation that we in the world of sound can only envy. Each time I coax a writer to open his vocal cords on my show I expect sudden magic; expect verbal rabbits snatched from the top hat of his subconscious.

Of course, I am habitually disappointed. Last year's Dobie Fellow, hungrily surfacing from under Los Angeles's thick sky, had spent six months staring through the barb-wire fence at the milling livestock, his vocabulary locked in constipation. On the air, so full of his oneness with the land and its manure, he had had the opposite problem. I purposely omitted mention of his work in progress, lest it never progress.

I had high hopes that this year's visiting writer would be better. For one thing he possessed the irresistibly German name of Gruene Albrech; for another, his brooding voice, accepting my invitation to appear on my interview show, had suggested a prodigal son come home to confront an archetypal father—to kill or to forgive him (depending on the size of the Dobie grant).

Now, considering him through the pane of glass, he didn't look as I expected. He was not brooding at all; in fact, he seemed eager as a kid on his first day of school all decked out in new clothes, which he was—board-stiff jeans, creased Western pearl-snapped shirt, hand-tooled glossy leather boots. Even, sticking from his back pocket, a red bandanna with the price tag still on it.

Right off I could see he was no German. Looking closer at his wide face whose skin stretched across high cheekbones tight as a drum, I decided he must be Slavic. His deep almost golden tan gave him a general yellow wash that appeared to color even the whites of his eyes and his teeth, and darkened to copper his bow-shaped mouth. In the manner of symmetrical faces, his chin was cleft in the center, Czech, there was no question.

That charade was all right with me; I was used to that. Things are seldom what they seem. None of us are as we present ourselves.

The old men in this fenced-in town in Central Texas, named for Prince Solms, the nobleman who brought their ancestors from the old country inland from the coast to this rolling edge of a ring of weathered hills, purport to live in a German-speaking hamlet.

In fact, they dream of a remembered past; today they make up less than half the town. Beer-bellied, polka-dancing Mexicans, heirs of the original land-grant holders, now outnumber the beer-bellied, polka-dancing German descendants of the prince's immigrants. Nor is this the lush verdant farmland they claim to their grandsons, hoping to keep them close at hand; only the thinnest veneer of grass and scrubby shrubs covers the rocky soil of this insular place whose factions shut themselves off from their neighbors as surely as its rivers cut apart its three hills.

We aren't what we claim either, here on my beloved Mole in the Tunnel. Our very show pretends one thing as it delivers another. KPAC, a remote broadcast station, sells itself as Pasture Radio, down home sound brought to you from the land of the Aberdeen Angus and Poland Chinas. Actually, although we pipe our audience the picking sounds of country and western's finest, we sit ten miles out of town on a rise so that we can beam our advertisers to the Porsche drivers and politicians in both San Antonio and Austin. We are no more authentically rural than Neiman-Marcus custom-cut blue jeans.

Otto, my sidekick, who gives the news and weather in heavy German accent, is really a forty-five-year-old Mexican, with Pancho Villa mustache, who works afternoons (out of his lederhosen and into his stiff black suit) as the cemetery sexton.

Nor am I, Avery Krause, the cowgirl my faded jeans and blue work shirts would imply. I am, rather, as my mama is, a Swede sitting like a burr in the saddle of a large German family. A corn on the sole of the old grandfather's foot.

For twenty years in the coal-burning state, as Papa in his German way called the black, gutted mountains of eastern Kentucky, Mama and I were mistaken for any other Appalachian towheads. Which angered Papa into deep silences over his journals and ledgers. I, so like the other schoolgirls with blue eyes pale as watercolor—all of us blanched, bleached, with peaked faces—made faint impression on the eye. We were Polaroid shots not yet developed. Now, come back here last year to bury Papa and replant ourselves, Mama and I are set apart from the Germans we married or were born into by our near-white curls, our wide thighs, even our sweet Swedish smiles.

If my appearance was the same in Kentucky, so was my manner of dealing with the world. I was a drama teacher, which, if you think about it, is not too different from what I'm doing now. In both settings I present illusions as real. In both theater and radio the audience is let in on the hoax; together we share the thrill of belief suspended. Here, by consent, coconut shells pound into horses' hoofs and squeaking doors signal mysterious entries and ominous departures. There, small white faces grew bold with greasepaint and eager hands slew dragons with broom handles.

So it was fine with me if today's prince was after all a golden impostor, faking his German birthright; I too make my living by delusion.

As I stared at his large dark head and wide palms which seemed designed to compensate for lack of height, he flashed a hesitant grin of greeting.

Wanting to get the feel of him before we went on the air, I put on the easy sounds of Willie Nelson's "Remember Me" and left the control booth to Otto, who was assembling the good tidings of local news and the usual bad tidings of local weather.

"Good morning, I'm Avery Krause. We talked on the phone."

"I'm here early." Gruene Albrech rose, short in the leg as I had perceived.

I shook his firm hand, deciding that the touch was worth coming out for. "Would you like a cup of coffee?"

"If it's no trouble. I left in a hurry. It looked farther on the map. I thought it would take me longer to get here."

"You were good to drive out at eight o'clock in the morning."

"I've never been on radio."

Which must explain the scrubbed look. People always forget we on radio see only with our movie-making minds.

"We're very informal," I tried to put him at his ease. "I'll ask a few questions, play some music. We'll let the listeners call in their comments. They like to feel they're taking part in the show."

Which in fact they did. The weekday interview hour was now the station's most popular feature, and the high point of Otto's and my shift. This was satisfying to me as last year, returned home and job hunting, I had sold KPAC's managers on the idea that visiting dignitaries and celebrities from San Antonio and Austin, and even stammering ordinary citizens from Prince Solms, telling their versions of daily events, would create a wider advertising market than followed their existing mix of country sounds, news, and weather.

"You can ask me about my book," the writer told me. "That's why I'm here."

I was more interested in him than in his proposed translation of himself into fiction, but, guessing he wanted a dress rehearsal, I asked, "What is your novel about?"

He cast about as if he hadn't thought of it before. "It's about these people."

Clearly he needed to warm up. Some writers obviously grew tongue-tied in the morning. Leaving his work, I moved to him, a matter of more concern to me anyway. "How long have you been away from Texas?"

He studied his cup. "Uh—since I left high school. Several years."

"Do you have family back here?" The Dobie grant as I recalled had to be bestowed on a native Texan.

"Uh—that's right. My mom's folks are from Veramendi."

"Czech?"

He looked relieved, as if the business of disguises bothered him. "How could you tell?"

"Long practice at observing dissembling."

"I guess I do that. Writing, I mean."

"Is Albrech your real name?"

"Actually it's Billy Wayne Williams." He looked sheepish at this admission.

"Why did you change it?"

"Who reads books by Billy Wayne Williams? If your name is Gruene Albrech they take you seriously. They give you a grant to the Dobie Ranch." He grinned. "They ask you to appear on radio shows."

"So they do." I smiled my blondest smile.

"Besides, I thought the German name would prepare me to tell my story."

"About these people . . ." I chided him.

"I'll tell about it when we're on the air. I don't want to waste myself now. I'm saving up for when it counts."

"Is that the way you write?"

"What?"

"Keeping it all inside until it goes down on paper?"

"I guess so. I never thought about it."

His crisp just-purchased clothes must also be a way to get into his tale and into this part of the country again. They did not look like the tweeds and Shetland sweaters I imagined for Connecticut. "How do you like being back here?" I asked.

"That's part of what we'll talk about." With that, he went back to the guest chair and turned his attention to waiting. Moving his knees apart and planting his feet squarely as a peasant, he simply sat.

It came to me I was observing an actor, offstage, getting into his role. A fine development, and one that I had missed.

Most people did not know that when the first sounds gave the cue that the curtain had gone up, we were on our invisible stage. Most people played to me, thinking me their audience. Most gestured to me, looked to me for confirmation, took my silent nods as answers. Most people did not believe that anyone was Out There; it would be grand to work with an actor again.

It took me back to another actor who had seemed, for a time, to be a prince of a fellow. An actor with a fine hairy belly against which I slept for five years of weekends. Remembering that earlier tale (or perhaps a later one) made me wonder about the writer before me—did he make love as the Czech rodeo rider or as the moody German?

However, I knew that such thinking was unproductive. After all, I had only taken one guest to bed, and he was no prince. Still, you had to consider it again each time; otherwise you ceased to take the risk that goes with looking.

Otto wrapped up his good tidings of local news with, "It vill be a goot day, as ve shall see." Popping his alpine suspenders, he plugged in a public service cartridge and signaled for me to take over.

"Pronounce my name *Green.*" My guest spoke up suddenly. "That is the German way."

Then back in the booth the sorcery began again; we were crackling out over the air waves into the waiting cars. "Hello out there, this is Avery Krause on KPAC, Keep Peace, the station which brings you morning. Our guest today is that distinguished novelist Gruene Albrech, returned to the land of his forefathers in search of an ancient tale. You at home refill your freeze-dried and you in your economy cars move closer to your FM while we listen to his story. It isn't every day we get a real live word wizard on our show, so stay tuned and be sure to call in your own questions for him." At home in my eyeless world, I beamed myself to my unknown intimates.

"Tell us, Gruene, how does it feel to be back here in your homeland coming to terms with your past?" I fed him the cue.

With the first answer he was before the floodlights. His hands led him; his planted stance anchored him. He was Everyman, struggling to find himself and, in the process, each of us. As he talked he brushed his brown hair continually away, as if brushing aside deception or falsehood.

In the heavy tones of a Günter Grass he shared the anguish of going home again. He was the tortured expatriate, returned to wring the truth from the meager lives of his ancestors.

"And what is your novel about?"

"My book is a fable of a grandfather blinded by his villagers. It is a parable; for we are all that grandfather, the world is that village. Do you know the works of ——?" He plunged into a comparison of himself and a little known but powerful German writer, exiled from his home soil, writing of alienation.

Now I was not thinking of him in bed, but with his pencil and pad. Wondering if he wrote as this fine actor, the tormented Albrech, or as the golden cowboy. Most of all wondering did he write well?

"Do you write from your own experience?"

"I am everyone I invent, but they each transcend me."

"How do you know when your writing is good?" This was something I had never understood, as the actor is dependent on immediate response. The kids would put on a tablecloth, a bandit's cape, and ride their chairs backwards, and it was a good performance if their watchers shouted and clapped. And if they didn't, it wasn't. But for a writer the lapse from entrance to applause required a far vaster attention span to approval.

"Not until it's read. And then, if it comes from your deepest level of consciousness, you can only hope it will speak a truth to the deepest level of the reader."

He spoke then not of theater but of a message in a bottle, of himself stolidly gathering clams until the tide went out and came in again. Nodding my admiration of such patience, as well as such fine answers, I gave us both time to catch our breath and myself time to answer the blinking red phone that flashed a listener's call. Putting on John Prine's bittersweet ballad of "Donald and Lydia," I spoke into the off-air receiver. "Good morning, Keep Peace."

"How would you like to interview me tonight?" It was the all too familiar voice of the mayor of San Antonio. I felt a flush rise to my face. Wasn't it enough that I was still engaged in a shabby affair with this burgher in white socks; did he have to intrude himself into my ear as well on that ultimate invasion of privacy, the telephone?

"I can't talk now, Sterling, I have a guest."

He drew in his breath. It excited him to call when I was on the air, knowing he couldn't be heard by the audience but knowing it rattled me. He liked getting a reaction from me whenever it appealed to him—the usual attitude of a man to his mistress. "I can be at the cabin at a quarter to seven." Breathless, aroused by his call, he proffered the weekly rendezvous.

"How long will you have?" I did not relish the drive to our hideaway, a trip that took me more than an hour.

"I don't have to be at the reception until nine. Plenty of time for what I have in mind."

"I'll try to come."

"See that you do." He laughed, titillated by the double meaning. He knew I would appear; after a year it had become a foregone conclusion.

After a year he knew that he could count on my weekly treks to hear how things were going with his boys. He had surmised that whatever thrill the clandestine provided him, I was willing to settle for the feel of a man again.

As the music faded and Otto stroked his mustache in disapproval of the call, I invented a final question for our writer. "How long have you had this story in your mind?"

Through the pane of glass he acknowledged my invention, meeting my eyes above my flushed cheeks. "The blind old man surrounded by others," he concluded, "represents the primal scene in my life. I have never been without it."

If he writes badly, I admitted, I cannot bear it.

"Thank you for being with us, Gruene Albrech, and now stay tuned while Otto brings you news of the outside world from our fertile field among the mooing Angus."

Out in the front, I shook the writer's hand in thanks.

"Otto is Mexican, isn't he?" He studied the newscaster through the glass.

"His name is Ramirez. He's the cemetery sexton."

"He does a good imitation of the language."

"None of us is really German, are we?" I looked about the studio where we had each performed in costume. "Not to the grandfathers, anyway."

"I guess not." He looked away.

I studied his face, not knowing how to proceed. I had never known how to make overtures to men. If they wanted you then you either said yes or you said no, but it was their question before it was your answer. I had never learned how to move things along with the ones who didn't ask.

In Kentucky where I taught drama there had been a school principal who supported me in my attempts to get the mountain children to loosen their bodies, to wrestle a smile to the floor, or to pretend to be a caterpillar crawling in the dirt. He was one of those rumpled, dedicated men you always mean to end up with, conscientious and underpaid. Educated but with some flaw visible as a rip in his jacket which meant he had settled for a poor rural school in a backwater. In three years we never got past his encouragement and my redoubled efforts in the classroom. We never got past ending up at the same lunch table with our sacks of sandwiches and apples.

The one who finally did ask, the extravagant actor, had also, as Gruene had, rechristened himself. He had given himself, as he liked to pun, three *given* names. Called himself Charles Henry David in a takeoff on the famous whose parents give them three surnames at birth (Custer Lincoln Grant). To his delight, people could never remember whether he was Charles David or David Charles. I called him Henry; I never knew his real name. At least this time, with the writer, I had got that far.

"Do you have time for another cup of coffee?" I asked, finally. "We could go watch the cows eat grass."

"Sure. I set the morning aside from my work."

We took our refills outside and leaned against the fence. There were no Angus in sight, nothing in the rolling green fields but air waves whispering messages.

"What did Billy Wayne do to eat in Connecticut?"

"How do you mean?"

"Nothing deep. English faculty?"

"Uh—yeah. The usual stuff. Teaching. Writers' workshops."

"Does Texas seem changed to you?"

"Everything stays pretty much the same down here."

I tried another tack. "When we were on the air, who were you talking to?"

He cast his eyes about, as if trying to visualize. "Just someone out there, I guess. Someone I don't know."

"I beam myself to a woman who is clearing the table, grabbing her things, getting into her sports car to go to work, taking me along with a fresh cup."

He considered. "I couldn't imagine anyone specific like that. If I did I would get involved in where he was going to work and what kind of car he had and then I would get into his wife and kids and their fights and that personal business and then I couldn't talk to him. I guess I was talking to the same person I write to: just someone out there."

"How long do you have at Dobie?"

"Six months. Isn't that standard?"

"Sometimes they give the grant for a year—"

"I figure if I can't get my book started in six months then I can't do it anyway."

"Do you write every day?"

"The research is what slows me down. I thought I knew my people but it is taking me longer than I planned."

It couldn't be going slower than my research on him. I could only guess that he had put on the new country clothes in order to leave behind the world of the teacher and method act his fictional villagers. "You made your tale very convincing to our listeners."

"I have never been on radio before."

Which was where we came in. Stymied, I watched as his hazel eyes focused on some scene out there past the fields.

Unexpectedly, he asked a sudden question of his own. "Who were you talking to?"

"I told you. Just a woman in her car—"

"I mean on the phone. When you made up that question for me."

"Oh." I felt the red come back again. "The mayor of San Antonio. A friend of mine." Which I guess spelled out the whole thing for him. But I didn't know what else to do but tell the truth; I did not bill myself as what I was not.

"You got opaque."

"How do you mean?"

"You closed up."

"I may do that a lot."

"That's not good for you."

I shrugged. Some things it was better not to stay open to. "It's self-defense."

"I know about that," he said.

"Around here you have to . . ." But he must remember all that.

". . . Well," he said.

I asked one parting query. "Do you write in those clothes?"

"I never wore these before."

I didn't press further. Maybe he wrote in turtlenecks and corduroys, or, emulating the grandfather, in an old man's nightshirt. Maybe he got up every day and sharpened all the pencils in his cigar box, in the nude. Maybe I would never know.

We emptied our cups and scanned the horizon—toward Prince Solms and the lavender hills to the north, toward Veramendi and distant Mexico to the south. I had run out of inquiries. If not out of all I wanted to know, at least what it was possible to ask. Holding out my hand one last time, I called it a morning. "Thank you for coming. Otto will have to move onto ag news and polkas if I don't rescue him."

"Here . . ." He tugged the bandanna from his back pocket and stuck it in my hand. "I don't need this."

I tried to leave things open. "Stop by on your way back to see the folks in Veramendi."

He left them closed. "Right now I'm working out the village in my head." Getting into a car as new as his name, his Levis, and his performance on my show, he backed out onto the unpaved access road.

I tied the bandanna on my tow head. Sometimes you had to make do with souvenirs.

Stephen Brook ————————————————————

Stephen Brook is a British-born author with a background as a travel writer who in 1984 flew to Austin to visit a friend, then rented a car and proceeded to tour the state for a year, covering thousands of miles of backroads and freeways.

SURGICAL SPIRITS

"This is it? It all happens in this tiny room?"

"Yes."

As Apollo made its spidery descent onto the surface of the moon, or as Skylab spun lazily around the Earth, I'd assumed that the operations would be controlled from a vast complex of computer terminals and backup systems attended by teams of bespectacled scientists and calm shirt-sleeved technicians wearing headphones, while excitable assistants collided into one another as they rushed about carrying vital charts under their arms. Not a bit of it. Mission Control Center at the National Aeronautics and Space Administration some twenty-five miles south of Houston is the size of a small lecture hall. Four rows of consoles, twenty-two in all, face six large screens that fill an entire wall; during a mission the two outer screens on either side relay data, while the two middle screens usually display a map. At the rear is a glassed-off VIP gallery, which during tense moments on space missions is packed with politicians and their molls. The technological achievement of going to the moon and back should, one feels, be rooted in a ground support and communications system more outwardly elaborate than this modest bank of gibbering consoles. It was somehow mildly alarming as well as awesome that the greatest adventures of our century should be so discreetly monitored.

All of NASA's Johnson Space Center, the president's most munificent gift to his native state, is laid out on this unassuming scale. Most of the buildings are no more than two or three stories high, dotted over lawns and reflected in pools. A stranger stumbling across it might think it was a high school, not the command center for an enterprise that, after all, is described in quasi-religious terms as a mission. Visitors are free to stroll through half a dozen buildings; there is no obsession with security, though I daresay an unauthorized foray into the wrong building without an identification badge could result in swift zapping. From a visitor's viewpoint, NASA is well run, and mockups and old modules retired from active service are laid out for close inspection. I was especially enthralled by the dental kits and the equipment required to rehydrate astronautical "food"; it was these details that brought home to me the heroism of space travel more than photographs of astronauts floating through nothingness. Cramped hours inside a command module no larger than a his-and-hers coffin, constant monitoring not just of scientific procedures but of body responses to the fierce jostlings of space travel, manipulation of devices with such splendidly blunt names as Thumper Geophone Assembly, and above all, not being able to take a piss without a bank of instruments giving a complete analysis to the wizards in Houston—it adds up to a peculiar form of bravery.

I was filled with admiration but not with awe. I wanted some awe. I eventually found it at Rocket Park, an open-air museum on the edge of the NASA compound. Here, lying on its side, is the Saturn V rocket, which was used from 1968 to 1973 to propel Apollo and Skylab into space. It is 363 feet high, and if it were set upright inside St. Paul's Cathedral, there would be only two feet to spare under the dome. A few feet away from Saturn V is the vertical form of the Mercury-Redstone rocket that took Alan Shepard on his fifteen-minute flight in 1961. It's no taller, and not even wider, than an average oak or beech, and I wasn't sure which alarmed me more: the power of the huge Saturn rocket, or the frailty of this pencil that launched the first American into space.

I drove back into Houston on the busy highway, unable to resist the modish reflection that while NASA is effectively building a space shuttle to provide rapid transit from here to nowhere, the city which conceived it hasn't managed to devise an adequate transportation system for its three million residents. After town planners and administrators and politicians emerged from a decade-long huddle, the best they could come up with was the idea of special bus lanes, which, in fact, already exist in Houston. Drive toward the airport in the rush hour and you'll see buses hurtling toward you down one of the contraflow lanes. Terrifying until you get used to it.

Driving around large American cities can be strangely pleasurable. Cruising at a steady speed up broad highways with as many lanes as most people have fingers, the pace is oddly relaxing. I'd roll down all the windows, turn up the radio, tan an elbow on the sill, and sling my other arm along the unoccupied passenger seat beside me. I might whistle or sing, and idly look about me, though outside the central areas there's little to observe from the elevated highways—just tract housing and shopping malls and warehousing and light industrial plants and hospitals, barely distinguishable from each other. The view will be the same whether you are twenty miles north of downtown Houston or twenty miles south. Only the names change: the shopping precincts will be called Cottonwood Plaza or Heritage Oaks Mall or Spring Valley Center, each with its K-Mart and Safeway and Sears Auto Center, liquor stores and gun shops, late-night 7-Elevens and a battery of fast food huts.

Culturally this endlessly repetitive urban landscape ought to be deeply depressing, yet I've always found it soothing, and in part it's the satisfaction of knowing I don't live in it. At a dollar a gallon, driving aimlessly is cheap entertainment, and at the first sign of fatigue I can revive myself by dipping off the highway and onto empty side streets, where I could be sure of remaining lost for half an hour. Driving into Houston one day on I-10, a narrow brute of a highway, I felt a yawn flowering in my mouth and I decisively headed for the nearest exit ramp and drove south. I found myself in a small incorporated township, one of many embedded within greater Houston, called Hunters Creek Village. The main road crossing the suburb is Memorial Drive, a pleasant parkway that meanders westward from Memorial Park through a number of choice communities. From time to time I'd turn off Memorial and crawl up dead-end lanes lined with houses that in many cases were still unfinished.

They were, most of them, white brick boxes embellished with grand architectural features. Here was a mansard roof to give height to a building easily a hundred feet long and filling one whole side of its acre lot; the house opposite was embraced by a portico that was extended into an arcade that ran around all visible sides of the structure. Yet in all these cases the architects never had the courage of their pretensions.

The grand purposeless arcade—for no family would ever sit out on this porch shelling peas or spooning in the hammock—was supported on spindly columns with what in a kind mood I'd call Doric capitals, though the builders' merchant probably describes them as square flat tops. The front door of this monstrous house was a full two stories high, panelled with clear glass, so that the envious passerby could gaze into a hall that also rises to the full height of the house. . . .

There are hundreds of such streets in suburban Houston, and there must be thousands of people who both want, and can afford, to buy these hypertrophied houses. As Hank the Dallasite unkindly observed: "Houston's an example of what happens when you let unimpeded greed run its course. Houstonians are like kids in a candy store who eat everything in sight and then can't figure out why they're sick."

When Houstonians do get sick, there's never any doubt about what action to take. They go straight to the Texas Medical Center, which is more than just a large hospital. Let me dazzle you, as they dazzled me, with statistics. There are 29 institutions here, both public and private, employing 30,000 people. In 1982, 2 million outpatients paid visits, while 68,000 patients were admitted to beds. While the institutions are independent of each other, they do share libraries, laundries, and parking facilities. To be part of the center, hospitals may not restrict their activity to patient care; laudably, they must also be involved in teaching and research.

It's not just the size of the center that makes it peculiarly Texan. This is the home of free enterprise surgery. When Dr. Michael DeBakey pioneered open heart surgery at one of the hospitals, a rival surgeon, the equally celebrated Dr. Denton Cooley, broke away and established his own base at the Texas Heart Institute. Those readers contemplating being opened up by one of these two doctors might like to know that at Dr. DeBakey's Methodist Hospital, the luxury suites serve food specially catered by Jamail's, Houston's best-known delicatessen. Whoever makes the incision, the operation is going to cost you $25,000 or more. At the M. D. Anderson Hospital, which specializes in cancer treatment, in-patients pay up to $700 a night for a bed. Not all the hospitals are private. The Ben Taub Hospital, which is also the Baylor University teaching hospital, has special rates for the "indigent and needy," and the Shriners Hospital for Crippled Children is free. Women about to give birth should give serious attention to the merits of Hermann Hospital, at which happy new mothers, on returning to home and husband, are treated, courtesy of Hermann, to "a gourmet candlelight dinner."

I lunched one day on the terrace of the Café Moustache on West-heimer with an acquaintance who runs a scanning unit at one of the hospitals. Only the breeze saved us from asphyxiation under a surf of exhaust fumes. As I tucked into a seafood salad she echoed Ed by telling me that the center, like the Galleria, was swamped by South Americans. Like ailing Arabs in London, they stumble off the plane, check into a classy hospital, and then, if they survive, settle the account in cash.

"That's all very well for obscure dictators who can rob the peasantry to earn their living, but most of us aren't in that league," I protested. "What happens if you're at death's door but just can't afford tens of thousands of dollars for your operation?"

She shrugged. "Guess you die.". . .

The Texas Medical Center was, it seemed, the only major group of buildings in the state that Jack Rains's company 3D/International hadn't designed: the Galleria, the Johnson Space Center, half a dozen hotels, the Bass towers of Fort Worth, the Johnson Library—not to mention a couple of new cities and palaces in Saudi Arabia. Rains de-scribes his company as "a supermarket" that oversees a project from start to finish: from feasibility studies to the master planning stage to architectural and engineering design. They'll take care of purchasing, construction, and all interior design.

3D/I is as corporate in its structure as many of its august clients. Rains himself is no architect, but an administrator who identifies with an entrepreneurial spirit that is quintessentially Texan. The desire to make money is universal, but in Texas it's exalted into an ideology in which prosperity and the good life are more likely to come into being if free enterprise is encouraged to flourish without restraint. I also suspected Rains was typically Texan in his bragging, but I did him an injustice. When I said I thought I. M. Pei was the architect of the Texas Commerce Tower, he replied: "We're associated architects with Pei. We did the engineering, the interior architecture. Mr. Pei is responsible for the aesthetic sculpturing, but our design team worked very closely with him. It's common for a developer to bring in a design consultant—someone like Pei or Philip Johnson—while the local boys really execute the project. It's good marketing."

From the top of 3D/I's twenty-two-story tower, we looked out over the loop to the area just inside it. Rains, burly but impeccably groomed, from the cut of his hair to the shine on his shoes, gestured out over the landscape. "Houston is a construction site, an unfinished symphony. There's a saying here that the national bird of Texas is the building crane. See over there? In a few years that will all be high rise. The land price is now one hundred dollars a square foot, and that dictates that all those low apartment blocks you see will eventually come out. They're just warehousing the land. Come back in the year two thousand and it'll be much more interesting to look at.

"These developments are all private initiative. That's what distinguishes Texas. We rely on the marketplace, free enterprise. People will say to you, 'Look how little money Texas puts into the arts—it's forty-ninth out of all the states.' That's very true. We don't do it through taxes, but there's more money spent on the arts here per capita than most places in the world, with the possible exception of New York City, which has a lot of tax-funded art and endowments. In time we'll have those endowments here too. But we don't believe that taxpayers should subsidize cultural stamps, like food stamps for the rich. It's just a different philosophy and a different approach. We're more individual and self-reliant. And that carries over into the way we run our cities, our state, our institutions. We believe that the private sector creates jobs. Our low taxes attract business here, and we think that's the way to help people rather than to tax everyone and redistribute income."

I hadn't asked for this crystalline exposition of the trickle-down theory but it was clearly something Rains wanted me to appreciate. Yet surely, I argued, private initiative could create wealth but not determine how, indeed whether, it could be used to benefit those in need. Or, for that matter, to deal with such banal yet pressing problems as the immobilized traffic on the loop two hundred feet below where we stood.

Rains was untroubled. "When a problem gets bad, you develop a political concensus. Public pressure's built so that we've got to do something about the freeways. The state will double gasoline tax, which will still keep us very low, but that'll create a billion dollars annually for road improvements. And much of the city's growth is user paid-for. A developer goes out, he creates a water district, he sells his own bonds, he paves his own streets, and then the people who buy the lots have to pay for it. Then one day the city gets out there and annexes it, but it's the users who've paid for it."

It's a peculiarity of Texas law that cities can vote to annex neighboring areas, except where other cities already exist. Houston can't annex Galveston, but it can, and did, annex the land around the Johnson Space Center. In, for example, Boston, the suburbs are all separate townships; as inner-city residents moved out to the suburbs, the city was unable to recoup the taxes they had formerly contributed. In Houston, on the other hand, annexation expands the tax base, and this in turn helps the city to provide services.

Houston, with thirty-five percent of its economy dependent on the energy industry, had, its citizens repeatedly told me, suffered more than most other Texan cities in recent years. But was it as bad as all that? A prominent attorney claimed that native Texans hadn't suffered too badly. He pointed out that "overpaid union workers" had flooded into the city a few years ago, but as soon as the recession hit, "most of those people turned around and went back to Michigan." Judge Tom Phillips didn't agree with the overpaid lawyer: "I can get a good indication of how hard times are from the number of bankruptcy cases that come through my court."

Jack Rains had no doubts about his assessment. "The city has the resources to overcome its problems. We're not recession-proof. We were hit by our export business here, by the strong dollar. Mexico went absolutely on its back, and that was our major trading partner, the oil industry went down at exactly the same time, and agriculture did not have an outstanding year. You combine all those things and we still created new jobs and grew."

R. E. Smith

R. E. Smith traces his Texas roots back to 1848. The author of fifteen published stories, many set in Texas, he is an associate professor of communications at Purdue University.

JANICE, BOBBY, AND SARAH

Janice Dalton glanced at the clock which seemed to have slowed down since she last checked it, still an hour to go before closing time. She looked again at the headline of the *Rio Ancho Bugler*, "Series of Thefts Continues." She had already been through the classifieds twice but had found nothing for which she was suited. She was lucky to have this job, clerking in the new Quickke Shoppe, lousy hours and all.

She reached for a cigarette. She was smoking too much. She was eating too much, too. In high school, in Rio Ancho, she had a knockout figure, but now she needed to lose thirty pounds. She wore knit slacks that were becoming pilly and an old, loose sweater that hid rather than displayed her body.

Maybe she could lose weight if she didn't work in a place that sold so much junk food. Maybe if things were quieter at home, she could cut down on the smokes. She was still upset from the conference that afternoon with the fourth grade teacher who said that Bobby was not doing his work and was behaving as if he wanted to get into trouble.

She had fewer cigarettes than she should have. Randy, she thought, and became angry at him again. Always sneaking around. She had caught him twice trying to take money out of her purse. Just like his father. Taking what he could and not giving anything back. Randy treated dinner and clean clothes as if he expected them and then pitched a fit if you asked him to do anything around the house.

Still, she thought, calming down, better his taking a few cigarettes from her than shoplifting them and getting in trouble again with the police. When they caught him the second time in Gibson's, she had to pay out money they could not spare to get him off the hook. That was what finally moved her back to Rio Ancho.

Out of high school, she could not wait to leave, to get away from her parents and the rounds of arguments about her not going to church, staying out late, dating boys they did not like. Rio Ancho was a hick little town, and she was sure not going to stay there and dry up the way they had.

Now, she had come dragging back so her parents could help look after the kids. At least they wouldn't be running loose after school the way they had been at the apartment complex in San Antonio. Bobby and Sarah were good about going to their grandparents'. Half the time, Randy just disappeared after school. She had several arguments with him about it, but they did not do any good.

Headlights swept into the store, and she looked up to see Phil Jackson's truck. She blew out a tight-lipped stream as she watched him saunter toward the door with a can of beer in his hand, his gimme cap pushed back on his head.

"How you doing?" he asked as he came in.

"Just fine," Janice said. She motioned toward the gas pumps in front. "You need to move your truck. You're blocking the pumps."

"Nobody's going to be wanting gas this hour of the night," he said. He pulled a sack of potato chips off the rack and opened them with his teeth.

"That's thirty-five cents," Janice said and hit the register keys. "And you owe me thirty-five cents for the last time you were in here and left without paying."

Jackson grinned and handed over the money. "Don't spend it all in one place," he said.

He munched a few chips before asking, "How're your kids doing?"

"All right," Janice said.

She wanted to say more, to tell someone of the problems with Bobby, her worries about the others. But she knew he was only trying to warm her up. When he stopped by the house, he regarded the kids as nuisances.

"I was just thinking," he said, "that you and me might go to the dance at the Longhorn this Saturday night."

"Sorry," she said, "I have to work every night this week."

"You can take off," he said.

"No, I can't," she said. "I need the money."

"We could have us a lot of fun," Jackson said.

"Thanks, but no," she said.

"I'd better be going," he said. "You better watch this store real close. Don't want any of that stealing in here."

"How much of that do you think is really going on?" she asked.

"No telling," he said, "but I lost a fishing rod out my truck last week. I never thought I'd have to lock up a truck in Rio Ancho, but I'm sure doing it now. You sure you don't want to go to that dance?"

" 'Fraid so," she said.

"All right then," he said as if she were missing a big opportunity. He walked back to his truck and drove off with a wave.

She found herself wishing she had said yes to the dance, but she corrected herself. She knew what would happen if she went. He wasn't any different from any other man.

He had pestered and pestered her until she had gone to a dance with him two weeks before. After it was over, he took her home and came inside. She let him kiss her, and before he even came up for air, he was forcing his hand inside her blouse. Then he was offended when she jerked his hand out and told him to leave.

She wanted the warmth of another person, to forget for a little bit the kids and the money and the job always grabbing at her. All he wanted was what they all wanted. Get on, get it off, and get gone.

Her first husband was hot to get into her pants, but when Randy came along, her husband decided that a man needed freedom and could not be tied down. Bobby and Sarah's father was no different. He

Janice, Bobby, and Sarah | 355

would spend half his paycheck on booze, but he wouldn't spend a quarter for a rubber. When money got tight, he was gone too.

Not all men were that way, she had to admit. At least Harold wasn't. She met him in a grocery store when he started a conversation with Sarah, who was riding in the shopping cart. Harold was a steelworker on a project at Brooks Army Hospital, and he made good money. He moved in with them after Janice had four dates with him. He bought groceries, paid the rent, and was smart enough to help make sure they did not have a kid.

"I have a son," he told her one night as they lay in bed. "He's ten. Lives with his mama in Wichita Falls. I feel bad I can't be with him and do the things I'm supposed to do, but she and I don't get along, and I got to go where the work is."

Harold took the kids to the park and to ball games, and in the fall, he borrowed some rifles and took the boys deer hunting. They did not get anything, but they talked about it for the next six months.

By then Harold was gone. The project was finished and the company sent him to Thailand. Janice could not go packing the kids over there.

After Harold, she lived with Larry for a while, or rather, Larry lived with them. She never would have let him in if she had not been missing Harold so much. She caught Larry messing with Sarah one day, and she ended up changing all the locks and obtaining a restraining order to keep him away.

Lights swung into the pump area again, and she looked up to see a big Oldsmobile pull in. The man came inside, leaving the woman in the car and two kids, about Bobby and Sarah's ages, asleep in the back seat. Janice recognized the man as a local rancher.

"Hate to keep the kids out late on a school night," he said as he bought some cigarettes, "but we got tickets to the Ice Capades in San Antonio." He grinned with pleasure. "The kids sure got a kick out of it. You ought to take your kids in."

"I'd like to," Janice said and stopped at that.

Janice watched them drive away. They probably had problems like everybody else, but she sure would like to be like them with a nice car and money for something special.

Nobody else stopped by, and she swept out and closed five minutes early. It did not make much sense to stay open so long in a small town, but Quickke Shoppe was a chain, and they all followed company policy. To save wear and tear on her old Buick, she walked to and from work. The streetlights at the corners cast pools of light, and she moved from one to the next, past dark and quiet houses.

The rent house where they lived was a wooden box on concrete blocks. The front door opened into the living room which, with the kitchen behind it, took up one side of the house. The other side had a bedroom at each corner and a bathroom between them. She looked in on the boys and found them sleeping. Sarah rolled over but did not wake up when Janice slid into bed next to her.

The clock radio showed a little after two-thirty when she woke up. Movement and voices came from down the hall. She moved, the bedsprings creaked, and the voices were suddenly silent, a sure sign the boys were up to something. Janice reached for her robe on the chair and went down the hall.

"Okay, what's going on?" she asked irritably, squinting against the glare of the light she flipped on. The boys lay propped on their elbows looking at her.

"I just wanted to ask him something," Randy said as if she were silly to ask.

"Ask him what?" she pressed.

"Nothing important," Randy said and looked at Bobby.

Bobby looked at Randy and then at her and then at the bed.

With all those looks going back and forth, they were hiding something. She drew in a deep breath and let it out through pursed lips.

"I'm not taking 'nothing' for an answer," she said emphatically.

"I can't tell you," Bobby said, on the verge of tears.

"And why not?" she demanded.

Bobby was crying now and trying not to.

"He'll beat me up," he said.

Janice looked at Randy who simply stared back at her. She turned back to Bobby and looked at the oddly placed bruise on his arm and the red spot under his eye. Yesterday he had said he got them while playing; now they no longer looked like accidents. Sarah, too, had a red spot on her face, and when asked, had mumbled something about running into a bush at school.

Janice stormed up to Randy's bed. "Why were you hitting him?"

"I didn't hit him," Randy said sardonically and turned away.

Janice caught his face in her hand, pinching his cheeks between her thumb and fingers, and jerked him back to face her.

"Why did you hit him?" she asked through clenched teeth.

Randy pulled his head out of her grasp. "He was messing with my stuff."

"Did you hit Sarah?"

"Maybe once or twice."

Janice, Bobby, and Sarah | 357

"She's six years old. What were you hitting her for?"

"She was messing with my stuff."

Janice was so mad, she almost hit Randy. Repeating a line like that, lying to her. She whipped back to Bobby.

"Why was he hitting you?"

"I was messing with his stuff," Bobby replied, sniffling.

"Don't you lie to me," Janice threatened.

Bobby broke out in a sob, and she let him cry for a few moments, then repeated the question more quietly.

"He wanted me to go back outside," Bobby said, then plunged on. "To take things."

The answer puzzled her. "What kinds of things? From where?"

Bobby shrugged. "Anything. Off porches, out of cars, out of yards."

"Whatever for?" she asked.

"He said he was going to sell them and get some money."

Bobby and Sarah's bruises were bad enough, but they suddenly became part of something bigger that stunned her, a sickening possibility that moved far beyond her house to newspaper headlines, conversations in the store, speculations over coffee. Surely not. Not a ten-year-old. Not Bobby.

"Where are the things?" she asked, surprised at how calm she sounded.

Bobby pointed toward the closet.

Afraid of what she would find but knowing she had to look, Janice went to the closet and pulled on the light. In a corner, under a blanket, she found two tackle boxes, a fire extinguisher, three fishing rods, several flashlights, and, incongruously enough, an infant's car seat.

"Is this all?" she asked, turning back to the boys.

"We threw some stuff down the gully 'cause he said they weren't any good." Bobby paused, then said, "There's something under his mattress."

Randy looked at him malevolently and pulled back the edge of the mattress. "See, nothing," he said.

"Don't push me," Janice said.

Randy got out of bed and pulled the mattress all the way back. He had been sleeping on a twenty-two rifle.

Janice stared at it, shocked, then forced herself forward and picked it up. "Where did you get this?"

"Out of a truck somewheres," Randy said.

"Do you have any bullets?"

"A couple," Randy shrugged.

"Don't just stand there," Janice said.

Randy sullenly rummaged in a dresser drawer and handed her three battered twenty-two shorts.

Janice looked at him for a moment and then, just to be sure, checked the drawer herself. She found two boxes of long rifles.

"Where did you get these?" she demanded.

"Hardware store," Randy said.

"They don't sell ammunition to kids," Janice said.

"I didn't buy them," Randy confessed.

Shoplifting again. Janice was so angry she did not know what to do except that she had to do something with the rifle before somebody was hurt.

She crossed back to her room. She put the bullets in her dresser drawer, pulled out the bolt and put it in one of her shoes and put a sock in the shoe. She grabbed her keys and went outside where she locked the barrel and stock in the car trunk.

She had hoped it was over, the mess in San Antonio, but they were as bad off as ever, worse even. Randy was stealing again and lying and beating up on Bobby. No wonder Bobby was having a hard time at school. And Sarah. No telling what would happen to her if Janice didn't watch Randy like a hawk.

As she came back into the house, she heard Randy's voice from the back. "You little shit."

She moved quickly to the boys' room to find Randy beside Bobby's bed and Bobby protecting his head with his hands and arms.

Janice did not stop moving. With both hands she pushed Randy back toward his own bed. The mattress caught him at the knees, and he fell back, hitting his head on the wall. Before he could recover, Janice had one knee on the bed and slapped him twice.

"Damn you!" she shouted. "Can't you leave anybody alone?"

She started to hit him again but stopped. Hitting him wasn't helping anything.

"Get your pillow and sheets," she ordered. "Go get on the sofa."

Randy massaged his face and glared at her but pulled off the sheets and left. Bobby was backed as far away from her as he could get. Janice sat down on his bed and held out her arms.

Cautiously, Bobby approached and let himself be held.

"I'm sorry," she said. "This is a hell of a thing to put you through."

She felt him relax a little.

"Mama," he said, "I'm scared."

"I know you are," she said. "I am too."

She gave him a hug and tucked him back into bed.

"What's going to happen now?" he asked.

"I don't know," she said truthfully.

She moved back into her room for her cigarettes and saw Sarah was still sleeping. Going into the kitchen, Janice noticed that Randy was already asleep on the sofa.

In the dark kitchen, Janice allowed herself the luxury of smoking a cigarette without thinking of anything. Then she put on water for coffee and drank coffee and smoked her way through half a pack while she tried to figure out what to do.

She had not accomplished anything with Randy. Bobby and Sarah might have a chance if Randy didn't pull them down.

But Randy was her son. She'd changed his diapers and looked after him the best she could. She wanted him to turn out all right, but the moment her back was turned, he was in trouble. He had a rifle and bullets. He was beating up Sarah and Bobby.

He could not stay. She knew that. And the sooner he left, the better. She would not even wait for morning.

She dressed and decided that it was better for Bobby to know where she was going than for him to wake up in a dark, near-empty house.

"I'm going to the sheriff's office," she told him.

"Are they going to arrest me?" he asked.

"No," she said and hugged him. "You'll be all right."

Looking at Randy, she hesitated. He was just a skinny fourteen-year-old kid with pimples. He didn't look as if he could hurt anybody.

She knew better now, though. She shook his shoulder.

"Grandma and Grandpa aren't going to like it," he said as he pulled on his clothes, "waking them up."

"You'd just sneak off at Grandma and Grandpa's," Janice said. "We're going to the sheriff's office."

"Like hell I am," Randy said.

"Like hell you are," Janice replied.

Randy backed down a little. "I'll take all that stuff back tomorrow."

Janice wavered. It would be so nice if he would. People would be forgiving. They could just start all over.

But she knew he was just saying whatever he could think of to stall her. If he meant to return things, he would have done it already.

"I'm sorry," she said. "I can't let you stay, and I'm not pushing you off on my parents. Come on." She took hold of his arm to urge him to move.

He pulled away roughly. "Damn it, I said I'm not going."

She stood uncertainly. If she lost this round, she would never have any control again.

Suddenly, she reached down, grabbed his arm with both hands, and heaved. Randy was forced to stand to keep from falling. While he was off balance, she pushed him toward the door and kept pushing.

At the door, he whipped around to face her. "Get your hands off me."

"They're off," Janice said. "Get in the car."

"I'm not going and you can't make me."

Janice did not hesitate but stepped forward. She saw his fist rising when it was too late to dodge. Her jaw grated sideways as the blow landed.

"I'll do it again," Randy threatened.

Janice wavered only for an instant and moved toward him again. Randy started to bring his fist up, but she caught his upper arm and deflected the blow. She pushed him as hard as she could into the wall. Randy bounced back and caught her in a headlock.

She tried to remember what she had done when she wrestled with her brothers. Randy jerked her around but did not seem to know what to do with her once he had control.

She wrapped her arms around his waist and squeezed as tightly as she could. She straightened up and lifted him off the ground. The move startled him enough that she shook her head free and threw him off.

He caught himself and rushed at her. His shoulder hit her in the chest and she went down backward, cracking her head on the floor.

Randy's head was caught under her arm, and he was trying to get on top of her. She pulled her arm back and brought it down, ramming her elbow into his temple. The next blow caught him on the face, the next on the ear.

She rolled out of his grasp and threw herself on top of him and caught his wrist. He hit at her and missed and she caught his other wrist. She ended up sitting on his chest, pinning his arms to the floor.

She took several ragged breaths, then said, "Had enough?"

"Go to hell, you old bitch!" Randy hissed.

Janice turned loose of his arm and slapped him across the face so hard she felt her hand sting.

"Listen!" she shouted into his face. "You're not going to hurt us any more."

She felt the fight go out of him.

She got to her feet and commanded. "Get up and get in the car."

Randy got to his feet and did not look at her. Neither said anything on the short drive to the courthouse. The deputy looked up from his western paperback when they came in.

"This is my son," Janice said simply. "You have to lock him up."

Janice told him about the stolen items, that Randy was beating up on his brother and sister.

"Well, ma'am," the deputy said, "I can put him into custody on your accusations, but I can't hold him beyond twenty-four hours."

"That's good enough for now," Janice said, "but he can't come back home."

"You'll have to talk to the sheriff about that," the deputy said. "He comes on duty at eight."

"I'll do that," Janice said.

"Come with me, son," the deputy said, stepping out from behind the counter.

Randy gave her a last, sardonic look.

"I'm sorry," Janice said and suddenly felt as if she were going to break down right there in the office. She held herself together as Randy left the room, and when the deputy returned, she was able to answer his questions evenly and thoroughly.

Getting out of the car at home, she heard the first birds of the morning.

She sat at the kitchen table with her jaw hurting, her head hurting, and more than that, feeling whipped and defeated. She went to the cabinet and checked behind the dishes on the top shelf. The bottle was gone. Randy must have taken it.

He wasn't even in the house and he was still causing problems.

She lit a cigarette and took a beer out of the refrigerator. The beer tasted awful, but having opened it, she could not waste it, so she continued sipping at it.

She heard a noise and turned to see Bobby peering around a corner.

"Are you all right?" he asked.

She nodded. "I'm all right. How about you?"

"I was scared," he said. "I kept hearing all those noises, like you and Randy were fighting."

"We were," Janice said.

"But you're okay now?" Bobby asked.

"Yes, I'm okay," Janice said and held out her arms. "Come here."

Bobby stepped out slowly and Janice discovered that Sarah had been hiding behind him.

The two edged across the floor to her. She bent and hugged them both.

"Would you like some hot chocolate?" she said.

That was what she should have had instead of that stupid beer.

She put the water on the stove and sat back down.

The kids looked so helpless, just standing there in their underwear.

"Come on," she said and patted her lap.

They climbed up and leaned back against her.

"Where's Randy?" Sarah asked.

"He went away," Janice said.

"When's he coming back?" Sarah asked.

"I don't know," Janice said. "Maybe never."

"Am I going away?" Sarah said.

"I hope not, honey," Janice said.

She hugged the kids again and looked out the window at the new day.

"I sure hope not."

William Goyen

William Goyen (1915–1983) is considered one of America's finest short story writers (Joyce Carol Oates called him "the most mysterious of writers . . . a spiritual presence in a national literature largely deprived of the spiritual"). Often set in a pastoral, tree-shaded, bewitched East Texas peopled by vivid, strange, ill-fated characters, Goyen's stories reveal a sure ear for dialogue, humor, and the simple force of storytelling. This selection in particular expresses the voice of the unconscious in the cadence of the colloquial, a contemporary version of St. Paul's "tongues of men and of angels."

TONGUES OF MEN AND OF ANGELS

I started out to tell about what became of two cousins and their uncle who loved them, according to what the older cousin told me. But some of their kinfolks' lives would have to be told if you're going to talk at all about the cousins and their uncle. So what I have to tell about first is all one family, what I heard told to me and what I watched happen. I have been here in this family's town longer than any of the family, and have in my long time noted—and wonder if you have, ever—the turning around of some people's lives, as if some force moved in them against their will: runaways suddenly arrived back, to the place they fled; berserk possessed people come serene; apparently Godblessed people overnight fall under malediction.

Joe Parrish

Blanch, Louetta's mother, ran away from everybody—mama, papa, husband, child—with a good young Mexican that had worked on the East Texas place, named Juan Melendrez from the Rio Grande Valley. Blanch's husband, Louetta's father, named Joe Parrish, went *loco* at this. He was found lying in the mud of the pigpen, sockeyed and slobbering from what was thought to be a stroke, staring up at the mud-caked pigs grunting over him. And again, some fishermen came upon him prostrate in the steaming weeds of the river. Cottonmouth water moccasins glided all around him yet no snake bothered him. He's gone crazy, said the town, and tried to persuade Blanch's folks to put him in the insane asylum, but they would not. A black woman was brought by Kansas Tate to pull out the devils that had taken hold of Joe Parrish, but she said that they were deeper into him than any she had ever witnessed. She told how devils put roots into a person that thread around his liver and his lights and rope his heart and grow thorns into his lungs. This is why he foams and screams and pants for breath. But then Joe Parrish quieted for a while and sat on the porch, calm. Until one night he was missing. He was gone, leaving Louetta a tragic orphan in her grandparents' house at fourteen.

Now a lot of years later, Joe Parrish came back one night, and he wanted to see his daughter and to get her to help him, but found no one left on the place but the uncle. Joe Parrish told that he was escaped from the penitentiary, a murderer-convict that had killed six Mexicans in the Rio Grande Valley. A winged man with black wings had come near him and unfurled and curled back again a thin black tongue like a horned toad's and said, "Get even. Pay back the Mexicans." Now he had broken out and had come back barefooted and in rags, wanting to hide on the place.

When told that Louetta had drowned in the well, his old bedevilment took him again, and again the black-winged figure came and licked out his black tongue and suggested that at the bottom of the well Joe Parrish would possibly find better times for himself. Before the uncle's eyes Joe Parrish lept into the very well, which had long been without water and was only a cistern of deep thick mud. Flashlights revealed only the yellow soles of Joe Parrishes naked feet lying on a floor of black mud, like a pair of turned-over houseshoes. When the rescuers, about fifty of them gathered from all over the country, threaded through the well-wheel a rope with an iron claw at the end of it and hooked it to Joe Parrishes feet (some said the claw looked like the devil's pitchfork but it was used to grab along the riverbottoms for bodies of the drowned) they strained together as if they were lifting an enormous bucket of wellwater. Suddenly there was a socking sound deep in the well and its echoing was a sound of horror, and then the tuggers, who had fallen back upon one another upon the ground, saw swaying at the crest of the well-wheel, dripping of mud and blood and clawed by the iron claw, two naked feet. Joe Parrishes feet had been pulled from their ankle sockets. The whole town was sickened for a time by the feet of Joe Parrish. They poured bag after bag of lye into the accurst well on the back porch of the old house and then strong men laid a cement hood over the top of what was now Joe Parrishes tomb. Except for his feet, which of course many thought ought to have been thrown into the well. Instead, they were stolen from the Funeral Home where they had been taken—where else could you take them?—and it was not known whether they were embalmed or whether they were just rank feet in the hands of the thief.

And then began the rumors of the feet of Joe Parrish, one foot or both, cropping up here and there. Some reported seeing a footless man crawling through the woods, howling for his lost feet. But the two feet of Joe Parrish began to haunt people. One person said she saw one of the feet walking on the railroad track one moonlight night and that it chased her; another screamed that a foot was in her bed when she got in, but nobody in her household could find it; and sure enough a woman at a dinner table, wanting the butter, asked somebody to please pass the foot—the town was so foot-haunted; and another, way down in the Rio Grande Valley in a Mexican town, reported being followed home from the midnight shift by two steadily tromping feet. Finally this all stopped. Joe Parrishes feet were never found, or haven't been yet. God knows where they came to rest. You will say that every town old enough to have its stories has some hand or a head or has something walking without peace to haunt people. This town was not any different. But since I am interested in the old places that are lost and the stories in them and how they were almost lost until they were saved by some who had ears and tongues and mouths, I thought I'd mention the story of Joe Parrish.

But one question: What had Joe Parrish done to deserve all this? Is there no meaning to some lives? Doesn't it sometimes seem that a life has reeled through its time without making any sense to the rest of us? Or is it that Joe Parrish was just a toy of a bad angel, a poor soul crazed by jealousy-madness and vengeance, that lept headfirst into a well of mud at the bidding of a bad angel. Are there such angels?

But I have some more to tell.

Inez Melendrez McNamara

Two women arrived in town one day. One was an older but beautiful woman, and the other a beautiful brown young girl of some fifteen years with flowing coarse black hair. It was Blanch and her Mexican daughter, Inez Melendrez. Juan Melendrez had been killed beside Blanch and Inez in the truck as they drove along a road back of Refugio, Texas. They said that three gunshots shot out of the fruit groves. Blanch saw Juan burst into blood as though he were a punctured wine sac, and had enough composure to grab the wheel and put on the brake. Inez was thrown through the door and into the air and came down like somebody under a parachute of black hair into a watermelon field and landed astraddle a large watermelon. Blanch couldn't stop screaming. A car stopped and helped. Juan Melendrez was dead, faceless, in Blanch's lap of blood. Inez was badly hurt—her womb was crushed—and she was told that she could never bear a child.

Blanch thought to come back home. Did she think they would all be waiting with open arms? There was no one there to tell her the story of all that happened, of Joe Parrishes fate and of Louetta's, her daughter's. Her sister and brother in Houston had long ago disowned her and had left their home place to rot and fall in upon their drunken brother, the uncle I will tell you more about (and his two nephews—maybe you will remember) in a while.

When mother and daughter came to the family house, they found doors and windows all boarded up. Blanch came face to face with the forbidding riding figure on the glass pane. She fell back for a moment and felt a cold shudder over her, but then, being a strong woman of Texas prairie and valley, she tore open the front door. The odor of the house was of death and rot, and when she found the well cemented over and read the words drawn with a nail in the cement, THIS WELL ACCURST, and the figure of a skeleton head in the embrace of cross-bones, she felt a chill of horror. When she was later told of the content of the well, she pulled her daughter Inez Melendrez to her and told her the tale of Joe Parrish and of Louetta, her daughter, and of Juan Melendrez and of the uncle, her brother and of the red nigger. She was told that the uncle had gone off to Houston to seek his sister and brother and just as she was making plans to go there and find him and to bring him back home, the uncle arrived, but as a wasted corpse in the hands of his nephew. You have already heard of the funeral.

Blanch and Inez Melendrez went on living in the house with the accurst well. She had an altar built over the well and kept a candle burning on it night and day, but you can sure enough believe and will want to know that evil spirits were not in the least held away by the burning light of any candle.

Blanch began to be worried by the sound of somebody walking on the roof. She placed a ladder to the roof so that she was often climbing the ladder day and night, staring at the roof. She had climbed the ladder so many times that she had blisters bleeding in the palms of her hands and the soles of her feet. No sooner had she come down the ladder than up she had to go again. Up and down the ladder she went, night and day. Inez Melendrez feared for her mother's sanity because she herself had not heard anything. One night Inez heard a crash and when she ran outside she found that it had come from her mother Blanch who had fallen off the ladder in the dark and was dead in the canna lilies from a broken neck. At last Blanch had peace. But who knows who has peace? It is told that when Inez found her mother dead in the lilies, a black-winged person stood near and with a long black tongue going in and out of its mouth said, "Joe Parrish won." Inez cried out and the figure vanished. She lifted up her mother and carried her into the house, where she laid her in her bed and lit candles around her. That night when Inez dozed, the house burned to the ground, burning Blanch to ashes in it as Inez fled for her life. Nothing but the well was left.

I later came to the place to see what was left of the door. I found in rubble on a jagged piece of glass the perfect head of the horse rearing passionate and proud in his curling delicate mane, and took it. I looked for the rider but never found him. He must have lain on the burnt ground in a thousand pieces of blackened glass. I would give anything to have found the rider of that precious horse, horseman lost forever.

Inez the Chicana was now seventeen. She saw suffering, persecution and unfair treatment of the Mexican people in her county. She deplored the exploitation of her people by rich Anglo Texans. "I am a *Tejana,*" she said. "I am a Texan as well as a *Mejicana.*" She was widely sought after since she was so haughty and beautiful with her fountainous coarse black hair. A rich independent oil man name Ralston McNamara pursued Inez Melendrez and he happened to be one of those who confiscated land wherever he wanted it to drill for oil from it. He took away land from Mexican people, then hired them as cheap labor to work on it with his drilling company, promising a share of profits, which they never got, since they did not know numbers or how to speak English. How could they figure anything out? They seemed to be naturally in disgrace everywhere. Why was this? Many towns would not allow Mexican people to eat in their cafés or to come into their stores. "I'll tell you, give me a nigra anytime over a greasy mescan" is what you heard.

Ralston McNamara continued to pursue Inez Melendrez and in some time Inez Melendrez married Ralston McNamara. His big wells which he gave to his young bride (she was nineteen) as a wedding present, *Inez No. 1* and *Inez No. 2,* had come in like earthquakes and explosions bursting open the earth and splattering with thick oil mud a countryside of grazing cows and blooming cotton fields and tomato and pea farms, and bringing overnight power and riches to Inez Melendrez McNamara. She at once moved to invest and to buy and to accumulate. She bought a hotel in the Panhandle, acreage in the small town of Houston adjacent to what would one day be a great international airport, and some several miles of the early Houston Ship Channel, along which she built docks and warehouses for cotton and grain. She bought automobile agencies in some small towns like Tomball and Conroe, Texas, and a radio station in the state capital of Austin. Ralston McNamara was amazed at her avarice and her clutching sense of money and was already experiencing spells of impotence with his young wife. Within two years of their marriage he was dead from a split skull brought about by the blade of a machete that fell from a rigging. His head had been sliced in two to the end of his nose. For a time there had been suspicion of foul play among the Mexicans since it was known that the Mexicans were not fond of Ralston McNamara even though he had a Mexican wife. Now all the McNamara fortune fell into Inez's hands and at twenty—and miraculously pregnant—she was perhaps the most powerful person in all Texas and no doubt in the whole Southwest, probably in half the country. Soon after McNamara's death Inez Melendrez McNamara gave birth to an Irish-Mexican boy, who was named Juan McNamara. This boy was the idol of Inez McNamara's eyes. He was not out of her sight. She held him against her breast wherever she went, whatever she did. He slept beneath the cool cover of her coarse black hair. But the shining glory of an immense fortune was darkened by the sickness of a child. Juan McNamara was attacked by a mysterious illness when he was two years old and he lay in a pale languor night and day. The beautiful ivory-colored child could not be healed. Famous doctors came and were of no help. Inez's investments fell; she did not care. She closed shops and offices and warehouses, canceled contracts. People embezzled from her and stole her property. She was in a trance of dread, clutching her dying child to her. She pawned and sold for a nuisance her silver and furs to pay for exorbitant miracle medicines and to bring healers and holy men to her child. But Juan McNamara died. He was three years old and had withered to look sixty.

Inez Melendrez McNamara turned her back on her former life. She brought a bag of cash money and jewels to a Carmelite nunnery in the fields near San Antonio, Texas, and entered it, taking a vow of renunciation and total silence.

No one from the outside world has ever seen her or spoken to her again. Not once has she opened the little door to her cell. The nuns who feed her and take care of her have been pursued by people from all over the world for information about the hidden beautiful woman of sorrows. And some have come with business papers, leases, titles and contracts. The sisters would not speak to them, although some needed immediate life-saving answers that only Inez could give. Some begged to slip a piece of paper under the door for Inez's signature. There was even one incensed man on the roof of Inez's cell crying down to her to help him salvage some few dollars of his lost fortune, but there was no answer. The sisters would not speak to anyone of Inez Melendrez McNamara, as though she did not exist. Only one little novitiate, who was missing and was found in the Shamrock Hotel in Houston wearing a huge emerald and ordering elaborate room service for a bunch of conference salesmen in a penthouse orgy, told some news of Inez before she passed out, champagne-sodden. She told how Inez Melendrez McNamara weighed 350 pounds and that her huge body was cloaked by her coarse black hair, which dragged on the floor, like a shaggy black cape. When the novitiate sobered up she found herself back in the nunnery, raped so many times that it took some weeks to heal her.

But time has almost carried off forever the story of Inez Melendrez McNamara. I've saved a little of it here.

Gary Cartwright

Gary Cartwright (b. 1934) worked for twelve years as a daily reporter for Fort Worth and Dallas newspapers. Later, he became a writer of choice fiction and nonfiction that reveal a controlled sense of the anarchic and the absurd.

THE DEATH OF THE MARLBORO MAN

A world big enough to hold a rattlesnake and a purty woman is big enough for all kinds of people.

—OLDTIME COWBOY SAYING

I never realized that the Marlboro cowboy was real until I read last May that he had drowned on a bucking bronco. *Drowned* . . . incredible . . . drowned on a nervous young colt in a newly dug stock tank on the Bill Flowers Ranch near Old Glory, in the starkly beautiful Marlboro country north of Sweetwater. No one knows exactly how it happened; as usual, Carl (Bigun) Bradley was alone at the time.

Bigun and his daddy, Carl (Banty) Bradley, had just sold the colt to Bill Flowers, but Flowers's foreman couldn't handle him. Bigun saddled the horse late that afternoon, cinching the flank rope tight as he could so the horse would feel pain every time he bucked, then he rode off toward what they call Cemetery Pasture.

Bigun was thirty-six and for as long as anyone could remember his workday started before sunup and ended after sundown, never varying except for the two days he took off to get married and the few times he was off in South Dakota doing a Marlboro commercial. It was seven days a week, week after week; it was the repetition as well as the work that kept him at it. But this particular day, for no particular reason, Glenda Bradley was worried. She telephoned Susann Flowers at ranch headquarters just after dark.

"You know how cowboys are," Susann Flowers told Glenda. "You gotta hit them in the head to get them off their horse. He'll be in in a while." Nevertheless, Bill Flowers and his foreman would take a pickup out to Cemetery Pasture and see about Bigun. "I'll call you back," Susann told Glenda.

The Flowerses were not only Bigun's employers, they were his friends, and Glenda's too, a couple about their own age. Bill Flowers was a famous rodeo roper and heir to old Pee Wee Flowers's four-ranch spread of eighty thousand acres. Bill was a real cowboy, too, but not in the way Bigun was—Bigun was a working cowboy, the son of a working cowboy, the grandson of a working cowboy, all of them born and raised on the same tenant ranch outside of Knox City, simple men working for wages and living their unrelenting existence in a world that could go mad without them knowing or even caring. Bill Flowers and Bigun Bradley had ridden together when Bigun was wagon boss of the Four Sixes (6666) Ranch near Guthrie—"neighboring," they call it, helping out when there is branding or gathering to be done—there was one stretch, Bill recalled, when they were out forty-one days, miles from the nearest asphalt or bathtub or woman or child or roof or television set. But there was always this difference—Bill Flowers was rich. He could quit anytime and go back to running his own ranch and rodeoing. Bigun Bradley never had time for the rodeo. And he didn't live long enough to own his own spread.

Bill Flowers and his foreman found nothing in Cemetery Pasture, but returning to the ranch house later that night they saw something in the headlights that sent cold chills up their boots—a horse's leg and part of a saddle blanket protruding from the muddy water near the edge of the new stock tank.

"Get the rope," Bill yelled, jumping from the pickup before it had even stopped rolling. But they had made a mistake that Bigun Bradley would never have made: they had forgotten their rope.

About midnight, Bill and Susann Flowers drove over to Glenda's house and told her they had found the horse. There was no trace of Bigun, except his lip ice, gloves, and a package of Kools. Sheriff Marvin Crawford and other volunteers had come over from Aspermont, and the dragging operation had begun. The Flowerses drove Glenda and her eighteen-month-old son, Carl Kent Bradley, back to the ranch house, where they could wait out the night.

"It was the longest night ever," Susann Flowers would say later. "We kept hoping that maybe he had been bucked and was unconscious somewhere out there. Almost the same thing had happened to my daddy's foreman in Pecos—they found his body in the Pecos River. We never knew what happened."

Working in the lights of a circle of pickup trucks and a fire truck beacon, the cowboys told stories and speculated. There were three possibilities: Bigun could have been bucked off; the horse could have spooked and charged into the water, taking Bigun with him; or Bigun could have deliberately ridden the bronco into the tank. "Some people think every horse will swim, but every horse won't swim," Sheriff Crawford said. "I've rode horses up to drink tubs . . . you get a bronco around water, the cinches tight up, they're liable as not to turn and pitch. You get a horse in water, most of them will swim right across, but they's a few'll just turn on their sides and go straight to the bottom."

"Bigun has been known to ride 'em into water," another cowboy recollected. "I seen him one time after a big rain take his chestnut right into the Little Wichita, trying to get the cattle to follow him."

Back at the ranch house, George Humphrey, an old-time cowboy who managed the Four Sixes for forty years (Bigun left the Sixes when George retired four years ago), told stories to the gathering of women and children. How in the old days when cattle were cheap the best way to subdue an old mossy horn was to shoot it through the thick part of the horns, aiming for dead center so that the pain would calm the steer and make it manageable. "What if you misshot?" Glenda Bradley asked, laughing the nervous schoolgirl laugh that was maintaining her. "You'd kill the animal," George Humphrey said. "Cattle was cheap and it was an advantage to get rid of these outlaws at any price. They spoiled the other cattle. They had to be either shot or driven off."

They dragged Bigun Bradley's body from the tank around two A.M. There were signs of a blow over one eye and behind his ear. "Either one was hard enough to kill him," Sheriff Crawford told Glenda Bradley.

Glenda went outside and cried, then she came back and helped fix breakfast.

"He preferred to work alone," Glenda Bradley is telling me. Her voice has started to quiver, and she clasps her hands tightly in her lap. "That's very dangerous, but he was so good . . . I think anyone will tell you this . . . he *was* good with horses. He just wasn't afraid. He didn't think anything could happen."

We are sitting in the kitchen of her parents' home in Westbrook, a tiny farming town near Colorado City. This is where Glenda grew up, and this is where she returned after Bigun's death. It has been two months since the funeral: only yesterday Glenda finally forced herself back to Old Glory, and having made the trip she feels better. Old friends and memories are too dear to ignore.

"I interviewed for a job teaching homemaking at Jayton High School—that's east of Knox City. When we were first married and Bigun was wagon boss of the Four Sixes, I taught homemaking in Guthrie. It's a comfort to at least know what I'm going to do. People in that part of the country, especially around Guthrie, they're not very progressive. They want things the way they were in the old times and do a pretty good job keeping it that way. Oh, they use pickups and butane branding irons, but that's about it. At first I thought I could never go back, but . . ."

Carl Kent Bradley, called Kent, now twenty months old, rides a stick horse around the table where we talk.

"I guess he'll be a cowboy, too," Glenda says. "I hate for him to do it, but that's what Bigun would want, and I know Banty (Bigun's daddy) is going to have it that way. Bigun was never allowed to be a little boy. Banty had him out breaking horses when he was old enough to ride. I mean breaking *horses . . . colts . . .* not riding old nags." Glenda says this without rancor. She is more composed now, and there is that nervous, laughing edge to her voice. "Bigun and Banty and all their people, cowboying is all they've ever known or wanted. To be on a horse chasing a cow was what Bigun enjoyed. Kent has already turned that way. Unless I ever remarry and my husband is so different . . . but I don't think I'd like any other life except cowboying."

Glenda Bradley is pretty, the way a high school majorette is pretty, a way that is difficult to describe. She is what you would call "a sweet girl," but tough and proud. As she talks about her five-and-one-half-year marriage to Bigun Bradley, she admits that she never knew him very well. No one did. "The truth is," she says, "we never had much time together, and when we did he didn't say much. He'd leave the house at three or four in the morning and come home after dark. He'd eat and go to bed. Every day, no days off. About the only socializing we did, every July Fourth the cowboys would take off and go to the Stamford Cowboy Reunion Rodeo."

Bigun was a thirty-year-old bachelor when Glenda met him at a rodeo dance. She was twenty-two and had just graduated from Texas Tech. He was the Marlboro man and wagon boss of the 6666. She had never met Bigun Bradley, but she knew him, knew him in a way that always embarrassed Bigun when she told the story.

"Bigun would kill me for telling you, but . . . well, it was a big joke at school [Texas Tech] that I liked *cowboys.* A friend of mine cut out Bigun's picture from a Marlboro ad in *Life* magazine . . . here's your cowboy, Sis, she said. . . . I said, fine, I'll just *marry* him, and put the picture on my dorm wall . . . you know, a silly girl thing. That summer another friend sent an article out of *Western Horseman* that gave his name—Carl B. Bradley, Jr. He got the name Bigun from his Uncle Guy who used to call him Bigun and his little brother (Doug Bradley) Littleun. Actually, Bigun wasn't all that tall, only about five eleven, but very strong. Anyway, on July Fourth that summer I went to the

Stamford Cowboy Reunion Rodeo Dance with a girlfriend and there he was. He took my girlfriend home that night. Two nights later, I went back to the dance and he pretty well ignored me, but he did ask me for a date."

Six months later, after a courtship that consisted of going to an occasional cowboy movie in Bigun's pickup, they were married. As wagon boss at the Four Sixes, Bigun was making $310 a month, but Glenda started teaching and there was extra money from the Marlboro commercials, not all that much, but enough to get by. The Marlboro people had "discovered" Bigun Bradley while shooting some background film at the Four Sixes. He was one of several real cowboys who posed for commercials.

"One of the first things he told me," Glenda says, "is about the Marlboro deal—he'd been offered a full-time contract that included a part in a movie. He'd turned it down, but now, with us getting married, he didn't know if he'd done the right thing. But he decided he wouldn't be happy not cowboying . . . and he wouldn't, 'cause he was good and he liked it."

Bigun did not speak of the future, but it was his dream to someday own a small ranch. They put a little money in the bank . . . $120 every time Marlboro used him on TV, $1,500 for a few cover ads in *Life* or *Look* . . . and Bigun bought a few horses and cattle and went in partnership with Banty, who was now leasing the land where they had always worked for wages. Then the government banned cigarette commercials on TV. Glenda had to quit her job when Kent was born, and the savings account quickly evaporated. Bigun hadn't posed for a commercial in the two years before his death. "We were barely getting by," Glenda says. "And I mean barely."

It cost money to cowboy. Four hundred dollars for a saddle . . . forty dollars for a pair of chaps . . . one hundred dollars for shopmade boots. Except on the rare occasion when he accompanied Glenda to the First Methodist Church ("He never felt comfortable in a crowd"), Bigun wore Levis, white shirt, boots, hat, and, in the winter, a neck scarf. He never walked outside without his hat and boots.

"He was always giving things away," Glenda recalls. "Bridles . . . spurs . . . if he thought someone wanted his boots he'd sit down and take them off right there. That's just how he was. He was the most patient, most courteous man I ever knew. Even after we were married and had the baby, he would still open doors for me . . . yes, ma'am and no, ma'am . . . he wouldn't even take a serving of food off the table until I'd served myself first. That's the way May (Bigun's mother) raised her two boys.

Even after we were married, whatever Mama and Daddy said do, he'd do, regardless of my opinion."

J. Frank Dobie once described the cowboy as "a proud rider, skilled, observant, alert, resourceful, unyielding, daring, punctilious in a code peculiar to his occupation, and faithful to his trust."

That's a pretty good description of Bigun Bradley.

Joe Thigpen, the young county attorney of Stonewall County, tosses a pack of Kools on his desk and tilts his straw hat on the back of his head. In his wilder days, before he finished law school, Thigpen worked for Bigun Bradley at the Four Sixes.

"I knew about the Marlboro cowboy—everybody around here did," he tells me. "It was a thrill meeting him." The first thing Bigun Bradley did was send Joe home for his saddle and bedroll; it hadn't occurred to Joe that he would need a bedroll. This was 1968, and the Four Sixes still had a chuck wagon drawn by four mules, a kind of traveling headquarters; they slept under the stars, bathing maybe twice a month. The wagon was already out when Joe Thigpen hired on, and they stayed out another two and a half months.

Joe Thigpen tells me: "I never met a man as patient and completely dedicated as Bigun. I never knew a man who worked harder. I don't think he ever asked for a day off. He'd wake me up every morning and tell what we had to do that day. Then we'd do it.

"Now I'm not saying he couldn't be tough on you. There was one day we were flanking cattle and I was always in the wrong place, spooking the yearlings. Bigun roped this calf . . . must of weighed four hundred fifty pounds . . . and said, 'You been messing up all day so you just flank [i.e., throw] this one by yourself.' Now there's no way one man can throw a four-hundred-fifty-pound yearling. The calf stepped on my toes and like to of broke them . . . I was sweating and puffing, all the way given out . . . never did get that yearling down. Another fellow finally had to help me. But Bigun wasn't doing it for meanness—he was teaching me a lesson."

I asked Joe Thigpen what it is that makes a man cowboy. He thought for a while, then said, "I can't tell you exactly, but I loved it better than anything I've ever done. You're outdoors, doing what you like to do. I probably never would of gone back to school, except Bigun told me that's what I ought to do. It was the best advice I ever got—a cowboy can't afford a family."

Thigpen took a check stub from his wallet and showed me his final month's pay at the Sixes—$162.50. Then he offered me a Kool and told me a story: "We had about a hundred twenty-five horses in the remuda. We were moving them one day . . . I guess we must of rode twenty-two miles . . . me being the low man on the totem pole, I had to ride drag . . . you know, back at the end, hollering and yelling and pushing horses. It was just dusty as the dickens. I was trying to smoke those Marlboros . . . I thought that's what I oughta smoke . . . but they were burning me up . . . I'd take one puff and throw it away. That's when Bigun came riding back. He didn't say a word. He just took a pack of Kools out and offered me one."

Joe Thigpen takes another cigarette and shakes his head. Hard to believe that a man who knew so much about horses could be killed by one. "It's something I'll never be able to get out of my mind," he says.

It doesn't take long to tour the Old Glory community, but the tour is fascinating. Seated in a flat, green valley of windmills and skeleton mesquites that have been poisoned because they take too much water from the land, Old Glory is an abandoned cotton gin, a general store and post office, and a scattering of quaint old homes. One of the homes is the old Raynor Court House, which sits now like a feudal castle on a high mound. It looks like the house in the movie *Giant,* I think as I drift below on the farm road from Aspermont, and it turns out they modeled the movie set after the Raynor Court House. An old couple whose name I didn't catch live there now. No one ever goes up there, they told me at the general store.

The Germans who settled here called the spot New Brandenburg until World War I when, in a fit of patriotism, they decided the name sounded too un-American and asked the oldest woman in town, Mrs. Weinke, what they should do about it. She told them to change it to Old Glory, and that's what it's been ever since.

I'm in the passenger side of a station wagon with Susann Flowers and her two young boys. Bill Flowers has been off since before daylight, buying cattle in a market that is on the verge of Nixonian panic, and Susann is showing me the ranch. We drive through Cemetery Pasture, where the old German cemetery is preserved by a fence—judging from the gravestones, an unusual number of children died here in the late 1800s, a time of epidemic, perhaps—and now we slow down near the stock tank where Bigun Bradley died.

"You know what I always think when I drive by here?" Susann Flowers says. "I think about Bigun's hat. We never found it. It's down there somewhere.

"Bigun couldn't swim, you know. Neither can Bill. It scares the hell out of me to see them swimming their horses, but they do it all the time. There's no reason for it, it's just something they do. We're not supposed to question what happens on this earth, but I can't help wonder what happened that night. He could have been bucked, or the horse could have gone into the tank, but I can't help feel that Bigun rode in on purpose."

We stop in a warm summer rain while Susann fills the tank of her station wagon from a gasoline drum near the foreman's house. In an adjoining pasture there is a modern house trailer where old Pee Wee Flowers still comes occasionally to play dominoes with the hands. Susann wants to change the name of the Bill Flowers Ranch to "something Spanish," but Bill and Pee Wee won't hear of it. Susann Flowers doesn't want her two children to cowboy, but that's what they will do—cowboy like their daddy, not like Bigun Bradley. Meanwhile, Susann is organizing a college scholarship fund for little Carl Kent Bradley.

"Bigun wasn't afraid of anything," she says as we drive back to the ranch headquarters. "I heard him say one time . . . he was talking about this cowboy we all knew . . . Bigun said, 'Charley's afraid of dying.' It was something Bigun couldn't understand. He was tough as hell—that's what he was. Yet he was the most considerate, most dependable man I ever knew. I'd known him for years before he stopped calling me Mrs. Flowers—and I was younger than he was."

Jeff Flowers, age five, tells me what he remembers about Bigun—Jeff remembers Bigun brought him a tiny rabbit they caught in a post hole. Jeff wears spurs on his little boots and has two horses. They're not very good horses, he tells me.

In a driving rainstorm, I turn toward Knox City, thinking about women and glasses of beer.

I stop to consult my crude map. The rain has stopped and the sun is slipping behind Buzzard Peak when I find the muddy, rutty, unmarked road that leads to the tenant house where Bigun and all his people grew up—the ranch that Banty Bradley now leases. A sign at the main-gate cattleguard identifies this as the "General American Oil Co.," and it is still another ten miles to the house, which sits on a crest overlooking miles of green hills and naked brown peaks. Fat quail and jackrabbits big as dwarf deer bounce in front of my car, and horses and cattle look me over without judging my intentions.

Banty and May Bradley are out by the stable, hoeing weeds. There are miles of weeds, weeds far as you can see, but the apron of ground around the stable is clean as a dinner plate. They hoe patiently, like people listening to the radio, like they don't care if there is an end to their struggle.

Banty is a short, husky, red-faced cowboy with wide spaces between his teeth to spit tobacco through. They say Bigun was a younger exact replica of his daddy. May, though, is pure Texas mule iron, a lean, severe, outspoken woman who hasn't smiled since Christmas. There is no telephone here; I couldn't call in advance, and now they decline to be interviewed. I stand by my open car door, asking questions, while they go on hoeing. Then I get an idea. I tell them that I saw "Sis" (Glenda's nickname) yesterday, she says hidy and she's feeling much better. She's got a new teaching job at Jayton. Banty and May brighten as I play them a part of the tape I did with Glenda.

"Did you see Bigun's boy?" Banty asks, eagerly breaking the silence.

I describe meeting Carl Kent Bradley.

"That baby of Carl B.'s is a natural-born cowboy," May says. May is the only person I met who doesn't call her son Bigun. She calls him Carl B. "Look at him ride his rocky horse . . . natural saddle gait."

"It's getting harder," May says, "harder to go on. There is very little neighboring any more. It's every man for himself. You used to be able to tell a cowman by his boots," she tells me. "If he was worth a speck, he had hundred-dollar shopmade boots. Nowdays, you tell a cowboy by his woreout brogans. Real cowboys can't hardly afford boots. One thing about Carl B., he couldn't care less about money. There was a pattern in his life. Things came his way. He didn't ever ask for things, we taught him that, but things came his way. He didn't ask for all that publicity. He got plenty of it, but he wasn't a *seeker.*"

May does most of the talking, deferring occasionally to Banty, reminding him of a particular story. They tell me about Banty buying Bigun's first saddle when Bigun was three. May talks about their other son, Doug, how Doug never wanted to be a cowboy. Doug drives a bulldozer. Doug was always building things, while Bigun played cowboy. Blocks and stick horses. "Bigun wore out many a stick horse before he could ride," May says. "He'd play cowboy and Doug was always his calf. Doug had all the hide wore off his neck by the rope."

At May's urging, Banty tells me about Bigun snitching the latch pin off the barn door, and how Bigun was afraid of the dark but Banty made him go back alone in the dark and replace the latch pin. Bigun never again messed with the barn latch. They tell me about the agonizing weeks it took before Bigun would mount his first wild bronco. And how, once he had done it, he never stopped. Why does a man cowboy? I ask.

Banty grins and points to his head, as though to say that's where his heart is. If Bigun was as good as they say, and I believe he was, why didn't he join the rodeo circuit? "Too many people," Banty grins.

Later, May takes me up to the house and shows me her clippings, the clippings describing the deeds of the Marlboro cowboy. Best all-around boy at Knox City High, senior class favorite, FFA president, co-captain of his football team, honorable mention all-district. Carl B. (Bigun) Bradley, Jr.'s, plain moon face, his eyes tinted Paul Newman blue, barely seen in the shadow of his hat, smoking what is alleged to be a Marlboro cigarette. Why? Why would Marlboro pick Bigun Bradley? I guess because they saw he was a real cowboy.

There is a Marlboro sunset as I slide back along the mud road and turn toward Guthrie. Two horses in the road ahead turn flank and trot off into the brush. There is a silence that lasts forever—if there were such a word, *forever*. A windmill is silhouetted against the dark fire of the horizon, and I can't help thinking it's a long way home.

Al Stricklin with Jon McConal

Alton M. Stricklin (b. 1908 near Grandview) played piano for Bob Wills and the Texas Playboys for most of the legendary swing band's successful years from 1935 to 1971.
Jon McConal (b. 1937 in Pecos) is a national award-winning columnist for the Fort Worth Star-Telegram.

REMEMBERING BOB WILLS

I keep hearing people talking about the good old days. Often those good old days were the 1930s when I was playing with Bob. I guess they were good old days.

Beef was selling for nine dollars a hundred. That was fat beef, too, that had been on feed for several months. You could buy a complete set of false teeth for thirty-five dollars. I remember reading one ad that said that. It went on to say, "They are built to suit your own facial looks.

Even your uncle won't know that you're wearing them when he talks to you up close."

There were a lot of people who thought being a Texas Playboy would be the best way to live in them good old days. A lot of them auditioned for us, as I've already noted.

Taking it all the way around, I mean as far as instruments were concerned, I think Leon and his steel guitar had to be the most popular instrument in our band. Bob worked it perfectly. Leon loved it. As a result of Bob's famous "Take it away, Leon" and Leon's equally famous playing the hell out of that steel guitar, there were hundreds of kids wanting to learn to play the steel guitar. I remember standing around one day listening to a kid audition with a steel guitar. When he finished, I thought he sounded like two cats that had been high lifted and put inside a rusty barrel. I asked him as he was leaving why he was learning to play the steel guitar (and believe me he was learning). He stood up tall and said, "I want to play it the way Take-it-away-Leon McAuliffe does."

One time about fifteen minutes before our radio show, we got a request for an unusual audition. About a dozen people came up and asked if their little girl could play the radio show with us. Bob always gave everybody a chance, if he could. But, this seemed a bit too much.

"Tell you what folks," he said, tilting his big white hat back on his head. (You could see some sweat popping out and you knew that Bob didn't want to hurt these people's feelings.) "Why don't we audition her first and then maybe sometime in the future we can put her on?"

"Okay," said the father. "We understand. We'll bring her back sometime."

They started out. Bob looked out and he saw only one child with them. He really pushed his hat back then. The girl had no arms. She just had shoulders. Absolutely no arms.

"Go get them folks and bring them back," he said.

One of us stopped the people and brought them back. Bob was looking at the little girl. He began talking, his voice deep with emotion. He said, "Is this the little lady that plays the steel?"

"Yes, sir, Mr. Wills, this is her," said the mother.

Bob reached down and put his arms around the little girl and hugged her. He said, "Honey, you can play on my radio show anytime you want."

I know that Bob was being kind and generous. I felt good that he was. But, I know, and I figured the rest of the band felt the same way, and probably Bob did too, that this little girl could no more play the steel guitar than I could be the Pope. And there was no way I could be the Pope. I'm not even Catholic. But, there are other reasons too.

But, we helped this little girl get her steel guitar set up. The band tuned our instruments so we were all together. Then the show began. We played a couple of numbers. All of us kept wondering what was going to happen and how Bob was going to introduce this little girl. He finally did. He said, "Friends out there in radio land, we've got a beautiful little lady who is with us today. She's going to entertain you now. She is going to play the steel guitar."

Let me tell you. She surprised everyone. She cut loose on the "Steel Guitar Rag." She played the hell out of it. She played it much like Leon did and never lost time or music. She did that with her toes. She used those toes like we use our fingers. She was an instant hit. Not only with the band, but with the fans.

After the show, I went up to her and said, "Sweetheart, you can play with me anytime."

"Make that 'us' anytime," said Bob.

She just grinned widely, then played with us some more. We kept up with her for a long time. I don't know what ever happened to her, but I'll bet she was a success. She made her own dresses, cooked and combed her hair. She did it all, just like she played that steel. Like a professional.

Really, I wasn't surprised when Bob let that girl play on the show. That was in his nature. It was carved into his being. He'd have let that girl play even if she had struck notes that would have made a church choir frown. He just loved people!

When we were out on the road or at dances, people would write down requests for Bob to play on his radio program the next day. Bob never overlooked a request. He gave me the responsibility of writing down the requests.

"Al, don't you ever throw them away. There's people out there depending on us for these," he told me. I never threw them away.

Many of these requests would be for old people, or shut-ins, or people who were sick. It meant a lot to Bob to help these people. He'd always made it a point to say something nice to them before the request. I always figured that part of his wanting to do that might have gone back to the days when he was thinking about being a preacher and he figured this was his own kind of missionary work.

That's what caused him on many occasions to take off in the daytime, when he was tired and desperately needed some rest, and go and sing at someone's funeral or visit a shut-in or help some relative or friend. He was eager to do this.

I remember one woman who lived in a nursing home out from Tulsa. She was a daily listener to Bob's show. She asked Bob to play her a tune on his fiddle one day. That day was her 112th birthday. We played the song. Then Bob said, "Lady, we are going to come out to your party. You must be a real sweet person and I have just got to have a piece of your cake."

Bob didn't go by himself. The whole band went. We played a concert for this woman and the other folks there. The audience had tears in their eyes when we were through. We all walked out and started talking to them. One grabbed Bob's hand, her fingers wrinkled and with veins that stood out like long pieces of spaghetti. She said, "God bless you, Mr. Wills. Mr. Bob Wills, God bless you!"

The old lady who was having the party was blind. But she could hear. Her face broke out in a wide smile. As the music went along, she would let out with little hollers.

"I may be too old to dance to the music, but I'm not too old to appreciate it," she said.

She died about a year after that. We went to her funeral. Bob played. As usual, there were about six of us who went to these. Bob always played one special song. It was "There is No Disappointment in Heaven." He not only played it, he sang it. And, how he could sing that song!

He had a fine, clear voice that enunciated every word. You could almost see water pouring clear and pure from one of those old windmills out on the wind-battered West Texas landscapes as he sang. The words went:

> There is no disappointment in Heaven.
> No weariness, sorrow or pain.
> No hearts that are bleeding or broken.
> No song with a minor refrain.
> No clouds of the earthly horizon
> Will ever appear in the sky.
> Where all will be sunshine and gladness
> With never a sob nor a sigh.
> I'm bound for that beautiful city
> Our Lord has prepared for His own.
> Where all the redeemed of all ages
> Sing glory around the white throne.

Sometimes I grow homesick for Heaven
And, the joys my eyes shall behold.
Oh, what joy that will be when my Savior I see,
In that beautiful City of Gold.

That song was beautiful. But Bob would sing or play any song that was requested of him. It didn't make any difference who the request was for or from. Even people in prison. Bob played for them. He felt close to these men. One time we went to the state prison at McAlester, Oklahoma and played for the inmates. The warden had invited us. But, I'm sure it was Bob's missionary desires that were as responsible for us being there as the warden's invitation.

We played our noon broadcast from the men's dining room. You talk about applause. I've never heard anything like it. It sounded like someone firing shotgun blasts from inside a concrete culvert.

"These boys like you," said the warden. "They listen to you every day while they're eating dinner. That's probably why they're applauding so much. Here you are right up in front of them."

That probably was right. But I think it was Bob's appeal that turned them on so much. His music did everyone that way. I've often thought, and many more people back me up on this thinking, that Bob, having once been a servant of the land, put the land and life into his music. That's why the people loved it. That's why the convicts went so wild.

We were taken on a guided tour of the prison. We visited the shops and working areas. We visited death row. We met a young man who was really nice to us. He talked and said, "Man, I really like your music. It makes me glad I'm alive."

He wouldn't be alive long. He was to be executed in the electric chair in forty-eight hours.

The prison band played for us. They were really good. We reciprocated the applause they had given us earlier. Then we went to the women's unit.

As I recall, there were about four hundred women in there. Some of them were real beauties. There was one particularly good-looking woman who kept near Leon as he played. He didn't miss her attention.

When we finished the concert, Leon walked over and began talking to the good-looking woman. He said, "You let me know when you get out and how I can get in touch with you."

She smiled, then said, "It may be a while. But I certainly will let you know."

"Well, how long will it be?" asked Leon.

"I really don't know," she said.

"It can't be that long. What are you in for anyway?" he asked.

"I murdered my husband. I'm here for life," she said.

Leon was speechless. It was one of the few times I ever saw him that way.

There was an interesting thing that happened at the prison while the inmates were playing. They had a young man about twenty who played the trombone. He was out of this world. Not only could he play, but he was good-looking and had a great personality. Bob was attracted to him.

He was looking for a trombone player at the time. So he got with the warden and found out that this young man was due to get out in a few months. The warden agreed to let him go early if Bob would agree to take his custody. Bob readily agreed to that. Within a few days, Bob had his trombone player.

He fit right in. He was a real good sport. The people liked him and he was simply great on the trombone. Since he had heard us so much, he already knew all our songs. But one of Bob's bitterest disappointments was about to happen.

It seemed that not all of the people liked the new trombone player. As much as the Oklahoma people loved Bob Wills, there was some self-righteousness there.

As soon as it got out that Bob had a jailbird in his band, we began to get nasty letters. People began saying they would not come to his dances if he didn't get rid of the convict. Bob was furious. He said, "I really don't give a damn what those self-righteous bastards think. There but for the grace of God and a lot of good luck, would be a lot of us."

So he bowed his head. He kept the trombone player.

But it didn't do any good. The criticism got worse and Bob finally had to face the reality that society was based on conventionalities. These people were going by the book. Bob let the young man go.

"That was the hardest thing I've ever done," he told me later. "It was like someone had my heart in a vice and they just kept on twisting it and I couldn't get a wedge in there to stop it."

He gave the guy two hundred dollars and told him if he ever needed any help to let him know. He had tears in his eyes the day the young man left.

I kept up with the young man. About a month later, he broke into a store and took some clothes. He was sent back to prison. I've got a theory on that. I think the kid did that because he didn't want Bob to have the responsibility of taking him back. He broke into that store to get Bob off the hook. But I will always have a fondness and a sadness in my heart for that young trombone player.

The trombone player, the little girl, the shut-ins and the sick are all good examples of how far Bob would go to help people. He did it for his band, too. There was no limit to how far he would go.

Sometimes these involved touchy issues. Like the time one of the boys who was married came to Bob. He was downcast. He said, "Bob, I've been fooling around. I got a girl pregnant."

He told Bob all about it. It had started at the dances at the Trianon Ball Room. The girl had put the heavy rush on him. But he was true to his wife. But, she was good-looking and she kept on after him, like an old hound dog that has struck a fox's path on a rocky trail, and there's just enough scent there to start him baying, and he knows sooner or later he's going to pick up the full trail. That's what this girl knew.

She was successful. She convinced the young man that the sky had no stars in it unless he was her star. If he would just love her fully one time, she could endure her drab life and would never bother him again. So he went to her room one night. The hound was baying on full trail.

About two months later, he went back to see her. He hadn't seen her in all that time. When he walked up, she said, "I've got news for you. I'm pregnant. I'm carrying your child." She broke into tears, then said, "I'll do anything to protect you. I'll kill myself."

The band member was shook! But he wasn't that shook. He had rather have a deceived wife than a dead woman on his hands. While he was struggling with his emotions, the girl said, "There is a solution. I know a doctor who can fix me for one hundred and fifty dollars."

That was high money in those days. Musicians didn't make that kind of money and have it lying around. That's why the young man was so desperate. That's why he went to Bob.

Bob listened. His eyes were directly on the young man's face. When he got through his story, Bob said, "This may hurt, but I'm going to tell you something about your new true love. She is nothing but a fraud. She's a cheat. She's a tramp! Now here's what you do. You call her and you be real nice and sound concerned about her. But you tell her that you have a friend, a longtime high school buddy who went to medical school and is now a doctor and he will take care of her for you. Tell her that you will come and get her, bring her to Tulsa, put her in a room, and see that she gets expert care. Tell her you want to be near her and you want to be sure she is all right and you will pay for everything."

The young man called her and told her exactly what Bob had told him to. Guess what. He never heard from the girl again. About six months later, Bob asked him, "What ever happened to your lady friend?"

"I never heard from her since I called her," said the band member.

Bob shook his head and walked away grinning.

Bob helped me out many times. One of them was a very sad time in my life. It came when my wife died. She had gotten ill not too long after we moved to Tulsa. Eventually it was diagnosed as cancer. It was incurable.

The last few months were rough ones. She was in pain. No medicine helped her much. But I kept looking for something. Rather the doctors kept looking and I kept paying. By the time she died, all my savings were gone. I had also spent a bunch of borrowed money.

I went to Bob before the funeral. I told him my troubles. I said, "Bob, I need to borrow some money."

"How much do you need, kid?" he asked.

"I need six hundred dollars," I said.

He didn't say anything else. He turned to Mayo and told him to write me out a check. I had the money in a matter of minutes.

I took my wife's body back to Texas for burial. I also took a week off. I wanted to take more, but I kept thinking about how pressed I was for money. A friend had told me that I'd probably be better off back with the band where I wouldn't be spending so much time moping.

I kept my nose to the grindstone. I finally started getting things in order. My finances were shaping up. So after about five months, I asked Bob if I could talk to him. He, like always, said sure.

"Bob, I'm getting my finances back in shape and things are rolling pretty smoothly. I think I can start paying you that six hundred dollars back," I said.

"Kid, what are you talking about?" he asked.

"The money I got from you after my wife died. That six hundred dollars," I said.

"I didn't loan you six hundred dollars," said Bob.

"Yes you did, Bob. You had Mr. Mayo write out the check. You loaned it to me," I said.

"I *gave* you six hundred dollars, kid. I didn't loan you nothing. And, I don't want to hear any more about it. You've got a lot of necessary things to worry about. Okay?" he said.

I stumbled out of his office that day. I couldn't talk. I walked out and the air smelled so good. There was a little wind kicking up. It felt cool on my face. It was drying my tears. That old Oklahoma sunshine looked like someone had sprinkled gold in front of me. Bob Wills had made it that way.

Lola Scobey

Lola Scobey, native Tennesseean educated in Texas, has written extensively on country music including books on Willie Nelson and Dollie Parton. She now lives in Florence, Alabama.

JUST AS I AM: WILLIE NELSON, COUNTRY OUTLAW

The University Baptist Church in Austin is an affluent, respectable congregation, nestled close to the multimillion-dollar towers of the University of Texas. Here, comfortably set, heaven-bound Southern Baptists faithfully attend services and conscientiously fulfill their three-times-weekly obligation to God.

In 1975, the minister, about forty-two years old and a friend of Darrell Royal's, got the unorthodox idea of inviting Willie Nelson to participate in a Sunday-night church service.

Although he had darkened few church doors over the past twenty years, Willie was intrigued, and said okay.

Arriving in tennis shoes and T-shirt, Willie sat up on the podium with the preacher. He brought his guitar, and Bobbie came, too, to play piano.

Willie was supposed to sing some songs, and the preacher, deeply elated over this public meeting—this reconciliation, he hoped—between organized religion and outlawry, had prepared some questions.

After cordial introductions, the service began. "How did you envision Jesus as a boy?" the preacher first asked.

"Well," Willie remembered and smiled, "we had pictures of him."

"Where do you think you would find Jesus, if you were going to look in Austin for him today," the preacher continued.

Willie paused, observing the congregation sitting in stately pews below and in the big white balcony above. "I think you might find him at the Armadillo World Headquarters," he replied simply. "It would have been a good spot, and he would have enjoyed it."

No one gasped, but the reaction of the conservative Baptists was unclear. Then Willie sang. After his first song, the sedate congregation burst into loud applause—right in church. And each time Willie sang a familiar hymn like "Amazing Grace" or a song like "Family Bible," they would applaud. Willie was obviously elated—and moved by this unexpected acceptance.

"What do you think about God?" the preacher continued. "Well, he's somewhere up there above Jesus," Willie offered. "We are the image of God—or he's the image of us. I'm not sure which," he hesitantly added.

Then with obvious pleasure, he reminisced about his boyhood, about sitting on his front porch in Abbott listening to the Christians sing, about how he'd "been to church a lot of times" that way "without going."

"I live day to day, one day at a time," he explained of his nomadic ways to the stable, well-established Christians. "I've always moved around, because I like to move. The human race," he observed, "is a moving thing."

Well, the preacher gingerly proposed, hadn't Willie in his day been accused of being a bit "loose"?

"I've been accused of being a little loose," Willie frankly admitted, then added with conviction, "I believe in looseness, too."

In that case, the preacher wondered, what would Willie consider a sin? Willie responded vaguely.

What, in his mind, is wrong? the preacher more boldly probed. "A person can answer what is right or wrong for themselves," Willie finally assured the preacher with quiet confidence. "If they think long enough, they'll come up with the answer."

With each song that he sang, and each round of joyous applause from the congregation, Willie was obviously becoming more deeply moved and inspired by this reunion with the roots of his childhood.

He told of his confrontation with the Metropolitan Baptist Church in Fort Worth; remembered the days of his first hit, "Hello Walls"; and even regaled the assembly with the tale of Ray Price and the rooster. "I used to tell Ray Price I owed him a lot of money for an education," he joked. "I'd just look at him and do the exact opposite."

As the service neared its end, Willie, eyes heavenly bright with the memories and the moment, began softly singing with Bobbie playing gently behind.

"Just as I am . . . without one plea . . . but that thy blood . . ." The congregation spontaneously joined in, sweet and low, and Willie's voice faltered, ". . . was shed for me. . . . Upon thy promise I believe . . ." Willie choked out the words, "Oh, Lamb of God, I come to thee, oh . . ." Willie was no longer singing. His guitar slid slackly into his lap, and tears streamed down his rough, bearded cheeks.

For years acutely tuned to her brother's most subtle emotional change on stage, Bobbie leaned into the keyboard and the beautiful, pleading strains of Mama Nelson's girl, playing "Just As I Am," backed by a whole congregation singing softly in unison from pews below and balcony above, filled the huge auditorium. In a time, Willie was able to pull his guitar to his chest and lead the final words, "Just as I am . . . I come to thee . . . Oh, Lamb of God, I come . . . I come."

There was no applause. But into the poised silence, the preacher introduced one more question.

How, he gently asked, would Willie want the world to remember Willie Nelson?

Willie, eyes glistening with tears, looked at his interrogator. The congregation sat, waiting, still as a band of angels paused in flight.

"Just tell them I meant well," he quietly answered.

Benjamin Alire Saenz ———————————————

Benjamin Alire Saenz is a writer living in El Paso. This essay reflects the author's actual experiences living along the border and offers a most dramatic contrast between rich and poor nations.

BORN IN THE U.S.A.

Do you know what exile is?
I'll tell you,
            exile

is a long avenue
where only sadness walks.
—ROQUE DALTON

El Paso

That morning, when the day was beginning, I looked out my window and stared at the Juarez Mountains. Mexican purples—they were mine. That was the first time it ever happened, the spring of 1985. It had happened to others, but never *to me*. And when it happened, I didn't like it.

And it will never be over.

As I walked to school, I remember thinking what a perfect place Sunset Heights was. Turn of the century houses intact. Remodeled houses painted pink. The rundown Sunset Grocery store decorated with the protest art of graffitti on one end and a plastic-signed "Circle K" on the other. Bordering the University. Bordering the freeway. Bordering downtown. Bordering the border. People from Juarez knocking on doors and asking for jobs—or money—or food. Small parks filled with people whose English was apparently nonexistent. The upwardly mobile living next to families whose only concern was getting enough money to pay next month's rent. Some had lived here forever, others would live here a few days. A bazaar of colorful people who lived in the shadows of the Juarez Mountains. Sunset Heights: a perfect place with a perfect name, and a perfect view of the river.

After class, I went by my office and drank a cup of coffee, and smoked two or three cigarettes. Lawrence, my office mate, turned on his fan and told me I smoked too much. "Yeah," I nodded, "I smoke too much—but I'm going to quit." I had no intention of doing so, and he knew it. It was a game we played.

At about three o'clock I put my things together in my torn backpack and started walking home. I made a mental note to sew the damn thing. *One day everything's gonna come tumbling out—better sew it.* I'd made that mental note before.

Walking down Prospect, I thought maybe I'd go for a job. I hoped the spring would not bring too much wind this year. The wind unsettled the desert—upset things—ruined everything. My mind wandered: searched the black asphalt littered with torn papers; the chained dogs in the yards who couldn't hurt me; the even bricks of all the houses I passed. I belonged—the thoughts entered like children running through a park. This year, maybe the winds would not come.

I didn't notice the green car drive up and stop right next to me as I walked. The border patrol interrupted my daydreaming: "Where are you from?"

I didn't answer. I wasn't sure who the agent, a woman, was addressing.

She repeated the question in Spanish, *"¿De donde eres?"*

Without thinking, I almost answered her question—in Spanish. A reflex. I caught myself in midsentence, and stuttered in a nonlanguage.

"¿Donde naciste?" she asked again.

By then I'd regained some composure and quietly spit out, "I'm a U.S. citizen."

"Were you born in the United States?"

She was as brown as I was. I might have asked her the same question. I looked at her for a while—searching for a human being.

"Yes," I answered.

"Where in the United States were you born?"

"In New Mexico."

"Where in New Mexico?"

"Las Cruces."

"What do you do?"

"I'm a student."

"And are you employed?"

"Sort of."

"Sort of?" She didn't like my answer. I looked at her expression and decided it wasn't hurting anyone to answer her questions. It was all very innocent. Just a game we were playing.

"I work at U.T.E.P. as a teaching assistant."

She didn't respond one way or another. I looked at her for a second and decided she was finished with me. I started walking away. "Are you sure you were born in Las Cruces?" she asked again.

I turned around and smiled, "Yes, I'm sure." She didn't smile back. She and the driver sat there for a while and watched me as I continued walking. They drove past me slowly, and then proceeded down the street.

I didn't much care for the color of their cars.

"Sons of bitches," I whispered, "pretty soon I'll have to carry a passport in my own neighborhood." I said it to be flippant. I wasn't angry—not at first. In less than ten minutes I was back in my apartment playing the scene again and again in my mind. It was like a video I played over and over—memorizing the images. Something was wrong.

I was embarrassed—ashamed because I'd been so damned compliant. Just like a little kid in the principal's office—in trouble for speaking Spanish. "I should have told that bitch exactly what I thought of her and her job." *Are you sure you were born in Las Cruces?* Piss on her and her green car and her green uniform. I lit a cigarette and told myself I was overreacting. "Breathe in—breathe out—no big deal—you live on a border. These things happen—just one of those things. Just a game. . . ." I changed into my jogging clothes and went for a run. At the top of the hill on Sunbowl Drive, I stopped to stare at the Juarez Mountains. I felt the sweat run down my face. I kept running until I could no longer hear *Are you sure you were born in Las Cruces?* ringing in my ears.

School let out in early May. I spent the last two weeks of that month relaxing and working on some paintings. In June I got back to working on my novel. My working title was *Adagio for Strings: An American Fairytale.* I liked the title more than I liked the story.

From my window I could see the freeway. It was then I realized not a day went by that I didn't see someone running across the freeway or someone walking down the street looking out for someone. They were people who looked not so different from me—except they lived their lives looking over their shoulders.

One Thursday, I saw the border patrol throw a couple of guys into their van. Threw them. Threw them like they were pieces of meat— dead bucks after a deer hunt. The *illegals* didn't even put up a fight. They were aliens, from somewhere else. They just hung their heads— practically scraping the littered asphalt. I sat at my typewriter and tried to pretend I didn't see it. *That's what I get for looking out windows.* I didn't write the rest of the day. I kept seeing the border patrol woman against a blue sky turning green. I thought of rearranging my desk so I wouldn't have to be next to the window. But I thought of the mountains. . . .

Two weeks later I went for a walk. I couldn't stand sitting at my desk for another second. The novel wasn't going well that day. My writing was getting worse instead of better. I needed a break. My characters were getting on my nerves. I hadn't taken a shower—hadn't shaved. I looked in the mirror and talked to the image, "You need a haircut. You need a shave. You need . . ." I threw some water on my face and walked out the door. God, it was hot. I wiped the sweat from my eyelids. Sweat—stinging and blinding. I laughed. It was a hundred degrees, the middle of the afternoon. *I'm crazy—a shower would have been a better idea.* I turned the corner and headed back home. I saw the green van. It was parked right ahead of me.

A man about my height got out of the van and approached me. Another man, taller, followed him. *"¿Tienes tus papeles?"* he asked me. His gringo accent was grating.

"I can speak English," I said. I started to add, "I can probably speak it better than you," but I stopped myself. No need to be aggressive.

"Do you live in this neighborhood?"

"Yes."

"Where?"

"Are you planning on making a social visit?"

He gave me a hard look—cold and blue—then looked at his partner. He didn't like me. I didn't care.

I watched them drive away and felt nothing.

There were other times when I felt watched. Sometimes, when I jogged, the green vans would slow down—eye me. I felt like prey. I pretended not to notice them. I started noting their presence in our neighborhood more and more. I started growing suspicious of my own observations. Of course, they weren't everywhere—I had just been oblivious to their presence—had been oblivous because they had nothing to do with me. The green cars and the green vans were clashing with the purples of the Juarez Mountains. I never talked about their presence to other people. Sometimes, the topic of the *Migra* would come up in conversations. I felt the anger—would control it. I casually referred to them as the Gestapo and everyone would laugh—I was only playing. I hated them.

When school started in the fall, I was stopped again. Again I had been walking home from the university. I heard the familiar question, "Where are you from?"

"Leave me alone," I stared back.

"Are you a citizen of the United States?"

"Yes."

"Can you prove it?"

"No. No, I can't."

He looked at my clothes—jeans, tennis shoes, and a casual California shirt. He noticed my backpack—full of books.

"You a student?"

I nodded and stared at him.

"There isn't any need to be unfriendly. . . ."

"I'd like to be left alone."

"Just trying to do my job," he laughed. I didn't smile back. Terrorists, I thought. Nazis did their jobs, too. Death squads in Guatemala did their jobs, too. An unfair analogy, I knew. I thought it, anyway.

The Juarez Mountains were not as purple that fall.

In early January, I went with Michael to Juarez. Michael was from New York, and had come to work in a home for the homeless in South El Paso. We weren't in Juarez for very long—just looking around and getting gas. On the way back, the customs officer asked us to declare our citizenship. "U.S. citizen," Michael followed. The customs officer lowered his head and poked it in the car, "What are you bringing over?"

"Nothing."

He looked at me. "Where in the United States were you born?"

"In Las Cruces, New Mexico."

He looked at me a while longer. "Go ahead," he signaled.

I noticed he didn't ask Michael where he was from.

That winter, Sunset Heights seemed deserted to me. The streets were empty like the river. One morning, I was driving up Upson Street towards the university—the wind blowing the limbs of the bare trees. Nothing to shield them—unprotected by green leaves. I noticed two border patrol officers were chasing someone. One of them put his hand out, signaling me to slow down as they ran across the street in front of my car. They were running with their billy clubs in hand. *So it had come to that.*

I wanted the wind to blow them out of existence.

In late January, Michael and I went to Juarez again. A friend of his was in town and we wanted to take him to Juarez to have a look around. We took him to the cathedral and the marketplace, and talked about how markets were a much more civilized way of doing business than going to Safeway. We stopped at the Kentucky Club and had a couple of beers. Walking back over the bridge, we stopped at the top and looked out at the city of El Paso. "It actually looks pretty from here, doesn't it?" I remarked. Michael nodded. It *did* look pretty. We looked off to the side—down the river—and watched the *illegals* looking for a way to cross the Rio Grande. We watched them for a long time. Michael's friend said that this was just like watching the "CBS Evening News."

As we reached the customs building, we noticed that a border patrol van pulled up behind the building where the other green cars were parked. The officers jumped out of the van and threw a handcuffed man against one of the parked cars. It looked like they were going to beat him. Two more border patrol officers pulled up in a car and jumped out to join them. One of the officers noticed we were watching. They straightened him out, and walked him inside—like gentlemen. They would have beat him had we not been watching—that's what I thought. But things like that don't happen.

My fingers wanted to reach for the wire fence. To touch it. I felt guilty for living on the freedom side of the fence. That fence—it separated me from myself.

The first day of February I was walking to the Chevron station in downtown El Paso. On the corner of Prospect and Upson a green car was parked—just sitting there. A part of my landscape. I was walking on the opposite side of the street. For some reason I knew they were going to stop me. My heart clenched like a fist. My back tightened up. Maybe they'll leave me alone, I told myself. I wanted to believe it. I should've taken a shower this morning. I should've worn a nicer sweater. I should've put on a pair of socks—worn a nice pair of shoes. . . .

I should've dyed my skin.

The driver of the car rolled down his window. I saw him from the corner of my eyes. He called me over to him—*whistled me over*—much like he'd call a dog. I kept walking. He whistled me over again. *Here, boy.* I stopped for a second—only a second. I kept walking. The border patrol officer and a policeman rushed out of the car and ran toward me. I was sure they were going to tackle me—drag me to the ground—handcuff me. They stopped in front of me.

"Could I see your driver's license?" the policeman asked.

"Since when do you need a driver's license to walk down the street?" Our eyes met. "Did I do something that was against the law?"

The policeman was annoyed. He wanted me to be passive, to say, "Yes, sir,"—to approve of his job.

"Don't you know what we do?"

"I know exactly what you do."

"Don't give me a hard time. I want to see some identification."

"I'd like to know why I was stopped."

"I'm asking you for some identification."

I looked at him. Just looked. He stared back. He hated me as much as I hated him. He saw the bulge of my cigarettes under my sweater and crumpled them.

I backed up a step. "I smoke. It's not good for me, but it's not against the law. Not yet, anyway—and don't touch me. Don't ever touch me. Read me my rights, throw me in the can or leave me alone. Understand?" I smiled.

"No one's charging you with anything."

"Good. Very good." I nodded—and kept nodding.

They walked back to their green car.

My eyes followed them. I'd won. It was an empty victory.

This spring morning I wake up. I sit at my desk, wait for the coffee, and look out my window. *This day, like every day, I look out my window.* Across the street a border patrol van stops and an officer gets out. So close I could touch him. On the freeway—this side of the river—a man is running. I put my glasses on. I am afraid he will be run over by the cars. I cheer for him. *Don't get run over. Be careful.* So close to the other side he can touch it. The border patrol officer gets out his walkie-talkie and runs toward the man who has disappeared from my view. I go and get my cup of coffee. I take a drink—slowly it mixes with yesterday's tastes in my mouth. The officer in the green uniform comes back into view. He has the man with him. He puts him in the van. I can't see the color in their eyes. I see only the green. They drive away. There is no trace that says they've been there.

No one knows what I have seen. Except the mountains.

The green van. They are taking something from me. The green vans. This is my home, I tell myself. But I don't know if I want this to be my home, any more. The thought crosses my mind to walk out of my apartment without my wallet. The thought crosses my mind that maybe the *Migra* will stop me again. I will pretend I cannot speak English. I will say nothing. I will bow my head, and let them put me in a detention center for a month or two. I will let them warehouse me. I will let them push me in front of a judge who will look at me like he has looked at the millions before me. I will be sent back to Mexico. I will let them treat me like I am *illegal.* But the thoughts pass. I am not brave enough to let them do that to me. And I never will be.

Today, the spring winds blow outside my window. The reflections I see on the pane have words written on them—graffitti: *Sure you were born? . . . Identification? . . . Do you live? . . .* The winds will unsettle my desert—cover Sunset Heights with green dust. The green vans will stay in my mind forever—I cannot banish them. I cannot banish their questions—*Where are you from?* I no longer know.

EPILOGUE

John Graves

John Graves (b. 1920) lives on Hardscrabble Ranch in Somervell County, and is a master of the "ruminative essay" that combines acute reflections on the natural world with shrewd observations on human nature. His writings on the parts of Texas being lost to rural sprawl have won many prestigious awards from literary and environmental groups. The present selection comes nearest to being a reflection on his own approach to the creative act of observation.

NOTICING

A good long while back as time goes for us individual mortals, I lived for slightly more than a year in a small dingy apartment on East Fifteenth Street in New York City, poking more or less continually at the keys of a Corona portable and hoping for better days ahead. While Manhattan has never been exactly my idea of a spiritual home, I think I was farther from considering it one that year than during any of several other stays, even if it did give me what I was looking for when I went there: anonymity, release from the pressures of family and friends, mental scope for some knotty apprentice work.

My sixth-floor windows in that habitation gave onto an airshaft whose disused and littered courtyard was patrolled by rats in search of edible rubbish and cats in search of edible rats, though two or three times during my tenancy the rats ganged up and managed to eat themselves a cat, nor was the ingestion of cousins and offspring unknown. The view was not much improved by glimpses of sad clerks in the back ends of offices around the shaft, or by what I could see of the goings-on in one of the ladies' rooms of S. Klein's On The Square cut-rate department store. Its big window, open in warm weather, was opposite my worktable and occasionally there were some pretty good free-for-alls over package mixups or who was to get first go at a particular toilet stall, made more complex by the fact that some shoppers used the place for trying on skirts and blouses and things. But on the whole the ladies came across as just a quarrelsome aggregation of pale bulging flesh and I learned to ignore them most of the time, along with the cats and rats and filing clerks.

I achieved indifference also to the horrific mood music against which these scenes were enacted, the airshaft being a sounding box for all the racket of Union Square—the Square that S. Klein's was On and a zone of convergence for several bus lines and three subways. Even at three or four in the morning I could listen unheeding and unmoved, drifting toward sleep, to the amplified farting of great diesel engines, the squall of steel wheels on steel tracks, and frail piercing cries for succor rising up from murderous alleys here and there. To do so was a matter of functioning, of survival.

Though I remember that obliviousness clearly enough, I can't recapture its feel and indeed have a hard time these days believing it was really I who experienced it, so different was it from the sort of casual but constant observation of detail, the *noticingness,* of the rural life I've led for most of the past two decades. It would be simplistic to ascribe this contrast to some supposed superiority of a country existence over the city kind, for I've known some dull and unobservant rustics and have had some urban friends who missed very little of what went on around them, from obscure marital tiffs on subways to the fairyland glitter of mica in certain downtown sidewalks. I've even liked certain cities well enough myself and have lived awarely in them. But the country attitude I mean is in some ways of another sort. It comes from having a personal stake in the landscape that envelops you, in the various beasts and fowls and crops and objects it contains whose ownership you claim, and in the activities of many wild things that own themselves. To take stock of all this daily, to exercise surveillance, is about as much a requisite for survival as was my Fifteenth Street indifference—survival for your chattels alive or inert and therefore for you as a countryman. Because if you grow careless about what's happening on the land, you stand a good chance of ending up broke and back in town. In the country you *need* to notice things, and even fairly fogheaded fellows like me attain a degree of alertness.

Bugs, for instance, are a part of human experience in almost any surroundings—flying up before one's feet in grass, building ingenious nests under caves or webs behind austere computer panels, fluttering or zooming from tree to tree in search of nectar or prey or love, expending their entrails on windshields, scurrying beneath the water heater when the kitchen light goes on, fiddling long sleepy heat-songs throughout afternoons in August, stinging or biting mammalian surfaces when such is their inclination. Yet in town only a few species of them are ever much thought about, and most of those few by suburbanites jealous of the well-being of the miniature farms they call yards. A countryman who runs his place right, however, while he's unlikely to be an expert entomologist or even an adequate one, often has to be familiar with the look and habits of dozens.

At a minimum, in my region, he knows greenbugs, grubs, aphids, armyworms, ticks, fleas, lice, stinkbugs of three or four varieties, flies of six or eight, mosquitoes, various wasps and ants, crickets, grasshoppers, numerous kinds of spiders, and a host of specialized epicures like corn earworms, Colorado potato beetles, spotted and striped cucumber beetles, beeswax moths, peachtree borers, plum curculios, grape leafrollers, tomato hornworms, and squash bugs. Most matter to him as potential pests and enemies to be dealt with harshly, but others—predatory characters like ladybugs and mantises and spiders and some wasps, pollinators, soil-enriching earthworms, and so on—are friends and allies in his often doomed attempt to thwart rank nature's resolve to go her own sweet way.

He sees both sorts and their signs as he goes about his daily rounds, fleetingly for the most part but consciously enough that if they add up to a problem—clouds of hornflies tormenting his cattle, for instance, or a proliferation of cabbage loopers in the garden's lettuce—he can take some needed action. You may on occasion catch him doing queer things such as crumbling mud-dauber nests between his fingers to see what sort of anesthetized spiders have been stored there to feed the growing larvae. At least you could have caught me doing that last summer when the black widow spider population burgeoned alarmingly—which pleased the daubers greatly and set them off on a reproductive binge stoked with black widow meat, so that by autumn not only could I stick my hand into dark corners more or less without qualms, but the armatures of all unprotected electric motors were jammed with mud nests and among the materials composing my barn, adobe may have outweighed wood and sheet iron.

Bees make a botanist of their owner as he watches for blooms and nectar; in fact, the more varied the activities to which someone commits himself on and with the land, the keener his powers of observation are likely to become. Flat, rich, monocultured country with wide expanses of wheat or milo or cotton and very little else requires no whetted perceptions on the part of its proprietor save in terms of soil conditions, weather, and a few sorts of weeds and insects. But an archaic type with a recalcitrant, rocky, up-and-down domain, who indulges his outworn notions of self-sufficiency by gardening, tending an orchard, sowing three or four field crops in their seasons, keeping poultry and bees and a milk cow, running goats and beef cattle and sheep, and even worrying over the fish in his stock ponds, needs to utilize such awareness as he can muster just about full-time, which I guess ought to add up to tension and neurosis but doesn't often seem to. More usually it comes out as the sort of equanimity that fitting in with one's world can give.

The real ones of this breed, those who have soaked up country habits and knowledge since childhood, grow older and fewer and amount perhaps to little in times geared to specialized agribusiness and the urban public it serves. Yet a good many of us latecomers and part-timers in the country admire the best of them and their ways, learning a little of what they know when we get a chance and imitating them as best we can in the privacy of our own terrain, like a movie-struck kid taking off Steve McQueen before the bathroom mirror. Having learned the hard way that ignorance vis-à-vis the landscape can cost dearly in dead or strayed or ailing animals and failed crops and whatnot, we pick up what we can from books and county agents and maybe evening ag college courses, but this other kind of skill is seldom peddled in such places. It comes from living attentively on your own land and sometimes, when you're lucky, getting to watch someone intelligent who's spent a lifetime living that way.

If on a clear day in October there is a single dark puff of cloud on the northwestern horizon, such a man sees it within moments of coming outside (that swift eye-sweep of the sky that you find in all old rurals, even those ending their days in rest homes and wheeled onto a terrace for air) and gauges its probable meaning. Bouncing through a pasture in a pickup and passing a cow on her left side, he somehow discerns a wire cut on her right shoulder and checks it out for screwworms, hemorrhage, or infection. At supper he may rise from the table in response to sounds that others have not heard, and go to the porch to learn where a pack of marauding dogs is running or a family of coyotes has its base. On a dusty path in the hills he can tell you, if asked, what creatures meek or fierce have trotted and slithered and shuffled there the night before. Distant columns of smoke have messages for him, as do neighbors' tractor sounds, shots, the urgent cries of jaybirds and crows, the alarm coughs of unseen deer, hillside seeps, and the tinge of blooming sweetclover on damp evening air. All these things lodge in him and combine into understanding, for they are a part of his world, and so quite integrally is he.

Such honed vigilance is ancient, of course, tracing back to primitive tribesmen with eyes like falcons' and noses like setter dogs', and to the half-wild trappers and frontiersmen who felt out our continent for conquest not very long ago. In the best of their heirs it is by no means always economic in slant but adds up in part to "useless" wisdom, because having been led by circumstance into focusing good brains on natural phenomena instead of the civilized world's bright clutter and jabber and stink, they follow curiosity where it leads like academics, amassing knowledge for its own sake.

Many have read a good bit, and some have college degrees. I have one ranching friend, an Aggie ripe in years, who is always good for a couple of hours' ruminative, expert discussion of wild vegetation in our area, utile or not, and long ago I knew a laconic old Hill Country native who had more information on red ants than I've seen in books (admittedly I'm no deep reader on the subject), and admired them so much that he hated to disturb their beds in the course of farming and was hostile toward people who poisoned them. I liked him and respected his knowledge but was not converted, and to this day rather enjoy any chance to discommode the testy little bastards and get a measure of revenge for the many times one has climbed up my pants for a bite. Plowing is one way, though in certain years other small beings are upset by it too and express enough resentment for both themselves and the ants. Roaring along on your tractor you may find yourself suddenly in the middle of a towering cloud of bumblebees or the stubby yellowjackets that hive up by the thousands in burrows, and full many a crooked furrow or indeed a deserted machine has resulted from such attacks.

Days are when you see and touch things; nights are when other senses come most into play. Partly for this reason I don't much like closed bedrooms and really prefer sleeping on a screened porch, as I used to do all year long till a couple of arctic winters in a row chased me back inside. Ensconced on a porch with your head sticking out of the covers and only a film of wire gauze between you and the vast starred blackness outside, you're in tune with the night, or at any rate as much in tune with it as your perceptions will let you be.

The far-off rising groan of big Macks and Whites as they shift to low gear on the hills of U.S. 67 means a drift of air from the southeast, and means also that its Gulf moisture may give the region a shot at wanted rain within the next few days. A standard whiff of polecat, not unpleasant, tells you only that one is foraging somewhere, but a stouter whang indicates he may be at your hives again, scrabbling with his claws at the entrance to bring the bees out in their dudgeon, then gobbling them up with stings for piquant seasoning. Cows with milk-taut bags bawl urgently for roving offspring, and if one hungry answer comes from a wrong direction and lasts too long and sounds a trifle desperate, you know a calf has blundered through a fence and you'll have to do something about it in the morning. Coyotes on the hill to the east yap and wail and trill in sudden chorus for a minute or so to establish hunting contact or possibly just for love of music, then go silent; owls talk; a cottontail shrieks as something (what?) grabs it; a being unknown says *hark-o-hark-hark* in the west. A dog's voice goes softly *woo-woo* in the distance and you know that the Edwards kid is out with his mongrel "silent trailer" again and they've treed something, which leads you into reflection on the high pelt prices that have all furred varmints under siege. Hens on a live-oak branch beside the house stir and mutter in sleep; leghorns rescued by your daughter from the biology lab at school, they grew up as gentle pets and refuse to roost in the barn where the rape-minded gamecock and his combative harem of one hold sway. The sheep dog snores and snuffles on the concrete floor beside your bed, but wakes to growl in his throat at something, maybe old Woo-woo. . . .

Nights are thus very rich, right on into that zone of fading consciousness where real noises and smells blend with dozing illusion, and afterward too for that matter, since the sleep of attunement is light, if sound, and doesn't much mind interruption. I remember once having a dream in which a buzzing, clucking, angry, continuous voice took on the shape of whirlpooling points of light, then waking and going out into frozen moonglow to find that Blue, our only dog then, had treed a ringtail in a hackberry beside the garden, and I didn't resent the waking or the cold or the effort since they served to teach me the exact origin of that sound I'd heard before in ignorance, thinking it was probably coons. But I confess it may take a special sort of picayunish concern with natural things to see the matter so.

Picayunish or not, it is a sort of concern—sometimes practical, sometimes not—that I share with a lot of other people out beyond the cities' rims. And if it is a far far cry from being able to slumber rosily through the pandemonic nightly din of Union Square and to glance with unseeing eyes at the antics of fat ladies squabbling half-clad in a restroom, I guess what the difference really has to do with is belonging. What it may show is that when you're somewhere you don't especially want to be and don't belong, you tend to wall yourself off from sentience like a hibernating bear, whereas in surroundings that you care for and have chosen, you use eyes, ears, nose, tastebuds, and whatever other aids you can muster for reception. You notice. And, noticing, you live.